Handbook of Investment Research

Economic and Financial Indicators as Market Movers

Conrad Mattern

Handbook of Investment Research

© Conrad Mattern 2002

Language translation © by Palgrave Macmillan 2002

Praktiker-Handbuch Investment-Research Copyright © 2000
by Schäffer-Poeschel Verlag GmbH & Co.KG

Published by arrangement with Schäffer-Poeschel Verlag GmbH

This edition published 2002 by
PALGRAVE MACMILLAN
Houndmills, Basingstoke, Hampshire RG21 6XS and
175 Fifth Avenue, New York, N. Y. 10010
Companies and representatives throughout the world

PALGRAVE MACMILLAN is the global academic imprint of the Palgrave Macmillan
division of St. Martin's Press, LLC and of Palgrave Macmillan Ltd. Macmillan® is a
registered trademark in the United States, United Kingdom and other countries.
Palgrave is a registered trademark in the European Union and other countries.

ISBN 0–333–96869–7

This book is printed on paper suitable for recycling and
made from fully managed and sustained forest sources.

A catalogue record for this book is available
from the British Library.

Library of Congress Cataloging-in-Publication Data
Mattern, Conrad, 1964–
    Handbook of investment research: economic and financial indicators as
market movers/Conrad Mattern.
        p. cm
    Includes bibliographical references and index.
    ISBN 0–333–96869–7
        1. Economic indicators—United States—Handbooks, manuals, etc.
    2. Economic indicators—European Union countries—Handbooks, manuals, etc. I.
Title.
HC106.83 .M388 2002
330.9'001'5195—dc21   2001057743

10   9   8   7   6   5   4   3   2   1
11   10   09   08   07   06   05   04   03   02

Printed and bound in Great Britain by
Antony Rowe Ltd, Chippenham and Eastbourne

Commerce

Contents

List of Figures

List of Tables

Preface

Nowadays, very few financial market operators can afford to make their buy or sell decisions without an in-depth analysis of the respective circumstances. For this purpose there are two basic ways to go. Technical analysis aims to explain market activities largely from within and therefore focuses primarily on information contained in trading prices, which are visualized in the form of charts. Fundamental analysis, by contrast, attempts to explain market activity on the basis of exogenous factors. Analysis is based on economic relations and refers to a whole set of economic indicators.

We are all familiar with phrases we have read in this context, such as 'The retail price index was way above expectations, leading to a strong rise in interest.' However, the problem many market operators encounter in this context is that, although they have some idea of what lies behind such economic indicators, it is virtually impossible (given the large number of indicators) to have all the methodological information on the most important information to hand all the time. It is precisely this problem that this book addresses. Key indicators from the USA and the Euro-zone are described in detail with links between the individual indicators. With the help of this book no one will be at a loss for words when asked to explain why unemployment has risen in the USA, where so many new jobs have been created outside the agricultural sector, for example. One possible explanation for this phenomenon could be that both figures are taken from different jointly published surveys. Consequently, they can portray opposite pictures of the labour market situation, without any necessary contradiction in terms of faults in the survey.

This book attempts to provide a comprehensive summary of the key economic indicators in the USA and the Euro-zone, but there is always the problem that new indicators may be added or the structure of existing indicators changed, as has happened frequently of late. This book was published in German in September 2000. Since then, for many indicators from the Euro-zone the methodology has been updated. The same is true for some US indicators where they have started to use the North American Industry Classification System (NAICS) instead of the Standard Industrial Classification (SIC) system. This may also happen (to a lesser extent) in the future. In spite of these inevitable problems, the book is a helpful guide for all those who are not just interested in the foreground data but want to look 'behind' the figures in order to produce even better analysis. For these people the book should represent a useful source of reference.

Through my research I was directed to a great many different sources. This primarily took the form of personal contact. Consequently, I would like to take this opportunity to thank first Henning Ahnert from the EZB, Richard Curtin from the University of Michigan, Angela Grobler from NTC Research, Michael Holstein from DZ Bank, Franz-Josef Klein from the EU Commission, Alamaiz Ozyildivim from The Conference Board, Klaus Reeh from Eurostat, Joachim Scheide from the Kiel Institute of World Economics and Hermann Seyler from the Ifo Institute for Economic Research, as well as Ulrich van Suntum from the University of Münster for their help in producing this book. Without their willingness to provide me with information, which only someone involved in creating economic indices could do, a number of sections in this book would have been poorly described or omitted. In addition I would also like to thank Nils Domann and Bob Sinnige from Thomson Financial/Datastream. Of course, I take full responsibility for any inconsistencies remaining. Moreover, those mentioned are to be exonerated from all responsibility, other than my heartfelt thanks for the useful information in this book. And finally, I would like to thank my wife Karin and my two children Enya and Joshua who had to forgo a lot of time with me and encouraged me throughout the time the book was in production, in spite of all the difficulties.

It is a myth that Mark Twain once said the art of prophecy is very difficult, especially with respect to the future. As it cannot be proved whether he is the true source of this quotation, one can see how difficult it is to analyze what has happened in the past. In addition (as mentioned in the quotation), it is by far more difficult to forecast what will happen in the future. These problems are two of the many that market participants are faced with each day. I hope I have been able to provide all the people working with fundamentals with a useful, handy guide to make their work at least a little bit easier.

Conrad Mattern

List of Abbreviations

BEA	Bureau of Economic Analysis
bop	balance of payments
BLS	Bureau of Labor Statistics
c.i.f.	cost, insurance and freight
COF	Costs of funds
CPI-U	Consumer Price Index for all Urban Customers
CPI-W	Consumer Price Index for all Urban Wage Earners and Clerical Workers
DEA	Data Envelopment Analysis
ECB	European Central Bank
EMU	European Monetary Union
ESA	European System of Accounts
ETA	Employment and Training Administration
f.a.s.	free alongside ship
FISIM	Financial Intermediation Services Indirectly Measured
f.o.b.	free on board
GAFO	General merchandise, Appliance, Furniture, and Other
GNI	gross national income
ILO	International Labour Organization
IMF	International Monetary Fund
INSEE	Institut National de la Statistique et des Études Économiques
ISAE	Instituto di Studi e Analisi Economica
ISM	Institute for Supply Management
LIFO	last in, first out
MFI	monetary financial institution
MIG	Main Industrial Grouping
m/m	month on month
MZM	Money, Zero Maturity
NAHB	National Association of Home Builders
NAICS	North American Industry Classification System
NAPM	National Association of Purchasing Managers
NAR	National Association of Realtors
NBER	National Bureau of Economic Research
nsa	not seasonal adjusted
OECD	Organization for Economic Co-operation and Development
OPEC	Organization of Petroleum-Exporting Countries
PMAC	Purchasing Management Association of Chicago
q/q	quarter on quarter

rhs	right-hand scale
sa	seasonal adjusted
saar	seasonal adjusted at annual rates
SIC	Standard Industrial Classification
SITC	Standard International Trade Classification
TRAMO/SEATS	Time Series Regression with ARIMA-Noise, Missing Observation and Outliers/Signal Extraction in ARIMA Time Series
ULC	Unit Labour Costs
y/y	year on year

Part I

Introduction

1
General Introduction

In recent years, the general public has become increasingly aware of economic activities, aided and abetted by the growing involvement of private individuals in the stock market. As decisions in financial markets have become no longer a matter of luck but based on structured decisions, the investor or adviser has been left with two options. First, decisions can be based on technical indicators or charts. This is the field of technical analysis, whose importance has steadily increased in recent times. In addition, there is fundamental analysis, which boasts a far longer history, although considered 'elitist' for a long time, whereby national economic indicators are calculated and their importance and effect explained in a somewhat cryptic form. Any investors basing their decision to some extent on economic performance should therefore have at least some idea of what individual economic indicators mean and their relation to other indicators.

The effects of economic values on financial markets or fixed income markets are therefore comparatively simple. References to strong (weak) economic growth and therefore related to higher (lower) inflation have a mainly negative (positive) impact on these financial markets, as they imply higher (lower) interest and therefore lower (higher) market rates. This apparently simple link is no longer so easy to identify in relation to other financial markets. High economic growth frequently produces high inflation, which in turn prompts the central bank to tighten monetary policy more by raising interest. This, however, makes company lending more expensive, thereby narrowing the profit margin. At the same time, the higher economic growth also means that companies can sell more because demand rises. Due to the increase in demand they also probably have greater scope to increase prices. In this respect higher economic growth positively influences company profits. The question therefore remains as to the overall effect on a company and on the trend on the stock markets. The situation in the currency markets is different again. High interest rates tend to suppress economic growth. Falling growth rates adversely affect the exchange rate of a currency. High interest rates make investment in this country attractive, boosting capital inflows, thereby in principle positively affecting the exchange rate.

It is not the aim of this book to explain the fundamental factors of performance and their interdependencies within the financial markets. Instead, it aims to form a basis for appreciating the fundamentals in the USA and the Eurozone, the European Monetary Union (EMU) region. This can then be taken as the starting point for fundamental analysis of these national economies and their effects on the financial markets.

The importance of a national economic indicator ultimately depends on a number of factors:

1. **Time of publication**

   The importance of an indicator depends on how up-to-date the information is. If economic figures are published after several months' delay, the underlying information can be estimated in advance with the help of the other indicators, thereby reducing the importance of the indicator itself.

   Example

   One of the reasons why so much notice is taken of the ISM Purchasing Managers' Index for Manufacturing Business is that it is published on the first working day of the month and provides one of the earliest bits of information on the economic situation in the preceding month.

2. **Scope of new information**

   Information is partly published in the form of a number of statistics and individual information can be estimated on the basis of other statistics. The importance of an indicator therefore directly increases as more new information is published with this indicator.

   Example

   One of the most important publications of US economic indicators is the *Labor Market Report*. With the help of this report, conclusions can be drawn about economic growth, inflation pressure, the profit situation of companies and international competition. As a result the *Labor Market Report* (in conjunction with producer prices and consumer prices) is given top priority among US statistics.

   Nevertheless, little notice is taken of the statistics on housing completions in the USA as the situation in this market sector can be assessed with adequate accuracy using other indicators already published for the construction sector.

3. **Accuracy of statistics**

   Indicators fluctuate over time and are also often subsequently adjusted. The more volatile an indicator, the more difficult is its use to identify economic trends. At the same time, adjustments can cause the picture produced by the indicator to become unsustainable. Consequently, the importance of an indicator becomes greater, the more the economic situation is portrayed clearly and the number of false signals lowered, reducing the need for subsequent revisions.

Example

Retail sales normally provide a good summary of consumer demand in a national economy. In Germany, the significance of this statistic is, however, limited by the fact that it fluctuates dramatically from month to month and that there are frequent adjustments.

4. **Importance for economic policy decisions**

   The more weight economic policy decision makers attach to an indicator, the more significant this indicator is to the financial markets. It is worth noting, however, that this significance is not independent of the aforementioned points. Indicators, which frequently provide false signals, are only given minor weighting in economic policy decision-making. The significance of an indicator also depends on how closely it is linked to the respective target value. However, as this link can change over time, it inevitably follows that the relative significance of indicators can also change over time. Moreover, indicators in different countries do not all have the same significance.

Example

Since the mid-1970s monetarism has become so well established in economic policy practice that most central banks responded to monetary trends with monetary policy regulation. The Deutsche Bundesbank played a pioneering role in this, and this still characterizes their significance inside the European Central Bank (ECB) even today. In recent years the significance of these indicators has suffered as a result of financial innovations. The Federal Reserve, for example, has since largely begun to focus on actual trends rather than specific targets. In addition, individual central banks have switched to direct inflation targeting so that the money supply is now only one indicator with equal weight in a whole series of indicators. The importance of indicators can therefore change over time and also differ between nations.

With regard to fundamentals in particular there is the problem of the data being extremely difficult to assess accurately. Market operators are frequently surprised by data releases. In the forefront of such vital statistics market operators and high street bank economists are questioned about their expectations. The results are then published in the form of a market consensus. The markets frequently clearly anticipate certain results in advance; that is, they act on expectations. The more important an indicator is for the financial markets, the greater the false expectation is in a publication and the stronger the market response is to the data published. Therefore, the chance of achieving profits via the respective positioning in terms of the market consensus increases and also the results published can be estimated more accurately.

The importance of knowing how indicators are constructed to forecast economic developments can be seen in a publication from the International Monetary Fund (IMF). The private organization, Consensus Forecast, publishes each month an overview of forecasts made by large banks on GDP growth, inflation unemployment and so on for all the major countries. While evaluating the performance of Consensus Forecast of GDP growth for industrialized and developing countries from 1989 to 1998, it was found that from 60 recessions, only two had been forecast in the year before they happened. Looking at the average forecast, it is still worse. All forecasts had been too optimistic. In the year before a recession, the forecast growth exceeded actual growth in all cases.

In principle, the analysis of economic data involves providing answers to the following questions:

- How high is economic growth?
- How high is inflation?

And consequently:

- What impact will these have on interest rates, stock prices and currency markets?

The most comprehensive measurement of economic performance and thereby economic growth is the GDP. In simple terms, GDP can be taken as the sum of consumption, investment, government purchases and net exports. As publication of the GDP is subject to relatively long delays in most countries, it is helpful to estimate sections of the individual components which have already been published in advance and economic growth can be approximated with the help of these. The most important component is consumer demand, which accounts for over 70 per cent of the GDP in some nations. Consumer demand is only subject to slight fluctuation. However, with its share of the GDP this slight fluctuation is clearly noticeable in terms of economic growth. Key indicators for assessing consumer demand include retail sales, consumer confidence surveys, income trends and the demand for consumer credit. The demand for investment is far more volatile in comparison to consumer demand, so that the largest proportion of fluctuations in economic growth can be attributed to this smaller component. This figure is estimated with the aid of data on production of investment goods, inventories and construction activity. Finally, data on the balance of trade and balance of payments are particularly essential for the analysis of international demand.

The aforementioned division of the GDP into components considers economic performance in terms of the consumer. At the same time it is also useful to analyze the production side. Here, data on industrial production are particularly relevant as fluctuations in industrial production tend to have the greatest impact on fluctuations in economic performance. In addition, industrial production trends are strongly influenced by exchange rate fluctuations and relative price trends in the respective individual nations. This means that this sector is of great importance for the analysis of global economic growth.

Apart from the 'standard' data on economic performance, company surveys can also provide information on the economic situation. Surveys have an advantage over production data in that they reflect people's attitudes, which can trigger a response to developments far earlier than production plans. In addition, short-term distortions, such as extreme weather conditions or differences in the number of working days are short-lived or not reflected at all in surveys.

The labour market data need to be considered between the data from the production side and the consumer side. On the one hand, they are affected by the economic position of the enterprises, and on the other, the labour market situation affects demand for goods and services in turn. In addition, labour market data can provide information on rising inflation pressure.

Finally, inflation can be measured using a number of methods. Apart from the GDP price deflator, which represents the broadest measure of price trends, these primarily include producer and consumer prices. Nevertheless, for policy-making and market trends it is important not only to be informed about the current inflation rate but also (and at least as important) to assess the inflationary pressure that may be building.

According to monetarist theory, inflationary trends can only develop in the long term when the central bank fails to keep a tight enough grip on monetary trends. This is why monetary aggregates have been so important for financial markets in the past. As was explained in the above example, the importance of monetary aggregates for inflation trends in the past has been somewhat reduced by the introduction of financial innovations. In spite of this, these numbers continue to play an important role in monetary policy and still serve as a guide on potential interest rate decisions by the central banks.

It has already been intimated that individual indicators can provide early forecasts of trends for other indices or economic performance in general. Some indicators largely change direction in line with cyclical trends, whereas others only change direction after the turning point of an economic cycle. Such indicators are called leading indicators, coincident indicators or lagging indicators. Leading indicators are characterized by the fact that they reflect turning points in economic cycles before these turning points are actually visible. As expectations have great influence on market trends in financial markets, leading indicators are therefore of great importance. These include, amongst others:

- New orders
- Building permits
- Information on overtime
- Monetary trends
- Consumer expectations
- Business climate indices

By contrast, coincident indicators are characterized by the fact that they develop mostly parallel to the economic cycle. They make it possible to assess economic cycles more accurately as national accounting data is normally subject to time delays and only published quarterly. These include, amongst others:

- Labour market figures
- Information on available income
- Data on industrial production
- Sales figures at various production levels and in the retail sector

Lagging indicators, on the other hand, usually only supply information on changes in the cyclical situation after the situation has changed. They therefore normally change direction after the coincident indicators. They can be used to check whether the coincident indicators have given the correct signal. On the other hand, they also act as a guide as to whether major structural imbalance is to be expected within a national economy, which could be averted via economic policy measures. Lagging indicators include, among others:

- Average period of unemployment
- Inventory to sales ratio
- Ratio of consumer installment credit outstanding to personal income

In addition to the leading indicators on the business cycle there are also indices for assessing inflationary pressure. On the one hand, it should be noted that inflationary trends often occur in waves through all levels of the production process. As a result, price increases in crude materials, for example, are initially reflected in the crude material price index, then in the producer price indices for intermediate products and finally in the producer price indices for finished products. Only then does a price change affect consumer prices for goods, thereby finally also affecting prices for services.

To what extent price changes affect the individual stages depends on the scope within the company for passing on price increases. In a sector with marked competition between companies there is far less potential than, for example, in a sector with only a few highly specialized companies. On the other hand, price trends are also affected by cost factors occurring within the production stages such as wages, individual taxes and profit margins. The following are some of the leading indicators for consumer price trends:

- Unit labour costs
- Labour market figures
- Capacity utilization
- Commodity prices
- Producer prices
- Purchasing power of currencies
- Surveys on expected price trends

Literature

Clark, Peter *et al.*, *Exchange Rates and Economic Fundamentals*, International Monetary Fund Occasional Paper, Washington, DC, 115, December 1994.

Fleming, Michael J. and Remolona, Eli M., 'What Moves the Bond Market?' in Federal Reserve Bank of New York, *Economic Policy Review*, December 1997, pp. 31–50.

Fleming, Michael J. and Remolona, Eli M., *The Term Structure of Announcement Effects*, Bank for International Settlements, BIS Working Paper No. 71, Basel, June 1999.

Galati, Gabriele and Ho, Corinne, 'Macroeconomic news and the euro/dollar exchange rate', Bank for International Settlements, BIS Working Paper No. 105, Basel, December 2001.

Holstein, Michael and Moersch, Mathias, 'Reaktion der Finanzmärkte auf Wirtschaftsdaten: Deutscher Rentenmarkt und US-Konjunktur' [The Reaction of Financial Markets to Fundamental Indicators: German Bond Market and US Business Cycle], Michael Stierle (ed.), *Wirtschaftsdaten, Konjunkturprognosen und ihre Auswirkungen auf die Finanzmärkte* [*Economic Indicators, Economic Forecast and the Impact on Financial Markets*], INFER Studies Vol. 2, Verlag für Wissenschaft und Forschung, 2000, pp. 67–85.

Loungani, Prakash, *How Accurate are Private Sector Forecasts? Cross-Country Evidence from Consensus Forecast of Output Growth*, IMF Working Paper No. WP/00/77, April 2000.

Moersch, Mathias, 'Predicting Market Movers: A Closer Look at Consensus Estimates', *Business Economics*, April 2001, pp. 24–9.

Schröder, Michael and Dornau, Robert, 'What's on their Mind: Do Exchange Rate Forecasters Stick to Theoretical Models?', Zentrum für Europäische Wirtschaftsforschung, *ZEW Discussion Paper No. 99–08*, Mannheim, 1999.

Thomas, Lloyd B. Jr. and Grant, Alan P., 'Forecasting Inflation – Surveys versus other Forecasts', *Business Economics*, July 2000, pp. 9–18.

2

Index Values versus Rates of Change

Most economic indicators are published in the form of indices, from which the direction and degree of change to the underlying factors can be calculated. Base years, to which indices relate, and against which change is measured, are often used. The value of a base year is often standardized: 0, 1 or 100 being the most popular starting values. Rates of change in terms of preceding years or the base period can be calculated from the index values. The percentage change between two periods is normally calculated using the following formula:

$$\left(\frac{\text{Index value in period } t}{\text{Index value in period } t - 1} - 1 \right) * 100$$

Example

If an index value increases from 131 to 132, this corresponds to a percentage change of:

$$\left(\frac{132}{131} - 1 \right) * 100 = (1.00763 - 1) * 100 = 0.763\%$$

The disadvantage of this method is that positive and negative changes are treated differently.

Example

Assuming a value of 100, a reduction of 10 units is first undertaken and then a further rise of 10 units (i.e., the original and end value are identical). The resulting percentage changes calculated then amount to:

$$\left(\frac{90}{100} - 1 \right) * 100 = -10.00\% \quad \text{and} \quad \left(\frac{100}{90} - 1 \right) * 100 = +11.11\%$$

If, on the other hand, an identical positive and negative percentage change is assumed, the original and end values no longer correspond. If, assuming a value of 100, an initial increase and then a decrease of 10 per cent is undertaken, the result is:

$$100 * 110\% = 110 \quad \text{and} \quad 110 * 90\% = 99$$

This is avoided by applying the formula for symmetrical percentage changes as follows:

$$\left(\frac{\text{Index value in period } t - \text{Index value in period } t - 1}{\text{Index value in period } t + \text{Index value in period } t - 1} \right) * 200$$

When a percentage change is calculated with this formula and the same percentage change occurs with a different sign in the following period, the index value reverts to its original value.

Example

In the same way as with the above example, assuming a value of 100, an initial decrease of 10 units and then an increase of 10 units again is undertaken. The resulting percentage changes then amount to:

$$\frac{90 - 100}{90 + 100} * 200 = -10.53\% \quad \text{and} \quad \frac{100 - 90}{100 + 90} * 200 = 10.53\%$$

The base period is chosen according to a number of factors. This can be the period in which the index is calculated for the first time. In this case, the index relates to a specific day, month or year, which is established as the initial value. It is also possible, however, to incorporate the average value of such a period. In addition, the base year can change over the years. This is mostly the case when the index is aligned to changed conditions. One example of this is the regular adjustment of a basket of goods to calculate rates of price changes.

Basically, indices can be calculated in two ways. First, the weighting of the components in the index may remain constant over the period. A change only occurs therefore when the individual components change. Second, the weighting of the individual components may change over the period. This is normally applied when the weighting of the components no longer corresponds to the circumstances they are supposed to portray. One example of this is the increased weighting of information technology, which up to a few years ago was far less important and was therefore represented by a lower weighting in the government statistical baskets of goods. This has been adjusted in recent years.

A change in the composition of an index can occur for two reasons. First, a change in the index can arise as a result of a change in the components (similarly to the index with constant weightings), but can also be due to a change in the weightings themselves. In this case, the index with the new weighting is normally calculated subsequently for a number of preceding periods to obtain a measure for comparison. The old weightings continue to be announced in some cases for the interim period.

Example

Components	Original weightings	Adjusted weightings	Price in Period 1	Price in Period 2
A	10%	30%	3	1
B	50%	30%	2	2
C	40%	40%	1	3

The resulting index values for the original weightings are:

$$(0.1 * 3) + (0.5 * 2) + (0.4 * 1) = 0.3 + 1.0 + 0.4 = 1.7$$

and,

$$(0.1 * 1) + (0.5 * 2) + (0.4 * 3) = 0.1 + 1.0 + 1.2 = 2.3$$

The values with the new weightings, however, produce the following:

$$(0.3 * 3) + (0.3 * 2) + (0.4 * 1) = 0.9 + 0.6 + 0.4 = 1.9$$

and,

$$(0.3 * 1) + (0.3 * 2) + (0.4 * 3) = 0.3 + 0.6 + 1.2 = 2.1$$

The index thereby changes on the basis of the original weightings by:

$$\left(\frac{2.3}{1.7} - 1\right) * 100 = 35.3\%$$

according to the new weightings, however, only by:

$$\left(\frac{2.1}{1.9} - 1\right) * 100 = 10.5\%$$

3
Real versus Nominal Figures

Most statistics are published both as nominal and real figures. Nominal values are figures measured in terms of current prices, whereas real values are figures relating to the prices in a specific base year. The reason for this method is to exclude distorting effects, as a result of price changes, from the measurement. Changes in real figures therefore only occur as a result of changes in quantity, whereas changes in nominal figures represent a combination of quantity and price changes.

Example

Wine sales are to be measured within a national economy. The starting point is Year 1. Sales and average prices are shown below.

	Year 1	Year 2	Year 3	Year 4
Unit volume of sales	100	120	120	110
Average unit price	20	25	30	35

Accordingly, in Year 1 in nominal terms $100 * 20 = 2000$ monetary units were generated, compared with 3000 monetary units in Year 2. Therefore sales from Year 1 to Year 2 rose in nominal terms by:

$$\left(\frac{3000}{2000} - 1\right) * 100 = 50\%$$

The remaining sales and growth rates are shown below.

	Year 1	Year 2	Year 3	Year 4
Unit value of sales (nominal)	2000	3000	3600	3850
Change on preceding year		50%	20%	6.9%

If we now examine the individual rates of change more closely, the price distorting effects can be identified. In Year 2 the change occurred as a result of a simultaneous increase in quantity and price. In the subsequent year the quantity sold remained constant at 120 units, whereas prices continued to rise. And Year 4 still shows a nominal rise, although sales were down from 120 to 110 units.

These distorting effects are excluded from the consideration of real sales, although there is then the problem of the selection of a base year, (i.e., the year on which the prices are based). If, for example, Year 1 is chosen as the base year, real sales are obtained by multiplying the relevant quantity by the price of year 1. Consequently, in Year 2 the following sales are effected: $(120 * 20) = 2400$.

Base year 1	Year 1	Year 2	Year 3	Year 4
Unit value of sales (real)	2000	2400	2400	2200
Change on preceding year		20%	0%	−8.3%

For Year 2 a rise of 20 per cent is reported with no change in real sales in the following year and for Year 4 a fall of 8.3 per cent.

On the other hand, if Year 4 is chosen as the base year the rates of change remain the same as when Year 1 is the base year even if the real sales values change.

Base year 4	Year 1	Year 2	Year 3	Year 4
Unit value of sales (real)	3500	4200	4200	3850
Change on preceding year		20%	0%	−8.3%

The measurement of real and nominal values is simple as long as only one product is examined. However, this changes dramatically as soon as a number of products are considered at the same time. One reason for this lies in the problem of determining the relative importance of individual goods. However, there are various options for measuring change. Each of these is statistically correct, although they can produce completely different results, so in reality it can be difficult to measure the 'real' real values. The problems arising can be illustrated in an 'economy' with two goods.

Example

It is assumed that only two goods are produced in a national economy: cars and computers. The respective quantities and prices are shown below:

	Year 1	Year 2	Year 3
Quantities produced:			
Cars	10	15	13
Computers	10	20	30
Unit prices:			
Cars	10	12	15
Computers	10	10	8

The nominal GDP and the respective shares of the two components in the GDP are obtained by multiplying the quantities by the relative prices and then by adding them.

	Year 1	Year 2	Year 3
Nominal unit value of GDP:	200	380	435
Cars	100	180	195
Computers	100	200	240

The respective rates of change of the factors can be seen in the table below. Thus, in Year 2 for example, the number of cars produced rose by 50 per cent on the preceding year with prices up by 20 per cent in contrast. Consequently, cars as a share of GDP rose by 80 per cent, whereas total GDP was up by 90 per cent.

Rates of change	Year 1	Year 2	Year 3
Quantities produced:			
Cars		50%	−13.3%
Computers		100%	50%
Unit prices:			
Cars		20%	25%
Computers		0%	−20%
Nominal unit value of GDP:		90%	14.5%
Cars		80%	8.3%
Computers		100%	20%

In order to obtain the real GDP, a base year now has to be established. If Year 1 is chosen as the base year, all quantities are multiplied by the prices in Year 1. Real figures are thereby obtained by the following calculation:

	Year 1	Year 2	Year 3
Real GDP at Year 1 prices:	200	350	430
Cars	100	150	130
Computers	100	200	300

Rates of change	**Year 1**	**Year 2**	**Year 3**
Real GDP at Year 1 prices:		75%	22.9%
Cars		50%	−13.3%
Computers		100%	50%

Real GDP thereby increased in Year 2 by 75 per cent, whereby the individual components were up by 50 per cent and 100 per cent respectively.

For the level of the inflation rate it is now crucial that the right measuring procedure is used. With the publication of the GDP figures a price deflator is always calculated as well to take into account both quantity and price changes. A price deflator is calculated by dividing nominal GDP by real GDP.

Example

On the basis of the national economy described above the following price deflator was calculated for Year 2:

$$\frac{380}{350} = 1.086$$

The values for the other years and the resulting rates of change are shown below.

	Year 1	Year 2	Year 3
Price deflator	1	1.086	1.012
Rate of change		8.6%	−6.8%

The economic impact of a price deflator lies in the fact that it expresses the inflation components for a nominal change in GDP. In the above example the economy rose by 90 per cent in nominal terms. This constitutes a 75 per cent increase in the real components and a rise of 8.6 per cent in the price components. The total increase is therefore a product of these two components ($1.75 * 1.086 = 1.90$).

Another way of calculating inflation is to employ the relative weightings which the individual components have in certain years. Either the actual years (Paasche Index) or a specific base year in the past (Laspeyres Index) may be selected, and this is then regularly adjusted.

Example

In a case where Year 1 is employed as the base year, the two components are incorporated into the calculation of the index with equal weighting, as both have a 50 per cent share in GDP. With the calculation of the index the prices in the respective years are multiplied by the weightings in the base year and shown as nominal figures, so that the index in the base year assumes a value of 1. For Year 2, for example, the following index value is obtained:

$$\frac{10 * 12 + 10 * 10}{10 * 10 + 10 * 10} = \frac{120 + 100}{100 + 100} = \frac{220}{200} = 1.10$$

Laspeyres Index	Year 1	Year 2	Year 3
Price index	1.00	1.10	1.15
Rate of change		10.00%	4.55%

On the other hand, if the respective current year is taken as the weightings the following index value is obtained for Year 2, for example:

$$\frac{15 * 12 + 20 * 10}{15 * 10 + 20 * 10} = \frac{180 + 200}{150 + 200} = \frac{380}{350} = 1.09$$

Paasche Index	Year 1	Year 2	Year 3
Price index	1.00	1.09	1.01
Rate of change		8.57%	−6.82%

The individual methods of calculation show that it is difficult to obtain the 'real' inflation rate. Consequently, for example, according to the Laspeyres Index for Year 3, a positive inflation rate is produced, although the price deflator and the Paasche index show a negative inflation rate. The reason for these different results lies in the relative weightings which the individual components have in the respective indices. As the individual price indices show different values, we may therefore conclude that different real GDP figures and growth rates will also be calculated with them, depending on which price indices are used to calculate the real values.

Another form of inflation accounting is the use of a chain-type index, whereby the weightings are regularly adjusted by identifying the relative

importance over several years with the aid of a moving average. Cases are
frequently encountered where the average calculation is obtained via geometric
means.

Example

For the above 'economy' it is assumed that relative weightings from the
current and preceding year form the basis of the calculation of the chain
index. Thus in Year 2 the following relative weighting occurs in the
calculation of the inflation rates for the automobile sector:

$$\frac{10*10+15*12}{(10*10+15*12)+(10*10+20*10)} - \frac{100+180}{(100+180)+(100+200)}$$

$$= \frac{280}{580} = 48.28\%,$$

with a relative weighting for the computer sector of:

$$\frac{10*10+20*10}{(10*10+15*12)+(10*10+20*10)} = \frac{100+200}{(100+180)+(100+200)}$$

$$= \frac{300}{580} = 51.72\%$$

If, on the other hand, geometric averages are calculated, the relative
weightings are:

$$\frac{\sqrt{(10*10)*(15*12)}}{\sqrt{(10*10)*(15*12)}+\sqrt{(10*10)*(20*10)}} = \frac{134.164}{134.164+141.421}$$

$$= \frac{134.164}{275.585} = 48.68\%$$

and,

$$\frac{\sqrt{(10*10)*(20*10)}}{\sqrt{(10*10)*(15*12)}+\sqrt{(10*10)*(20*10)}} = \frac{141.421}{134.164+141.421}$$

$$= \frac{141.421}{275.585} = 51.31\%$$

4
Seasonal Adjustment

The overriding majority of economic indicators are not just published in the form of their original values, but also contain seasonal adjustments. The reason for this is that cyclical trends cannot normally be identified from raw data as they reflect seasonal patterns which conceal the basic trends (see Figure 4.1). In certain individual data series, 95 per cent of periodic change is solely for seasonal reasons. Possible reasons for these seasonal patterns, among others, are:

- Regular change in weather conditions over the year
- Different number of working days within a period
- Routine pattern in a time series over the year, such as increased demand for non-durable goods in pre-Christmas business

These effects can be approximately eliminated by calculating rates of change in terms of the preceding year's figures. This procedure has the disadvantage that the values obtained in this way reflect cyclical trends over the entire preceding twelve months, whereas the question of the dynamic rate of the last few months remains unanswered.

By using seasonal adjustment methods and eliminating regularly recurring influences, one can try to identify cyclical basic trends and thereby make the values comparable with one another irrespective of the period under investigation. This is effected by eliminating seasonal patterns, different numbers of working days, or irregular influences, such as strikes or large orders.

The most popular seasonal adjustment procedure to date is the so-called Census X-11 ARIMA program, which was further developed and refined in the 1970s by the Federal Statistical Office in Canada from the X-11 procedure, developed in the 1960s by the US Bureau of the Census. In recent years, for example, as a result of information technology trends, the US Bureau of the

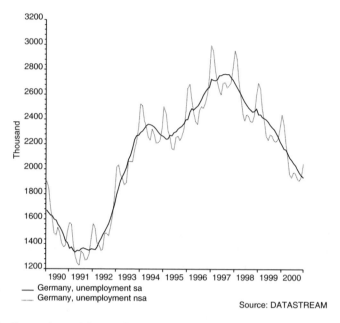

Figure 4.1 graph content:

Source: DATASTREAM

Figure 4.1 Comparison of data with and without seasonal adjustment

Census primarily produced the X-12 ARIMA procedure, which largely adopted the methodology from the X-11 ARIMA program but which also included additional new modules not yet employed. With this new procedure it is now easier to identify and classify extreme values. Apart from the so-called isolated blips which occur only in periods with bulk orders or extreme weather conditions, structural breaks (increase in direct tax) and unexpected special influences (which subsequently disappear), such as changes in demand following price changes, are taken into account in models of economic processes as well as their consequences for economic policy.

With aggregate figures in particular there is the question of what level of aggregation is effected in seasonal adjustment. Although seasonal adjustment at the highest level of aggregation is the simplest, this may mean the seasonal pattern is no longer correctly identifiable, particularly where contradictory trends occur within earlier levels.

Example

With the calculation of US unemployment figures various classes of employees are grouped together. Whereas unemployment with 'normal' employees is highest in the winter due to the weather conditions, youth unemployment regularly peaks in the summer when the school-leavers join the labour market. With seasonal adjustment for these earlier stages, different trends can be taken into account, whereas this is only possible to a limited extent at the aggregate level, as contradictory effects partly offset one another.

At the highest aggregate level, adjusted data therefore frequently produce different results from data which are subject to seasonal adjustment in terms of earlier periods and then shown as aggregates. Above all, in association with the data published by Eurostat, the so-called direct method of seasonal adjustment is employed, i.e., non-adjusted or trading-day adjusted data is first converted into aggregates and then subject to seasonal adjustment. The reason for this procedure is that Eurostat normally employs seasonal adjustment procedures which differ from those employed by the national bodies. Whereas most national statistical offices (in Germany this is the Deutsche Bundesbank) either use the X-11 ARIMA or the X-12 ARIMA method, Eurostat employs the TRAMO/ SEATS procedure (TRAMO = Time Series Regression with ARIMA-Noise, Missing Observation and Outliers; SEATS = Signal Extraction in ARIMA Time Series). Comparisons of the data series adjusted using these two methods have shown that the differences are not very great, yet minor discrepancies are unavoidable. As the national bodies for most economic indicators also calculate and publish national values with seasonal adjustment based on the procedure selected by them, the situation arises where values adjusted at national level differ from those adjusted based on the TRAMO/SEATS procedure by Eurostat. In order not to add to the confusion, it was decided that Eurostat would not publish any seasonally adjusted figures of national data. For this reason, national statistics are shown as aggregates first and seasonal adjustment is then conducted.

In addition to the seasonal adjustment procedures described above, in the surveys conducted on its behalf, such as the EU industrial survey, the EU Commission uses the Dainties method, which is another seasonal adjustment method featuring time series decomposition of various terms similar to the X-12 ARIMA model.

Normally, the calculation of seasonally adjusted data is based on the following pattern:

$$SAD = \frac{NSAD}{SAF}$$

where
SAD = Seasonally adjusted data
$NSAD$ = Non-seasonally adjusted data
SAF = Seasonal adjustment factor

It should be noted that the effects of seasonal adjustment factors offset one another within a year (see Table 4.1). The total of adjusted data within a year therefore corresponds to the total for non-adjusted data within a year. This does not, however, apply for adjustments occurring as a result of various calendar-related effects, but only for the 'real' seasonal pattern and weather conditions.

Table 4.1   Comparison of figures with and without seasonal adjustment

Number of unemployed in Germany 2000	Non-adjusted figures	Adjusted figures
January	4293	3970
February	4277	3942
March	4141	3944
April	3986	3932
May	3788	3900
June	3724	3897
July	3804	3882
August	3781	3859
September	3685	3838
October	3611	3811
November	3645	3797
December	3809	3772
Monthly average	3879	3879

However, as seasonal patterns can also change over time, the adjustment factors, have to be monitored and aligned regularly. This normally occurs every six to twelve months, in some cases even monthly. The latest data are taken into account for the alignment of the seasonal adjustment factors. However, the data are not all input into the calculation with the same weighting. The most up-to-date values are given top priority, and others are given less priority the older they are. The recalculation of the seasonal adjustment factors normally includes revision of earlier values in a series which have already undergone seasonal adjustment and are recalculated with new adjustment factors to ensure comparability of the data.

'Normal' seasonal fluctuations can be eliminated by using the seasonal adjustment method. However, in exceptional circumstances, although the new X-12 ARIMA procedure can determine the type of irregular influencing factor in most cases, it is not possible to exclude this effect. For this reason, some of the organizations producing seasonally adjusted data explicitly point out when such influencing factors distort basic trends.

Example

The US Federal Reserve noted on the publication of the US industrial production statistics for September 1999 that the data was somewhat lower as a result of Hurricane Floyd than it would have been without the extreme weather conditions.

Literature

Dagum, Estela Bee, *The X-ARIMA-Seasonal Adjustment Method*, Statistics Canada Catalogue No. 12–564E, January 1983.

Deutsche Bundesbank, 'The Changeover from the seasonal adjustment method Census X-11 to Census X-12-ARIMA', *Monthly Report*, September 1999, pp. 39–50.

Deutsche Bundesbank, *Einheitliche Saisonbereinigung der Deutschen Bundesbank und des Statistischen Bundesamts für Ergebnisse der vierteljährlichen Volkswirtschaftlichen Gesamtrechnungen* [*Uniform seasonal adjustment by Deutsche Bundesbank and Statistical Office for results of quarterly national accounts*], Press statement 29 May 2000, Frankfurt-am-Main.

European Central Bank, *Seasonal Adjustment of Monetary Aggregates and HICP for the Euro Area*, August 2000.

European Commission, 'The joint harmonised EU programme of business and consumer surveys', *European Economy*, No. 6, 1997, Luxembourg, Annex A.1.

Findley, D. *et al.*, 'New Capabilities and Methods of the X-12-ARIMA-Seasonal-Adjustment Program', *Journal of Business and Economic Statistics*, Vol. 16 (1999), pp. 127–52.

Higo, Masahiro and Nakada, Sachiko Kuroda, 'How can we Extract a Fundamental Trend from an Economic Time Series?', Bank of Japan, *IMES Discussion Paper*, No. 98-E-5, Tokyo.

Höpfner, Birgit, 'Ein empirischer Vergleich neuerer Verfahren zur Saisonbereinigung und Komponentenzerlegung' [Empirical comparison of new seasonal adjustment and competency assignment methods], *Wirtschaft und Statistik* 12 (1998), pp. 949–59.

Kirchner, Robert, 'Implications of the new seasonal adjustment method Census X12-ARIMA for current economic analysis in Germany', *Discussion Paper of the Economic Research Group, Deutsche Bundesbank*, No. 7 (1999).

Shiskin, Julius, Young, Alan and Musgrave, John, *The X-11 Variant of the Census Method II Seasonal Adjustment Program*, Technical Paper No. 15, Bureau of the Census, 1967.

Speth, Hans-Theo, 'Unterschiedliche Verfahrensweisen der Statistischen Ämter in der Europäischen Union bei der Saisonbereinigung' [Different methodology in statistical offices in the European Union for seasonal adjustment], *Wirtschaft und Statistik* 1 (1999), pp. 23–7.

5
Annualization

Data are frequently annualized or expressed in the form of an annual rate. The reason for this is to make it comparable if it relates to different periods. To achieve this, a number of methods are available, although their results may vary and they therefore have different advantages and disadvantages. It is generally assumed that the trend occurring in the preceding period will continue. An annual rate therefore does not contain any prediction about how the trend will continue over time. Instead, it is a description of how the trend would be if the trend in the last period continued.

The simplest way of calculating an annual rate is by multiplying the values obtained within a month or a quarter over 12 months or four quarters.

Example

In March 2001 approximately 85 000 new houses were sold in the USA following seasonal adjustment, thereby giving an annual rate of:

$$85\,000 * 12 = 1\,020\,000 \text{ new homes.}$$

Growth rates, on the other hand need to be treated differently. Assuming a base period, a time series changes and thereby produces periodic growth. In the following period a new base period occurs. It is then necessary to link the individual time sections together in order to calculate an annual rate for a specific period. As it is assumed that the respective change will remain constant, the monthly rate is exponentiated by twelve for the annual rate, whereby the exponential is four for quarterly changes.

Example

GDP in the USA for the first quarter of 2001 was USD9422.8 billion at a seasonal adjusted annual rate, in the preceding quarter it was USD9393.7 billion. This produces an annualized growth rate of:

$$\left(\left(\frac{9422.8}{9393.7}\right)^4 - 1\right) * 100 = (1.0030978^4 - 1) * 100 = (1.0124490 - 1) * 100$$

$$= 1.2\%$$

The US economy thus grew in the first quarter of 2001 by an annual rate of 1.2 per cent.

The producer price index in the USA in April 2001 was up, being 142.1 compared with the preceding month's value of 141.7. This produced an annual rate of:

$$\left(\left(\frac{142.1}{141.7}\right)^{12} - 1\right) * 100 = (1.002822865^{12} - 1) * 100$$

$$= (1.034405286 - 1) * 100 = 3.4\%$$

Producer prices thus rose in April 2001 by an annualized rate of 3.41 per cent.

Annual rates are calculated to make trends in periods of different lengths comparable with one another. Nevertheless, the so-called base effect also has to be taken into account. This is the position on which various figures are based from different points, and thereby from which different trends can be shown.

Example

The trend of the real GDP for Germany for the years 1997 and 1998 can be seen in the following table:

	GDP (in billion DEM, 1991 prices)	Change on preceding quarter, annual rate	Change on preceding year's quarter
1st quarter 1997	767.5		
2nd quarter 1997	775.3	4.1%	
3rd quarter 1997	779.1	2.0%	
4th quarter 1997	783.1	2.1%	
1997 Average	776.5		
1st quarter 1998	793.3	5.3%	3.4%
2nd quarter 1998	793.2	−0.1%	2.3%
3rd quarter 1998	800.2	3.6%	2.7%
4th quarter 1998	797.2	−1.5%	1.8%
Average 1998	796.0		2.5%

The different methodology is particularly apparent in the fourth quarter of 1998. Whereas annual growth was −1.5 per cent on the preceding period, the value on the preceding year's period was up by 1.8 per cent. In extreme cases it can happen that positive growth is shown for the annual average, although over the entire year there was not one quarter where positive annual growth was reported. The reason is that in the first half of the base year, for example, there was very low growth, whereas in the second half high growth was reported. Consequently, the annual average is not very high. When the values in the quarters of the second year fall slightly, the annual average in the second year is above that of the previous year. Then positive growth for the averages of the two years is reported although all the individual quarters of the second year show negative growth. This phenomenon is called 'statistical overhang'. An explanation for this is described below:

	Time series values	Change on preceding quarter, annual rate	Change on preceding year's quarter
1st quarter	100		
2nd quarter	103	12.6%	
3rd quarter	107	16.5%	
4th quarter	110	11.7%	
Year 1 average	105		
1st quarter	109	−3.6%	9.0%
2nd quarter	108	−3.6%	4.9%
3rd quarter	108	0%	0.9%
4th quarter	107	−3.7%	−2.7%
Year 2 average	108		2.9%

Although there was not one quarter with positive growth throughout year 2, a positive annual average growth rate of 2.9 per cent is reported. The different trend in the first quarter of the second year is very clear. On the preceding quarter there is a negative annual growth rate of −3.6 per cent, whereas growth on the preceding year accounts for +9.0 per cent

In the last example, reference was made to the statistical overhang. This phenomenon arises from the difference between the last value of a period and the average value of this period. It is the value that would be created if, in the new period (normally one year), only a zero growth existed. In this case, the average value of this period would equal the last value of the period before. As a result, the average of the second period would be higher than the average of the first period, even if there was not one sub-period with a positive growth rate. This statistical overhang is higher the larger the difference between the last value and the average value of a period is. It is also higher the more dynamic a time series is.

Literature

European Central Bank, 'Carry-over effects on annual average growth rates of real GDP', *Monthly Report*, December 2001, pp. 47–8.

6
Benchmarks

Individual data series are normally based on surveys with a sub-group of all potential participants. On this basis the results published are then estimated. This can, however, produce considerable errors for a wide variety of reasons (see Chapter 8 on reasons for revisions). For these reasons more comprehensive surveys are conducted regularly using a larger database and where participation is obligatory frequently, in contrast to the monthly or quarterly surveys. The results of the full survey are only available a long time after the survey has been conducted due to their scope. As a result of these surveys, which are normally conducted annually or every five or ten years, it is possible to define benchmarks via which regular services can be orientated. They give an accurate summary of the number and composition of the companies or households questioned so that the results of the surveys can be used for estimates. Normally, the results of the benchmark surveys differ from the results of regular survey. In this case, the monthly or quarterly survey results have to be aligned to the benchmark results. To prevent breaks in the data series, earlier survey results also have to be revised. In particular, the method of distributing the difference between the results of the last monthly survey and the benchmark survey equally over all the survey results since the last benchmark revision is frequently employed.

7
Diffusion Indices

Diffusion indices can be used to check whether a change of an indicator or a group of indicators occurs as a result of one comprehensive change or change in a number of components, or whether a change is primarily due to one or more components which distort the overall position.

Example

An indicator composed of five components, for example, of which four remain unchanged, while the fifth rises by 100 per cent, corresponds to a rise of 20 per cent overall for components with equal weighting where the unequal distribution of the rise is not expressed.

To calculate diffusion indices it is therefore necessary first to examine how many components rise, remain unchanged and fall in order to allocate values to the respective components. Normally, a distinction is made between two cases in the calculation of diffusion indices:

- Case A
  Components with increases are allocated a value of 1, components with no change a value of 0.5 and components with decreases a value of 0.
- Case B
  Components with increases are allocated a value of 1, those with no change a value of 0 and components with decreases a value of -1.

In this method the conditions under which components are allocated to the individual categories have to be defined first. Frequently an approach is chosen whereby a component with no change constitutes one where the change on the preceding period is within an interval of, for example, $+/-0.05$ per cent. In addition, the allocation depends on the respective context. If economic performance is to be examined with the index, for example, and one of the components is the unemployment rate, for the calculation a decrease (in unemployment) is seen as a rise (in economic performance).

In a further step, the values allocated to the respective components are added together. This sum is then frequently divided by the number of components and then multiplied by 10 or 100 to standardize the final value. Diffusion indices, which are calculated on the basis of method A, therefore normally fluctuate between the values of 0 and 1 (or 100), whereas indices which are calculated according to Method B fluctuate between −1 (or −100) and +1 (or +100). The neutral points, i.e., the values with no change in value (on average), for Method A accounted for 0.5 (or 50), and for Method B, 0.

Example

For the calculation of a diffusion index five components are to be considered.

	Component 1	Component 2	Component 3	Component 4	Component 5
Period 1	5	3	7	1	6
Period 2	5	5	6	3	7
Case A	0.5	1	0	1	1
Case B	0	1	−1	1	1

In case A the total is 3.5. If we divide this value by 5, the number of components, and then multiply it by 100 the total value of the diffusion index is 70. In Case B, on the other hand, the total is 2.0 with a total value of 40.

To compare a diffusion index calculated using Method A with an index from Method B, the value of the index calculated with Method B is divided by 2 and added to 50. Vice versa, 50 is subtracted from the index which was calculated with Method A and the remainder is multiplied by 2. As can be seen from the above example, a value of 70 with the index calculated using Method A corresponds to a value of 40 with an index calculated using Method B.

As long as all components do not change on average, the diffusion index produces a neutral value. In Case A this value is 50; in Case B, 0. Depending on the underlying components the actual neutral point can shift and be higher or lower.

Example

The ISM Purchasing Managers' Index for Manufacturing Business in the USA by definition reports positive economic growth as long as a value of over 50 is produced. Empirical studies have, however, shown that zero growth is already achieved at a value of around 44. Each percentage point above this threshold value accounts for an additional annual growth rate for the GDP of approximately 0.3 percentage points. One reason for this is that rapidly growing, newly founded companies are taken into account with a time lapse, whereas established companies are still surveyed when they are on the brink of bankruptcy. Due to the random sampling the results can become distorted which can lead to a shift in the neutral value in the diffusion index.

Literature

Getz, Patricia M. and Ulmer, Mark G., 'Diffusion Indexes: A Barometer of the Economy', *Monthly Labor Review*, April 1990, pp. 13–21.

8
Reasons for Revisions

When defining economic indicators, errors can occur due to a wide range of circumstances, leading to an incorrect reflection of the economic situation and a distortion of the data point. These errors are partly caused by the fact that normally only a random sample is taken and not all relevant economic subjects are surveyed. The inaccuracies arising from error sources such as this do not occur as a result of incorrect calculations, but represent limitations in the informative value of the individual statistics. Each random sample will produce a somewhat different result. This result more closely approximates the result for the group overall, the larger the random sample. As a full survey is normally impracticable, a random sample is often conducted instead. The differences between random sample results and the 'real' results can then be quantified using standard deviation.

In addition there are also sources of errors which are independent from the sample chosen. This type of error can have far more serious consequences for the informative value of statistics than the sources of errors mentioned above as the scope of their influence is extremely difficult to quantify. Distortions in statistics which are independent of a specific random sample normally occur as a result of:

1. **Errors in the selection of subjects surveyed**
   Consequently, there is always a chance that people are surveyed who may not be part of the target group or economic subjects may not be questioned although their answers are relevant for the evaluation of the data. This can lead to distortions in the underlying database.
2. **Errors in the consideration of changes in the underlying database**
   This problem occurs above all in the calculation of price indices, as prices change frequently when new models or new products come onto the market.
3. **Errors as a result of incorrect time allocation of responses**
   Frequently the questions set are related to periods. Consequently for industrial production, for example, the number of goods produced within a certain

period is required. Errors can occur in this case where goods are allocated to another period, instead of the one in which they were produced. Moreover, errors can occur if the individual parts required for a product which is produced over several periods are not properly allocated to the individual periods.

4. **Errors in recording responses**

   This problem increases in proportion to the number of bodies involved in the process between the economic subject surveyed and the final evaluation. Such errors can also occur where the responses are based on incorrect recollections of initial data. In addition, misleading questions or interviewers distorting the responses via their survey method or the question may also constitute a source of error.

5. **Errors due to missing responses and data substitution**

   Frequently, data are unavailable in some parts because it was not possible to locate some of those surveyed or the responses were sent too late. This can mean that other data are used which are assumed to approximately reflect the trends for the missing data, where data are not available. This can, for example, occur when data from the preceding period are employed where the actual values differ considerably from the previous values.

6. **Errors in processing responses**

   Normally, surveys are evaluated using electronic data processing programs. For this the responses have to be in a form which can be processed first. Errors can thereby occur in the data conversion. They can also occur in the form of incorrect statistical processing, where statistical requirements are not taken into consideration.

With statistical methods it is possible to quantify at least the scope of errors from a sample survey and estimate confidence intervals within which the 'real' result is likely to be with some degree of certainty. In some publications, confidence intervals and levels are also published with them.

Example

In April 2001 construction was started on 1 586 000 privately-owned houses in the USA on an annual basis. This level is around 1 $(+/- 7)$ per cent below the revised April 2000 rate of 1 626 000.

This statement means that on the basis of the survey there was a drop of 1 per cent on the same month in the previous year. Due to the potential sources of error in the survey, the real values may well differ from this figure. There is a 90 per cent chance of the change being between -8 per cent and $+6$ per cent. The uncertainty is thereby so great that even with a probability of just 90 per cent it is not possible to say whether the number of new construction starts rose or fell on the same months of the preceding year.

Confidence intervals for errors which occur independently of the scope of the random sample are not, however, published, as they would also occur if all the possible economic subjects were surveyed.

Frequently the database is not completed on publication of the statistics. To account for late responses, revisions are often conducted in the following months to take the new results into consideration. Such revisions can take place one or more times. In some cases data are not immediately revised in the month following publication but only after a certain period when the database has increased enough to ensure that no further revisions will be required.

Example

The data on the GDP growth in the fourth quarter of 1998 were revised up in the preliminary report from 5.6 per cent (as shown in the advance report) to 6.1 per cent. One of the main reasons for this was the foreign trade deficit, which was considerably lower than expected, in the light of falling imports and rising exports. These data were not known at the time of publication of the advance report and therefore had to be estimated.

Other reasons for revisions include amongst others:

1. **Consideration of a new benchmark and alignment of earlier data to this new basis**

Example

In June 2001 the Bureau of the Census switched from the Standard Industrial Classification (SIC) system to the North American Industry Classification System (NAICS) and started to publish the retail sales data based on this new classification. One effect was that all data going back to January 1992 were reclassified and the benchmark is now based on the years 1992 and 1997. Thus all data going back to January 1992 had to be adjusted retrospectively and thereby revised (Data prior to 1992 are no longer available.)

2. **Change in data allocation**

Example

With the publication of the GDP data for the third quarter of 1999 software expenditure was no longer classed as consumer goods but as an investment. Consequently, the time series had to be recalculated retrospectively from the year 1959. One consequence of this was that average growth in the USA for the period from 1991 to 1999 was revised up from 3.1 per cent to 3.5 per cent.

3. **Errors in calculations/data transmission**

Example

In January 2001, Eurostat released the producer price index for November 2000, only to withdraw the release shortly after the initial publication. They explained that the German Statistisches Bundesamt had transmitted the wrong data to Eurostat which was then used for the calculation of the published index. They finally released the corrected numbers a few days later.

Not all data series are revised and aligned to new results. Whether this is carried out depends on the area of responsibility of the publishing body. In some cases revisions are not even conducted when it is determined that they are based on incorrect data.

Example

The data for the ISM Purchasing Manager's Indices in the USA is only revised in the January after publication when the new seasonal adjustment factors are incorporated. Subsequent revisions of the reasons for changes in the underlying database or input errors in previous months are not conducted.

One major problem arising from the revision of economic data is that it is hard to use this data as a basis for econometric models if one wants to forecast financial data. Once a price for one single stock, for a bond or an exchange rate is fixed, this price will not be revised. Thus if you have a time series of financial prices you can be sure what price was paid for an asset on a specific day. This is totally different from economic data. As mentioned before, these data will be revised for a number of reasons. The problem with econometric data is that financial markets react to the data as they were initially released. Sometimes the markets will notice revisions of the prior month, but everything before is of no interest to the financial markets.

If you compare the data as they were initially released with those available in data bases you will notice that there can be huge differences between these two sets of numbers. It is possible that a negative number could become a positive one, a number initially indicating no change now points to a large rise or decline and sometimes there is no change due to revisions. Thus it is not possible to find any major direction of the revisions.

Example

If you check the US GDP numbers you can find all sorts of impacts of revisions. Numbers were revised up, down or were unchanged. Positive

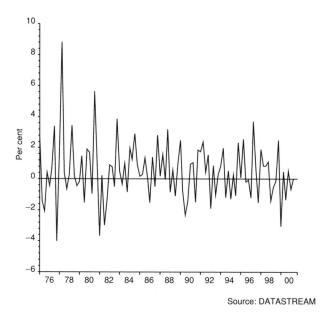

Source: DATASTREAM

Figure 8.1 Difference between initially released and actually available US GDP numbers, measured with quarter-on-quarter change (saar)

numbers became negative and vice versa. In addition, the amount of the revision varies. The advance data for the first quarter of 1978 has initially shown a 7.5 per cent saar increase against the quarter before. This was revised to 8.0 per cent as shown in the final report, released in June 1978. After several benchmark revisions, the numbers now show an increase of 16.3 per cent for this quarter. Thus the difference between the first release and the actual numbers for this quarter is 8.8 percentage points, more than the initial release.

The advance data for the second quarter 1981 showed an economic decline of −0.8 per cent. This was revised to +0.9 per cent in the final report. Now the data show an annualized increase of 4.9 per cent against the first quarter of 1981.

For the first quarter of 1991, the advance data showed an increase of 1.2 per cent against the quarter before. This number was revised down to 0.3 per cent. After all the benchmark revisions the data now show an increase of 2.3 per cent which is nearly twice the value of the initially released number.

The problem with revisions becomes worse if you compare countries because revisions happen in all countries but not necessarily in the same direction. For instance, if you want to find out if the growth differential between two countries

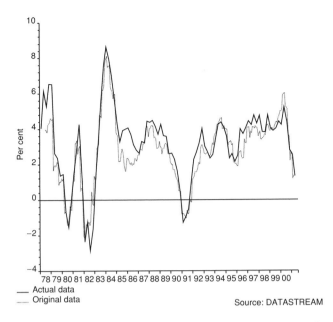

Figure 8.2 Change in US GDP on preceding year, based on initially released numbers and actual available data

had an impact on the exchange rate you have to use the numbers as they were initially released because these were the numbers the market was looking at. But nearly all statistical offices do not have a time series with the original data. Thus you have to collect these data yourself, which is very time consuming. The Federal Reserve Bank of Philadelphia has a database with originally released data but for quarterly data only one number per quarter is available.

Literature

Croushore, Dean and Stark, Tom, *A Real-Time Data Set for Macroeconomists: Does Data Vintage Matter for Forecasting?*, Federal Reserve Bank of Philadelphia Working Paper No. 00–6.

Mattern, Conrad, 'Wie sich Revisionen auf die Fundamental analyze auswirken' (How revisions affect fundamental analysis), *Boersen-Zeitung*, 22 March 2001.

Runkle, David E., 'Revisionist History: How Data Revisions Distort Economic Policy Research', *Federal Reserve Bank of Minneapolis Quarterly Review*, Fall 1998, pp. 3–12.

9
International Comparability of Data

Not all statistics are produced in all countries. In most countries, at least, approximations of these are available. If these statistics are used as the basis for a comparison of the economic situation in the individual nations, however, one soon encounters the problem that the individual indicators differ in fundamental ways. This leads to distortion and adversely affects the comparability of the data. Such distortions among others can occur as a result of the following reasons:

1. **Different definitions**
   One of the main causes of distorted statistics is the different allocation of individual sub-sections. This can also mean that individual figures are not included in some cases, or they are allocated to different components.
2. **Different survey periods**
   Some indicators are only surveyed on certain days, whereas others are monitored over a specific time period.
3. **Different survey methods**
   Whereas some indicators are generated via direct surveys, others are based on written or telephone polls, or are even calculated only on the basis of other statistics.
4. **Different seasonal adjustment methods**
   Many statistics are published in both forms with and without seasonal adjustment, yet the individual adjustment methods often differ slightly from one another. The main difference is probably whether an adjustment for working days is conducted or not. Differences can also occur as a result of different methodology in the production of adjustment factors (for details see Chapter 4).
5. **Different base years**
   Statistics, which are published in the form of indices, frequently relate to a base year. The basis for the calculation of the base is the respective economic situation in this year or a specific time period. As the respective situation

normally changes over time, regular adjustment of the base years is frequently required. The older the base year is, the greater the probability
that the underlying situation no longer corresponds to the current one. If
indicators are then compared with different base years, this can compound
the distorting effect.

6 **Publication period**

A distortion in the international comparison of statistics, which primarily
occurs with current (and, to a limited extent, with historical) values, occurs
where one country has only provisional figures and the other has the final
figures available.

7. **Different component weightings**

When indices consist of several components, these individual components
have to be assigned weightings. Normally these components correspond to
the situation to be described in the individual nations. If the differences
between the nations are very great, this is reflected in the composition of the
indices. This has to be taken into account in the interpretation of statistics
for comparison.

For the main indices it is at least possible to resort to statistics from common
sources. Consequently, statistics are calculated and published by the OECD or
the IMF on the basis of national indicators, whereby most of the differences
leading to definitional problems are eliminated. But the differences in survey
methods and periods cannot be eliminated as long as no independent surveys
are conducted.

10
Structure of the Book

The book is divided into four sections in total. In the introduction, general principles about the construction of economic indicators are described and the problems that are sometimes encountered when analysis is conducted, using cyclical indicators, are pointed out. In addition to the general knowledge on the construction of rates of change, real figures and annual rates, methods for seasonal adjustment are described in this context and the attributes of the diffusion index are explained.

The two main sections relate to the description and analysis of key economic indicators from the US and Euro-zone. Each of these two sections is identically structured and divided into the following sub-sections:

- General introduction
- Overall activity
- Company surveys
- Labour market indicators
- Consumer indicators
- Investment indicators
- International transaction indicators
- Inflation figures
- Financial activity
- Address list

In the general introduction section peculiarities of the respective currency area are described. In addition, there is also a summary of the key economic indicators in order of importance. The section on overall activity covers indicators such as national accounts, industrial production or leading indicators. This sub-section is therefore concerned primarily with indicators which directly illustrate the business cycle.

The company survey section describes indicators which do not relate to business activity on the basis of metric measured sales figures or investment decisions, but on the basis of surveys including primarily qualitative questions. One example of this is, 'How do you assess business activity compared to the preceding month? Higher, equal or lower?' The responses are regularly collected and evaluated using diffusion indices. One advantage of this method is that information can be collected directly from companies and the official statistics can then be usefully supplemented. Examples for this include purchasing management indices, as well as the Ifo Survey on Business from Germany or the EU Industrial Survey conducted by the EU Commission.

The labour market indicators section aims to explain economic indicators relating to the situation in the labour market. The most prominent example of this is the unemployment rate, which is often calculated differently in various nations. As a result values from different nations can only be compared with one another with extreme caution. Other key factors describing the labour market situation include new non-farm payrolls, the number of employed and change in working hours.

The consumer indicators section covers two main types of economic data. In addition to the retail trade sales, with which demand performance is measured, consumer confidence indices are also relevant. Since good progress has been made in this area in the analysis of consumer demand in the USA, there are now also similar indicators for the Euro-zone.

With regard to investment indicators, construction trade figures are the most interesting. Yet, particularly in this sector, the data position in the Euro-zone is clearly a long way behind the USA. Whereas the US construction industry can be analyzed with indicators covering everything from the planning to completion and sale of existing buildings, the Euro-zone only has access to a survey on the construction sector by the European Commission and, since 2001, an Index of the Production in the Construction Sector. Furthermore, there is US data on new orders for investment goods, whereas there are to date no comparable publications for the Euro-zone.

The international transaction section focuses primarily on data relating to international trade and balance of payments. However, these data are normally only made available subject to long delays so their importance for current analysis is limited. Instead, international transaction indicators in particular can be used to explain long-term relations or for background analysis. Balance of payments data are particularly helpful in this context for examining international capital flows, which are not just crucial for the currency markets but also affect the stock and bond markets.

Inflation figures are primarily concerned with producer prices, consumer prices and cost factors in the production and trade sectors. Whereas data on cost factors can be seen as a leading indicator for price trends, consumer price data provide information on price trends in a specific period. Producer prices, however, are in between. On the one hand they are a measure of price trends, and on the other they measure the inflation pressure to be expected with a time delay in consumer prices.

Financial activity is mainly described by monetary aggregates. These indicators illustrate how different the importance of individual factors is in different countries and how strongly their importance over time can change. Whereas monetary trends are one of the cornerstones of monetary policy at the ECB and publications can prompt strong repercussions on the financial markets, the importance of US monetary aggregates has steadily diminished in recent years, although the Federal Reserve Board still publishes money supply targets. The reason for this reduced importance is that failure to achieve the targets does not normally elicit any change in monetary policy and monetary aggregates are now no more than a minor figure within a whole set of economic indicators, which are used as the basis by the Federal Reserve Board for the analysis of the economic position.

The postal and internet addresses of the data providers producing the economic indicators in the book are listed in the final sub-section. Internet addresses are useful for accessing current publications, as most data providers produce at least a summary of the indicators on the internet.

A uniform approach was chosen to explain the individual indicators. The following points were covered for each indicator:

- Data source
- Importance for the financial markets
- Description
- Periodicity/revisions
- Seasonal adjustment
- Notes
- Key Datastream mnemonics
- Literature

Data source provides information on data producers for the respective economic indicators. Also provided are Internet addresses where a copy of the publication can be accessed. Other publications containing economic data in full or in part are also listed.

Importance for the financial markets employs a uniform grading of A to E. Indicators with an A grading are those which have the greatest influence on financial markets, whereas indicators graded E are of more minor importance. The aim was to make the evaluation of US and Euro-zone indicators comparable. For classification, studies were employed analyzing the effects of indicator publications on financial market prices. A survey with experienced financial market operators was also conducted and the results incorporated. It should, however, be noted that classification also changes again in the respective category, as has already been demonstrated in the example on the monetary aggregates. Economic indicators are also subject to fashion trends. This cannot be reflected in the book. For this reason the evaluation should be seen more as a rough guide providing general tips on the importance of each indicator and not as an absolute valuation standard.

Description is the most extensive section for the majority of indicators. It provides methodological information, sample calculations and peculiarities in data surveying, processing and limitations of data. Historical information is also provided.

Periodicity/revisions explains when data are surveyed, the date and time of publication and whether and to what extent data can be revised. Seasonals also contains explanations of whether economic indicators are subject to seasonal adjustment and if so what method is used.

Notes is the second largest description for each indicator. This summarizes all the key points which are important for the analysis of financial market trends. It indicates which sub-indicators impact on the financial markets and gives the connection to the other economic indicators. Explanations are illustrated with graphs where applicable.

Key Datastream mnemonics give mnemonics for the respective indicators and for other key sub-indicators, as provided by Datastream. This is not possible for all indicators and not all sub-indicators published are available from Datastream. In the tables, the names of such time series are mentioned, too. And there is space left to add important missing mnemonics when they become available in the future. This is also the case for the few indicators that are missing.

Usually the mnemonics for index values or absolute figures are accessible and can be used to calculate rates of change. In particular, for indicators from the Euro-zone there are frequently already rates of change on the preceding month, quarter or year and annual rates of change available. In such cases the special mnemonics are listed separately.

Literature supplies additional references and helps interested readers who want to study the material in greater depth.

The book finishes with an appendix that relates to indicators and financial data not explained in the two main parts of the book. This book is intended to help people who work in the field of financial markets to make the access to data on these markets more convenient. Thus, the appendix delivers a broad number of Datastream mnemonics on stock markets, bond markets, currency markets, commodities and some other economic indicators. It is far from being a complete survey but many of the major data series are included.

Part II

United States of America

11
General Introduction

The economic situation of the USA is reputed to be the most thoroughly surveyed and documented with the most up-to-date information. Some time series, for example, date back to the early nineteenth century. Most of the economic indicators are published by federal organizations, such as the Bureau of the Census and the Bureau of Economic Analysis at the Department of Commerce, the Bureau of Labor Statistics at the Department of Labor and the Federal Reserve Board. In addition there are a number of private organizations, such as the Institute for Supply Management (ISM) or the Conference Board.

The US economic data are not just of interest in analysis of the USA but also impact on the situation in other nations. The individual indicators each have a different significance for the economy and thereby also for the financial markets. A surprisingly positive or negative index result can initiate strong price movements on Wall Street, the bond market for US treasuries or the currency markets and influence prices in Europe or Asia correspondingly, due to the interdependencies in the markets. Consequently the analysis of the situation in the USA, the largest economy in the world, is fundamental to the analysis of all other industrial nations and should always be an integral component of a financial market analysis.

The individual indicators have been assigned values for their importance to the financial markets, whereby A represented the most important and E the least important. The most important US indicators are as follows:

1. **A grading**
   - Labor Market Report;
   - Producer prices;
   - Consumer prices.
2. **B grading**
   - National Accounts;
   - Industrial production and capacity utilization;

- Manufacturing ISM Report on Business;
- Retail sales;
- International trade;
- Labor Cost Index.

3. **C grading**
   - The Conference Board U.S. Business Cycle Indicators;
   - Federal Reserve Bank of Philadelphia Business Outlook Survey;
   - Personal income and personal consumption;
   - Index Consumer Confidence, The Conference Board U.S.;
   - Consumer Sentiment Index (University of Michigan);
   - Report on durable goods orders;
   - Report on New Housing;
   - Homebuilders Survey;
   - Balance of payments.

The Bureau of the Census divided up the USA into four sections with nine regions, which were employed for the various indicators. These are:

1. **Northeast**
   with the regions:
   - New England (Maine, New Hampshire, Vermont, Massachusetts, Rhode Island, Connecticut);
   - Middle Atlantic (New York, New Jersey, Pennsylvania).
2. **Midwest**
   with the regions:
   - East North Central (Ohio, Indiana, Illinois, Michigan, Wisconsin);
   - West North Central (Minnesota, Iowa, Missouri, North Dakota, South Dakota, Nebraska, Kansas).
3. **South**
   with the regions:
   - South Atlantic (Delaware, Maryland, District of Columbia, Virginia, West Virginia, North Carolina, South Carolina, Georgia, Florida);
   - East South Central (Kentucky, Tennessee, Alabama, Mississippi);
   - West South Central (Arkansas, Louisiana, Oklahoma, Texas).
4. **West**
   with the regions:
   - Mountain (Montana, Idaho, Wyoming, Colorado, New Mexico, Arizona, Utah, Nevada);
   - Pacific (Washington, Oregon, California, Alaska, Hawaii).

12
Overall Activity

12.1 National Accounts

Data Source

The data are published by the Bureau of Economic Analysis (BEA) at the Department of Commerce. The press release is available on the Internet at www.bea.gov/bea/dn1.htm. Data are also published in Tables 1, 5, 7 and 8 in the Survey of Current Business.

Importance for the Financial Markets   B

Description

The GDP is the most comprehensive measure of the economic activity of a nation. Data are collected on the basis of output by economic subjects both in terms of current prices (nominal) and constant prices (real). The current base year is 1996. To calculate the real figures a chain-type index is currently used, whereby the weightings of the relative shares in the GDP are continuously aligned. In preceding years the real figures were always published in a form where the components for the period under review were fixed. This type of publication is still conducted, although now only in parallel with the chain-type method.

In addition to data on economic activity, various inflation measures are also published. The most important are the implicit price deflator and the GDP price index. Both figures only reflect domestic prices. Price changes for reasons of higher import prices are neglected (in contrast to the calculation of consumer prices). The implicit price deflator takes into account both price changes and changes in the composition of an underlying basket of commodities. It can be taken as the average price of all goods and services which is weighted with shares of the GDP produced in the current period. The implicit price deflator thereby corresponds to the GDP at current prices, divided by the GDP at constant prices. However, with the price index, the basket of commodities remains constant, only price changes are reflected. The basket of commodities therefore relates to a specific base year.

Periodicity/Revisions

Quarterly data is published in the three months following the respective quarter. The advance report is published at the end of the first month after the end of a quarter. At the same time, the BEA publishes an overview of their assumptions. As for the advance report, data for all three months of a quarter are available only for sub-source series. An overview with the months available is given in Table 12.1. One month later, at the earliest on the twenty-third day of this month, however, the preliminary report is released, containing possibly major revisions. The reason for this is that the database has grown substantially by this point and sub-indicators for additional figures have been published in

Table 12.1 Source data availability for the advance GDP report

GDP component and monthly source	Months available
Personal consumption expenditures	
Retail trade and food service	3
Unit auto and truck sales	3
Non-residential fixed investment	
Unit auto and truck sales	3
Value of construction put in place	2
Manufacturers' shipments of machinery and equipment	2
Net exports of machinery and equipment	2
Residential investment	
Value of construction put in place	2
Housing starts	3
Change in business inventories	
Manufacturing and trade inventories	2
Unit auto inventories	3
Net exports of goods and services	
Merchandise exports and imports	2
Government purchases	
Federal outlays	2
Value of construction put in place by state and local government	2
GDP prices	
Consumer Price Index	3
Producer Price Index	3
Non-petroleum merchandise export and import prices indices	3
Values and quantities of petroleum imports	2

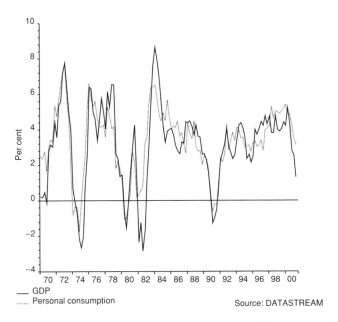

Figure 12.1 Change in GDP and personal consumption expenditure on preceding year

the meantime. Final figures, which are normally only slightly altered (final report), are then published in the third month after the end of the quarter. The preliminary and final reports are normally released on a Wednesday or Thursday. Publication of all data takes place at 08.30 ET (14.30 CET) in the form of a press release. This and selected summary tables which are later published in the Survey of Current Business are available on the BEA Internet site. Figures for the whole of the previous year are published with the data for the fourth quarter.

Each July, with the advance report for the second quarter, a revision going back two and a half years is published. In addition, there are also regular comprehensive revisions going back several years which may be accompanied by a new definition of individual sub-sectors. The last revision of this kind was published with the advance report for the second quarter of 1999 and related to individual series from 1959. The two most important changes were that software expenditure for companies and government organizations was now to be classed as an investment and no longer as a non-durable good. On the other hand, state pension systems were made equal to private ones. One consequence of this is that economic growth is now higher than before: average annual economic growth since 1991 is now 3.5 per cent instead of a previous 3.1 per cent due to the revision. The private savings ratio has also been increased, despite the consistently falling trend since the beginning of the 1980s.

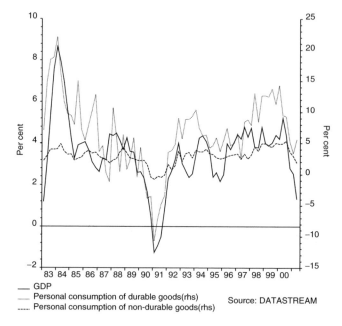

Figure 12.2   Change in GDP and personal consumption expenditure on durable consumer goods as well as non-durable consumer goods on preceding year

Seasonal Adjustment

Data are subject to seasonal adjustment.

Notes

The most important components of the GDP are personal consumption, private investment, government consumption, inventories and foreign demand. As these indicators apply to most of the components on publication of the GDP figures, the data have been easy to estimate and surprises have been rare. This applied in particular to the preliminary and final report. But with the switch from the Standard Industrial Classification (SIC) system to the North American Industry Classification System (NAICS) for many monthly indicators such as Retail Trade and Food Services, Durable Goods Orders and others, forecasting GDP has become more difficult. The NAICS grouping is considerably different from the old system and the source data will only be converted to the NAICS over a four-year period. The difficulties in forecasting arise because, during this four-year period, the new source data will not conform to the SIC data still used in GDP. Many of the old relationships break down. Until the switch is completed, it is necessary to translate the NAICS data to an SIC basis before forecasting GDP growth. Thus an extra layer of complexity and a new source of possible errors has appeared.

Table 12.2 Composition of GDP in 2000 as percentage of total GDP

Personal consumption	67.6%
Private investment	19.8%
Government expenditure	17.0%
Exports	12.1%
Imports	16.5%

Source: DATASTREAM

Figure 12.3 Ratio of gross private domestic investment to GDP

The market focuses on annualized quarterly change in real growth. Volatility is, however, high. Inventories and the ratio of inventories to sales is also important as high inventories in relation to sales implies weaker economic growth in the future quarters.

In the USA the Business Cycle Dating Committee at the National Bureau of Economic Research (NBER) was commissioned to determine the beginning and end of economic cycles. Two quarters in succession with a fall in GDP are often taken as a definition of recession. The NBER, however, uses a different definition. According to them, a recession is identified as sustained low growth in the overall economy, income, jobs and demand. A period of weak growth, on the other hand, is when there is continued positive growth, which is well below the long-term average. The NBER also employs the term 'depression'. This is a recession of exceptional scope and length. The Business Cycle Dating

Committee's last pronouncement was on 26 November 2001, when it announced a recession had started in March 2001 (exactly 10 years after the end of the last recession), when a peak in business activity occurred in the U.S. economy. The economic peak and trough points since 1854 are shown in Table 12.3.

Table 12.3 Business cycles in the USA

				Duration of economic cycles	
Economic trough	Economic peak	Duration of contraction (from peak to trough)	Duration of expansion (from trough to peak)	From trough to trough	From peak to peak
December 1854	June 1857		30		
December 1858	October 1860	18	22	48	40
June 1861	April 1865	8	46	30	54
December 1867	June 1869	32	18	78	50
December 1870	October 1873	18	34	36	52
March 1879	March 1882	65	36	99	101
May 1885	March 1887	38	22	74	60
April 1888	July 1890	13	27	35	40
May 1891	January 1893	10	20	37	30
June 1894	December 1895	17	18	37	35
June 1897	June 1899	18	24	36	42
December 1900	September 1902	18	21	42	39
August 1904	May 1907	23	33	44	56
June 1908	January 1910	13	19	46	32
January 1912	January 1913	24	12	43	36
December 1914	August 1918	23	44	35	67
March 1919	January 1920	7	10	51	17
July 1921	May 1923	18	22	28	40
July 1924	October 1926	14	27	36	41
November 1927	August 1929	13	21	40	34
March 1933	May 1937	43	50	64	93
June 1938	February 1945	13	80	63	93
October 1945	November 1948	8	37	88	45
October 1949	July 1953	11	45	48	56
May 1954	August 1957	10	39	55	49
April 1958	April 1960	8	24	47	32
February 1961	December 1969	10	106	34	116
October 1970	November 1973	11	36	117	47
March 1975	January 1980	16	58	52	74
July 1980	July 1981	6	12	64	18
November 1982	July 1990	16	92	28	108
March 1991	March 2001	8	120	100	128

Average values of cycles:

1854–1991 (31 cycles)	18	35	53	53
1854–1919 (16 cycles)	22	27	48	49
1919–1945 (6 cycles)	18	35	53	53
1945–1991 (9 cycles)	11	50	61	61

Key Datastream Mnemonics

Gross Domestic Product and Related Measures (saar)	Datastream
Gross domestic product (GDP)	USGDP...D
GDP (%q/q, saar)	USGDP%..D
Personal consumption expenditures	USCONEXPD
Durable goods	USCNDURBD
Non-durable goods	USCNNONDD
Services	USCNSERVD
Gross private domestic investment	USGDPRIND
Fixed investment	USGPDFXID
Non-residential	USNRSINVD
Structures	USNRSSTRD
Equipment and software	USINVPDED
Residential	USGPDRESD
Change in private inventories	USBUSINVD
Farm	USBINFRMD
Nonfarm	USBINNFMD
Construction, mining and utilities	USBINCOND
Manufacturing	USBINMFGD
Wholesale trade	USBINWTWD
Retail trade	USBINRT.D
Other industries	USBINOTHD
Net exports of goods and services	USBALGSVD
Exports	USEXPGSVD
Goods	USEXPTMCD
Services	USEXS...D
Imports	USIMPGSVD
Goods	USIMPTMCD
Services	USIMS...D
Government consumption expenditures and gross investment	USPUG...D
Federal	USPUGC..D
State and local	USPUGZ..D
Residual	USRSGDP.D
Addenda:	
Final sales of domestic product	USFINSLSD
Gross domestic purchases	USPUDG..D
Final sales to domestic purchasers	USSFPU..D

Gross Domestic Product by Major Type of Product (saar)	Datastream
GDP	USGDP...D
Final sales of domestic product	USFINSLSD
Change in private inventories	USBUSINVD
Residual	USRSGDPID
Goods	USGNPGDSD
Final sales	USFINSLGD
Change in inventories	USBINVGCD
Durable goods	USGDPCD.D
Final sales	USFINSLDD
Change in inventories	USIOCD..D
Non-durable goods	USGDPCN.D
Final sales	USFINSLND
Change in inventories	USIOCN..D
Services	USGNPSRVD
Structures	USGNPSTRD
Residual	USRSGDPPD
Addenda:	
Motor vehicle output	USGDPMV.D
GDP less motor vehicle output	USGDPXMVD

Gross Domestic Product by Sector (saar)	Datastream
GDP	USGDP...D
Business	USGNPBUSD
Non-farm	USGNPNFMD
Non-farm less housing	USGNPNFHD
Housing	USGDPBH.D
Farm	USGDPBA.D
Household and institutions	USGDPHI.D
Private households	USGDPHH.D
Non-profit institutions	USGDPNI.D
General government	USGDPGG.D
Federal	USGDPGC.D
State and local	USGDPGZ.D
Residual	USRSGDPSD

Relation of Gross Domestic Product, Gross National Product, and National Income (saar)	Datastream
GDP	USGDP...B
Plus: Income receipts from the rest of the world	USICFRC.B
Less: Income payments to the rest of the world	USICFPM.B
Gross national product (GNP)	USGNP...B
Less: Consumption of fixed capital	USCCF...B
Less: Indirect business tax and nontax liability	USTXL...B
Less: Business transfer payments	USTB...B

Relation of Gross Domestic Product, Gross National Product, and National Income (saar)	Datastream
Less: Statistical discrepancy	USSYNIA.B
Plus: Subsidies less current surplus of government enterprises	USSBXGE.B
Equals: National income	USNATINCB
Addenda:	
Gross domestic income	USGDIC..B
Net domestic product	USNDP...B

National Income by Type of Income (saar)	Datastream
National income	USNATINCB
Compensation of employees	USCOMEMPB
Wages and salaries	USWAGSALB
Proprietors' income with inventory valuation and capital consumption adjustment	USICOWAQB
Rental income of persons with capital consumption adjustment	USRENTPSB
Corporate profits with inventory valuation and capital consumption adjustment	USPROFTSB
Net interest	USNETINTB
Addenda:	
Corporate profit after tax with inventory valuation and capital consumption adjustment	USCPATAXB
Net cash flow with inventory valuation and capital consumption adjustment	USMFNWA.B
Less: Inventory valuation adjustment	USCPFIVAB
Equals: Net cash flow	USCNCASHB

Gross Product of Corporate Business (saar)	Datastream
Gross product of corporate business	USGDPCB.B
Gross product of financial corporate business	USGDPCF.B
Gross product of non-financial corporate business	USGDPCNFB
Gross product of non-financial corporate business (in 1996 USD)	USGDPCNFD

Personal Income and Its Disposition (saar)	Datastream
Personal income	USPERSINB
Wage and salary disbursements	USWAGSALB
Less: Personal tax and nontax payments	USPERTAXB
Equals: Disposable personal income	USPDISPIB
Less: Personal outlays	USPERSOTB
Equals: Personal saving	USPERSAVB
Addenda:	
Disposable personal income, bio. of chained (1996) USD	USPDISPID
Personal saving as a percentage of disposable personal income	USPRSAVRE

Personal Consumption Expenditures by Major Type of Product (saar)	Datastream
Personal consumption expenditures	USCONEXPD
Durable goods	USCNDURBD
Non-durable goods	USCNNONDD
Services	USCNSERVD
Residual	USRSCP..D
Addenda:	
Energy goods and services	USCNENGYD
Personal consumption expenditures less food and energy	USCONXFED

Government Current Receipts and Expenditures (saar)	Datastream
Current receipts	USFSLRECB
Current expenditures	USFSLEXPB
Current surplus or deficit (-)	USFSLBALB
Social insurance funds	USFSLSOCB
Other	USFSLOTHB
Federal government surplus or deficit	USFGV...B
State and local government surplus or deficit	USSLC...B
Addend:	
Net lending or borrowing (-)	USNLBG..B

Gross Saving and Investment(saar)	Datastream
Gross saving	USGROSSVB
Gross private saving	USGROSPSB
Personal saving	USPERSAVB
Gross government saving	USSVG...B
Gross investment	USGROSINB
Gross private domestic investment	USGDPRINB
Gross government investment	USGROSGIB
Net foreign investment	USIVWN..B
Statistical discrepancy	USSYSVIGB
Addendum:	
Gross saving as a percentage of gross national product	USSV%GNPB

Corporate Profits by Industry (saar)	Datastream
Corporate profits with inventory valuation and capital consumption adjustment	USPROFTSB
Domestic industries	USCPICDIB
Financials	USCPICFNB
Non-financials	USCPICNFB
Rest of the world	USCPICRWB

Corporate Profits by Industry (saar)	Datastream
Corporate profits with inventory valuation	USCPITOTB
Domestic industries	USCPIDOMB
Financials	USCPIFINB
Non-financials	USCPINFNB
Rest of the world	USCPIRWDB
Addenda:	
Corporate profits after tax with inventory valuation and capital consumption adjustment	USCPATAXB
Net cash flow with inventory valuation and capital consumption adjustment	USMFNWA.B
Less: Inventory valuation adjustment	USCPFIVAB
Equals: Net cash flow	USCNCASHB

Chain-Type Price Indexes	Datastream
GDP	USGDP..CE
Personal consumption expenditures	USCE...CE
Gross private domestic investment	USIVP..CE
Net exports of goods and services	USEXN..CE
Government consumption expenditures	USPUG..CE
Addenda:	
Final sales of domestic product	USSFDP.CE
Gross domestic purchases	USPUDG.CE
Final sales of domestic purchasers	USSFPU.CE
Gross national product	USGNP..CE

Implicit Price Deflators	Datastream
GDP	USIPDGDPE
GNP	USIPDGNPE

Literature

Berns, Richard B., 'Corporate Profits: Critical for Business Analysis (and not just for Wall Street)', *Business Economics*, January 2002, pp. 7–14.

Bils, Mark and Kahn, James A., 'What Inventory Behavior Tells Us about Business Cycles', *Federal Reserve Bank of New York Staff Reports*, No. 92 (November 1999).

Dotsey, Michael, 'The Predictive Content of the Interest Rate Term Spread for Future Economic Growth', *Federal Reserve Bank of Richmond Economic Quarterly*, Vol. 84/3, (Summer 1998) pp. 31–51.

Duecker, Michael J., 'Strengthening the Case for the Yield Curve as a Predictor of U.S. Recessions', *Federal Reserve Bank of St. Louis Review*, March/April 1997.

Grimm, Bruce T. and Parker, Robert P., 'Reliability of the Quarterly and Annual Estimates of GDP and Gross Domestic Income', US Department of Commerce, *Survey of Current Business*, (December 1998), pp. 12–21.

Landefeld, J. Steven and Fraumeni, Barbara M., 'Measuring the New Economy', US Department of Commerce, *Survey of Current Business* (March 2000), pp. 23–40.

Landefeld, J. Steven and Grimm, Bruce T., 'A Note on the Impact of Hedonics and Computers on Real GDP', US Department of Commerce, *Survey of Current Business* (December 2000), pp. 17–22.

McConnell, Margaret M. and Quiros, Gabriel Perez, 'Output Fluctuations in the United States: What has Changed since the Early 1980s' *American Economic Review*, Vol. 90, No. 5 (2000), pp. 1464–76.

Millard, Stephen, Scott, Andrew and Sensier, Marianne, 'Business cycles and the labour market: Can theory fit the facts?', *Bank of England Working Paper Series* No. 93 (March 1999).

Moulton, Brent R., Parker, Robert P. and Seskin, Eugene P., 'A Preview of the 1999 Comprehensive Revision of the National Income and Product Accounts – Definitional and Classificational Changes', US Department of Commerce, *Survey of Current Business* (August 1999), pp. 7–20.

Moulton, Brent R. and Seskin, Eugene P., 'A Preview of the 1999 Comprehensive Revision of the National Income and Product Accounts – Statistical Changes', US Department of Commerce, *Survey of Current Business* (October 1999), pp. 6–17.

Moulton, Brent R. and Sullivan, David F., 'A Preview of the 1999 Comprehensive Revision of the National Income and Product Accounts – New and Redesigned Tables', US Department of Commerce, *Survey of Current Business* (September 1999), pp. 15–28.

Ritter, Joseph A., 'Feeding the National Accounts', *Federal Reserve Bank of St. Louis Review*, Vol. 82, No. 2 (March 2000), pp. 11–20.

Seskin, Eugene P. and Parker, Robert P., 'A Guide to NIPAs', US Department of Commerce, *Survey of Current Business* (March 1998), pp. 26–68.

Seskin, Eugene P. and Sullivan, David F., 'Annual Revisions of the U.S. National Income and Product Accounts: Annual Estimates, 1997–1999 and Quarterly Estimates', US Department of Commerce, *Survey of Current Business*, (August 2000), pp. 6–33.

Smets, Frank and Tsatsaronis, Kostas, 'Why does the Yield Curve predict Economic Activity?', *Bank for International Settlements, BIS Working Papers* No. 49, September 1997.

US Department of Commerce, 'BEA's Chain Indexes, Time Series, and Measures of Long-Term Economic Growth', US Department of Commerce, *Survey of Current Business*, May 1997.

12.2   Industrial Production and Capacity Utilization

Data Source

Data are published by the Federal Reserve Board. The press release is available on the Internet at www.federalreserve.gov/releases. The data are also published in Tables 2.10, 2.12 and 2.13 in the Federal Reserve Bulletin.

Importance for the Financial Markets   B

Description

The industrial production and capacity utilization indices measure the physical output of companies, as well as US mining, gas and electricity suppliers on the

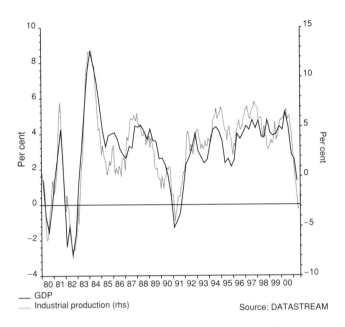

Figure 12.4 Change in GDP and industrial production on preceding year

basis of the value-added method. The input factors are deducted from the output of the individual industries to eliminate duplication. When calculating the indices the production of water supply companies and the construction sector are not taken into account, although the Federal Reserve Board has been considering including these sectors for some time. The individual industrial sectors are calculated separately and grouped with fixed values from 1992 (manufacturing industry 85.4 per cent, mining sector 6.9 per cent and utilities 7.7 per cent). In addition the index on industrial production is also calculated according to individual market sectors (final products 46.3 per cent, intermediate products 14.2 per cent and materials 39.5 per cent). Final products include goods which are purchased by consumers, companies or the state as the end user. Intermediate products, in contrast, are goods bought by companies outside industry (agriculture, construction or service sector) for further processing, whereas materials are bought by other industrial companies for use in production.

Industrial production is currently divided into a total of 264 sub-sections. The calculation of the sub-index by the survey bodies is based as far as possible on physical production numbers, such as tonnes of paper produced or barrels of crude oil. These figures are calculated by the Bureau of the Census and account for approximately 40 per cent of total production. This type of approach is not always useful, however, as the number of cars or computers produced, for example, does not have much informative value due to the different models

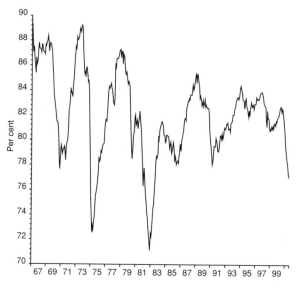

Figure 12.5   Capacity utilization

and performance. In these cases production is estimated using input factors for the production process, such as requisite working hours (this method is applied for around 30 per cent of production and is calculated on the basis of data from the Bureau of Labor Statistics) or energy expended (approximately 30 per cent, calculated by the Federal Reserve Board).

In addition to industrial production the Federal Reserve Board also publishes the capacities of the individual industries and the capacity utilization thereby derived. Overall, indices are published for 76 industrial sectors. Utilization is calculated by dividing industrial production by capacity. It therefore describes production as a percentage of production capacity. Capacity is a measure of economically viable potential output and is defined as the largest level of production that a production plant can achieve within a realistic working period with normal shutdown times. When calculating capacity it is assumed that adequate primary products are available to operate the machinery and other equipment. It is clear that capacity, by definition, cannot be accurately measured but has to be estimated by the Federal Reserve Board. The Board therefore assumes that the capacity of the industrial sectors will increase in a straight-line basis over time.

Furthermore, diffusion indices are also published for industrial production. Changes on the previous month and on the preceding three or six months are thereby calculated for the individual sectors. Diffusion indices are calculated by

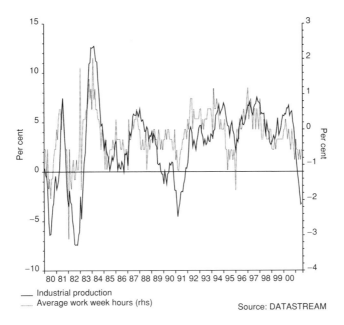

Industrial production
Average work week hours (rhs)

Source: DATASTREAM

Figure 12.6 Change in industrial production and average work week hours in manufacturing sector on preceding year

adding half of the number of sectors that remained unchanged to the number of sectors with increases within the respective period.

Periodicity/Revisions

Preliminary data is published between the fifteenth and eighteenth days of the month following the survey period. Revisions are possible over the next three months and the report is then regarded as final, although further retrospective adjustments may be made reflecting seasonal factors in the autumn. The indices are published at 09.15 ET (15.15 CET).

The monthly data on capacity utilization is meant to be consistent with the monthly data for industrial production and the quarterly data on capacity. As there are no direct monthly data on capacity, the data required for this are estimated monthly using interpolation.

The weightings of the individual sectors are based on company surveys in the manufacturing and mining sector, which are conducted every five years. As soon as data are available, the weightings are aligned to the new data.

Figure 12.7 Change in industrial production on preceding year and ISM Purchasing Managers' Index for Manufacturing Business

Seasonal Adjustment

Data are seasonally adjusted and adjustment factors are realigned annually. However, seasonal influences in individual industrial sectors differ and are also dependent, to a certain extent, on the weather. In principle it can be assumed that (non-seasonally-adjusted) production in the summer is higher than in the winter. In extreme weather conditions this can, however, produce contradictory effects. Whereas, for example, in a very cold winter, output in the manufacturing industry can fall considerably, it can rise substantially in supply companies with the increased demand for energy for heating. The same applies to very hot summers in terms of the energy requirement for air conditioning. In such cases, the Federal Reserve Board normally makes specific mention of such special factors. In addition to these seasonal adjustments, data relating to hours worked and energy consumption are also adjusted on the basis of the long-term relationship between the input and output level as a result of the cyclical link.

Notes

The value of production goods at 1992 price levels amounted to USD2878 billion in 2000, whereas the real GDP accounted for USD9318.5 billion. Although this share is relatively small, industrial production is still largely responsible for cyclical fluctuations in the GDP and therefore is a very good indicator for estimating overall economic performance. Initial indications of industrial production values can be taken from the data on new non-farm payrolls, average work week hours and changes in overtime which are announced by the Bureau of Labor Statistics 2–3 weeks prior to the initial publication of the industrial production figures. Moreover, there are close parallels between industrial production and the ISM Purchasing Managers' Index for Manufacturing Business. The primary focus in industrial production is on the monthly change in total production and in the manufacturing industry, although there are still individual sub-indices (e.g., the automobile industry) which are extremely volatile and can distort the entire index. For this reason special aggregates are also published simultaneously which do not take into consideration the influences of individual sectors.

On publication of the preliminary report nearly all of the data from the Bureau of Labor Statistics sources is available, whereas only an approximate 40 per cent is available from the data based on physical production numbers. Figures produced by the Federal Reserve Board are only transmitted at the end

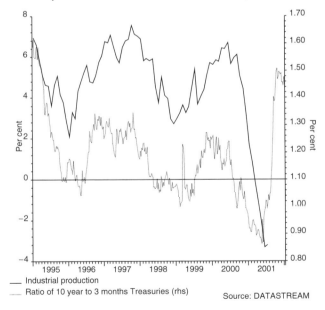

Figure 12.8 Change in industrial production on preceding year and ratio of 10 year to 3 month US Treasuries with a lag of 6 months

of the month for the preceding one and are therefore not included in the preliminary report. They are only incorporated with the subsequent revisions. The Federal Reserve Board calculated that in the 1987–97 period the scope of revisions without regarding the direction of the revision for the level of the index between the initial announcement and the final publication was around 0.28 per cent, whereas revisions of the percentage change in the same period amounted to 0.21 per cent. The signs in the initial publication corresponded to the final figures in 87 per cent of cases.

Values for capacity utilization should be regarded with caution in light of the possible revisions and above all the difficulties described with the survey. In an average economic cycle capacity utilization is a little over 80 per cent. Values of over 84 per cent are considered to be a danger to price stability in general. The peaks and troughs in capacity utilisation in the latest business cycles are 84.5 (in 1995), 85.4 per cent (in 1988/89) and 78.1 per cent as the lowest (in the actual downturn, the trough has not been seen. The latest and lowest value was 74.2 in Jaunary 2002) (in 1990/91). In the preceding business cycles the values amounted to 87.3 per cent (1979/80) and 71.1 per cent (1982), 89.2 per cent (1973) and 72.6 per cent (1975) respectively. Utilization of over 90 per cent has not yet been achieved in peacetime. Since the late 1960s the peak of the capacity utilization has been on a declining trend. The 1979/80 peak was below the 1973 peak, the 1988/89 one was below the 1997/80 one and so on. The reason for this is that the service sector became more important and now has a larger part of the whole economy than before. But because industrial production does not cover the service sector, the capacity utilization numbers are somewhat misleading. Nevertheless, the market focuses on capacity utilization in total industry and in the manufacturing industry as the largest sub-sector.

Key Datastream Mnemonics

Industrial Production: Industry Groups (sa)	Datastream
Industrial production	USINPRODG
Manufacturing	USMANPRDG
Durable goods	USDURBLIG
Non-durable goods	USNONDBIG
Mining	USMININGG
Metal mining	USIPMETMG
Coal mining	USIPCOALG
Oil and gas extraction	USIPOILGG
Stone and earth minerals	USIPSTONG
Utillities	USUTILTIG
Electric	USIPELCUG
Gas	USIPGASUG

Industrial Production: Industry Groups (sa)	Datastream
Special Aggregates (sa)	
Energy	USIPENERG
Non-energy	USIPNENGG
Selected high-technology industries	USIPIMHTG
Computer and office equipments	USIPMOFFG
Communications equipment	USIP366.G
Semiconductors and related electronic components	USIP367SG
Non-energy excluding selected high-technology industries	USIPNEXCG
Motor vehicles and parts	USIPMVHPG
Excluding motor vehicles and parts	USIPNEXMG
Measures excluding selected high-technology industries	
Total industry	USIPTXHTG
Manufacturing	USIPMFXHG
Durable	USIPDMXCG
Measures excluding motor vehicles and parts	
Total industry	USIPTXMVG
Manufacturing	USIPMFXMG
Durable	USIPDMXMG
Primary processing	USMFPRPIG
Advanced processing	USMFADPIG
Memo: Motor vehicle assemblies	
Total	USPMV...O
Autos	USPAUTO.O
Trucks	USPTRUCKO

Industrial Production: Market Groups (sa)	Datastream
Industrial production	USINPRODG
Products, total	USIPPRDTG
Final products	USFINALIG
Consumer goods	USCONSMIG
Durable	USDURCNIG
Automotive products	USAUTOPIG
Other durable goods	USIPCTRKG
Non-durable	USNDRCNIG
Energy	USIPNDEPG
Non-energy	USIPNDNEG
Equipment, total	USIPEQUPG
Business equipment	USBUSEQIG
Defence and space equipment	USIPDEQPG
Oil and gas drilling	USIPOILDG
Manufactured homes	USIPMFHMG
Intermediate products	USINTGDIG
Construction supplies	USCNSTRIG
Business supplies	USIPIBSPG
Materials	USMATERIG
Durable	USMATDBIG

Industrial Production: Market Groups (sa)	Datastream
Non-durable	USMATNDIG
Energy	USIPENEGG
Special Aggregates	
Total excluding:	
Autos and trucks	USIPTXATG
Motor vehicles and parts	USIPTXMVG
Computers	USIPTXOMG
Computers and semiconductors	USIPTXCSG
Consumer goods excluding:	
Autos and trucks	USIPCXATG
Energy	USIPCXENG
Business equipment excluding	
Autos and trucks	USIPBXATG
Computer and office equipment	USIPBXOEG
Materials excluding energy	USIPMXENG

Industrial Production: Gross Value of Products (billions of 1996 dollars/saar)	Datastream
Products, total	USIPPRDTD
Final products	USIPFINLD
Consumer goods	USIPCONSD
Equipment, total	USIPEQUPD
Intermediate products	USIPDEQPD

	Industrial Production (sa)	Capacity (sa)	Capacity Utilization (sa)
Total industry	USINPRODG	USIC....O	USOPERATE
Manufacturing	USMANPRDG	USICIM..O	USCAPMANE
Primary processing	USMFPRPIG	USICIMPPO	USIUIMPPO
Advanced processing	USMFADPIG	USICIMAPO	USIUIMAPO
Durable	USDURBLIG	USICIMD.O	USIUIMD.O
Non-durable	USNONDBIG	USICIMN.O	USIUIMN.O
Mining	USMININGG	USICIX..O	USIUIX..O
Utilities	USUTILTIG	USIC49..O	USIU49..O
Electric	USIPELCUG	USIC49E.O	USIU49E.O
Selected high-technology industries	USIPIMHTG	USICIMHTO	USIUIMHTO
Computer and office equipment	USIPMOFFG	USIC357.O	USIU357.O
Communications equipment	USIP366.G	USIC366.O	USIU366.O
Semiconductors and related electronic components	USIP367SG	USIC367SO	USIU367SO
Manufacturing excluding selected high-technology industries	USIPMFXHG	USICMFXHO	USIUMFXHO

Diffusion Indexes of Industrial Production	Datastream
1 month earlier	USIPDIF1%
3 months earlier	USIPDIF3%
6 months earlier	USIPDIF6%

Electric Power Use: Manufacturing and Mining	Datastream
Total	USCELC..G
Manufacturing and mining	USCELCM.G
Manufacturing	USCELCMEG
Durable	USCELCMDG
Non-durable	USCELCMNG
Mining	USCELCMIG

Literature

Emery, Kenneth M. and Chang, Chin-Ping, 'Is there a Stable Relationship between Capacity Utilization and Inflation?', *Federal Reserve Bank of Dallas Economic Review* (First Quarter 1997), pp. 14–20.

Federal Reserve Board, 'Industrial Production: 1989 Development and Historical Revision', *Federal Reserve Bulletin*, (April 1990), pp. 187–204.

Federal Reserve Board, 'Industrial Production and Capacity Utilization: Historical Revision and Recent Developments', *Federal Reserve Bulletin* (February 1997), pp. 67–92.

Higo, Masahiro and Nakada, Sachiko Kuroda, 'What Determines the Relation between Output Gap and Inflation', Bank of Japan, *IMES Discussion Paper* No. 99-E-24.

Steindel, Charles and Stiroh, Kevin J., 'Productivity: What Is It, and Why Do We Care about It?', *Federal Reserve Bank of New York Staff Reports No. 121* (March 2001).

Stiroh, Kevin J., 'What Drives Productivity Growth', *Federal Reserve Bank of New York Economic Policy Review*, Vol. 7, No. 1 (March 2001), pp. 37–59.

12.3 Monthly Wholesale Trade: Sales and Inventories

Data Source

Data are published by the Bureau of the Census at the Department of Commerce. The press release is available on the internet at www.census.gov/cgi-bin/briefroom/BriefRm. Data are also published in the *Current Business Report*, BW Series.

Importance for Financial Markets   D

Description

The report on wholesale sales and inventories, the second stage of the production process, is based on data from surveys of companies operating primarily in the wholesale sector. These include merchant wholesalers that take title of goods they sell, and jobbers, industrial distributors, exporters, and importers. Excluded are non-merchant wholesalers such as manufacturer sales branches and offices, agents, merchandise or commodity brokers, and commission merchants and other businesses whose primary activity is other than wholesale trade. Wholesalers provide nominal data of wholesale sales, end-of-month inventories and the methods of inventory valuation. The wholesale report has been produced since 1946 and about 4000 selected wholesale firms are currently surveyed. There are, however, distinctions in terms of company size. Large companies are surveyed on a monthly basis and smaller companies only every quarter. In this case, however, they have to supply data for two months. The composition of the survey panel is reviewed quarterly so as to include recently set-up companies, which normally applies approximately nine months after the company foundation. In addition companies which close down or which no longer satisfy the criteria are deleted from the survey register. The survey methods are overviewed every 5 years, including an sample update. The latest sample began in 2001, when the Bureau of the Census decided to change from the Standard Industrial Classification (SIC) system to the North American Industry Classification System (NAICS). One result of this update was that some wholesale trade establishments are now redefined as retail trade establishments because the NAICS bases the classification on how each establishment operates rather than to whom it sells, as was the case under the SIC.

In addition to sales and inventories in the wholesale sector, the ratio between the two is calculated. The inventories to sales ratio gives the number of months it would take to use up the entire inventory at the current level of sales performance.

Periodicity/Revisions

Data is published monthly between the fifth and eighth working day of the second month after the end of the data survey. Revisions can extend over several months. Initial revisions to data are conducted around one week after publication of the figures when the report on sales and inventories is published. Annual revisions due to changes in seasonal adjustment factors are published every spring and can go back over several years. The data are always published at 10.00 ET (16.00 CET).

Seasonal Adjustment

Data are seasonally adjusted. For annual alignment of the seasonal adjustment factors, the seasonally adjusted data are revised going back a number of years.

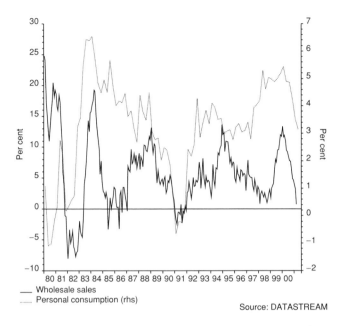

Wholesale sales
Personal consumption (rhs)

Source: DATASTREAM

Figure 12.9   Change in wholesale sales and personal consumption expenditure on preceding year

Notes

The relationship between wholesale sales and personal consumption is not very close. Consequently the markets do not pay much attention to publication of this data. Market response is greatest when inventories in the wholesale sector change dramatically, thereby affecting total inventories and the economic growth forecast.

Key Datastream Mnemonics

Monthly Wholesale Trade: Sales and Inventories (sa)	Datastream
Inventories, total	USINSW..B
Durable goods	USIN421.B
Non-durable goods	USIN422.B
Sales, total	USSWTOT.B
Durable goods	USSW421.B
Non-durable goods	USSW421.B
Inventories/sales ratio, total	USISSW..B
Durable goods	USIS421.B
Non-durable goods	USIS422.B

Literature

Parker, Robert P., 'The Impact of the North American Industry Classification System on U.S. Economic Data: In May 2001, NAICS Hits the Economic Indicators', *Business Economics*, April 2001, pp. 56–9.

12.4   Manufacturing and Trade Inventories and Sales

Data Source

Data are published by the Bureau of the Census at the Department of Commerce. The press release is available on the Internet at www.census.gov/cgi-bin/ briefroom/BriefRm. Data are also published in the *Current Industrial Reports* (M3 series for the manufacturing industry data) and in the *Current Business Reports* (BW series for the wholesale trade data and BR series for the retail trade data).

Importance for the Financial Markets   D

Description

The report contains data on sales and inventories for manufactures' activity, whole trade and retail trade. Data published in this report are based on three surveys: the Monthly Retail Trade Survey (see section 15.1), the Monthly Wholesale Trade Survey (see section 12.3) and the Manufactures' Shipments, Inventories and Orders Survey (see section 16.2). Starting with the data for April 2001, the Bureau of the Census switched from the Standard Industrial Classification (SIC) system to the North American Industry Classification System (NAICS).

In addition to sales and inventory data the ratio between the two (overall and for sub-indices) is also published. This figure gives the number of months it would take for the total inventories to be used up at the current level of sales performance. A relatively low proportion of inventories to sales can indicate that producers will produce more in the coming months in order to restock. This would subsequently boost industrial production and thereby economic growth. For the phases downstream (wholesale and retail) a low inventory/sales ratio can also indicate oncoming increased demand, which in turn positively affects economic growth. Inversely, a high ratio indicates a period of low growth.

Periodicity/Revisions

Data are surveyed monthly and published in the middle of the second month following the end of the survey period. The announcement is normally made on a working day after publication of the retail sales at 08.30 ET (14.30 CET). This is normally the tenth working day in the month. When retail sales are published on a Friday, the report on sales and inventories is released on the following Tuesday. As most of the data are already known at the time of publication the report is used for the initial revisions. These may apply several months retrospectively due to revisions of the sub-indicators.

Seasonal Adjustment

Data are seasonally adjusted.

Notes

The importance of this report is relatively minor as most figures are already known and the aggregated sales figures do not say much about private consumption. The market focuses on the monthly changes in total inventories and changes in the ratio of total inventories to total sales.

Total inventories, excluding components in automobile retail, are used by the Department of Commerce for an estimate of GDP inventories, excluding the agricultural sector. Automobile retail inventories are calculated on the basis of data from the automobile industry. As the report is only published in the middle of the second month after the end of the reporting period, the data for the third month of a quarter are not available on publication of the advance report of GDP figures. The data are therefore based on an estimate.

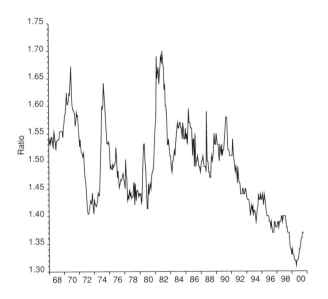

Source: DATASTREAM

Figure 12.10   Inventories to sales ratio

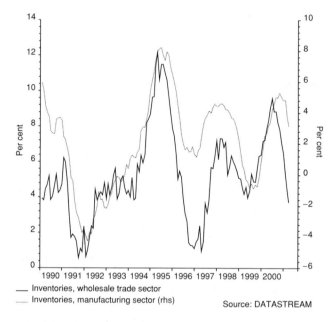

Source: DATASTREAM

Figure 12.11   Inventories in wholesale trade and manufacturing sector

Key Datastream Mnemonics

Manufacturing and Trade	Sales (sa)	Inventories (sa)	Inventories/ sales ratio (sa)
Total business	USBUSSALB	USBSINV.B	USISBUS.E
Manufacturing	USSHMFG.B	USINMFG.B	USISHMFGB
Durable	USSHDUR.B	USINDUR.B	USISHDURB
Non-durable	USSHNDURB	USINNDU.B	USISHNDUB
Retailers	USRETTOXB	USINRET.A	USISRET.B
Merchant wholsalers	USSWTOT.B	USINSW..B	USISSW..B
Durable	USSW421.B	USIN421.B	USIS421.B
Non-durable	USSW421.B	USIN422.B	USIS422.B

Retail Trade	Sales (sa)	Inventories (sa)	Inventories/ sales ratio (sa)
Retail trade, total	USRETTOXB	USINRET.A	USISRET.B
Total (excl. auto vehicles and parts	USSRXMVPB	USINRXMVB	USISRXMVB
Motor vehicle and parts dealers	USSR441.B	USIN441.B	USIS441.B

Retail Trade	Sales (sa)	Inventories (sa)	Inventories/ sales ratio (sa)
Furniture, home furniture, electr. and appl. stores	USSRFRELB	USIN442AB	USIS442AB
Building materials, garden equipment and supplies	USSR444.B	USIN444.B	USIS444.B
Food and beverages stores	USSR445.B	USIN445.B	USIS445.B
Clothing and clothing accessories stores	USSR448.B	USIN448.B	USIS448.B
General merchandise stores	USSR452.B	USIN452.B	USIS452.B
Department stores (excl. leased departments)	USSR4521B	USIN4521B	USIS4521B

Literature

Fitzgerald, Terry J., 'Inventories and the Business Cycle: An Overview', *Federal Reserve Bank of Cleveland Economic Review*, Vol. 33, No. 3, (third quarter 1997), p. 11–22.

Parker, Robert P., 'The Impact of the North American Industry Classification System on U.S. Economic Data: In May 2001, NAICS Hits the Economic Indicators', *Business Economics*, April 2001, p. 56–9.

12.5 The Conference Board U.S. Business Cycle Indices

Data Source

Data are published by The Conference Board. The press release is available on the Internet at www.globalindicators.org. Data are also published in the *Business Cycle Indicators* by The Conference Board.

Importance for the Financial Markets   C

Description

There are three business cycle indices published by The Conference Board. The Index of Leading Indicators is an index composed of published economic data, which is supposed to show turning points in economic activity in advance. The index is composed of indicators that summarize expectations and plans from various sectors (labour market, consumption, production and financial markets) and are an indication of future economic activity. In addition to the Index of Leading Indicators, there are also indices for coincident and lagging indicators. The Index of Coincident Indicators aims to identify turning points in current economic activity, whereas the Index of Lagging Indicators primarily shows whether production costs will rise or fall. Turning points in the Index of Lagging Indicators, as indicated by table 12.4, normally only occur after the turning points in economic activity.

Table 12.4   Leads and lags of the Business Cycle Indices

Leads and lags of indices (in months)			
Economic peaks	Leading indicators	Coincident indicators	Lagging indicators
April 1960	−11	0	+3
December 1969	−8	−2	+3
November 1973	−9	0	+13
January 1980	−15	0	+3
July 1981	−3	1	+2
July 1990	−6	−1	−12
March 2001	−14	−3	−4
Business cycle troughs	Leading indicators	Coincident indicators	Lagging indicators
February 1961	−3	0	+9
October 1970	−7	0	+15
March 1975	−2	0	+22
July 1980	−3	0	+3
November 1982	−8	+1	+6
March 1991	−2	0	+21

Source: NBER, The Conference Board.

Indicators for the three indices were selected on the basis of a number of empirical and theoretical criteria. These include:

- If one indicator can serve as a leading , coincident or lagging indicator
- Changes in direction in relation to the cyclical turning points in the economic cycle
- Consistency with the direction of the economic cycle
- Clear behavioural trends
- Quality of data
- Time of availability
- Scope of revision

Most of the underlying indicators are published before the announcement of the three indices, although they are incorporated into the calculation in a modified form. For the index of leading indicators, the two indicators of new orders are normally released shortly after the publication of the index. The individual indicators are as shown below.

1. Average weekly hours in manufacturing sector
   This indicator is employed as companies adjust the number of staff working hours first before aligning the number of staff to changes in economic conditions (see Section 14.1).
2. Average weekly initial claims for unemployment insurance
   This indicator normally responds more sensitively to changes in economic activity than the total number of employed or the unemployment rate. The monthly changes are incorporated into the calculation and the figures are inverted as the number of new jobless claims falls when the economy begins to pick up (see Section 14.2).
3. Manufacturers' new orders of consumer goods and materials (at 1996 prices)
   This value is taken into account as new orders directly influence the level of orders not yet executed as well as inventories, thereby influencing production decisions in companies (see Section 16.2).
4. Vendor performance
   This indicator measures the relative time within which industrial companies receive delivery from their suppliers. If the time increases this indicates that demand for primary products is rising and bottlenecks in delivery could occur. The sub-index of the ISM Purchasing Managers' Index for Manufacturing Business is used as the base value (see Section 13.1.1.1).

Figure 12.12 Change in GDP and Index of Leading Indicators on preceding year

5. Manufacturers' new orders of non-defence capital goods (at 1996 prices)
   This indicator is the counterpart on the producer side to the real new orders for non-durable goods and materials (see Section 16.2).

6. Building permits for private housing
   This indicator is normally several months ahead of the other production indicators (see Section 16.3.2).

7. Stock prices, measured on S&P 500 Index
   This indicator measures the rate of change for a large number of stocks and shares and therefore covers a broad market. Increases in stock prices can, amongst other things, signal the general mood of investors and therefore be a good indicator for future economic activity.

8. M2 monetary aggregate (at 1996 prices)
   The real change in money supply is taken into account as an expansion of money supply below the inflation rate can negatively impact credit issued by banks. This in turn can negatively influence future economic activity. Inflation adjustment is based on the implicit price deflator for private consumer expenditure (see Section 19.1).

9. Interest rate spread between Federal Funds Rate and 10-year Treasury Bonds
   This spread serves as an indicator of monetary policy behaviour as it normally rises when the money market interest rates are relatively low and the (bond) markets are expecting more restrictive monetary policy in the future. A negative value is also seen as a clear sign of an oncoming recession.

10. Index of consumer expectations
    This indicator is the only one based entirely on expectations. It relates to the survey by the University of Michigan. The expectation value is obtained from three sub-questions:
    - expectations on the financial situation of those surveyed for the next 12 months;
    - business expectations for the whole economy for the next 12 months;
    - business expectations for the whole economy for the next 5 years (see Section 15.3.2).

The following are included in the calculation of the index of coincident indicators.

1. Employees on non-agricultural payrolls
   This indicator includes both full and part-time employees and makes no distinction between permanent and temporary workers. As changes in the time series reflect current staffing behaviour, excluding agriculture and the state sector, this sub-indicator is one of the most significant (see Section 14.1).

2. Personal income less transfer payments (at 1996 prices)
   This indicator measures earnings and other income of all persons, and excludes state transfer payments. Staff bonuses are also excluded in part as the indicator should only measure income flows on which consumers base their consumption decisions now and in the future (see Section 15.2).
3. Index of industrial production
   Although this indicator only covers part of the total economy, there is still a close link between change in industrial production and change in overall economic activity (see Section 12.2).
4. Manufacturing and trade sales (at 1996 prices)
   This indicator is employed because it is strongly pro-cyclical (see Section 12.4).

Finally, the following indicators are taken into account in the calculation of the index of lagging indicators.

1. Average duration of unemployment
   The average duration of unemployment is measured in weeks and tends to rise in line with economic decline. Consequently the value is inverted by substituting the + or − sign in the rates of change. The term of unemployment recedes, however, as economic recovery gets under way, although the greatest increase is recorded shortly before the start of a recession (see Section 14.1).
2. Ratio, manufacturing and trade inventories to sales (at 1996 prices)
   Inventories frequently increase as the economy begins to slow and sales fall behind expectations. Record levels are normally recorded in the middle of a recession. Then the ratio gradually tails off again as companies begin to adjust production to the changes of the overall demand situation (see Section 12.4).
3. Change in labour costs per unit of output in the manufacturing sector
   This indicator is calculated by The Conference Board itself using a number of other indicators. As the monthly rates of change fluctuate erratically, a moving average over six months is input into the indicator calculation. Cyclical peaks for the moving average are normally reported during a recession, when production is declining faster than the number of employed.
4. Average prime rate charged by banks
   The prime rate is seen as a benchmark by which banks set the level of interest for all other credit. Changes to this, however, lag way behind economic activity.
5. Commercial and industrial loans outstanding (at 1996 prices)
   With the calculation of this figure both bank credits and the volume of commercial paper issued by non-financial institutions are taken into account. The indicator primarily reports record highs after the low point of a

recession, as falling profits cause the demand for credit to rise. Lows normally occur approximately one year after the end of a recession. The underlying time series was adjusted to a change in data employed in January 1998.

6. Ratio, consumer instalment credit outstanding to personal income
Consumers frequently wait until several months after a recession before taking out credit again. Consequently this indicator is usually at its lowest one year after the point where private income started to rise. The period between the turning points of the indicator and the turning points of the economy can, however, vary substantially (see Sections 15.2 and 15.4).

7. Change in Consumer Price Index for services
With the delay due to the perception of cyclical change and market rigidities, the costs of services tend to rise sharply in the first few months of recession, whereas they fall in the first few months of recovery (see Section 18.2).

The Conference Board publishes two different versions of the three business cycle indices. In addition to the indices, where 100 represents the average in 1996, diffusion indices are also published, where the number of rising subindicators is taken as a proportion of the total number of underlying indicators. Values in the diffusion index of over 50 indicate that more indicators are rising than falling.

To calculate an index like this, it has first to be determined which subindicators are rising, unchanged or falling. To this end, a sub-indicator which rises by over 0.05 per cent is allocated a value of 1. Indicators which change by less than 0.05 per cent are allocated a value of 0.5, and finally indicators falling by more than 0.05 per cent are assigned the value 0. For the interest rate spread, already available as a percentage, the change based on the difference in percentage points is calculated. First the values of the sub-indicators are added, then divided by the number of indicators (by the number 10 in the case of leading indicators) and finally multiplied by 100. In addition to the diffusion indices, which are calculated on the basis of monthly change, diffusion indices are also calculated using the same method on the basis of the change in indicators compared with their values six months before.

Example

Table 12.5 shows the values of the leading indicators for August and September 2001. The symmetrical monthly rates of change and respective diffusion values can be derived from these.

The total for diffusion values amounts to 3.0 in this example, thereby producing a value for the diffusion indicator of 30.

Table 12.5 Calculation of diffusion index of the Index of Leading Indicators

Indicator	August 2001	September 2001	Monthly change (in %)	Diffusion value
Index of Leading Indicators				
Average weekly hours manufacturing	40.7	40.5	0.49	0.0
Average weekly initial claims	399.5	455.0	(−)12.99	0.0
New orders for consumer goods and materials	166 625	166 626	0.00	0.5
Vendor performance	46.5	46.5	0.00	0.5
New orders for capital goods	52 099	51 870	−0.44	0.0
Building permits	1 571	1 524	−3.04	0.0
S&P 500	1 178.50	1 044.64	−12.04	0.0
M2	4 820.2	4 900.0	1.64	1.0
Interest rate spread	1.32	1.66	0.34	1.0
Index of consumer expectations	85.2	73.5	−14.74	0.0
Total of diffusion values				3.0

The composite index, on the other hand, is calculated in a completely different way. Based on the values in the current month ($X[t]$) and the preceding month ($X[t-1]$), the symmetrical percentage monthly change ($x[t]$) for each of the indicators is calculated using the following formula:

$$x[t] = \frac{(X[t] - X[t-1])}{(X[t] + X[t-1])} * 200$$

Changes in indicators, which are already available in percentage figures (such as the interest rate spread) are, on the other hand, calculated via simple subtraction. In a further step, monthly rates of change are adjusted with a separate value for each indicator by multiplying the rates of change by a factor. The adjustment is effected to take into account the same volatility for each indicator. The values of the respective factors are recalculated each year in December on the basis of the historical standard deviations for the series. Then the adjusted rates of changes are added together. The total of the indicator values ($i[t]$) produced is then linked with the last value of this indicator ($I[t-1]$) as calculated in the month before:

$$I[t] = I[t-1] * \frac{(200 + i[t])}{(200 - i[t])}$$

Table 12.6   Calculation of rates of change of the Index of Leading Indicators

Indicators (a)	August 2001 (b)	September 2001 (c)	Monthly change (in %) (d)	Adjust ment factor (e)	Adjusted change (d)*(e)
Index of Leading Indicators					
Average weekly hours manufacturing	40.7	40.5	−0.49	0.1836	−0.09
Average weekly initial claims	399.5	455.0	(−)12.99	0.0243	−0.32
New orders for consumer goods and materials	166 625	166 626	0.00	0.0490	0.00
Vendor performance	46.5	46.5	0.00	0.0275	0.00
New orders for capital goods	52 099	51 870	−0.44	0.0129	−0.01
Building permits	1 571	1 524	−3.04	0.0187	−0.06
S&P 500	1 178.50	1 044.64	−12.04	0.0308	−0.37
M2	4 820.2	4 900.0	1.64	0.3033	0.50
Interest rate spread	1.32	1.66	0.34	0.3317	0.11
Index of consumer expectations	85.2	73.5	−14.74	0.0182	−0.27
Total of adjusted rates of change					**−0.50**

According to this formula the three indices can be calculated recursively assuming the respective base year on consideration of the total of adjusted monthly rates of change.

The calculation of the value of the composite Index of Leading Indicators for September 2001 results in (August 2001 value = 109.7)

$$\text{Index of Leading Indicators in September 2001} = 109.7 * \frac{(200 + (-0.50))}{(200 - (-0.50))} = 109.2$$

Prior to 2001, an additional adjustment was made to equalize the volatility of the composite indexes by multiplying the monthly sum by an standardization factor. The Conference Board decided to remove this step as it was proved to make no meaningful difference to the indexes' analytical value.

The adjustment factors of the other sub-indicators are shown in Table 12.7.

The indices were previously calculated by the Department of Commerce. Since December 1995 responsibility has fallen to The Conference Board, a private research body with over 3000 member companies and business membership organisations in around 60 countries. The Conference Board also publishes the Help-wanted Advertising Index and one of the two Index of Consumer Confidence.

Table 12.7 Adjustment factors for 2002 of The Conference Board U.S. Business Cycle Indicators

	Adjustment factor
Index of Leading Indicators	
Average weekly hours manufacturing	0.1812
Average weekly initial claims	0.0241
New orders for consumer goods and materials	0.0456
Vendor performance	0.0277
New orders for capital goods	0.0131
Building permits	0.0191
S&P 500	0.0310
M2	0.3069
Interest rate spread	0.3330
Index of consumer expectations	0.0185
Index of Coincident Indicators	
Employees on non-agricultural payrolls	0.4805
Personal income less transfer payments	0.2814
Industrial production	0.1292
Manufacturing and trade sales	0.1090
Index of Lagging Indicators	
Average duration of unemployment	0.0367
Inventories to sales ratio, manufacturing and trade	0.1225
Unit labor costs, manufacturing	0.0611
Prime rate	0.2454
Commercial and industrial loans	0.1265
Consumer instalment credit to personal income ratio	0.2209
Change in consumer prices for services	0.1869

Periodicity/Revisions

Data are published around the 25th of the month. Publication takes place at 10.00 ET (16.00 CET). As these indices are composed of different indicators, they can also be revised for up to five months in parallel to the revisions of the sub-indicators. Every December a benchmark revision is conducted where, for example, the adjustment factors are aligned to the latest available data. As a result of these alignments revisions can go back several years.

Seasonal Adjustment

Most indicators are seasonally adjusted on publication. The indices produced by The Conference Board, however, are not seasonally adjusted again.

Notes

The most important indicator is the Index of Leading Indicators, as it indicates economic changes in the coming months. The monthly rate of change is of particular interest, as is the moving average over 6 or 12 months. As a basic rule, a decline in the index over three consecutive months indicates a recession within the next 12 months. However, the index has frequently given false signals in the past and the leads and lags compared to economic peak and troughs fluctuate strongly in the build up to a recession (see table 12.4). Each recession was predicted by a decline in the index over three consecutive months, but not all of these declining periods were indicating a recession. For instance, the index was falling in five consecutive months from January to May 1995, but no recession occurred. The amount of the decline should therefore also be analyzed. If there are some months where the index is falling but the decline is only gradual, one should be careful in arguing that a recession is unavoidable. In addition, the ratio of coincident to lagging indicators can provide extra information as it forecasts economic change to some extent before the Index of Leading indicators does. The ratio indicates whether profits in the coming months will rise or fall. When the coincident indicators rise more rapidly than the lagging indicators, it can be assumed that profits will rise, which indicates an improved economic situation.

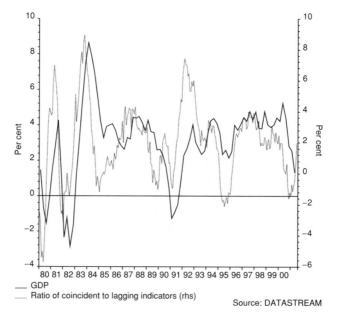

Figure 12.13 Change in GDP on preceding year and ratio of coincident to lagging indicators

Another misleading signal can occur if one looks only at the total change and ignores the change of single indicators. For example, the Index of Leading Indicators improved by 79 basis points from April to August 2001. The reason for this was that the Federal Reserve aggressively lowered interest rates, which lead to an expansion of money supply. Thus, the net contribution of the two indicators money supply and interest rate spread was 91 basis points, while all other indicators showed a small decline of 12 basis points. As a result, the improvement of the Index of Leading Indicators occurred only because of the expansive monetary policy of the Federal Reserve. There had been no indications for an improvement outside this part of the economy.

Key Datastream Mnemonics

The Conference Board U.S. Business Cycle Indicators	Datastream
Index of leading indicators (1996 = 100)	USLEADIN
1-month diffusion index	USDFILD1
6-month diffusion index	USDFILD6
Average work week, production workers (hours)	USAWHMANE
Average weekly initial claims, state unemployment insurance (1000)	USUNINSCE
Manufacturers' new orders, consumer goods and materials (million 1996 USD)	USCNORCGD
Vendor performance – slower deliveries diffusion index	USVENDOR
Manufacturers' new orders, non-defense capital goods (million 1996 USD)	USNOIDN.D
Building permits (1000)	USHOUSATE
S&P 500	US500STK
Money supply, M2 (billion 1996 USD)	USM2....D
Interest rate spread, 10-year Treasury bonds less federal funds University of Michigan Index of consumer expectations (1968:1 = 100)	USYSTNFF
Index of coincident indicators (1996 = 100)	USCOININ
1-month diffusion index	USDFICD1
6-month diffusion index	USDFICD6
Employees on non-agricultural payrolls (1000)	USEMPNAGE
Personal income less transfer payments (ann. rate, billion 1996 USD)	USPILESTD
Industrial production	USINPRODG
Manufacturing and trade sales (million 1996 USD)	USBSSALED
Index of lagging index (1996 = 100)	USLAGGIN
1-month diffusion index	USDFIGD1
6-month diffusion index	USDFIGD6
Average duration of unemployment (weeks)	USUNDURNE
Ratio, manufacturing and trade inventories to sales (chain 1996 USD)	USRBNSALE
Change in index of labour costs per unit of output, manufacturing (6-month percentage, ann.)	USLABCHN

The Conference Board U.S. Business Cycle Indicators	Datastream
Average prime rate charged by banks (%)	USPRIME.
Commercial and industrial loans outstanding (million 1996 USD)	USCOMILND
Ratio, consumer instalment credit outstanding to personal income	USRCRDPI
Change in CPI for services (6-month percentage, ann. rate)	USCPSCHN

Literature

Camacho, M. and Perez-Quiros, G., 'This is what the US leading indicators lead', European Central Bank *Working Paper No. 27*, Frankfurt-am-Main, August 2000.

The Conference Board, 'History of the Leading Economic Indicators and Composite Indexes', *Business Cycle Indicators*, May 1997 and June 1997.

The Conference Board, *Business Cycle Indicators Handbook*, 2001.

13
Company Surveys

In addition to the calculation of leading indicators, company surveys are also used to obtain early information on economic development. The most important of these is the monthly nationwide survey by purchasing managers, who are members of the Institute for Supply Management (ISM). Since June 1998 the ISM has published two indices. One index relates to purchasing managers in the manufacturing industry and the other to the non-manufacturing sector. There is a whole series of regional surveys. In addition, Federal Reserve Banks survey companies in their own districts. The most important are the surveys by the Federal Reserve Banks in Philadelphia and Richmond.

13.1 Purchasing Managers' Indices

13.1.1 ISM Purchasing Managers' Indices

The Institute for Supply Management (ISM), formerly known as the National Association of Purchasing Management (NAPM), is an organization of (purchasing) managers from around 180 sub-organizations with over 44 000 members in total from all over the USA and Puerto Rico. It is a non-profit making organization, which also promotes continuing education for its members. The ISM currently publishes two nationwide purchasing managers' indices. The Index of Manufacturing Business is far more important due to its long history. Its origins date back to the early 1920s and since 1931 the report has been published regularly with the exception of a four-year break during the Second World War. The Non-manufacturing ISM Report on Business has only been published since June 1998, with survey data going back to July 1997. In addition to these two indices, sub-organizations also publish purchasing managers' indices independently in various regions of the USA. These are only of relatively minor significance, however, the most important being the Purchasing Managers' Index produced by the Purchasing Management Association of Chicago.

The regional purchasing managers' indices are not incorporated in the calculation of the nationwide index.

13.1.1.1   Manufacturing ISM Report on Business

Data Source

Data are published by the ISM. The press release is available on the Internet at www.ism.ws.

Importance for financial markets   B

Description

The ISM Purchasing Managers' Index for Manufacturing Business, which was called NAPM Purchasing Managers' Index before January 2002, is a survey providing information on economic activity in the coming months. The index is composed of a number of sub-indicators which are grouped in a diffusion index with different weightings. The sub-indicators relate to the following sectors: new orders (with a 30 per cent weighting), production (25 per cent), employment (20 per cent), supplier deliveries (15 per cent) and inventories (10 per cent). The weighting was conducted in accordance with the significance of the sub-sectors as leading indicators of economic development. Companies are also questioned about backlogs of orders, prices, new export orders and imports. These four sectors are not, however, included in the overall index. Currently over 350 companies from 20 industrial sectors are surveyed in the USA, whereby the companies are representatively distributed over the entire nation.

The survey is used to determine how each of the sub-indicators have developed compared to the preceding month. The possible responses in the new order, production and new export order sectors are better, the same or worse. For the backlog of orders, inventories and imports the responses are greater, the same or less and for prices and employment higher, the same or lower. With supplier delivery the possible responses include slower, the same or faster.

Other information apart from these figures is included in the publication. There is information on individual sectors, and information on the ordering policy. There is also information on which raw materials prices are rising and falling, and what percentage of companies surveyed with backlogs of orders, new export orders, raw materials shortages.

The sub-indicators are published in the form of diffusion indices and then grouped in a weighted diffusion index. There the percentage values showing better economic development and half of the values representing no change in the situation are added together. The sub-indicators (excluding the backlog of orders which is not seasonally adjusted) are then divided by their respective

Table 13.1 Example of calculation of the ISM Purchasing Managers' diffusion indices (April 2001)

Sub-indicator (a)	Better (in %) (b)	Same (in %) (c)	Worse (%) (d)	Non-adjusted value (e) = (b) +0.5∗(c)	Seasonally adjustment factor (f)	Adjusted value (g)=(e)/ (f)	Weighting (in %) (h)	Weighted value (i)=(g)∗(h)
New orders	28	45	27	50.5	1.101	45.9	30	13.8
Production	21	50	29	46.0	1.073	42.9	25	10.7
Employment	10	59	31	39.5	1.038	38.1	20	7.6
Supplier deliveries	6	85	10	47.5	1.002	47.4	15	7.1
Inventories	16	49	35	40.5	1.024	39.6	10	4.0
Backlog of orders	16	55	29	43.5		43.5		
Prices	18	63	19	49.5	1.013	48.9		
New export orders	10	77	13	48.5	1.026	47.3		
Imports	9	78	13	48.0	1.017	47.2		
Total index (total of weighted values)								**43.2**

seasonal adjustment factors and totalled in accordance with the weightings for the total index. Table 13.1 contains an example of the calculation for April 2001.

Periodicity/Revisions

The ISM Purchasing Managers' Index is one of the first indices to supply information on the preceding month. It is always published on the first working day of the month and relates to survey results obtained from the third week of the preceding month. Publication always takes place at 10.00 ET (16.00 CET). Revisions are usually only conducted in January, when the seasonal adjustment factors are revised. However, subsequent revisions for changes in the database or input errors identified in preceding months are not conducted.

Seasonal Adjustment

The ISM Purchasing Managers' Index and the sub-indicators are seasonally adjusted with the exception of the backlog of orders. The underlying adjustment factors are recalculated each year by the US Department of Commerce. They are published in advance around the middle of January.

Notes

The ISM Purchasing Managers' Index is a good indicator of general economic activity in the coming months. Even if the monthly values of the index have

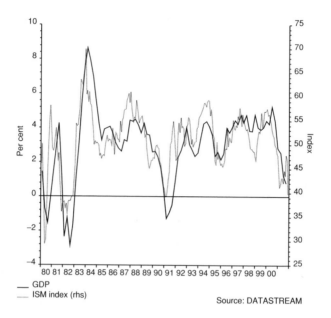

Figure 13.1 Change in GDP on preceding year and ISM Purchasing Managers' Index for Manufacturing Business

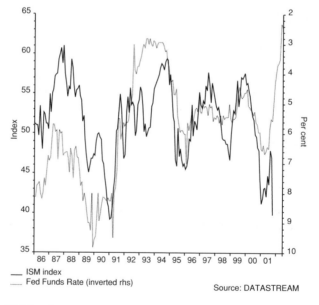

Figure 13.2 ISM Purchasing Managers' Index for Manufacturing Business and Federal Funds Rate with a lag of 7 months

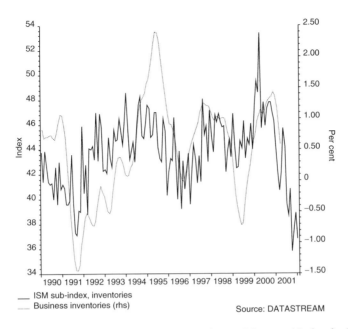

Figure 13.3 Sub-index for inventories in ISM Purchasing Managers' Index for Manufacturing Business with a lag of 3 months and change in business inventories on preceding quarter (moving average of 2 quarters)

only weak links with output in the manufacturing industry, the trends over three to six months provide clear signs of the economic situation in general.

The index can be criticized in that strict scientific criteria are only partly applied in the survey method and the questions set are very simple, with little differentiation. Also companies are only accepted into the survey panel from rapidly growing sectors when they are established, whereas existing companies are only removed when they stop existing. The companies surveyed also represent only around 1 per cent of the ISM members. The quota of responses varies from month to month, as responses not received by the deadline are not taken into account. By definition the diffusion index reports economic growth when the value exceeds 50. Empirical surveys, however, have shown that zero growth is reached at a value of 44. Each percentage point above the threshold value represents an additional annual GDP growth rate of approximately 0.3 percentage points. One reason for this is the rapidly growing newly founded companies which are only taken into account after a certain period, whereas established companies are still surveyed when they are on the brink of bankruptcy.

The markets are focusing primarily on the monthly change in the total index and the moving average of this value over three months. The price component is also a good indicator of future inflationary trends. The same applies to the sub-indicator relating to supplier delivery, as longer delivery times could signal bottlenecks in delivery, which can result in increased price pressure. The function of an economic leading indicator is undertaken, above all, by the sub-indicators for new orders, supplier delivery times and production. In addition, deductions on the future development of the balance of trade deficit in the USA can be made from the sub-indicators for export orders and imports.

Key Datastream Mnemonics

Manufacturing ISM Report on Business (sa)	Datastream
ISM Purchasing Managers' Index, total	USPURCHS
New orders	USNAPMNO
Better	USNPMONP
Same	USNPMONM
Worse	USNPMONN
Production	USNAPMPR
Better	USNPMP.P
Same	USNPMP.M
Worse	USNPMP.N
Employment	USNAPMEM
Higher	USNPME.P
Same	USNPME.M
Lower	USNPME.N
Suppliers deliveries	USVENDOR
Slower	USNPMLTN
Same	USNPMLTM
Faster	USNPMLTP
Inventories	USNAPMIV
Higher	USNPMINN
Same	USNPMINM
Lower	USNPMINP
Backlog of orders (nsa)	USNAPMBO
% Reporting	
Greater	USNPMBON
Same	USNPMBOM
Less	USNPMBOP
Prices	USNAPMCP
Higher	USNPMPPN
Same	USNPMPPM
Lower	USNPMPPP

Manufacturing ISM Report on Business (sa)	Datastream
New export orders	USNAPMEO
% Reporting	
Better	USNPMEOP
Same	USNPMEOM
Worse	USNPMEON
Imports	USNAPMIM
% Reporting	
Higher	USNPMIMN
Same	USNPMIMM
Lower	USNPMIMP

Literature

Bretz, Robert J., 'Behind the Economic Indicators of the NAPM Report on Business', *Business Economics*, July 1990.

Harris, Ethan P., 'Tracking the Economy with the Purchasing Managers' Index', *Federal Reserve Bank of New York Quarterly Review*, Fall 1991, pp. 61–9.

13.1.1.2 *Non-manufacturing ISM Report on Business*

Data Source

Data are published by the Institute for Supply Management (ISM). The press release is available on the Internet at www.ism.ws.

Importance for the Financial Markets   E

Description

Since June 1998 the Institute for Supply Management (ISM), formerly known as National Association of Purchasing Management (NAPM), has published an ISM Report on Non-manufacturing Business that is similar to the ISM Report on Manufacturing Business. The time series, however, only goes back to July 1997. Currently around 370 purchasing managers from the non-manufacturing sector are surveyed on the following sectors: business activity, new orders, backlogs of orders, new export orders, imports, changes in inventories, sentiment on inventories, prices, employment and supplier deliveries. Possible responses to the question of how a sector has changed in terms of the preceding month are higher, the same or lower for business activity, new orders, backlog of orders, new export orders, imports, inventory changes, prices, supplier delivery and employment, whereas with inventory sentiment they are too high, about right and too low. Those surveyed come from over 60 different sectors according to the Standard Industrial Code (SIC) system. As with the Purchasing

Managers' Index Manufacturing Business, the companies are selected in terms of regional factors, such as the importance of the sector for the overall economy.

In contrast to the other ISM Purchasing Managers' Index there is currently no total index for the non-manufacturing sector; available additional information on certain commodity price changes and difficulties with delivery is included in the press release. In the non-manufacturing sector computer experts and computer equipment (such as toners for printers) represent commodities.

The sub-indicators are published in the form of diffusion indices. There the percentage values showing higher activity and half of the values representing no change in the situation are added together. Only for supplier deliveries are the values for lower activity and half of the values representing no change summed. The sub-indicators of business activity, new orders, employment and imports are then divided by their respective seasonal adjustment factors. Table 13.2 contains an example of the calculation for April 2001.

Periodicity/Revisions

The index is published on the third day of business in the month for the preceding month. In the same way as for the Purchasing Managers' Index for Manufacturing Business, the data are only revised in mid-January.

Table 13.2 Example of calculation of the ISM Purchasing Managers' non-manufacturing diffusion indices (April 2001)

Sub-indicator (a)	Higher (in %) (b)	Same (in %) (c)	Lower (%) (d)	Non-adjusted value (e) = (b) +0.5*(c)	Seasonally adjustment factor (f)	Adjusted value (g)=(e)/(f)
Business activity	22	58	20	51.0	1.083	47.1
New orders	20	59	21	49.5	1.079	45.9
Backlog of orders	10	68	22	44.0		44.0
New export orders	22	67	11	55.5		55.5
Inventory change	17	57	26	45.5		45.5
Inventory sentiment	32	64	4	64.0		64.0
Imports	12	77	11	50.5	1.025	49.3
Prices	28	63	9	59.5		59.5
Employment	13	70	17	48.0	1.028	46.7
Supplier deliveries	6	86	8	51.0		51.0

Seasonal Adjustment

In January 2001 the ISM started to calculate seasonally adjusted indices for business activity, new orders, employment and imports. The underlying adjustment factors are recalculated each year by the US Department of Commerce. They are published in advance around the middle of January.

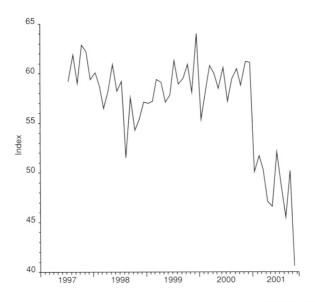

Source: DATASTREAM

Figure 13.4   ISM Purchasing Managers' Index for Non-manufacturing Business

Notes

The Purchasing Managers' Index for Non-manufacturing Business has not yet received much notice as it is still one of the newest economic indicators. The current time series is therefore still very short (data have only been surveyed since July 1997), which greatly limits the use of the indicator for the analysis of economic activity. No weighted total index is published either. This probably will change in the future. The key sub-indicator is business activity, which is comparable with the production of the Purchasing Managers' Index for Manufacturing. A comparison of the sub-indices is published in the press release for the Purchasing Managers' Index Non-manufacturing Business.

Key Datastream Mnemonics

Non-manufacturing ISM Report on Business (nsa)	Datastream
Business activity (sa)	USNPNBA.Q
Higher	USNPNBAPR
Same	USNPNBAMR
Lower	USNPNBANR
New orders (sa)	USNPNON.Q
Higher	USNPNONPR
Same	USNPNONMR
Lower	USNPNONNR
Employment (sa)	USNPNE..Q
Higher	USNPNE.PR
Same	USNPNE.MR
Lower	USNPNE.NR
Supplier deliveries	USNPNLT.R
Higher	USNPNLTPR
Same	USNPNLTMR
Lower	USNPNLTNR
Inventory change	USNPNIO.R
Higher	USNPNIONR
Same	USNPNIOMR
Lower	USNPNIOPR
Inventory sentiment	USNPNIN.R
Too high	USNPNINNR
About right	USNPNINMR
Too low	USNPNINPR
Backlog of orders	USNPNOU.R
Higher	USNPNOUNR
Same	USNPNOUMR
Lower	USNPNOUPR
Prices	USNPNPP.R
Higher	USNPNPPNR
Same	USNPNPPMR
Lower	USNPNPPPR
New export orders	USNPNEO.R
Higher	USNPNEOPR
Same	USNPNEOMR
Lower	USNPNEONR
Imports (sa)	USNPNIM.Q
Higher	USNPNIMPR
Same	USNPNIMMR
Lower	USNPNIMNR

13.1.2 Other Purchasing Managers' Indices

In addition to nationwide surveys other regional purchasing managers' indices are published by ISM sub-organizations. There are currently over ten such indices, which are available in the form of summary tables on the Internet site napm.org. The most widely regarded sub-index is the Purchasing Managers' Index of Chicago, which is produced by the Purchasing Management Association of Chicago (PMAC).

This index is largely identical in structure to the nationwide Purchasing Managers' Index and is published one day before the ISM Purchasing Managers' Index for the manufacturing sector. The survey of purchasing managers is always conducted in the second week of the month (compared to the third week for the ISM index). The PMAC index is also aligned to seasonal adjustment factors in January, which can be accompanied by revisions. Minor revisions are conducted throughout the year. The data are published at 10.00 ET (16.00 CET). The PMAC index can only be seen as an indicator for the nationwide index to a limited extent. For the period from 1980 to 1998 the direction of the monthly change in the nationwide ISM Index coincided with the PMAC Index in approximately two-thirds of all cases. And in some cases, they differ greatly. For instance, the PMAC indicator for October 2001 slipped by only 0.4

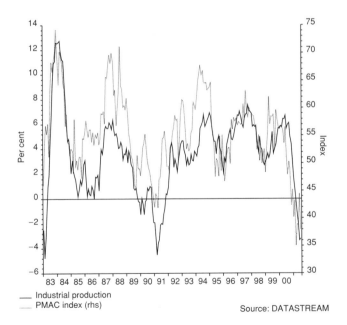

— Industrial production
········ PMAC index (rhs)

Source: DATASTREAM

Figure 13.5 Change in industrial production on preceding year and PMAC Purchasing Managers' Index

percentage points, indicating a stabilization of the economic situation, while the ISM Purchasing Managers' Index for Manufacturing Business, released one day later, fell by a considerable 7.2 basis points to the lowest level for more than ten years. The reason for this is that both indicators comprise different sub-indicators and weightings. In addition, only 200 companies are contacted for the PMAC index with an average response rate of 50 per cent. Thus, the sample is very small and the answers are very volatile.

13.2 Federal Reserve Bank of Philadelphia Business Outlook Survey

Data Source

Data are published by the Federal Reserve Bank of Philadelphia. The press release is available on the internet at www.phil.frb.org.

Importance for the Financial Markets   C

Description

The Federal Reserve Bank of Philadelphia Index (Philadelphia Fed Index) relates to a survey of the manufacturing sector in the district monitored by the Federal Reserve Bank of Philadelphia. It includes Delaware, the eastern part of Pennsylvania and the southern part of New Jersey. In the same way as the ISM indices it is composed of several sub-indicators, but there is no total composite index. The most important sub-index is the one relating to general economic activity. Companies are asked what they estimate its level will be. The possible responses are increasing, decreasing or not changing. They are also asked about their expectations for the next six months. These are a sign of optimism or pessimism among producers. Similar questions are also set for the sectors of new orders, shipments, unfilled orders, supplier delivery, inventories, prices paid (similarly to the price index for the nationwide ISM Index primarily for commodities), prices received (for end and intermediate products by producers, there is no comparable index in the nationwide ISM Index) and the number of employees. The expectations for the next six months are also surveyed for capital expenditure.

The Philadelphia Fed Index is published in the form of a diffusion index. In contrast to ISM Index the Philadelphia Fed index fluctuates between +100 and −100. The neutral value is 0, which corresponds to zero growth, in contrast to the ISM Index, where the neutral value is around 50.

Calculation example

In order to compare a value from the Philadelphia Fed Index with a corresponding value from the nationwide ISM index, the value of the

Philadelphia Fed Index has to be divided by two and 50 added. A Philadelphia Fed Index of 25.8 thereby corresponds to an ISM Index of:

$$\frac{25.8}{2} + 50 = 12.9 + 50 = 62.9$$

Periodicity/Revisions

Since June 2001, the index has been published at 12.00 noon ET (18.00 CET) on the third Thursday of each month instead of 10.00 ET as before. It relates to survey results received up to the first week in the current month. Consequently information from the preceding month also goes into the calculation. Revisions are only conducted in January when the seasonal adjustment factors are aligned.

Seasonal Adjustment

The data are seasonally adjusted. The seasonal adjustment factors are aligned annually in January when the data can be taken into account for a full year.

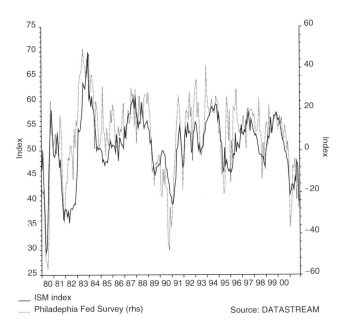

ISM index
Philadephia Fed Survey (rhs)   Source: DATASTREAM

Figure 13.6 ISM Purchasing Managers' Index for Manufacturing Business and Index of the Federal Reserve Bank of Philadelphia Business Outlook Survey

Notes

The most important sub-indices are those on general business activity, prices received and paid for in the current month and expectations for the coming six months. The sub-index for prices received is a good indicator for producer prices, where the relation between producer prices and intermediate products is particularly high. The focus is on the change in the sub-indices on the preceding month's values. The reason for the importance of the Federal Reserve Bank of Philadelphia Index to the markets is due to its contemporary and early release within a month. When interpreting this indicator one should not only have a look at the business activity indicator but also at the other sub-indicators to check if they are consistent with each other.

Example

In June 2001, the sub-indicator of business activity increased from −8.8 to −3.7. Most analysts were looking at these numbers and argued that Alan Greenspan's aggressive rate cuts showed first signs of an impact. Looking at the other activity sub-indicators, one could see that nearly all worsened. Only the unfilled orders increased from −15.1 to −10.5. In addition, the prices paid indicator rose while the prices received worsened, too. This depressed the manufacturers' earnings situation subject to the fact that that the situation was indeed deteriorating. The sub-indicators are shown in Table 13.3.

The importance of the indicator is somewhat restricted due to the high volatility of the time series. This volatility arises because there is no composite indicator. Comparing to the ISM Purchasing Managers' Index for Manufacturing Business, all sub-indicators are available. Thus one can calculate a composite

Table 13.3 Change in sub-indicators of the Federal Reserve Bank of Philadelphia Business Outlook Survey

	Diffusion Index May versus April	Diffusion Index June versus May	Change
General business activity	−8.8	−3.7	Increase
New orders	−4.8	−9.3	Decrease
Shipments	3.7	−0.8	Decrease
Unfilled orders	−15.1	−10.5	Increase
Delivery times	−10.7	−11.7	Decrease
Inventories	−10.5	−19.6	Decrease
Prices paid	1.5	17.8	Increase
Prices received	−2.2	−4.0	Decrease
Number of employees	−11.1	−14.3	Decrease
Average employee workweek	−14.6	−16.8	Decrease

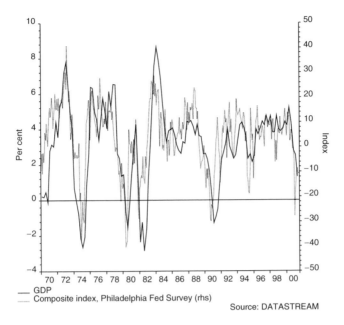

Figure 13.7   Change in GDP on preceding year and composite index, calculated with the sub-indicators of the Federal Reserve Bank of Philadelphia Business Outlook Survey

indicator using the same weights as the ISM (new orders 30 per cent, business activity 25 per cent, number of employees 20 per cent, delivery times 15 per cent, inventories 10 per cent). This creates an indicator with much less volatility without reducing its forecasting ability.

Another way of reducing volatility is to modify the indicator. The questions ask for the evaluation of the level of general business activity, compared to the preceding month. Thus one can sum up the monthly values to see how the assessment has changed from month to month. The resulting time series can be seen as an activity indicator. As with industrial production numbers, one is interested in the change against the year before. To get this information, the year-on-year change of this modified time series has to be calculated. The resulting numbers can then be compared to the year-on-year change of industrial production or GDP.

As the survey for the Philadelphia Fed Index is conducted at the beginning of the month and thereby differs strongly from the survey period of the ISM index, the correlation between the two indices is relatively slight. For the period between 1980 and 1998 the direction of the monthly change in the two indices coincided in only 65 per cent of cases. The correlation was just over 70 per cent when the PMAC Index and the Philadelphia Fed Index changed in the same direction compared to the preceding month.

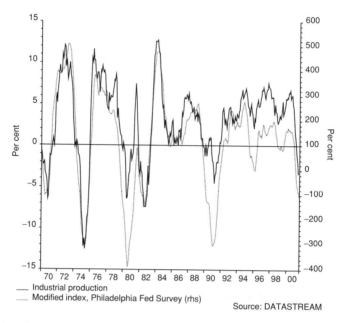

Figure 13.8   Change in industrial production and the modified Index of Business Activity from the Federal Reserve Bank of Philadelphia Business Outlook Survey on preceding year

In addition to the Federal Reserve Bank of Philadelphia, other Federal Reserve Banks also publish their own indices to measure economic activity in their region. Nevertheless far less notice is taken of these publications in the financial markets.

Key Datastream Mnemonics

Business Outlook Survey (sa)	Datastream
What is your evaluation of the level of change against the month before?	
General business activity	USFRBPIM
New orders	USFRBPON
Shipments	USFRBPSH
Unfilled orders	USFRBPOU
Delivery time	USFRBPLT
Inventories	USFRBPIN
Prices paid	USFRBPPP
Prices received	USFRBPPR
Number of employees	USFRBPE.
Average employee work week	USFRBPHW

Business Outlook Survey (sa)	Datastream
Expected change six months from now. What is your evaluation of the level of:	
General business activity	USFRPIM
New orders	USFRPFON
Shipments	USFRPFSH
Unfilled orders	USFRPFOU
Delivery time	USFRPFLT
Inventories	USFRPFIN
Prices paid	USFRPFPP
Prices received	USFRPFPR
Number of employees	USFRPFE.
Average employee work week	USFRPFHW
Capital expenditures	USFRPFIF

Literature

Crone, Theodore M. and McLaughlin, Michael P., 'The Philadelphia Story: A New Forecasting Model for the Region', *Federal Reserve Bank of Philadelphia Business Review*, September/October 1999, pp. 13–23.

Lacy, Robert L., 'Gauging Manufacturing Activity: The Federal Reserve Bank of Richmond's Survey of Manufacturers', *Federal Reserve Bank of Richmond Economic Quarterly*, Vol. 85, No. 1 (Winter 1999), pp. 79–98.

14

Labour Market Indicators

The situation in the US labour market is reflected by a number of indicators, which are calculated by various bodies and are published at different times. The most important publication is the *Labor Market Report*, which records the unemployment rate, the new non-farm payrolls and other indicators. This publication probably has the greatest influence on market development in association with the publication of producer prices and consumer prices. In addition there are the weekly jobless claims and the Help-wanted Advertising Index which supply further information.

14.1 *Labor Market Report*

Data Source

Data are published by the Bureau of Labor Statistics (BLS) at the Department of Labor. The press release is available on the Internet at stats.bls.gov/. More detailed figures can be found in the monthly publication *Employment and Earning*, available from the Bureau of Labor Statistics.

Importance for the Financial Markets   A

Description

The BLS's *Labor Market Report* is composed of two different sub-sectors. The Current Population or Household Survey, which has been produced regularly since 1940, provides information on the potential labour force as well as total employment and unemployment. For historical comparisons it should, however, be noted that survey methods were fundamentally amended in 1994. The Establishment Report or Current Employment Statistics Survey, on the other hand, supplies further information on the employment situation, hourly wage and hours worked per week.

The scope of those surveyed differs very greatly in the two surveys. Beginning in July 2001, the Bureau of Labor Statistics has increased the Current Population Survey sample size from 50 000 to about 60 000 households. In contrast to this, the Establishment Report covers around 390 000 companies with around 48 million employees (around 40 per cent of all those employed outside agriculture). All companies with over 250 employees, as well as many of smaller companies, are thereby surveyed via interviews, telephone polls, computer-assisted surveys and other methods. For the Household Survey, around one in 600 households in the nation are contacted.

In addition to the scope, the target groups of the surveys are also different. Whereas the survey for the Household Survey is people-related, the Establishment Report is a company-based survey. This can mean that those who have a secondary job in addition to their main employment are double counted. The same can apply to people who change jobs within the survey period.

The Household Survey is commissioned by the BLS and produced by the Bureau of the Census at the Department of Commerce. The required information is obtained in the form of a survey via interviews and telephone polls normally in the week of the nineteenth of the month. The relevant survey period relates to the week of the twelfth, a week before. Households taking part in the survey are not contacted every month. Normally a household is surveyed

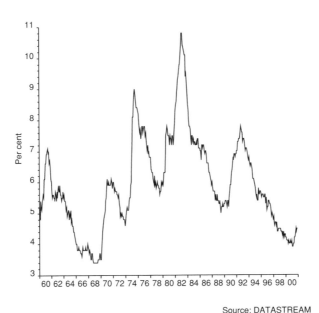

Source: DATASTREAM

Figure 14.1   Unemployment rate

over four consecutive months and then not surveyed for eight months. This means the composition of those surveyed is changed regularly.

To calculate the statistics it is necessary to differentiate between whether a person works or is seeking work or is not interested in a job. To decide in which category a person belongs, those surveyed are not questioned directly. Instead there is a series of questions to determine in which category a person belongs.

The following differentiation is made in the survey:

- People with jobs are employed
- People who are jobless, looking for jobs, and available for work are unemployed
- People who are neither employed nor unemployed are not in the labour force

The survey is designed so that everyone aged 16 or over who is not imprisoned or in a mental institution or on active duty in the Armed Forces is counted and classified in only one group. The potential labour force is therefore composed of the total of employed and unemployed. With this data the unemployment rate can be calculated. It is defined as the percentage share of the unemployed in the potential labour force. The number of employed and the ratio of the potential labour force as part of the population are also calculated. The

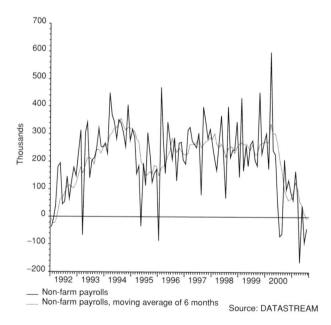

— Non-farm payrolls

······ Non-farm payrolls, moving average of 6 months

Source: DATASTREAM

Figure 14.2   New non-farm payrolls

population is thereby composed of the total potential labour force and those who are not classed as employed or unemployed.

The employed therefore include all those in paid full or part-time employment during the survey period. People who were employed during this period but were unable to work for certain reasons were classed as employed too. These reasons include holiday, illness, maternity leave, strikes, bad weather or temporary release for reasons of illness of a family member. People who did not/ could not take up employment for these reasons temporarily are shown separately in the statistics. People conducting unpaid work in a family business for at least 15 hours a week are also classed as employed.

The unemployed include all those who have no employment but actively looked for a job in the past four weeks and were available to the job centre. There is no need for a claim for unemployment benefit to be made for the assignment of this category. Active job seeking includes:

- Inquiries at companies, job centres or other employment agencies
- Responding to job offers or job advertisements, sending job applications

Passive methods of seeking work, on the other hand, are not taken into consideration. These include participation in further training schemes or reading job adverts.

All persons who are at least 16 years of age count as part of the potential labour force. All those not included in the above categories for various reasons are excluded from the calculation. Reasons for an exclusion are many:

- Imprisonment or institutionalization in a mental hospital
- Dependants of armed forces
- No intention of taking up paid employment

Persons to whom these reasons apply are listed as being outside the potential labour force. In the Household Survey, persons belonging to these categories are asked specific questions to obtain further information about the reasons for their decision. In particular, the aim is to determine how many unemployed people are disillusioned. These include those who would like a job and have been actively seeking work in the past 12 months, but have given up within the last four weeks because (according to those surveyed) it is hopeless.

From the aforementioned it is clear that the size of the potential labour force is not constant. In times of low unemployment some people are looking for jobs who then give up looking in times of high unemployment. These people are reconsidered in the calculation of the potential labour force when they start looking again. There can also be long-term changes due to social trends.

The Establishment Report produced by the BLS in collaboration with authorities in the federal states is probably the largest regular socio-economic survey in the USA. In contrast to the Household Survey, those surveyed do not include private households but, instead, private companies, businesses and state organizations. However, as primarily established companies are surveyed, adjustments are very slow. Thus, newly established, rapidly growing companies are included after some delay, although established companies in declining sectors continue to be surveyed until they shut down. This leads to underestimation of the new non-farm payrolls. Consequently, adjustment factors are used to estimate the companies not included. Data required from the state sector are provided by the Office of Personnel Management in time for the first revision. People are then reported who have been employed in state positions for over a calendar month. Only the defence ministry makes an exception. There only civilian personnel employed at the end of a month are registered.

In addition to the 'normal' influencing factors, data on the employed are also affected by strikes and lockouts. Strikes reduce the number of newly created jobs in the month in which the strike took place, whereas following strikes the number of job creations increase clearly. The BLS always publishes a separate strike report for the survey period in which strikes occur where at least 1000 employees were involved on Fridays before the publication of the labour market reporter. These data can provide indications on the labour market situation, but should be treated with caution as figures are produced from various sources and are only provisional.

Further important information on the labour market report can be found in the indices on average weekly hours and average hourly earnings. These figures are calculated on the basis of data from the Establishment Report and relate to the private sector of the economy only, whereas the state sector is also included in the new non-farm payrolls. To calculate the average weekly hours the total working hours registered in a week for which a wage is paid are divided by the number of employed.

For the wage data gross figures are calculated, i.e., wages and salaries are taken into account before social security deductions, unemployment insurance contributions, trade union membership and other deductions. Overtime bonuses, holiday entitlement and so on are included, whereas bonus payments and other one-off payments are not. The average hourly earnings are then calculated by dividing wages by the number of hours worked. This can be taken as a guide for wage costs, although the entire wage burden of the company sector is not included as the employers' contributions to social security, or tax, bonus payments and other special payments are not covered.

Diffusion indices are also calculated for the labour market data. For some years all 353 industrial sectors, excluding agriculture, have been included. For these sectors diffusion indices based on the change in employment on the

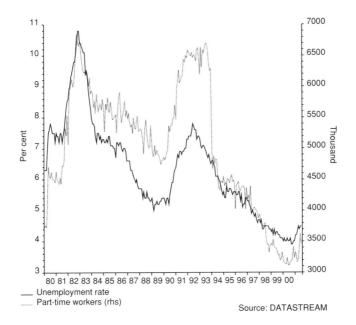

Figure 14.3 Unemployment rate and number of part-time workers

preceding month and the average change within 3, 6 and 12 months are calculated. In addition to the indices for the industrial sectors the same indices for the 136 sectors in the manufacturing industry are employed. With the diffusion index a measure has to be calculated to obtain information about how widespread a change in the employment situation is, as clear change in a few sectors with constant figures in most sectors has to be treated differently from a change in the same direction in the employment situation in most sectors. At the end of the 1980s the basis for the method of calculation was fundamentally changed; before, the manufacturing sector had above average weight. This was substantially reduced in the revision, although the change in the employment situation in the manufacturing sectors is still clearly given greater priority than a change in the service sector.

In addition to the above-mentioned difference in survey methods there are other important differences between the Household Survey and the Establishment Report. The Household Survey, for example, includes those employed in agriculture, the self-employed and unpaid workers in family operations, all of whom are omitted from the Establishment Report. People taking unpaid holiday are not included in the Establishment Report either, although they do figure in the Household Survey. In addition, the Household Survey is limited to people who are at least 16 years of age, a restriction that does not apply to the

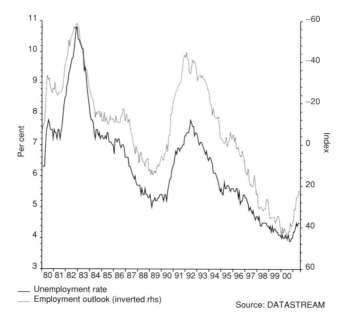

Figure 14.4   Unemployment rate and employment outlook as surveyed by The Conference Board's Index of Consumer Confidence

Establishment Report. Finally, the Household Survey also includes in-depth information on demographic characteristics, such as sex, age and socio-economic background.

Periodicity/Revisions

The Household Survey relates to the week (Sunday to Saturday) of the twelfth of the month. The survey then takes place a week later. The survey period for the Establishment Report, on the other hand, is the wage payment period including the twelfth. This can coincide with a calendar week but not necessarily. The results of the labour market report are published on the third Friday after the survey period for the Household Survey. This is therefore the first or second Friday in the month following the survey period. Publication varies due to the requirements of the survey methods. The respective week can end at the earliest on the twelfth of a month (when that is a Saturday) and at the latest on the eighteenth (when the twelfth is a Sunday). Consequently there are sometimes four or five weeks between survey periods. Publication occurs at 08.30 ET (14.30 CET). Revisions to the data in the Establishment Report can go back up to two months. With the first publication around 60 per cent or 230 000 companies are included, one month later the figure is around 80 per cent. But the report can only be classed as final with an adequate volume of data after the third month. This publication contains around 90 per cent of the companies surveyed. Responses received later are only incorporated with the annual benchmark revisions, which are announced with the labour market report for May. The old and revised data are thereby compared. The difference is then divided equally over the past 12 months. The data in the Household Survey is normally only revised with the report for December when the seasonal adjustment factors are aligned.

The BLS has announced plans for a comprehensive sample redesign of its monthly payroll survey. In June 2000, it has started to implement the first estimates from the redesigned sample for the wholesale trade industry. The remaining industry divisions will be phased in until 2003. The completion of the redesign in June 2003 will coincide with the conversion of the Current Employment Statistics series from the Standard Industrial Classification SIC system to the North American Industrial Classification System NAICS.

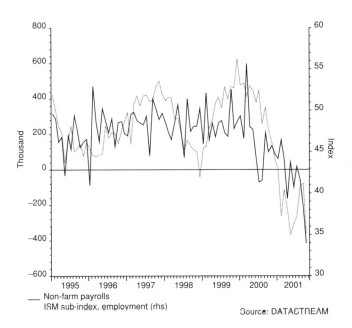

Figure 14.5 Non-farm payrolls and sub-index for employment in ISM Purchasing Managers' Index for Manufacturing Business

Seasonal Adjustment

Data are seasonally adjusted. There are still fluctuations over a year, however, which are due to exceptionally strong or weak seasonal patterns. In winter

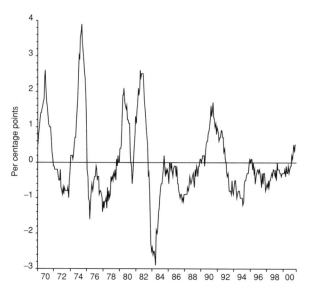

Source: DATASTREAM

Figure 14.6   Change in unemployment rate on preceding year

unemployment tends to rise due to the cold conditions in some parts of the country. In December, however, there is often a slight increase in retail employment figures due to Christmas trade. On the other hand, in June the number of employed and of unemployed rises as students start looking for and finding holiday jobs. Seasonal influences can account for up to 95 per cent of unadjusted fluctuation between two months.

The seasonal adjustment factors for the Household Survey are aligned twice a year. In January the data for the preceding year are taken into account. Then the seasonal adjustment factors for January to June are reassessed and the seasonally adjusted labour market data are recalculated, going back up to five years. Furthermore, in July the data for the preceding six months are used as the basis for calculation of the seasonal adjustment factors for the months from July to December. No revision of historical data is conducted in July, although adjustment factors for the Establishment Report for May to October are amended in June with the announcement of the results for May. Factors for the other months are aligned in December.

Notes

The *Labor Market Report*, together with producer prices and consumer prices, is the economic data publication which receives most notice from the financial markets. The new non-farm payrolls, unemployment rate, average hourly earnings and average weekly hours are particularly important. Due to the highly volatile data involved, moving averages over 3 or 6 months are incorporated for analysis of the labour market situation. The importance of the *Labor Market Report* is partly due to the fact that the data contain a great deal of new information for a whole series of sub-sectors of the economy. An increase in average weekly hours is therefore a leading indicator of rising economic growth. Industrial production trends are also closely linked to this indicator. At the end of an economic cycle or with very low unemployment in general, an increase in the average working week can also point to shortages in the labour supply, which can result in a build-up of inflationary pressure. Signs of such trends can also be seen in hourly wage trends.

In the past new non-farm payrolls and the unemployment rate sometimes developed at different rates. This was due to the different methods used in the data survey. With the substantially higher scope of survey in the Establishment Report, greater weighting is normally given to the new non-farm payrolls.

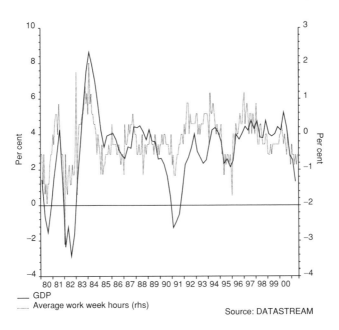

Figure 14.7 Change in GDP and average work week hours in manufacturing industry on preceding year

Key Datastream Mnemonics

Household Data (sa)	Datastream
Civilian non-institutional population	USCIVILPF
Civilian labour force	USLABFRCE
Participation rate	USLABFR%E
Employed	USEMPTOTE
Employment–population ratio	USEMPP%.E
Agriculture	USEMPLAGO
Non-agricultural industries	USPERNAGE
Unemployed	USUNEMP.E
Unemployment rate	USUNRATEE
Not in labour force	USLFNOT.O
Persons who currently want a job	USWANTJ.O
Part-time workers for economic reasons (all industries)	USPARTIME
Part-time workers for non-economic reasons (all industries)	USPTNONEO
Number of Unemployed	
Less than 5 weeks	USUNWK5.O
5–14 weeks	USUNWK14O
15 weeks and over	USUNPLNGE
Average (mean) duration, in weeks	USUNDURNE
Median duration, in weeks	USUNWKMDO

Establishment Data (sa)	Datastream
Employees on non-farm payrolls, total	USEMPNAGE
Employees on non-farm payrolls, total private	USEMPPRVE
New non-farm payrolls	USEMPNGME
Goods-producing	USEMPGPIE
Mining	USEMPMINE
Construction	USEMPCNSE
Manufacturing	USEMPMANE
Durable goods	USEMPDGDE
Non-durable goods	USEMPNDGE
Service-producing	USEMPSVPA
Transportation and public utilities	USEMPTRNE
Wholesale trade	USEMPWOLE
Retail trade	USEMPRETE
Finance, insurance and real estate	USEMPFIRA
Services	USEMPSERA
Government	USEMPGOVE

Average Weekly Hours (sa)	Datastream
Total private	USAWHPRVE
Goods-producing	USHWIQ..G
Mining	USHWIX..O
Construction	USHWIC..O

Average Weekly Hours (sa)	Datastream
Manufacturing	USAWHMANE
Overtime hours	USWOHMANE
Durable goods	USHWIMD.O
Overtime hours	USHOIMD.O
Non-durable goods	USHWIMN.O
Overtime hours	USHOIMN.O
Service-producing	USHWIH..G
Transportation and public utilities	USHWIT..O
Wholesale trade	USHWIW..O
Retail trade	USHWIR..O
Finance, insurance and real estate	USHWIF..O
Services	USHWIS..O

Average Hourly Earnings (sa)	Datastream
Total private in current USD	USAHEPNFB
In 1982 USD	USAHEPNFD
Goods-producing	USWHIQ..B
Mining	USWHIX..B
Construction	USWHIC..B
Manufacturing	USWHIM..B
Excluding overtime	USWHOIM.B
Service producing	USWHIH..B
Transportation and public utilities	USWHIT..B
Wholesale trade	USWHIW..B
Retail trade	USWHIR..B
Finance, insurance and real estate	USWHIF..B
Services	USWHIS..B

Indices of Aggregated Weekly Hours of Production (sa, 1982=100)	Datastream
Total private	USAWHPVTE
Goods-producing	USHWIQ..G
Mining	USHWIX..G
Construction	USHWIC..G
Manufacturing	USMNHOURE
Durable	USHWIMD.G
Non-durable	USHWIMN.G
Service producing	USHWIH..G
Transportation and public utilities	USHWIT..G
Wholesale trade	USHWIW..G
Retail trade	USHWIR..G
Finance, insurance and real estate	USHWIF..G
Services	USHWIS..G

Diffusion Indices of Employment Change (sa)	Datastream
Private non-farm payrolls, 353 industries	
Over 1-month span	USED1IP.G
Over 3-month span	USED3IP.G
Over 6-month span	USED6IP.G
Over 12-month span	USED12IPH
Manufacturing payrolls, 136 industries	
Over 1-month span	USED1IM.G
Over 3-month span	USED3IM.G
Over 6-month span	USED6IM.G
Over 12-month span	USED12IMH

Literature

Boyd, John H., Jagannathan, Ravi and Hu Jian, 'The Stock Market's Reaction to Unemployment News: Why Bad News is Usually Good for Stocks', *NBER Working Paper No. W8092*, January 2001.

Douglas, Stratford and Wall, Howard J., 'The Revealed Cost of Unemployment', *Federal Reserve Bank of St. Louis Review*, Vol. 82, No. 2, (March 2000), pp. 1–10.

Getz, Patricia M., 'Implementing the New Sample Design for the Current Employment Statistics Survey', *Business Economics*, October 2000, pp. 47–50.

Getz, Patricia M. and Ulmer, Mark G., 'Diffusion Indexes: A Barometer of the Economy', *Monthly Labor Review*, April 1990, pp. 13–21.

Harris, Ethan S. and Zabka, Natasha M., 'The Employment Report and the Dollar', Federal Reserve Bank of New York, *Current Issues in Economics and Finance*, Vol. 1, No. 8, (November 1995).

Juhn, Chinhui and Potter, Simon, 'Explaining the Recent Divergence in Payroll and Household Employment Growth', Federal Reserve Bank of New York, *Current Issues in Economics and Finance*, Vol. 5, No. 16, (December 1999).

Kosters, Marvin H., 'Wage and Job Trends in the U.S. Labor Market: An Assessment', Bank of Japan, *IMES Discussion Paper No. 98-E-17*.

Krane, Spencer and Wascher, William: 'The Cyclical Sensitivity of Seasonality in US Employment', Bank for International Settlements, *BIS Working Paper No. 67*, May 1999.

Millard, Stephen, Scott, Andrew and Sensier, Marianne: 'Business cycles and the labour market: Can theory fit the facts?', Bank of England, *Working Paper Series No. 93*, March 1999.

U.S. Department of Commerce, Bureau of Labor Statistics, 'Employment and Wages Covered by Unemployment Insurance', *BLS Handbook of Methods*, Ch. 5, April 1997, pp. 42–7.

U.S. Department of Commerce, Bureau of Labor Statistics, 'Employment, Hours, and Earnings from the Establishment Survey', *BLS Handbook of Methods*, Ch. 2, April 1997, pp. 15–27.

U.S. Department of Commerce, Bureau of Labor Statistics, 'Labor Force Data Derived from the Current Population Survey', *BLS Handbook of Methods*, Ch. 5, April 1997, pp. 4–14.

Valletta, Robert G., 'Changes in the Structure and Duration of U.S. Unemployment, 1967–1998', *Federal Reserve Bank of San Francisco Economic Review*, No. 3, (1998), pp. 29–40.

14.2 Unemployment Insurance Weekly Claims Report

Data Source

Data are published by the Employment and Training Administration (ETA) at the Department of Labor. The press release is available on the Internet at www.dol.gov/dol/media/main.htm.

Importance for the Financial Markets D

Description

In addition to the monthly labour market data, data on new jobless claims and the number of people on benefit are published weekly. Requirements for entitlement to unemployment benefit vary from state to state. In principle social security contributions have first to be paid during a period of employment.

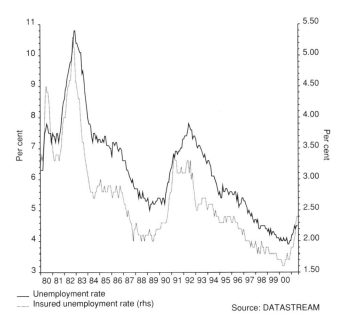

Figure 14.8 Unemployment rate (*Labor Market Report*) and insured unemployment rate (*Unemployment Insurance Weekly Claims Report*)

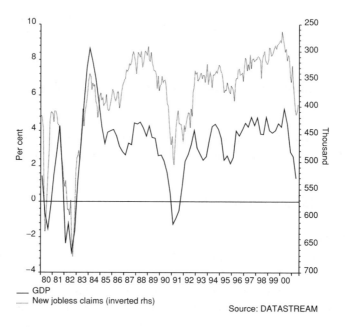

Figure 14.9   Change in GDP on preceding year and new jobless claims

Strikers have no entitlement to unemployment benefit, whereas staff in companies forced to stop production on account of strike activities in another company do receive unemployment benefit. In addition, people losing their jobs as a result of their own wrongful action are not entitled to unemployment benefit. Unemployment benefit is currently paid for a maximum of six months in the USA. Consequently, the number of people receiving benefit depends not only on the number of people who have found a job, but also those who are no longer entitled to benefit and are therefore no longer included in the statistics.

In addition to the aggregate weekly data a moving average of the number of new jobless claims over four weeks is published. Data on the situations in various states are also published, particularly if the number of new claims in these states changes by over 1000.

Periodicity/Revisions

Weekly data are always published on Thursdays at 08.30 ET (14.30 CET). Data on new claimants relate to the week ending on the Saturday before publication, whereas figures for those already on benefit are published with a lag of 12 days. Revisions normally take place one week after the initial release and in January/ February when the seasonal adjustment factors are updated.

Seasonal Adjustment

Data are seasonally adjusted.

Notes

The link between the change in the new non-farm payrolls and new jobless claims is not very close. The reason for this is that people seeking work were not necessarily entitled to unemployment benefit before. At the same time not all people who lose their jobs are entitled to benefit. Nevertheless the weekly data can still give some indicators on the labour market situation as measured by the monthly Labor Market Report. The trend between the two figures largely coincides. For a smoother outlook without weekly fluctuations, increased notice is being taken of the moving average over four weeks also published regularly by the Department of Labor. As a general rule, a recession is imminent when over 400000 new benefit claimants register per week. This accounts for a loss of around 100000 jobs per month outside agriculture.

It is important to assess the situation in the labour market and this means not just the level of new claims, but also the fluctuation in new weekly claims and above all the change in the moving average. The situation in the labour market is considered negative when, for example, 300000 new claims per week are registered. The situation is more critical when 300000 new claims are registered

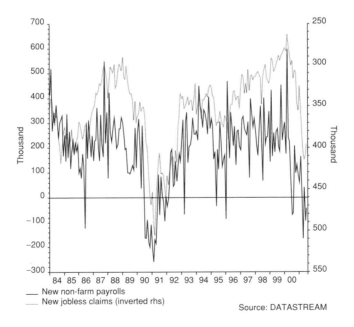

Figure 14.10   New non-farm payrolls and new jobless claims

and the trend is rising. A falling trend, on the other hand, indicates that the labour market is returning to normal.

Key Datastream Mnemonics

Unemployment Insurance (sa)	Datastream
Initial claims	USUNCLM
Initial claims, 4-weeks moving average	USUNCL4
Insurance unemployment	USUNIEM
Insurance unemployment, 4-weeks moving average	USUNIE4
Insurance unemployment rate	USUNIRT

Literature

McConnell, Margaret M., 'Rethinking the Value of Initial Claims as a Forecasting Tool', Federal Reserve Bank of New York, *Current Issues in Economics and Finance*, Vol. 4, No. 11 (November 1998).

14.3 The Conference Board Help-Wanted Advertising Index

Data Source

Data are published by the Conference Board. The press release is available on the Internet at www.conference-board.org.

Importance for the Financial Markets   E

Description

The Help-Wanted Advertising Index is a labour market indicator which summarizes in one index the number of job offers in 51 main daily newspapers in 51 cities throughout the country. The advertisements cover around half of the national labour market. The idea behind the index is that the volume of advertisements increases as the economic situation improves and companies require more labour. Each advertisement is only included once, even if this advertisement includes several jobs. Furthermore, it is not taken into consideration whether the advertisement appears in several newspapers at the same time or whether the same advertisement is published several times over a longer period.

Each of the 51 cities has its own indices, which are then grouped into the nine regions defined by the Bureau of the Census. The largest of these regions are Northeast Central, Pacific and Mid-Atlantic, whereas New England is the smallest. The nationwide index is then based on the nine regions. The weightings of the individual cities and regions are based on employment outside agriculture.

Periodicity/Revisions

Monthly data are published at the end of the second month following the survey period. Publication usually takes place on Thursdays at 10.00 ET (16.00 CET), normally one week prior to the publication of the labour market report.

Seasonal Adjustment

Data are seasonally adjusted, although the seasonal adjustment factors are still based on the year 1987. The factors are only very rarely aligned to changes in conditions.

Notes

Although there is no wide-scale correlation in the monthly changes between the Help-Wanted Advertising Index and the number of new non-farm payrolls, there is a much closer link between the trends of these two labour market indicators. The volume of job advertisements has fallen in recent years due to the increasing number of employment agencies and the increased use of the Internet for advertising jobs. This trend has not yet been taken into account

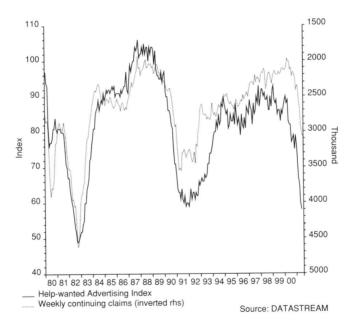

Figure 14.11 The Conference Board Help-Wanted Advertising Index and weekly continuing claims

in the calculation of the index, so the Help-Wanted Advertising Index tends to underrate the labour market situation.

Key Datastream Mnemonics

The Conference Board Help-Wanted Advertising Index (sa)	Datastream
Help-wanted Advertising Index	USHLPWANE
Proportion of labour markets with rising want-ad volume	USHLPWADQ

15
Consumer Indicators

15.1   Advance Retail Trade and Food Service

Data Source

Data are published by the Bureau of the Census at the Department of Commerce. The press release is available on the Internet at www.census.gov/cgi-bin/briefroom/BriefRm.

Importance for the Financial Markets   B

Description

Retail sales data are the economic data available which reflect consumer expenditure in the most up-to-date and comprehensive way possible, although data do tend to fluctuate strongly from one month to the next. One reason for this is the extremely erratic sales pattern in the automobile sector. For this reason, retail sales are also shown without sales in this sector. Data have been surveyed since 1951. The advance report has only been calculated since 1953 and between February 1970 and 1972 no advance report was published as revisions in this period between the advance reports and the final reports were so major that the use of the early information suffered greatly. Only after the survey method had been changed considerably did the Bureau of the Census decide to produce the advance reports again.

Starting with the April 2001 data, the Bureau of the Census switched from the Standard Industrial Classification (SIC) system to the North American Industry Classification System (NAICS) in order to better reflect the development of the retail trade sector with the published data. One outcome of this step is that new samples are designed to produce NAICS-based estimates and replace the SIC-based samples. Thus new retail categories, such as computer and software stores, warehouse clubs and superstores, are provided with the new system. In addition, the durable and non-durable goods categories have been eliminated.

One additional result of this update was that many wholesale trade establishments are now redefined as retail trade establishments because NAICS bases the classification on how each establishment operates rather than to whom it sells, as was the case under the SIC system.

Retail trade includes establishments engaged in selling merchandise in small quantities to the general public, without transformation, and rendering services incidental to the sale of merchandise. The sector includes both store and non-store retailers. Sales include merchandise sold by establishments primarily engaged in retail trade. The data are expressed in current dollars only. Services that are incidental to the sale of merchandise, and excise taxes that are paid by the manufacturer or wholesaler and passed along to the retailer, are also included. Deductions are made for refunds and allowances for merchandise returned by customers. Taxes collected directly from customers and paid directly to a local, state or federal tax agency are also excluded. Retail sales data measure the operations receipt rendered by stores that primarily sell at retail and represent the total sales and receipts of these establishments. Not included are the retail sales of manufactures, wholesalers, service establishments, and others whose primary activity is other than retail trade. The allocation of business categories is also conducted in terms of type of business and not type of product, so food sold at service stations, for example, is allocated to the gasoline sector and

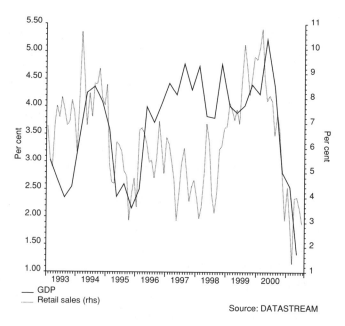

Figure 15.1 Change in GDP and retail sales on preceding year

not the food sector. Retail sales data are the sales of retailers during the reference month. In contrast to this, inventories are the value of stocks of goods held for sale through retail stores as of the last day of the report period.

Retail companies are surveyed by post. Questionnaires are sent out five working days before the end of a month and responses are due back at the Bureau of the Census at the latest three working days after the end of the month. Otherwise the Bureau of the Census telephones the companies to obtain the data. All the large retailers are surveyed, whereas only a proportion of smaller companies are included.

Around 13 300 companies operating primarily in the retail sector are currently surveyed monthly. Overall around 31 000 retail companies are involved in the survey, although they are not all included every month. There are currently three survey groups of 6 100 smaller retailers with only one business outlet. Only two of these three groups are surveyed at one time. In addition there are 2 200 smaller retailers with several outlets and a further group of large retailers who are surveyed every month.

The database is checked on a quarterly basis. However, not every retailer is incorporated immediately and there is on average a nine-month gap between a business start-up and initial inclusion in the survey. There is no differentiation

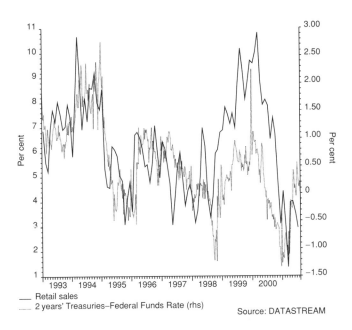

Figure 15.2 Change in retail sales on preceding year and difference of 2 years' Treasuries minus Federal Funds Rate

in terms of the type of distribution. This means that retailers distributing via the Internet are also included. Sales are also recorded from the date of the order and not the date of dispatch.

In addition to the monthly surveys, annual surveys have been conducted since 1951 (with the exception of 1954). Results of annual surveys have served as a benchmark for the monthly surveys since 1977. Currently around 22 000 retailers are surveyed. These include two of the three survey groups of small companies plus all the larger retailers. The interviews begin in the first week in January. Starting in April 2001, the restated estimates derived from the annual surveys were benchmarked to sales totals obtained from the 1992 and 1997 Economic Censuses. In addition, the monthly sales and inventories were benchmarked to the 1999 Annual Retail Trade Survey.

There are no figures on inventories for the respective companies in the retail sales report. These data are included in the manufacturing and trade inventory and sales report which is published after the retail sales.

Periodicity/Revisions

Data are published on the ninth working day of the month. If this falls on a Monday, publication is effected on the following Tuesday. Data in the advance report relate primarily to the month preceding the current month. The figures include results from retailers who have already responded on completion of the report. Data in the preliminary report, on the other hand, relate to the month two months previously and include data from all retailers surveyed. Each retailer is surveyed on average only once a quarter, although they have to supply information on the current month and the month before. Survey results from two months respectively (preceding month's results of the advance report and the preliminary results from the report) are then summarized in a final report.

Benchmark revisions relating to past years are normally carried out in March when the results of the annual survey of retailers are announced. These are obligatory, in contrast to the monthly questionnaires which are voluntary. Revisions serve to eliminate statistical discrepancies between the annual and monthly figures. However, the trend produced in the monthly data should be retained. In addition, every five years there is an alignment of the weighting within the indicator produced by the results of the census survey of retailers. The last revision was in 2001 on the basis of the surveys for 1992 and 1997. Publication always takes place around 08.30 ET (14.30 CET).

Seasonal Adjustment

Data are seasonally adjusted using the X-12 ARIMA program. The seasonal adjustment factors are aligned every month as soon as the latest sales are released. Starting in June 2001, new factors used to adjust sales and inventories

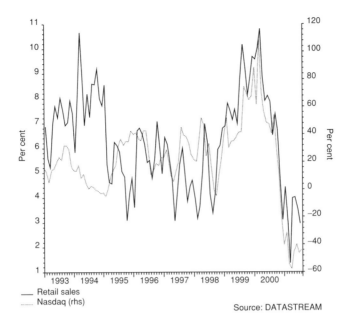

Figure 15.3 Change in retail sales and Nasdaq on preceding year

estimates for seasonal and trading-day variations have been developed and are used to adjust the revised estimates for January 1992 to March 2001.

Notes

Retail sales account for around 30 per cent of total GDP. As the monthly data are subject to considerable fluctuation and comprehensive revisions are standard, individual monthly figures are of little use for the analysis of economic development. For this reason, derived figures are used to improve results. First, the extremely volatile sales from the automobile sector are excluded, and second, information on discretionary expenditure is employed. These include retail sales excluding sales from the food industry, the energy sector and pharmacies. Particularly when energy prices are subject to extreme fluctuation, retail sales excluding expenditure on energy can be a good source of information. In the past it was established that a clear monthly change was frequently reversed in the subsequent month. For this reason it is also useful to employ a moving average over three months to identify the underlying trend. And finally there are close links between the retail data and the data published later on private consumer expenditure. Where the data for consumer expenditure reveal a similar monthly change, it can be assumed that revision of the retail sales would be relatively minor. It is also useful to calculate the retail 'control' to estimate consumer goods spending. This retail control consists of the retail sales excluding the sales of building materials, gasoline and motor vehicles.

Due to the major benchmark revision in June 2001, data before March 2001 should be used with caution, because historical data differ from previously published numbers as the results from the new NAICS-based samples were used in the benchmarking process. Data will be of much lower quality with NAICS codes that consist of more than one SIC component. Estimates from January 1992 to December 1996 are less accurate than estimates for later periods and the earlier the period, the less accurate the results are because the data for the January 1992 to December 1996 estimates depend more heavily on the conversion of SIC-based data to a NAICS basis than did data for later periods.

Retail sales figures are used by a number of other bodies as a basis for their own statistics. Consequently retail sales are input into the GDP calculation by the Bureau of Economic Analysis. The Bureau of Labor Statistics (BLS) uses retail sales figures for calculating consumer prices and productivity. The Council of

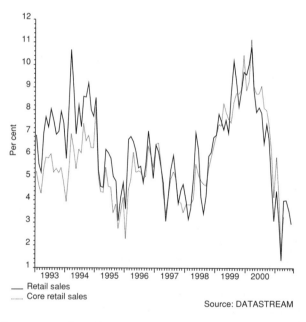

Source: DATASTREAM

Figure 15.4   Change in total retail sales and core retail sales on preceding year

Economic Advisers takes these sales into account in its analysis of economic activity and the Federal Reserve Board predicts consumer purchasing habits using retail sales figures.

The retail sales figures also include data relating to automobile sales. However, these data do not correspond to the figures regularly published by the automobile manufacturers. The main reason for this is that sales of used cars, repairs, car parts, motorbikes and boats are also included in sales by car dealers which form the basis for this publication, but are not included by the automobile producers.

Key Datastream Mnemonics

Retail Trade and Food Services (sa)	Datastream
Retail and food services, total	USRETTOTB
Total, excl. motor vehicles and parts	USSRAFSXB
Retail	USRETTOXB
GAFO	USSRGAFOB
Motor vehicles and parts dealers	USSR441.B
Furniture and home furniture stores	USSR442.B
Electronic and appliance stores	USSR443.B
Building material and garden equipment and supplies dealers	USSR444.B
Food and beverages stores	USSR445.B
Health and personal care stores	USSR446.B
Gasoline stations	USSR447.B
Clothing and clothing accessories stores	USSR448.B
General merchandise stores	USSR452.B
Department stores (excl. leased departments)	USSR4521B
Department stores (incl. leased departments)	USSRDPTLB
Miscellaneous store retailers	USSR453.B
Non-store retailers	USSR454.B
Food services and drinking places	USSR722.B

Literature

Harris, Ethan, S. and Vega, Clara, 'What do Chain Store Sales Tell Us about Consumer Spending', Federal Reserve Bank of New York, *Economic Policy Review*, Vol. 2, No. 2 (October 1996), pp. 15–35.

Parker, Robert P., 'The Impact of the North American Industry Classification System on U.S. Economic Data: In May 2001, NAICS Hits the Economic Indicators', *Business Economics*, April 2001, pp. 56–9.

15.2   Personal Income and Personal Consumption Expenditures

Data Source

Data are published by the Bureau of Economic Analysis at the Department of Commerce. The press release is available on the Internet at www.bea.gov/bea/dn1.htm. Supplementary data on private savings are also contained in Table 5.1 (Gross Saving and Investment) in the Survey of Current Business. Table 2.17 (Personal Income and Saving) in the Federal Reserve Bulletin and Table F.9 (Derivation of Measures of Personal Saving) in the USA's Flow of Funds Accounts also contain useful data for the analysis of the income and consumption situation.

Importance for the Financial Markets   C

Description

Data collected by the Bureau of Economic Analysis on personal income and personal consumption are a broad measurement of the respective figures. They are surveyed monthly and shown in an annualized form. The most important component of personal income is wages and salaries, which account for almost 60 per cent of total income. In addition there is rental income, state benefits (e.g., social security), interest and dividend income, transfer income and other labour income (e.g., contributions by the employer to health insurance and pension funds). In contrast income for changes in the value of assets, such as stocks, is not included. Personal consumption is divided into the categories of durable goods, non-durable goods and services.

In addition to personal income and personal consumption, the private saving rate is also published. This is defined as savings as a percentage of disposable income (personal income less direct tax). Private saving, on the other hand, is treated as a residual variable. All income not spent is thereby saved. Expenditure includes consumer expenditure and private interest payments on all loans outside the domestic sector as well as net transfer payments abroad.

Periodicity/Revisions

Monthly data are published at the end of the month following the survey period or the first day of the month thereafter, normally one working day after publication of the GDP figures. Published data can be revised over several months and revisions can be fairly substantial. The data are published at 08.30 ET (14.30 CET).

Seasonal Adjustment

All data are seasonally adjusted.

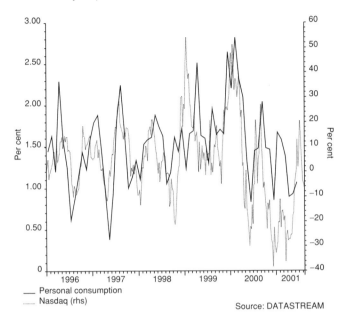

Figure 15.5 Change in personal consumption expenditure and Nasdaq on 3 months before

Notes

Personal income trends are a good indicator of future consumer development as consumption is largely dependent on income trends. As consumer demand is also dependent on other figures, such as future economic expectations, consumer trends cannot be assumed purely on the basis of income trends. In particular it should be noted that consumer demand falls as the economy begins to decline. The impact then snowballs and incomes begin to fall.

Consumer demand accounts for around two-thirds of the GDP. Data on personal consumption and personal income are therefore good indicators of the GDP trend, although conclusions can also be drawn from other publications on personal consumption and personal income. The demand for non-durable goods can be approximately derived from the retail data, whereas the demand for services is comparatively stable. However there are exceptions to this: for instance, strong price fluctuations in the stock market can affect broker fee levels.

Unusually hot or cold weather conditions can affect the expenditure of supply companies and major damage claims in the insurance business accompanied by high insurance contributions reduce the net expenditure on the acquisition of insurance policies. Wage data in the *Labor Market Report* are a good indicator of personal income trends. However, these figures can produce unusual distortions. As the monthly data are annualized, revenue received only once a year can distort the annualized monthly figures if several are grouped in one month. This effect is then offset in the subsequent month, although high monthly fluctuations may result.

The most difficult figure to interpret in this report is the private saving rate. The private saving rate has been falling substantially since the beginning of the 1990s and is now around zero. It should be noted, however, that figures from the Bureau of Economic Analysis only take into account income from the production process. Income from rising asset prices is not included. Rising stock prices and the resultant capital gain should specifically be taken into account.

In addition to the savings rate calculated by the Bureau of Economic Analysis, the Federal Reserve Board also calculates a savings rate as part of the Flow of Funds Analysis. Whereas the BEA bases its savings rate calculation on the difference between income and expenditure, the Board calculates the saving from the difference in the net rise of fixed assets and liabilities. These two procedures are conceptually identical but as they are based on a different database they produce different values. It should, however, be noted that the trends of both figures correlate, even though the underlying problem of the treatment of changes in assets cannot be solved by any procedure.

Apart from private saving, a distinction is also made between savings by business, savings by government and total savings. All three are clearly producing positive results; public savings are set to rise again according to future US government plans, thereby reducing state debt. Thus, in 2000 savings by government totalled USD528.0 billion, up from USD374.0 billion in 1999. Savings by the corporate sector totalled USD1305.6 billion and US gross savings totalled USD1825.1 billion. This accounted for 18.3 per cent of the GDP. In comparison, personal savings outside the corporate sector in 2000 showed a de-saving of USD−8.5 billion.

From the published data the key factors for the financial markets are the monthly changes in personal income and personal consumption as well as the personal savings rate. Given the conceptual problems with the calculation of the savings rate, and given that similar values for most data are already available, the importance of these figures is still limited.

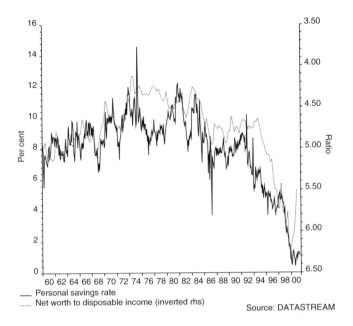

Figure 15.6   Personal savings rate and ratio of net worth to disposable income

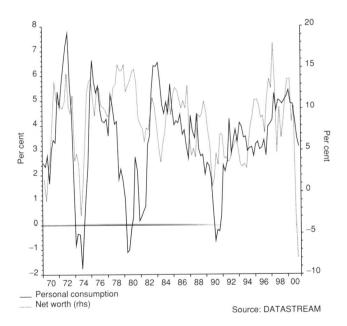

Figure 15.7   Change in personal consumption expenditures and net worth on preceding year

Key Datastream Mnemonics

Personal Income (saar)	Datastream
Personal income, total	USPERINCB
Wage and salary disbursements	USWSALARB
Private industry	USWSDIP.B
Government	USWSGOVTB
Other labour income	USOLABINB
Proprietors' income with inventory valuation adjustment and capital consumption adjustment	USICOWA.B
Rental income of persons with capital consumption adjustment	USRENTALB
Personal dividend income	USPDIVINB
Personal interest income	USPINTINB
Transfer payments to persons	USTRNPAYB
Less: Personal contributions for social insurance	USSOCIALB

The Disposition of Personal Income (saar)	Datastream
Personal income	USPERINCB
Less: Personal tax and non-tax payments	USPTAXNTB
Equals: Disposable personal income	USDPERSIB
Less: Personal outlays	USPEROUTB
Personal consumption expenditures	USPERCONB
Interest paid by persons	USINTCONB
Personal transfer payments to the rest of the world (net)	USTRFORB
Equals: Personal saving	USPSAVINB
Addenda	
Disposable personal income	
Chained 1996 USD	USDPERSID
Per capita (current USD)	USINPERCB
Per capita (chained 1996 USD)	USINPERCD
Population (1000)	USPOPNIA.
Personal saving as a percentage of disposable personal income	USPSVRATE

Personal Consumption Expenditures by Major Type of Product (saar)	Datastream
Personal consumption expenditures (billion current USD)	USPERCONB
Durable goods	USCONDURB
Non-durable goods	USCONNDRB
Services	USCONNDRB
Personal consumption expenditures (billion chained 1996 USD)	USPERCOND
Durable goods	USCONDURD
Non-durable goods	USCONNDRD
Services	USCONNDRD

Personal Consumption Expenditures by Major Type of Product (saar)	Datastream
Chain-type price indexes (1996 = 100)	
Personal consumption expenditures	USCP...CE
Durable goods	USCONDUCE
Non-durable goods	USCONNDCE
Services	USCONSRCE
Addendum:	
Personal consumption expenditures less food and energy	USCNXFECE

Literature

Board of Governors of the Federal Reserve System, *Guide to the Flow of Funds Accounts*, 1993.

Larkins, Daniel, 'Note on the Personal Saving Rate', U.S. Department of Commerce, *Survey of Current Business*, February 1999.

Ludvigson, Sydney and Steindel, Charles, 'How Important is the Stock Market Effect on Consumption?', in Federal Reserve Bank of New York, *Economic Policy Review*, Vol. 5 No. 2, (July 1999), pp. 29–51.

Seskin, Eugene P., 'Recent Trends in the NIPA Personal Saving Rate', U.S. Department of Commerce, *Survey of Current Business*, August 1998, p. 30.

Wilson, J.F. *et al.*: 'Measuring Household Saving: Recent Experience from the Flow-of-Funds Perspective', in R.E. Lipsey and H.S. Tice (eds), *The Measurement of Saving, Investment, and Wealth*, Chicago, 1989.

15.3   Consumer Confidence

Two key indices on consumer confidence are published in the USA, one by The Conference Board and the other by the University of Michigan. Both indices are based on a survey with five questions and are composed of two sub-indices in each case. The first is based on the current situation and the second one accounts for expectations.

15.3.1   The Conference Board U.S. Consumer Confidence Index

Data Source

Data are published by The Conference Board. The press release is available on the Internet at www.conference-board.org or www.crc-conquest.org. The full report is available for a fee from The Conference Board Consumer Research Center.

Importance for the Financial Markets   C

Description

The Consumer Confidence Index has been calculated since 1967. In the first few years it was only produced every two months but, since 1977, values have been produced monthly. Around 5000 households are currently surveyed on behalf of the Conference Board by NFO Research, Inc. of Greenwich, Connecticut. The following five questions are set for the overall index and the two sub-indices:

1. How would you rate the present general business conditions in your area? Good, normal or bad?
2. Six months from now, do you think they will be: better, the same or worse?
3. What would you say about available jobs in your area right now: plenty, not so many, or hard to get?
4. Six months from now, do you think there will be: more jobs, the same, or fewer jobs?
5. How would you guess your total family income to be six months from now? Higher, the same or lower?

Figure 15.8   The Conference Board U.S. Consumer Confidence Index and Dow Jones Industrials

The sub-index relating to the current situation is obtained from the responses to questions 1 and 3, whereas the other questions are used for the sub-index on expectations. The responses to all five questions are then input with equal weighting into the calculation of consumer confidence. This is indexed whereby $1985 = 100$.

In addition to the above five questions, there are separate questions on the purchasing intentions for houses (plan to buy a new home, a lived-in home or any home) or automobile (plan to buy a new automobile, an used automobile or any automobile) within the next six months. The full report also contains additional figures on consumer confidence in the nine US regions, as defined by the Bureau of the Census. Sub-indices in terms of the age of the head of the household and the family income are also produced.

Periodicity/Revisions

Monthly data are published on the last Tuesday in the month to which it relates. The survey is conducted in the first half of the month. Minor revisions take place one month after the initial publication. Publication of the index takes place at 10.00 ET (16.00 CET).

Seasonal Adjustment

Data are seasonally adjusted.

Notes

The Consumer Confidence Index is highly regarded as it is one of the first publications available (it is released on the last Tuesday of the month to which it relates). However, it has also been shown, particularly in recent years, that consumer confidence is strongly affected by stock price trends. At the same time the link between consumer confidence and consumer expenditure is not very close. Apart from the index level the monthly change is also of interest to the financial markets, However, it is worth noting that statistical inaccuracy is relatively high so monthly changes of under 10 points can be interpreted as 'interference' which has only a minor significance on consumer buying habits. For this reason it is useful to use a moving average over, for example, 3 months. The highest value obtained to date was 144.7 in January and May 2000 and the lowest was 43.2 at the end of 1974/1975.

The first indications of consumer confidence are provided in the provisional Consumer Value of the Index of Sentiment produced by the University of Michigan, which is released mid-month, i.e., before publication by The Conference Board. For the period of January 1991 to mid-2001 the correlation was nearly 0.94 between the provisional monthly values of consumer confidence calculated by the University in Michigan and The Conference Board.

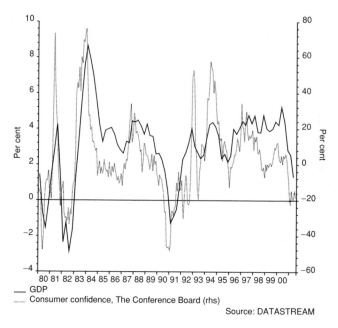

Figure 15.9 Change in GDP and The Consumer Board U.S. Consumer Confidence Index (Conference Board) on preceding year

Key Datastream Mnemonics

The Conference Board U.S. Consumer Confidence Index (sa)	Datastream
Consumer Confidence Index	USCNCONF
Index present situation	USCNPSIT
Index expectations	USCNEXPT
Index head of household:	
Under 35 years	USCNCA35
35–54 years	USCNCA44
55 years and over	USCNCA55
Business conditions currently:	
Good	USTCBBPP
Normal	USTCBBPM
Bad	USTCBBPN
Business conditions in 6 months:	
Better	USTCBBEP
Same	USTCBBEM
Worse	USTCBBEN

The Conference Board U.S. Consumer Confidence Index (sa)	Datastream
Jobs currently:	
Plentiful	USTCBEPP
Not so plentiful	USTCBEPM
Hard to find	USTCBEPN
Jobs in 6 months:	
More	USTCBEEP
Same	USTCBEEM
Fewer	USTCBEEN
Income in 6 months:	
Increased	USTCBIEP
Same	USTCBIEM
Decreased	USTCBIEN
Plans to buy auto within 6 months:	USTCBAEP
Plans to buy new auto within 6 months	USTCBAEW
Plans to buy used auto within 6 months	USTCBAEU
Plans to buy any auto within 6 months	USTCBAEM
Plans to buy home within 6 months:	USTCBHEP
Plans to buy new home within 6 months	USTCBHEW
Plans to buy lived in home within 6 months	USTCBHEX
Plans to buy any home within 6 months	USTCBHEM

Literature

Bram, Jason and Ludvigson, Sydney, 'Does Consumer Confidence Forecast Household Expenditure? A Sentiment Index Horse Race', Federal Reserve Bank of New York, *Policy Review*, June 1998, 59–78.

15.3.2   Surveys of Consumers (University of Michigan)

Data Source

Data are published by the Survey Research Center at the Institute for Social Research at the University of Michigan. Full results of the survey are only issued to subscribers. In addition to a fax service providing a summary, the University of Michigan also publishes a monthly report with the results and a so-called Yellowbook containing the survey results in tabular form. Historical data are published in the so-called Redbook. These publications are only available from the Survey Research Center at the Institute for Social Research at the University of Michigan. Historical data are also published on the Internet at athena.sca.isr.umich.edu or on the Internet site of the University of Michigan (www.umich.edu). Summaries of the survey results are distributed by the news services.

Importance for the Financial Markets   C

Description

Apart from The Conference Board U.S. Consumer Confidence Index, the index of Consumer Sentiment published by the University of Michigan is the second most important index for the assessment of consumer buying habits. The index has been produced largely in its current form since 1966, although there has been a comparable survey since November 1952. In the early years the report was not produced on a regular basis (around three times a year), but then was produced quarterly after 1960. Monthly results have only been available since January 1978. Around 500 households (250 to 300 households for the preliminary report) in 48 states (excluding Alaska and Hawaii), including the District of Columbia, are currently selected randomly and surveyed via a telephone poll. Each household therefore has the same chance of being selected. Around 9 per cent of US households currently have no telephone. This circumstance is taken into consideration in evaluation so the responses can be seen as representative.

Overall there are around 21 questions which, in addition to preset multiple-choice answers, also allow descriptive answers. The questions for evaluating consumer Sentiment represent a fraction of these. The questions cover three main sectors and are aimed at obtaining consumer estimates (i.e., estimates of personal financial situations, general business conditions and purchasing habits). These sectors are questioned by mentioning expectations about nominal family income or the real income situation. There are also specific questions on inflation, unemployment, interest rate trends or government economic policy. Finally interviewees are questioned about their assessment of the housing market, automobile market or market for durable goods.

The most important part of the whole survey, however, is the Consumer Sentiment Index, which is calculated from five sub-questions. In addition to the overall index, similarly to The Conference Board U.S. Consumer Confidence Index, two additional indices are produced for assessment of the economic situation and consumer expectations. The questions are shown below (possible answers in brackets).

1. We are interested in how people are getting along financially these days. Would you say that you (and your family living there) are better off or worse off financially than you were one year ago? (Better off, same, worse off, don't know/not applicable)
2. Why do you say so? (Higher income, lower income, higher prices)
3. Now looking ahead – do you think that a year from now you (and your family living there) will be better off financially, or worse off, or just about the same as now? (Better off, the same, worse off, don't know/not applicable)

4. During the next twelve months, do you expect your (family) income to be higher or lower than during the past year? By about what per cent do you expect your (family) income to increase during the next 12 months? (Expect increase of 1–4 per cent, 5 per cent, 6–9 per cent, 10–24 per cent, 25 per cent or more, don't know how much up, expect the same, expect down, don't know/not applicable)

5. How about the next year or two – do you expect that your (family) income will go up more than prices will go up, about the same, or less than prices will go up? (Income will go up more than prices, income will go up same as prices, prices will go up more than income, don't know/not applicable)

6. During the last few months, have you heard of any favourable or unfavourable changes in business conditions? What did you hear? (Heard favourable news, heard unfavourable news, no mentions)

7. What did you hear? (Favourable news: government, elections, employment, higher consumer demand, lower prices, easier credit, stock market, trade deficit/Unfavourable news: government, elections, employment, lower consumer demand, higher prices, tighter credit, energy crisis, stock market, trade deficit)

8. Would you say that at present time business conditions are better or worse than they were a year ago? (Better now, same, worse now, don't know/not applicable)

9. And how about a year from now, do you expect that in the country as a whole business conditions will be better or worse than they are at present, or just about the same? (Better, same, worse, don't know/not applicable)

10. Now turning to business conditions in the country as a whole, do you think that during the next 12 months we'll have good times financially, or bad times or what? (Good times, uncertain/good and bad, don't know/not ascertained)

11. Looking ahead, which would you say is more likely – that in the country as a whole we will have continuous good times during the next five years or so, or that we will have periods of widespread unemployment or depression, or what? (Good times, uncertain/good and bad, bad times, not ascertained)

12. How about people out of work during the coming 12 months – do you think that there will be more unemployment than now, about the same, or less? (Less unemployment, same unemployment, more unemployment, don't know/not applicable)

13. No one can say for sure, but what do you think will happen to interest rates for borrowing money during the next 12 months – will they go up, stay the same or go down? (Go up, stay the same, go down, don't know/not applicable)

14. During the next 12 months, do you think that prices in general will go up or go down, or stay where they are now? By about what per cent do you expect prices to go up, on the average, during the next 12 months? (prices will stay the same or go down, prices will go up by: 1–2 per cent, 3–4 per

cent, 5 per cent, 6–9 per cent, 10–14 per cent, 15 per cent or more, prices will go up by don't know how much, don't know/not applicable)

15. As to the economic policy of government – I mean steps taken to fight inflation or unemployment – would you say the government is doing a good job, only fair, or a poor job? (Good job, only fair, poor job, don't know/not applicable)

16. About the big things people buy for their homes – such as furniture, a refrigerator, stove, television, and things like that. Generally speaking, do you think now is a good or a bad time for people to buy major household items? (Good time to buy, uncertain; depends, bad time to buy)

17. Why do you say so?
    Good time to buy:
    Prices are low/good buys available
    Prices won't come down/are going higher
    Interest rates are low/credit is easy
    Borrow in advance of rising interest rates
    Times are good/prosperity
    Bad time to buy:
    Prices are high
    Interest rates are high/credit is tight
    Times are bad/can't afford to buy
    Bad times ahead/uncertain future

18. Generally speaking, do you think now is a good time or a bad time to buy a house? (Good time to buy, uncertain; depends, bad time to buy)

19. Why do you say so?
    Good time to buy:
    Prices are low/good buys available
    Prices won't come down/are going higher
    Interest rates are low/credit is easy
    Borrow-in-advance of rising interest rates
    Good investment
    Times are good/prosperity
    Bad time to buy:
    Prices are high
    Interest rates are high/credit is tight
    Times are bad/can't afford to buy
    Bad times ahead; uncertain future

20. Speaking now of the automobile market – do you think the next 12 months or so will be a good time or a bad time to buy a car?

21. Why?
    Good time to buy:
    Prices are low/good buys available

Prices won't come down/are going higher
Interest rates are low/credit is easy
Borrow in advance of rising interest rates
Times are good/prosperity
New fuel efficient models
Bad time to buy:
Prices are high
Interest rates are high/credit is tight
Times are bad/can't afford to buy
Bad times ahead/uncertain future
Price of gas/shortages
Poor selection/poor quality

To calculate the indices the percentage number of negative responses are deducted from the positive responses to questions 1, 3, 10, 11 and 16 and a value of 100 is added. The results are then rounded up to the next whole number. Subsequently, the Index of Consumer Sentiment (IoCS) is calculated using the following formula:

$$\text{IoCS} = \frac{X_1 + X_3 + X_{10} + X_{11} + X_{16}}{6.7558} + 2.0$$

where X_i represents the value of the respective diffusion indices for the five questions. It is then necessary to divide this by the constant 6.7558 to make the value comparable with the base year of 1966 and the constant 2.0 is added to take into account changes introduced in the fifties. The two sub-indices, of Consumer Expectations (ICE) and of Current Conditions (ICC), are calculated in the same way:

$$\text{ICC} = \frac{X_1 + X_{16}}{2.6424} + 2.0 \qquad \text{ICE} = \frac{X_3 + X_{10} + X_{11}}{4.1134} + 2.0$$

A value of 100 thus corresponds to the values obtained in the first survey in 1966. Most of those surveyed are surveyed again after a period of six months. Approximately 55 per cent out of the 500 or so surveyed are therefore contacted for the first time. The remaining 45 per cent are consumers who were surveyed for the first time six months before and are being re-surveyed.

In addition to responses to the above questions trend statements are also calculated for questions 1 and 3 as well as 8 and 9. The following categories are created for this: 'continuous increase' with the possible answers 'better off than a year ago' and 'better off a year from now'; 'intermittent increase' with the combination 'better/same' and 'same/better'; 'intermittent decline' with the combination 'worse' and 'worse', and 'mixed change' with the combination 'worse/better' and 'better/worse'.

Periodicity/Revisions

The publication of the preliminary report, which covers 250 to 300 households, occurs on the second or third Friday of the month, whichever is closer to the fifteenth of the month. The final report is published 14 days later, also on a Friday. This is normally the last Friday in the month. Information received a couple of days before publication is incorporated into the final report. The report is published at 10.00 ET (16.00 CET).

Consumer Confidence, Conference Board
Consumer Sentiment, University of Michigan (rhs)

Source: DATASTREAM

Figure 15.10   Consumer Confidence Index by The Conference Board and Consumer Sentiment Index by the University of Michigan

Seasonal Adjustment

Data are not seasonally adjusted.

Notes

The University of Michigan Consumer Expectation Index is used by The Conference Board for the calculation of the Index of the Conference Board's Leading Indicators. The provisional indicator value, which is published mid-month, can be used as the first indicator of The Conference Board's Consumer Confidence. For the period January 1991 to mid-2001 the correlation was nearly 0.94 between the provisional monthly values for consumer confidence measured by the University of Michigan and by the Conference Board.

Above all, the results of the additional questions can also serve as indicators of future economic trends. For the period 1960 to 1995 there is a correlation of 0.74 between expectations on future trends in interest rates and actual development with a six-month lead on expectations. The responses to questions on unemployment have a correlation of 0.80 with future labour market trends with a nine-month lead. The best results are for estimates of inflation trends. Here the correlation between inflation expectations and actual inflation amounts to 0.90 with a three-month lead on expectations.

Key Datastream Mnemonics

Surveys of Consumers (University of Michigan, nsa)	Datastream
Consumer Sentiment index	
Current Index	
Expected Index	
Current financial situation compared to a year ago	
Expected change in financial situation	
Expected family income change during the next 12 months	
News heard of recent changes in business conditions	
Current business conditions compared to a year ago	
Expected change in business conditions in a year	
Business conditions expected during the next 12 months	
Business conditions expected during the next five years	
Expected change in unemployment	
Expected change in interest rates	
Expected change in prices during the next 12 months	
Opinions about the government's economic policy	
Buying conditions for large houshold goods	
Buying conditions for houses	
Buying conditions for cars	

Literature

Bram, Jason and Ludvigson, Sydney, 'Does Consumer Confidence Forecast Household Expenditure? A Sentiment Index Horse Race', Federal Reserve Bank of New York, *Policy Review*, June 1998, pp. 59–78.

Otoo, Maria Ward, 'The Sources of Worker Anxiety: Evidence From the Michigan Survey', *Federal Reserve Board of Governors Working Paper*, 1997.

15.4   Consumer Credit

Data Source

The data are published by the Federal Reserve Board. The press release is available on the Internet at www.federalreserve.gov/releases. The data are also published in Table 1.55 Consumer Credit in the *Federal Reserve Bulletin*.

Importance for the Financial Markets   D

Description

Data on consumer credit relate to short- and medium-term credit extended to individuals which is used to finance consumer expenditure. Thus credit which is not repaid in instalments and loans for funding house and property purchases is excluded. Key items include credit for auto purchases, private loans for financing consumer expenditure and credit card payments. The volume of credit is therefore explicitly shown for credit card payments on which no interest is currently payable. Credit is also classified according to the individual creditors (commercial banks, savings institutions, non-financial business, etc.). The data

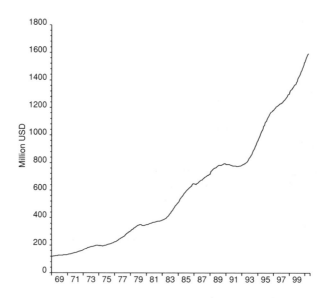

Source: DATASTREAM

Figure 15.11   Consumer credit

are only shown in the form of aggregate figures. Consequently, only the monthly change is taken into account, and not new loans or repayments.

Periodicity/Revisions

Data are surveyed monthly and published on the fifth working day of the month, two months after the survey period. Publication takes place at 15.00 ET (21.00 CET). Substantial monthly revisions are possible. These occur in the first month following publication. There are also annual benchmark revisions.

Seasonal Adjustment

Data are seasonally adjusted.

Notes

Consumer credit data are only of minor significance to the financial markets. First, publication is so late that other data is already available for the analysis of consumer demand. Second, the link between consumer credit and consumer demand is weak as only aggregate data and not the change in the components are published. From the data, both the percentage change on the preceding year and the annual volume are of interest. As the values are relatively volatile, it makes sense to use a moving average over 3 months, although it should be noted that consumer credit almost always rises. Even in times of deep recession lasting several months, credit will only fall at most over a single period. Borrowing causes the disposable income of households to rise. To investigate the credit burden on households it is therefore useful to cook at the volume of credit in relation to disposable income. However, the Federal Reserve Board stopped publication of a series of data showing the burden on households in relation to disposable income. The reason for this is that credit from credit card payments, on which no interest is currently charged, has risen dramatically in recent years. This development greatly affected the significance of the time series.

Key Datastream Mnemonics

Consumer Credit Outstanding (sa)	Datastream
Total	USCRDOUTB
Revolving	USCRDREVB
Non-revolving	USCRDNRVB

Terms of Credit at Commercial Banks and Finance Companies (nsa)	Datastream
Commercial banks	
Interest rates	
48 months, new car	USYLANDC
24 months, personal	USYLPDC.
Credit card plan	
All accounts	USYCCPDC
Accounts assessed interest	USDCFCDB

New Car Loans at Auto Finance Companies (nsa)	Datastream
Interest rate	USYLANFC
Maturity (months)	USFCLANMP
Loan-to-value ratio	USFCLANVP
Amount financed (USD)	USFCLFANA

Major Holders (nsa)	Datastream
Total	USCRDOUTA
Commercial banks	USBCCIC.A
Finance companies	USFCCIC.A
Credit unions	USTUCIC.A
Savings institutions	USTSCIC.A
Non-financial business	USBSCIC.A
Pools of securitized assets	USFICIC.A

Major Types of Credit (nsa)	Datastream
Revolving	USCICREVA
Commercial banks	USBCCICRA
Finance companies	USFCCICRA
Credit unions	USTUCIC.A
Savings institutions	USTSCIC..A
Non-financial business	USBSCICRA
Pools of securitized assets	USFICICRA
Non-revolving	USCICNRVA
Commercial banks	USBCCICNA
Finance companies	USFCCICNA
Credit unions	USCUCICNA
Savings institutions	USSICICNA
Non-financial business	USBSCICOA
Pools of securitized assets	USFICICNA

16
Investment Indicators

16.1 Advance Report on Durable Goods Manufacturers' Shipments, Inventories, and Orders

Data Source

Data are published by the Bureau of the Census at the Department of Commerce. The press release is available on the Internet at www.census.gov/cgi-bin/briefroom/BriefRm.

Importance for the Financial Markets   C

Description

The report on durable goods is part of the Manufacturers' Report, which is published about one week later. In addition to the data on new orders, which constitute the most important part of the report, shipments and the level of inventories are also calculated. The data are only published in nominal figures; there are no inflation-adjusted figures available. Durable goods are goods with an expected useful life of at least three years. They include intermediate and finished products. As this categorization depends on the respective branch of industry, individual goods in different sectors are taken into consideration. This can result in duplication, which somewhat falsifies the data. With new orders no differentiation is made for immediate or later delivery.

Starting with the data for April 2001, the Bureau of the Census switched from the Standard Industrial Classification (SIC) system to the North American Industry Classification System (NAICS), which resulted in major changes in the groupings of the time series. The advance report on durable goods now provides more detail than before. Time series, which were previously published in the Report on Manufacturers' Shipments, Inventories and Orders are now included in the advance report on durable goods. Inventory data on durable goods are now also included in the advance report.

In addition to the division into individual sectors, such as machinery and equipment, transportation equipment, electronic and other electrical equipment, a distinction is also made between capital goods and other goods. Whereas capital goods are divided into those for defence and non-defence use, in the other goods section transportation equipment is particularly important and so is shown separately.

Periodicity/Revisions

Publication normally takes place between the Tuesday and Thursday of the last full week in the month. Data relate to the preceding month and are revised one week after publication when the Report on Manufacturers' Shipments, Inventories and Orders is published covering all new orders in the manufacturing sector and not just durable goods. The revisions are relatively minor given the high monthly volatility of the data. Publication takes place at 08.30 ET (14.30 CET).

Seasonal Adjustment

Data are seasonally adjusted.

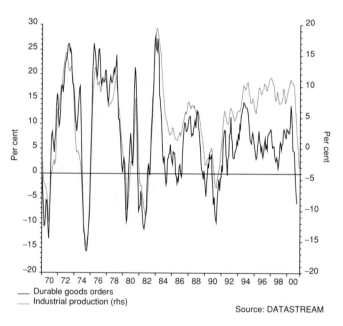

Source: DATASTREAM

Figure 16.1 Change in new durable goods orders and industrial production of durable goods on preceding year, moving averages over 3 months

Notes

The monthly change in data is very volatile. Key orders of transportation equipment continually produce very high fluctuations; however, these are frequently offset again in the following month. For this reason it makes sense to examine new orders without those from the transport sector. A moving average over three months also makes sense to facilitate identification of the underlying trend. Orders in the defence sector also vary enormously so they are frequently excluded from the trend calculation. A further reason for the high volatility of data is the way in which they are calculated. Companies do not report the level of new orders to the Bureau of the Census but just sales and unfilled orders. New orders are then calculated as the residual variable from unfilled orders at the beginning and end of the month and from sales. New orders are the most important part of the report, as they can be a good leading indicator of economic activity in the manufacturing industry. Above all, data on new orders outside the defence sector are a good guide to investment performance in private sector industries.

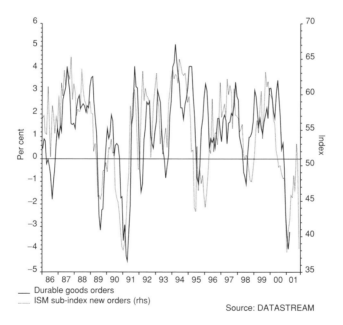

Source: DATASTREAM

Figure 16.2   Change in new durable goods orders on preceding quarter (moving average 2 quarters) and sub-index for new orders in ISM Purchasing Managers' Index for Manufacturing Business

Key Datastream Mnemonics

Durable Goods Manufacturers' Shipments and New Orders (sa)	Datastream
Total	
Shipments	USSHDUR.B
New orders	USNODUR.B
Excluding transportation	
Shipments	USSHMDXTB
New orders	USNOMDXTB
Excluding defence	
Shipments	USSHMDXDB
New orders	USNOMDXDB
Primary metals	
Shipments	USSH331NB
New orders	USNO331NB
Fabricated metal products	
Shipments	USSH332NB
New orders	USNO332NB
Machinery	
Shipments	USSH333.B
New orders	USNO333.B
Computers and electronic products	
Shipments	USSH334.B
New orders	USNO334.B
Computers and related products	
Shipments	USSH3341B
New orders	USNO3341B
Communications equipment	
Shipments	USSH3342B
New orders	USNO3342B
Semiconductors	
Shipments	USSHSEMIB
New orders	USNOSEMIB
Electronic equipment, appliances and components	
Shipments	USSH335.B
New orders	USNO335.B
Transportation equipment	
Shipments	USSH336.B
New orders	USNO336.B
Motor vehicles and parts	
Shipments	USSH3361B
New orders	USNO3361B
Aircraft and parts	
Shipments	USSH3364B
New orders	USNO3364B

Durable Goods Manufacturers' Shipments and New Orders (sa)	Datastream
All other durable goods	
Shipments	USSHDUROB
New orders	USNODUROB
Capital goods	
Shipments	USSHCAPMB
New orders	USNOCAPMB
Non-defence capital goods	
Shipments	USSHCAPNB
New orders	USNOCAPNB
Defence capital goods	
Shipments	USSHCAPDB
New orders	USNOCAPDB

Durable Goods Manufacturers' Unfilled Orders and Total Inventories (sa)	Datastream
Total	
Unfilled orders	USUODUR.B
Total inventories	USINDUR.B
Excluding transportation	
Unfilled orders	USUOMDXTB
Total inventories	USINMDXTB
Excluding defence	
Unfilled orders	USUOMDXDB
Total inventories	USINMDXDB
Primary metals	
Unfilled orders	USUO331NB
Total inventories	USIN331NB
Fabricated metal products	
Unfilled orders	USUO332NB
Total inventories	USIN332NB
Machinery	
Unfilled orders	USUO333.B
Total inventories	USIN333.B
Computers and electronic products	
Unfilled orders	USUO334.B
Total inventories	USIN334.B
Computers and related products	
Unfilled orders	USUO3341B
Total inventories	USIN3341B
Communications equipment	
Unfilled orders	USUO3342B
Total inventories	USIN3342B

Durable Goods Manufacturers' Unfilled Orders and Total Inventories (sa)	Datastream
Semiconductors	
Unfilled orders	USUOSEMIB
Total inventories	USINSEMIB
Electronic equipment, appliances and components	
Unfilled orders	USUO335.B
Total inventories	USIN335.B
Transportation equipment	
Unfilled orders	USUO336.B
Total inventories	USIN336.B
Motor vehicles and parts	
Unfilled orders	USUO3361B
Total inventories	USIN3361B
Aircraft and parts	
Unfilled orders	USUO3364B
Total inventories	USIN3364B
All other durable goods	
Unfilled orders	USUODUROB
Total inventories	USINDUROB
Capital goods	
Unfilled orders	USUOCAPMB
Total inventories	USINCAPMB
Non-defence capital goods	
Unfilled orders	USUOCAPNB
Total inventories	USINCAPNB
Defence capital goods	
Unfilled orders	USUOCAPDB
Total inventories	USINCAPDB

Literature

Parker, Robert P., 'The Impact of the North American Industry Classification System on U.S. Economic Data: In May 2001, NAICS Hits the Economic Indicators', *Business Economics*, April 2001, p. 56–9.

16.2 Preliminary Report on Manufacturers' Shipments, Inventories, and Orders

Data Source

Data are published by the Bureau of the Census at the Department of Commerce. The press release is available on the Internet at www.census.gov/cgi-bin/briefroom/BriefRm.

Importance for the Financial Markets   D

Description

The report provides broad-based monthly data on economic conditions in the manufacturing sector, because it measures current industrial activity and thus provides an indication of future business trends. A separate report on durable goods is produced and published before the overall report (see Section 16.1). In the Manufacturers' Report, there are three major sectors published: shipments, inventories and orders. In addition, the ratio of inventories to shipments (overall and for sub-indices) is published. This figure gives the number of months it would take for the total inventories to be used up at the current level of sales performance. A relatively low proportion of inventories to sales can indicate that producers will produce more in the coming months in order to restock. This would subsequently boost industrial production and thereby economic growth. For the phases downstream (wholesale and retail) a low inventory/sales ratio can also indicate oncoming increased demand, which in turn positively affects economic growth. Inversely, a high ratio indicates a period of low growth.

Starting with the data for April 2001, the Bureau of the Census switched from the Standard Industrial Classification (SIC) system to the North American Industry Classification System (NAICS), which resulted in major changes in the groupings of the time series. In addition, new sub-sectors are created to cover the whole industries producing electronic products and their components. As participation in the survey is voluntary and many companies operating in a number of sectors produce only consolidated data, 89 separately tabulated industry categories are combined into 55 publication levels for shipments and total industries. For new and unfilled orders and inventories by stage of fabrication, it has been necessary to introduce further combinations. Companies producing consolidated figures are thereby allocated to the sector with the most sales. The report has been produced since 1962. In the first few years companies were selected specifically according to the number of employees. Since participation in the survey by smaller companies began to decline companies are now primarily selected in terms of turnover. Currently almost all companies with an annual turnover of over USD500 million as well as a proportion of smaller companies take part in the survey.

The value of shipments data represent the net selling values, f.o.b. (free on board). Inventories are collected on a current cost or pre-LIFO (last in, first out) basis. New orders are net of order cancellations and include orders received and filled during a month as well as orders received for future delivery. Also included is the value of contract changes which increase or decrease the value of the unfilled orders to which they relate. Unfilled orders include

Source: DATASTREAM

Figure 16.3   Unfilled orders to shipments ratio

all orders that have not been reflected as shipments. Thus unfilled orders at the end of the reporting month are equal to unfilled orders at the beginning of this month plus net new orders received less net shipments.

The Manufacturers' Report survey data are benchmarked on a regular basis. Starting with the change of published data for April 2001, the series are benchmarked to the 1997 Economic Census, the 1998 and 1999 Annual Survey of Manufacturers and the 1999 MA-300 Unfilled Orders Survey.

Periodicity/Revisions

Publication takes place approximately one week after the report on durable goods (i.e., normally within the first four working days of the month). In relation to the volatility of the data series, minor revisions can occur within a report for a preceding month's report. There are also benchmark revisions going back a number of years. The data are published at 10.00 ET (16.00 CET).

Seasonal Adjustment

Data is seasonally adjusted using the X-12 ARIMA program. Many time series are also trading day adjusted.

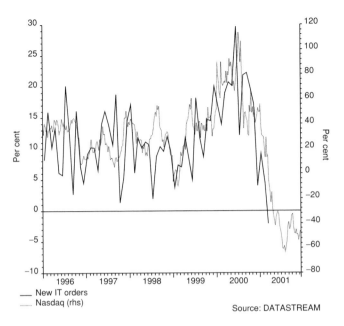

Figure 16.4 Change in new IT orders and Nasdaq (with a lag of 4 months) on preceding year

Notes

As provisional values for durable goods and the Manufacturing and Trade Inventory and Sales Report (see Section 12.4) have already been published and the values for non-durable goods are only subject to relatively minor fluctuation, the results of the report are clearly foreseeable. The influence of changes in prices on non-durable goods is frequently greater than the change in real demand. For this reason the importance of the Manufacturers' Report is minimal. To some extent the revision of new orders for durable goods receives most attention. Inventories are also only of limited significance. A rise implies that production is falling behind demand, which is a possible sign of rising prices. The inventories to shipment ratio is also worth noting as it shows for how many months inventories will meet production capacity, assuming sales remain constant. And finally the inventories to shipment ratio is an indicator of future economic activity. However, the trends in the individual components are worth noting. A fall in sales or rise in inventories signals possible production cuts in the coming months, whereas a rise in sales or decrease in inventories means rising production is likely. In addition, the large number of sub-categories shown can be a useful tool to analyze trends in the economy.

Key Datastream Mnemonics

Value of Manufacturers' Shipments for Industry Groups (sa)	Datastream
All manufacturing industries	USSHMFG.B
Excluding transportation	USSHMXTRB
Excluding defence	USSHMXD.B
Durable goods industries	USSHDUR.B
Wood products	USSH321.B
Non-metallic mineral products	USSH327.B
Primary metals	USSH331NB
Fabricated metal products	USSH332NB
Machinery	USSH333.B
Computers and electronic products	USSH334.B
Electrical equipment, appliances, and components	USSH335.B
Transportation equipment	USSH336.B
Furniture and related products	USSH337.B
Miscellaneous durable goods	USSH339.B
Non-durable goods industries	USSHNDURB
Food products	USSH311.B
Beverages and tobacco products	USSH312.B
Textile mills	USSH313.B
Textile products	USSH314.B
Apparel	USSH315.B
Leather and allied products	USSH316.B
Paper products	USSH322.B
Printing	USSH323.B
Petroleum and coal products	USSH324.B
Basic chemicals	USSH325.B
Plastics and rubber products	USSH326.B

Value of Manufacturers' New Orders for Industry Groups (sa)	Datastream
All manufacturing industries	USNEWORDB
Excluding transportation	USNOMXTRB
Excluding defence	USNOMXD.B
Durable goods industries	USNODUR.B
Primary metals	USNO331NB
Fabricated metal products	USNO332NB
Machinery	USNO333.B
Computers and electronic products	USNO334.B
Electrical equipment, appliances, and components	USNO335.B
Transportation equipment	USNO336.B
Furniture and related products	USNO337.B

Value of Manufacturers' Unfilled Orders for Industry Groups (sa)	Datastream
All manufacturing industries	USUOMFG.B
Excluding transportation	USUOMXTRB
Excluding defence	USUOMXD.B
Durable goods industries	USUODUR.B
Primary metals	USUO331NB
Fabricated metal products	USUO332NB
Machinery	USUO333.B
Computers and electronic products	USUO334.B
Electrical equipment, appliances, and components	USUO335.B
Transportation equipment	USUO336.B
Furniture and related products	USUO337.B

Value of Manufacturers' Inventories for Industry Groups (sa)	Datastream
All manufacturing industries	USINMFG.B
Excluding transportation	USINMXTRB
Excluding defence	USINMXD.B
Durable goods industries	USINDUR.B
Wood products	USIN321.B
Non-metallic mineral products	USIN327.B
Primary metals	USIN331NB
Fabricated metal products	USIN332NB
Machinery	USIN333.B
Computers and electronic products	USIN334.B
Electrical equipment, appliances and components	USIN335.B
Transportation equipment	USIN336.B
Furniture and related products	USIN337.B
Miscellaneous durable goods	USIN339.B
Non-durable goods industries	USINNDU.B
Food products	USIN311.B
Beverages and tobacco products	USIN312.B
Textile mills	USIN313.B
Textile products	USIN314.B
Apparel	USIN315.B
Leather and allied products	USIN316.B
Paper products	USIN322.B
Printing	USIN323.B
Petroleum and coal products	USIN324.B
Basic chemicals	USIN325.B
Plastics and rubber products	USIN326.B

Value of Manufacturers' Shipments, New Orders, Unfilled Orders, and Total Inventories for Topical Series (sa)	Datastream
Shipments	
All manufacturing industries	USSHMFG.B
Construction materials and supplies	USSHCON.B
Information technology	USSHINFOB
Capital goods	USSHCAPMB
Non-defence capital goods	USSHCAPNB
Excluding aircraft	USSHCAPXB
Defence capital goods	USSHCAPDB
Consumer goods	USSHCNSMB
Consumer durable goods	USSHCNSDB
Consumer non-durable goods	USSHCNSNB
New orders	
All manufacturing industries	USNEWORDB
Construction materials and supplies	USNOCON.B
Information technology	USNOINFOB
Capital goods	USNOCAPMB
Non-defence capital goods	USNOCAPNB
Excluding aircraft	USNOCAPXB
Defence capital goods	USNOCAPDB
Consumer goods	USNOCNSMB
Consumer durable goods	USNOCNSDB
Unfilled orders	
All manufacturing industries	USUOMFG.B
Construction materials and supplies	USUOCON.B
Information technology	USUOINFOB
Capital goods	USUOCAPMB
Non-defence capital goods	USUOCAPNB
Excluding aircraft	USUOCAPXB
Defence capital goods	USUOCAPDB
Consumer goods	USUOCNSMB
Consumer durable goods	USUOCNSDB
Total inventories	
All manufacturing industries	USINMFG.B
Construction materials and supplies	USINCON.B
Information technology	USININFOB
Capital goods	USINCAPMB
Non-defence capital goods	USINCAPNB
Excluding aircraft	USINCAPXB
Defence capital goods	USINCAPDB
Consumer goods	USINCNSMB
Consumer durable goods	USINCNSDB
Consumer non-durable goods	USINCNSNB

Value of Manufacturers' Inventories, by Stage of Fabrication, by Industry Groups (sa)	Datastream
Materials and supplies	
All manufacturing industries	USINMMFGB
Durable goods industries	USINMDURB
Non-durable goods industries	USINMNDUB
Work in progress	
All manufacturing industries	USINPMFGB
Durable goods industries	USINPDURB
Non-durable goods industries	USINPNDUB
Finished goods	
All manufacturing industries	USINFMFGB
Durable goods industries	USINFDURB
Non-durable goods industries	USINFNDUB

Ratios of Manufacturers' Inventories to Shipments and Unfilled Orders to Shipments, by Industry Groups (sa)	Datastream
Inventory to shipment ratio	
All manufacturing industries	USISHMFGB
Durable goods industries	USISHDURB
Non-durable goods industries	USISHNDUB
Unfilled orders to shipment ratio	
Durable goods industries	USUSHDURB

Literature

Goldberg, Linda S. and Crockett, Keith, 'The Dollar and U.S. Manufacturing', Federal Reserve Bank of New York, *Current Issues in Economics and Finance*, Vol. 4, No. 12 (November 1998).

Parker, Robert P. 'The Impact of the North American Industry Classification System on U.S. Economic Data: In May 2001, NAICS Hits the Economic Indicators', *Business Economics* (April 2001), pp. 56–9.

16.3   Construction Indicators

A series of indices on the construction sector is published in the US covering the entire sector from building permits to building completions and existing home sales. The vast majority of indices are published by the Bureau of the Census at the Department of Commerce. Separate indices, for example, on existing home sales are published by private-sector organizations. Most indices are shown as annual rates (i.e., monthly values are projected over a year).

16.3.1   Value of Construction Put in Place

Data Source

The data are published by the Bureau of the Census at the Department of Commerce. The press release is available on the Internet at www.census.gov/cgi-bin/briefroom/BriefRm. More detailed figures can be found in the publication *Current Construction Report – Value of Construction Put in Place* issued by the Bureau of the Census.

Importance for the Financial Markets   D

Description

Starting with the data for March 2001, the Report on Construction Put in Place has been presented using a new classification system. This new system allows the classification of all construction into one generalized coding design which bases project types on their end usage instead of building/non-building and ownership types. With these changes, comparisons of data with the previously published data can only be made at the total level. Although some categories seem identical to previously published data, there have been changes that make these values incomparable. The report is divided into expenditure on private construction versus public construction. The distinction is made on the basis of ownership during the construction period. In addition, private construction is divided into residential construction, non-residential construction, telecommunication buildings and all other private construction.

   In this report, construction includes the following:

- New buildings and structures
- Additions, alterations, conservations, expansions, reconstructions, renovations, rehabilitations and major replacements, such as the replacement of a roof or a heating system
- Mechanical or electrical installations such as plumbing, heating, electrical work, elevators, escalators or air-conditioning
- Site preparation and outside construction of fixed structures or facilities such as parliaments, highways or streets
- Installation of boilers, overhead hoists and cranes, blast furnaces, or other such equipment
- Fixed, largely site-fabricated equipment not housed in a building primarily used to support petroleum refineries and chemical plants
- Cost and installation of construction materials placed inside a building and used to support production machinery

Excluded are the following:

- Maintenance and repairs to existing structures or service facilities
- Cost and installation of production machinery and equipment items not specially covered above
- Drilling of gas and oil wells, including construction of offshore drilling platforms
- Land acquisition

The value of construction belongs to a given period and includes:

- Cost of materials installed or erected
- Cost of labour and a proportionate share of the cost of construction equipment rental
- Contractor's profit
- Cost of architectural and engineering work
- Miscellaneous overhead and office costs chargeable to the project on the owner's work
- Interest and taxes paid during construction

The total value for a given period is the sum of the value of work done on all projects underway during this period, regardless of when the work was started or when payment was made to the contractors.

As additional information the element of uncertainty is specified for this publication in the form of a statistical standard deviation with the margin thereby obtained with a confidence interval of 90 per cent. This can result in the interpretation that construction expenditure has changed by 1 per cent (+/−3 per cent) on the preceding month. This means that construction expenditure has changed with 90 per cent probability by an interval of between −2 per cent and +4 per cent on the preceding month. The statistical significance of such a change is therefore not very high.

As with virtually all indicators, a more comprehensive survey is undertaken every five years. All large and medium-sized construction companies and a proportion of smaller ones are surveyed. The results of these surveys are used as the basis for the monthly surveys.

Periodicity/Revisions

Data are normally published on the first working day of the second month after the month to which it relates. Publication of the data takes place at 10.00 ET (16.00 CET). As this is a survey, major errors can occur which sometimes result in

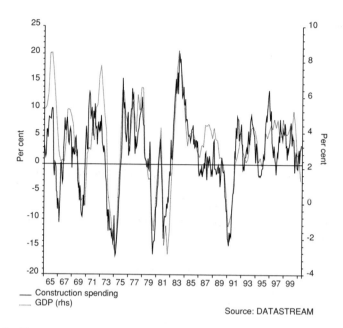

Source: DATASTREAM

Figure 16.5   Change in construction spending and GDP on preceding year

very extensive revisions. The average absolute change between the provisional and final value is 0.6 per cent for total expenditure according to the Bureau of the Census. For private construction expenditure, average revision is 0.6 per cent, whereas for private housing expenditure it is only 0.5 per cent. The data for private expenditure excluding the housing sector requires average revisions of approximately 1.3 per cent and public expenditure around 1.1 per cent.

Seasonal Adjustment

The data are seasonally adjusted as the construction sector is strongly influenced by weather conditions.

Notes

Data on construction expenditure form the basis of the construction component in the calculation of the GDP. This indicator has only limited importance for the financial markets as information on construction activity is available earlier via building permits or housing starts. In addition, construction sector figures excluding the housing sector and public construction are particularly volatile. The importance of construction expenditure is rather to round off the picture of the construction sector situation. For this purpose, the moving average over 3 months and percentage change on the preceding month should be particularly noted.

As the first estimates are subject to substantial revisions with each month's release, one should always pay close attention to the revised figures for the months before. The base to start from can change dramatically and this can lead to totally different values in the rates of change.

Key Datastream Mnemonics

Value of Construction Put in Place (saar, 1996 USD)	Datastream
Total construction	USNEWCOND
Private construction	USNCPRIVD
Residential building	USNCRESBD
New housing units	USICPHU.D
1 unit	USICPHU1D
2 units and more	USICPHU2D
Non-residential building	USNCNRESD
Industrial	USICPBI.D
Office	USICPBF.D
Hotels, motels	USICPBT.D
Other commercial	USICPBC.D
Religious	USICPBR.D
Educational	USICPBE.D
Hospital and institutional	USICPBH.D
Miscellaneous buildings	USICPBO.D
Telecommunications	USNCTELCD
All other private	USICPO..D
Public construction	USNCPBCND
Housing and redevelopement	USNCHOUSD
Industrial	USNCINDSD
Educational	USICBBE.D
Hospital	USICBBH.D
Other public building	USICBBO.D
Highways and streets	USICBHS.D
Military facilities	USICBML.D
Conservation and development	USICBCD.D
Sewer systems	USICBUS.D
Water supply facilities	USICBUW.D
Miscellanceous public	USICBO..D
Fixed-weighted price index (1996 weights)	USICNEWRF
Implicit price deflator	USICNEWDF
Monthly value of construction put in place (nsa)	USICNEW.A

Value of Public Construction Put in Place (saar)	Datastream
Total public construction	USNCPBCND
State and local construction	USICBZ..D
Total building	USICBBZ.D
Highways and streets	USICBHSZD
Conservation and development	USICBCDZD
Sewer systems	USICBUSZD
Water supply facilities	USICBUWZD
Miscellaneous nonbuilding	USICBOZ.D
Federal construction	USICBC..D
Total building	USICBBC.D
Highways and streets	USICBHWYD
Military facilities	USICBMLCD
Conservation and development	USICBCDCD
Miscellaneous non-building	USICBOC.D

Literature

US Department of Commerce, *Current Construction Report – Value of Construction Put in Place*.

16.3.2   New Residential Construction

Data Source

These data are published by the Bureau of the Census at the Department of Commerce. The press release is available on the Internet at www.census.gov/cgi-bin/briefroom/BriefRm. Detailed information on the data prior to April 2001 can be found in the publication *Current Construction Report – Housing Starts*, issued by the Bureau of the Census. Since 2001, these reports have been discontinued.

Importance for the Financial Markets   C

Description

Since April 2001, the Bureau of the Census has published a Report on New Residential Construction, which includes the former publications on housing starts and building permits as well as the housing completions. The data on housing starts and building permits relate to both private detached houses and apartment blocks. With apartment blocks a distinction is made according to the size of the houses (2–4 living units, 5 and more living units) and a separate classification is made for the geographical position (Northeast, Midwest, South, West). Mobile homes and manufactured houses are not incorporated but input into a separate statistic. Public-owned housing units are not included. However, privately built residential buildings, which are sold to the state, are included even if they are not completed. Hotels, motels and other residential complexes, such as student accommodation, are excluded. The data are shown as an annual rate in the same way as for construction spending.

Two categories, building permits and housing starts, affect the beginning of the procedure for housing construction, so they are good indicators of construction sector development in the coming months. Building permits are obtained when approval to start excavation is given. The average period between building permit and construction start is one month.

The data for building permits are obtained from a survey of construction authorities. However, such permits to build a house are only required in around 95 per cent of cases in the USA so this does not cover all construction activity. For this reason the number of housing starts regularly exceeds the number of building permits. Housing starts are also obtained via a survey of construction authorities, although the 850 bodies surveyed represent a far smaller number than the 8500 construction authorities with building permits, where almost half were surveyed by letter. Survey selection ensured that all large construction authorities in conurbation areas and around 10 per cent of the remaining authorities were surveyed. The first question posed how rapidly after permit receipt a construction was started. The total number of housing starts is calculated from the results. Before April 2001 the Bureau of the Census made two adjustments: first, construction activity in areas where no permit is necessary is taken into account and the second concerns building sites where construction was started before approval was obtained. Since then, the Bureau of the Census discontinued adjusting for construction in areas where building permits are required without a permit being issued, because the housing industry and trade groups have indicated that such unauthorized construction has virtually ceased. This adjustment did not phase out over time but was dropped completely in the revised estimates as of January 1999. In addition, the Bureau of the Census started a new grouping of the data. To estimate the total starts and permits, the Bureau of the Census estimates for smaller cells to sum up the total. They also now publish data only by the four Census regions and no longer by metropolitan and non-metropolitan areas in each of this regions. Another change belongs to the adjustment methods to account for late reports and non-response.

The total number of housing starts decreased by about 1.5 per cent compared to the data published before. This is a result of a decline of about 2.4 per cent in single family structures and an increase of about 1.8 per cent in structures with two or more units. The discontinuance of the adjustment on single family houses of 3.3 per cent accounts for a drop of about 2.4 per cent on total housing starts. The other methodology and processing changes resulted in an increase of about 0.9 per cent.

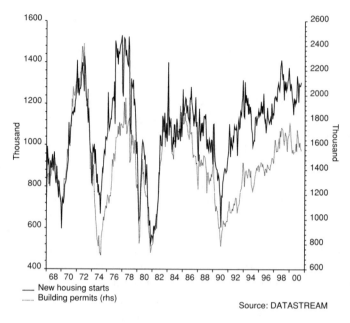

Figure 16.6   New housing starts and building permits

The statistics on housing completions has only been conducted since 1968. The reason for producing the data is to complete the picture of the situation in the construction sector. Data are divided up according to size and geographic location. In the same way as for the other statistics on the construction sector, the data are released as an annual rate. For the data without seasonal adjustment, a monthly rate is also published. In addition to the data on housing completions, the number of houses under construction is also produced.

Due to the new methods starting with the publication for April 2001, the total number of housing units completed decreased by about 2.1 per cent compared to the previously published data. This is a result of a decline of about 3.0 per cent in single family structures and an increase of about 1.8 per cent in structures with two units or more. The discontinuance of the 3.3 per cent adjustment on single family houses accounts for a drop of about 2.5 per cent on total completions. The other methodology and processing changes resulted in an increase of about 0.4 per cent.

Periodicity/Revisions

Data are published between the fifteenth and the twenty-second day of the month and relate to the preceding month. Revisions tend to be minor. The data

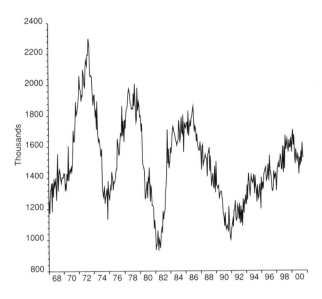

Figure 16.7 Housing completions

on housing starts is revised going back only one month, whereas the building permits are revised back over 2 months. The first revisions to building permits are announced around one week after the provisional publication, although revisions are conducted with an announcement of new provisional data. For the indicators on the construction sector, it should be noted that the data are obtained in the form of a survey. The results are therefore dependent on which of those surveyed is prepared to answer. This method can mean that the survey is not initially representative and the results therefore have to be amended subsequently as soon as more recent information is available. An annual benchmark revision is normally conducted in May.

Seasonal Adjustment

The data are seasonally adjusted. However housing starts are far more dependent on the weather than building permits. For this reason housing starts should be treated with caution in case of extreme weather conditions.

Notes

The most interesting parts of this publication are the housing starts and building permits in total and of single family structures and the change in the annual rate on the preceding month is of most interest to the financial markets. Due to the influencing factors described above housing starts are more volatile than building permits, and the Bureau of the Census consequently stresses that it takes five months for a trend to be visible in housing starts. With building permits, on the other hand, trends can be seen after three months.

As the time series of two units or more is far more volatile than the single family data, you always should notice this sub-series to watch the underlying trend. The volatility is a result of the calculating method. Each single family structure counts only once. Structures with two or more units count as being as many as there are units.

The residential construction sector only accounts for around 3 per cent of total GDP, yet it is one of the sectors which responds most sensitively to economic cycles and interest rate changes. Interest rate changes normally begin to affect the construction sector within 4 months.

Source: DATASTREAM

Figure 16.8   Change in new housing starts on preceding year and mortgage rate, lag of 4 months

Key Datastream Mnemonics

New Privately-Owned Housing Units Started (saar)	Datastream
Total	USPVHOUSE
1 unit	USPVH1UNE
2–4 units	USHB2TO4O
5 units and more	USHB5ANDO
Northeast	USHBRN..O
Midwest	USHBRM..O
South	USHBRS..O
West	USHBRW..O

New Privately-Owned Housing Units Started (nsa)	Datastream
Total	USHBEGUNP
1 unit	USHB1...P
2 units	USHB2...P
3–4 units	USHB3TO4P
5 units and more	USHB5ANDP
Northeast	USHBRN..P
Midwest	USHBRM..P
South	USHBRS..P
West	USHBRW..P

Privately-Owned Housing Units Authorized by Building Permits (saar)	Datastream
Total	USHOUSATE
1 unit	USHA1...O
2–4 units	USHA2TO4O
5 units and more	USHA5ANDO
Northeast	USHARN..O
Midwest	USHARM..O
South	USHARS..O
West	USHARW..O

Privately-Owned Housing Units Authorized by Building Permits (nsa)	Datastream
Total	USHAUTHPP
1 unit	USHA1...P
2 units	USHA2...P
3–4 units	USHA3TO4P
5 units and more	USHA5ANDP
Northeast	USHARN..P
Midwest	USHARM..P
South	USHARS..P
West	USHARW..P

Not Started at the End of Period (nsa)	Datastream
Total	USHNOTSTP
1 unit	USHN1...P
2–4 units	USHN2TO4P
5 units and more	USHN5ANDP
Northeast	USHNRN..P
Midwest	USHNRM..P
South	USHNRS..P
West	USHNRW..P

New Privately-Owned Housing Units Completed (saar)	Datastream
Total	USPVHOUCE
1 unit	USHC1...O
2–4 units	USHC2TO4O
5 units and more	USHC5ANDO
Northeast	USHCRN..O
Midwest	USHCRM..O
South	USHCRS..O
West	USHCRW..O

New Privately-Owned Housing Units Completed (nsa)	Datastream
Total	USHCOMPLP
1 unit	USHC1...P
2 units	USHC2...P
3–4 units	USHC3TO4P
5 units and more	USHC5ANDP
Northeast	USHCRN..P
Midwest	USHCRM..P
South	USHCRS..P
West	USHCRW..P

Privately-Owned Housing Units under Construction (saar)	Datastream
Total	USPVHCONE
1 unit	USHU1...O
2–4 units	USHU2TO4O
5 units and more	USHU5ANDO
Northeast	USHURN..O
Midwest	USHURM..O
South	USHURS..O
West	USHURW..O

Privately-Owned Housing Units under Construction (nsa)	Datastream
Total	USHUNDERP
1 unit	USHU1...P
2 units	USHU2...P
3–4 units	USHU3TO4P
5 units and more	USHU5ANDP
Northeast	USHURN..P
Midwest	USHURM..P
South	USHURS..P
West	USHURW..P

Literature

US Department of Commerce, *Current Construction Report – Housing Starts*.

16.3.3   New Residential Sales

Data Source

The data are published by the Bureau of the Census at the Department of Commerce. The press release is available on the Internet at www.census.gov/cgi-bin/briefroom/BriefRm. Detailed information on data prior to April 2001 can be found in the publication *Current Construction Report – New One-Family Houses Sold*, issued by the Bureau of the Census. These reports were discontinued in 2001.

Importance for the Financial Markets   D

Description

Data on new residential sales (formerly called new home sales) only relate to new builds of one-family homes, which are being sold for the first time. In addition to the annual rate, the median price and average price of homes sold as well as the number of homes for sale but not yet sold, are also published. The data are published both for the whole of the USA as well as for the four regions Northeast, Midwest, South and West. The data on new residential sales includes only around 60 per cent of one-family homes where construction has started. The rest are homes which are not for sale but are being built by the owners directly.

A confidence interval is also given for the provisional data on new residential sales, within which its real value lies. The standard deviations are based on surveys of the last six months ending in June or December respectively. Survey errors are therefore continuously adjusted.

Periodicity/Revisions

The data are published around the end of a month and relate to the preceding month (publication at the end of the month) or two months before (publication at the beginning of the month). With the survey method very extensive revisions can result going back over several months. Data are published at 10.00 ET (16.00 CET).

Seasonal Adjustment

The data are seasonally adjusted, although with new home sales the same applies as to other seasonally adjusted indicators in the construction sector (i.e., seasonal adjustment can only compensate for 'normal' fluctuations). Extreme influences can still distort the picture considerably.

Notes

The market focuses on monthly changes in total annualized sales. As the data are extremely volatile it is useful to use a moving average. The Bureau of the Census believes that a trend can be identified within four months, which is why a moving average over four months would be ideal. Frequently, however, standard moving averages over 3 months are used, which also produce good results. The number of new home sales can be seen as a leading indicator of

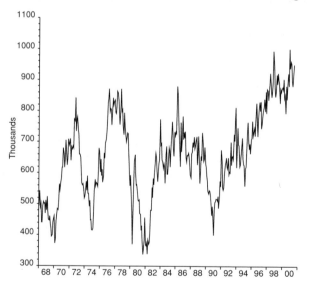

Source: DATASTREAM

Figure 16.9   New residential sales

the demand for fixtures and fittings. In addition to sales, the ratio of homes for sale to total sales is taken into account. When this ratio falls, this implies that demand exceeds the number of new builds. This normally results in increased construction activity after a few months to meet the increased demand. In an economic cycle it can be seen that the number of new home sales rises steeply at the beginning of a new cycle to meet built-up demand. Towards the end of the cycle, when demand is saturated, it begins to decline again.

New home builds account only for a very low proportion of GDP. However, the indicator reacts very strongly to cyclical trends and interest rate changes. As the data are very volatile and comprehensive revisions are conducted, the usefulness of the indicator for the analysis of the economic situation is limited. As a result, other indicators should be incorporated into an analysis of the construction sector. Above all, the sale of existing homes is of great interest as the database is approximately four times larger than the one for new builds. The survey by the National Association of Homebuilders can also indicate trends in the construction market.

Key Datastream Mnemonics

New One-Family Houses Sold (saar)	Datastream
Total	USHOUSESE
Northeast	USHSO1RNO
Midwest	USHSO1RMO
South	USHSO1RSO
West	USHSO1RWO

New One-Family Houses Sold (nsa)	Datastream
Total	USHSOLD1P
Northeast	USHSO1RNP
Midwest	USHSO1RMP
South	USHSO1RSP
West	USHSO1RWP

New One-Family Houses for Sale (sa)	Datastream
Total	USHSALE1O
Months' supply	USHSA%SOO

New One-Family Houses for Sale (nsa)	Datastream
Total	USHSALE1P
Northeast	USHSA1RNP
Midwest	USHSA1RMP
South	USHSA1RSP
West	USHSA1RWP
Months' supply	USHSA%SOP

Median and Average Sales Prices (nsa)	Datastream
Average	USHOUSEP
Median	USHOUSEM

Houses Sold, by Stage of Construction (nsa)	Datastream
Total	USHSOLD1P
Completed	USHCSO1.P
Under construction	USHUSO1.P
Not started	USHNSO1.P

Houses for Sale, by Stage of Construction (nsa)	Datastream
Total	USHSALE1P
Completed	USHCSA1.P
Under construction	USHUSA1.P
Not started	USHNSA1.P

Houses Sold by Sales Price (nsa)	Datastream
Under USD100 000	USHSU1HKA
USD100 000–124 999	USHS1HK.A
USD125 000–149 999	USHS125KA
USD150 000–199 999	USHS15OUA
USD200 000–249 999	USHS200UA
USD250 000–299 999	USHS250UA
USD300 000 and over	USHS300KA
Median sales price	USHOUSEM
Average sales price	USHOUSEP

Median Number of Months on Sales Market (nsa)	Datastream
Houses sold, measured from month of start (sa)	USHMSSO1O
Houses sold, measured from month of start	USHMSSO1P
Houses for sale, measured from month of start (sa)	USHMSSA1O
Houses for sale, measured from month of start	USHMSSA1P
Houses for sale, measured from month of completition	USHMSCO1P

Literature

Kahn, James A., 'Explaining the Gap between New Home Sales and Inventories', Federal Reserve Bank of New York, *Current Issues in Economics and Finance*, Vol. 6, No. 6 (May 2000).

US Department of Commerce, *Current Construction Report – New One-Family Houses Sold*.

16.3.4 Existing Home Sales

Data Source

The data are published by the National Association of Realtors (NAR). The press release is available on the Internet at www.realtor.org.

Importance for the Financial Markets   D

Description

Sales of existing homes are collated and published by the National Association of Realtors, a private organization, from a database of approximately 700 Boards or multiple listing services nationwide. As with statistics on the construction sector published by the Bureau of the Census, the NAR not only calculates total sales but also produces a classification in terms of the geographical regions Northeast, Midwest, South and West. Average prices and median prices are published, as well as the number of months it would take for all houses to be sold at the same level of business activity.

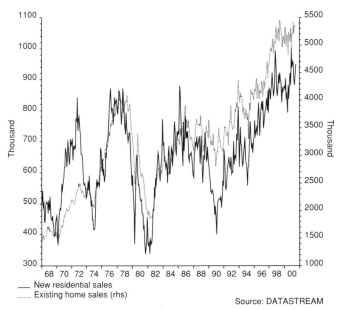

Figure 16.10 New residential sales and existing home sales

The data survey only includes one-family homes which are for personal use. Units housing more than one family and new builds, as well as houses in properties of over 10 acres and rented buildings, are therefore not incorporated.

Periodicity/Revisions

Data are published at the end of the month and relate to the preceding month. As the database is substantially more comprehensive than the one for new residential sales, there are fewer revisions for this indicator, although they go back over several months. Publication is always effected at 10.00 ET (16.00 CET).

Seasonal Adjustment

Data are seasonally adjusted.

Notes

The importance of sales of existing houses to the financial markets is somewhat less than the data on housing starts, as sales of new builds are more closely linked to construction activity. Although the database for the NAR statistics is far larger, around 85 per cent of all house sales consist of sales of existing housing stock. The NAR data series thereby gives a better summary of buying habits of the private sector. Both data series follow the same trend. The data are extremely dependent on mortgage rate trends. It has also been established that, after the end of a recession, sales rise sharply at first because purchase intentions (which were postponed during the recession), are then realized. Sales tail off as soon as the economic upturn slows and initial demand is satisfied.

Key Datastream Mnemonics

Existing Single-Family Home Sales (saar)	Datastream
Total	USEXHOUSE
Northeast	USHSOERNO
Midwest	USHSOERMO
South	USHSOERSO
West	USHSOERWO
Number of homes available for sale	USHSALEEP
Months' supply of homes on market	USHMSSAEP
Median sales price	USHPMEDEA
Average sales price	USHPAVGEA

Median Sales Price (nsa)	Datastream
Total	USHPMEDEA
Northeast	USHPMERNA
Midwest	USHPMERMA
South	USHPMERSA
West	USHPMERWA

Average Sales Price (nsa)	Datastream
Total	USHPAVGEA
Northeast	USHPAERNA
Midwest	USHPAERMA
South	USHPAERSA
West	USHPAERWA

16.3.5 Homebuilders Survey

Data Source

Data are published by the National Association of Homebuilders (NAHB). A summary of the report is available on the Internet at www.nahb.com/facts/hmi.htm.

Importance for the Financial Markets   C

Description

The survey is produced by the National Association of Homebuilders, which is a private organization. Its most important component is the so-called Housing Market Index, which includes surveys on the expectations of construction companies on the market situation for new, single-family homes. The index is composed of three sub-indices. The questions for these are:

1. How do you assess the current situation in the market for single-family homes? Good, fair or poor?
2. How do you assess the situation in the market for single family homes in six months' time? Good, fair or poor?
3. How is the traffic of prospective buyers? High/very high, fair, low/very low?

For the sub-indices, the following formula is applied to questions 1 and 2 first:

$$\frac{\text{Percentage of 'good'} - \text{Percentage of 'poor'} + 100}{2}$$

The formula for section 3 is as follows:

$$\frac{\text{Percentage of 'high/very high'} - \text{Percentage of 'low/very low'} + 100}{2}$$

The results of the sub-indices are totalled in an overall index with the following weightings: 59 per cent for current sales, 14 per cent for anticipated sales and 27 per cent for business contacts. In the past the weightings were obtained via a regression in order to best reflect the activity of housing starts. Around 900 building contractors are surveyed for the report, the vast majority of whom are selected at random. The number of responses is normally between 350 and 400, or lower. When the willingness to respond falls substantially, companies no longer involved in the survey are deleted from the list and new ones are added. The last reshuffle took place in November 1999.

Periodicity/Revisions

The data are obtained on a monthly basis via a survey. The questionnaires are sent by post. Publication of the results is always effected mid-month, normally one day before the announcement of housing starts at around 14.00 ET (20.00 CET).

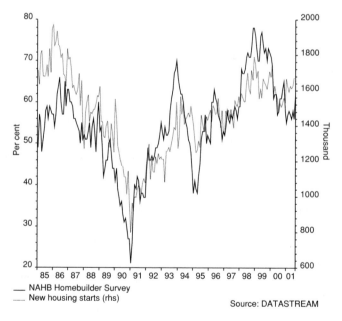

Figure 16.11   NAHB Homebuilder Survey and new housing starts

Seasonal Adjustment

Data are seasonally adjusted before the sub-indices are calculated.

Notes

The importance of this indicator has increased substantially recently as it is a good indicator of construction trends for housing starts. The short time span between the survey and the announcement of the figures is also an advantage.

Key Datastream Mnemonics

Homebuilders Survey (sa)	Datastream
Housing market index, total	USNAHBMI
Single family sales: present	USNAHB1P
Single family sales: next 6 months	USNAHB1E
Traffic of prospective buyers	USNAHBBT

17
International Transaction Indicators

The two most important statistics on international transactions are the data on international trade in goods and services and the balance of payments. The first indicator is published monthly by the Bureau of the Census, whereas balance of payments figures are released quarterly by the Bureau of Economic Analysis.

17.1 International Trade in Goods and Services

Data Source

Data are published by the Bureau of the Census at the Department of Commerce. The press release is available on the Internet at www.census.gov/cgi-bin/briefroom/BriefRm. The data are also published in Tables F and G in the Survey of Current Business.

Importance for the Financial Markets   B

Description

The statistical survey for US international transactions possibly has the longest history, as trading figures were recorded as early as 1821. They relate both to imports and exports of goods and services between the 50 states, the District of Columbia, Puerto Rico, the Virgin Islands and the free trade zones in the USA with the rest of the world. Consequently, trading patterns between the USA and US diplomatic representations or military units stationed abroad are not included. Imports are based on the prices reported to the customs authorities, although customs duty, freight costs and other fees incurred for transportation are excluded. Exports, on the other hand, are calculated f.a.s. (free alongside ship), i.e., all costs such as inland transport or insurance which are incurred transporting goods to the place of shipment where they are to leave US territory. All US exports with a value of over USD2500 are registered. For imports, the threshold value is USD1250 and for goods with an import quota the limit is USD250.

The flow of goods and services covers goods classification, quantity, value, country of origin and destination, destination or state of origin in the USA, as well as means of transport. In addition, exports are classified in terms of re-exports or original exports. Export values are primarily based on the export documentation. Exports to Canada are obtained with the help of the Canadian import statistics. US imports, however, are obtained by customs authorities, normally within ten days of the goods reaching the USA. The value of internationally traded goods, which is minimal, is estimated.

The individual figures are published in the form of a balance. Flows of goods and services are firstly divided into around 140 categories, which are based on the type of use of the goods. These categories then form the basis for the seasonal adjustment in six classes of goods: food, feeds and beverages; industrial supplies and materials; non-automotive capital goods; automotive vehicles and parts; non-durable goods and other goods. Detailed figures are also provided for specific goods classes, such as crude oil production, vehicles or the technology sector.

The services are grouped into seven classes. With exports these include travel, passenger fares; other transportation; royalties and licence fees; other private services; US government miscellaneous services and transfers under US military sales contracts. With imports, on the other hand, instead of transfers under US military sales contracts, direct defence expenditure is published. The individual categories are as shown below.

1. Travel: expenditure by travellers on food, accommodation, souvenirs, etc., and travel necessities. Travellers are those leaving their homeland for less than one year.
2. Passenger fares: this consists of income from US transport companies for transporting foreigners to and from the USA or between two points outside the USA. Payments by US citizens to foreign companies are only counted where they cover transport between the USA and abroad.
3. Other transportation: these include goods transport by ship, air, rail or pipeline between the USA and other nations. Only the freight costs, port or airport fees (as well as any rent incurred) are included.
4. Royalties and licence fees: these are payments for patents, copyrights and trade names. Transfers for trade names and copyrights are mostly booked under fees, whereas payments for patents are charged as licences.
5. Other private services: payments incurred as a result of US involvement in a foreign company or foreign involvement in a US company are registered under this item.
6. US government miscellaneous services: these cover non-military services.

7a. Transfers under US military sales contracts: this category only applies to exports and includes exports of goods and services involving military bases in the USA. Exports can take the form of repairs or equipment.
7b. Direct defence expenditure: by contrast this category only affects imports and includes, for example, payments by the US military to governmental employees outside the USA or costs for building activity by foreign companies on military bases outside the USA.

The service figures are based on surveys conducted quarterly, annually, and for the benchmark revisions. Transactions are shown at market prices.

The six classes of goods are published both in nominal and real terms. They are currently based on the export and import prices for 1996. In addition, figures for bilateral trade and trade between the USA and various groups of nations are published. Although these values are not seasonally adjusted and there is no price adjustment, it should be noted that individual nations could be duplicated. For example, Indonesia could be covered as part of the Pacific area or as an Organization of Petroleum-Exporting Countries (OPEC) nation. For services, on the other hand, only nominal figures are produced and there is no geographical division.

The data are obtained by the Bureau of the Census on the basis of a comprehensive survey. On this basis adjustments are made by the Bureau of Economic

Source: DATASTREAM

Figure 17.1   Balance of trade in goods and services

Analysis to enable the values to be employed within the balance of payments system. This adjusted data then form the basis for the quarterly balance of payments statistics, although they are already employed in the balance of trade statistics for certain aggregates.

Adjustments include, for example, changes in ownership, which occur without goods crossing the US border. Certain military exports are also included by the Bureau of the Census on the goods side, whereas the BEA books these under the category of military transactions on the service side. In addition, only commercial transactions are included by the Bureau of the Census, whereas in the balance of payments private transactions, such as gift parcels, are also incorporated. Finally, the value of gold purchased by private individuals in the USA from foreign government bodies is only included when it leaves the country, whereas for the balance of payments the change of ownership is already registered. A number of adjustments is also carried out on the import side. The customs value of imported goods is calculated on the basis of costs incurred abroad up to the point where they leave the country. In the case of Canada and Mexico this is the respective border with the USA, although customs authorities base some goods from Mexico and Canada on the producer price, excluding transport costs. To make these imports comparable with other imports the BEA adds the transport costs incurred up to the US border on to the import prices. The same applies to gold imports as to gold exports (i.e., they are included in the balance of trade when they cross the national border). And finally, there is a different definition of military imports in the balance of payments and balance of trade statistics.

Periodicity/Revisions

Data are published around the twentieth of the month and relate to the period two months prior to this. Publication is always effected at 08.30 ET (14.30 CET). Revisions are conducted for the statistics published in the preceding month. After this a further revision of balance of trade figures only takes place after quarterly figures for the balance of payments statistic have been published and revised where necessary. Revisions to the balance of payments are incorporated in the balance of trade publication following the balance of payments publication. This affects the preceding six months in each case. There is also a benchmark revision in July each year where methodological changes are conducted. These revisions relate to the entire preceding year.

Seasonal Adjustment

The aggregated data and some of the detailed figures are seasonally adjusted. Services are only seasonally adjusted where significant seasonal patterns are identified. Data on the geographic distribution of trading patterns are not subject to seasonal adjustment.

Notes

The market focuses specially on the nominal balance of trade figures. Export and import trends are also worth noting. A clear rise in exports is a sign that the USA is becoming more competitive and that the economic situation in the rest of the world is improving, whereas rising imports frequently signal rising domestic demand. However, there is often a certain time delay. In addition to the overall figures, individual country-specific figures are also important, particularly at times where in individual nations there is major imbalance in trade with the USA, which could lead to trading conflicts. One limiting factor here is the fact that the balance of trade figures are published with a long time lag.

The balance of trade figures are used by several other government bodies. First, the balance of payments statistics are based on the data. Second, the international trade sectors of the GDP statistics are also calculated on the basis of the balance of trade figures. This is also why, following publication of balance of trade statistics which clearly differ from market expectations, there are changes in expectations of economic growth as, on publication of the advance report on the GDP, the balance of trade statistics for the last month of the quarter are not known. The balance of trade therefore constitutes one of the main reasons for the first revision of the GDP figures. In addition to the Bureau of Economic Analysis, the balance of trade figures are also employed by the Bureau of Labor Statistics in the import and export price calculations.

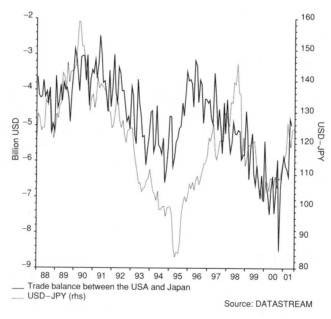

Source: DATASTREAM

Figure 17.2   Bilateral balance of trade for the USA and Japan versus USD–JPY

Key Datastream Mnemonics

US International Trade in Goods and Services (sa)	Datastream
Balance total	USBALTOTB
Goods	USVISBBLB
Services	USSERVBLB
Exports total	USEXPTOTB
Goods	USEXPTBLB
Services	USEXSERVB
Imports total	USIMPTOTB
Goods	USIMPTBLB
Services	USIMSERVB

US Services by Major Category (sa)	Datastream
Balance Services	USSERVBLB
Exports, total	USEXSERVB
Travel	USTRVRECB
Passenger fares	USPSFRECB
Other transportation	USOTRRECB
Royalties and licence fees	USRAFRECB
Other private services	USOPRVSVB
Transfers under US military sales contracts	USSVRMILB
US Government miscellaneous services	USMISRECB
Imports, total	USIMPTOTB
Travel	USTRVEXPB
Passenger fares	USPSFEXPB
Other transportation	USOTREXPB
Royalties and licence fees	USROYLICB
Other private services	USOPVSERB
Direct defence expenditures	USSVPDEFB
US Government miscellaneous services	USMISEXPB

US Trade in Goods (sa)	Datastream
Total, balance of payments basis	USVISBBLB
Total, census basis	USVSBALNB
Exports, total balance of payments basis	USEXPTBLB
Net adjustments	
Exports, total census basis	USEXPRTSB
Foods, feeds, beverages	USEXFFBVB
Industrial supplies	USEXISUPB
Capital goods	USEXCAPGB
Automotive vehicles, etc.	USEXAUTOB
Consumer goods	USEXCONGB
Other goods	USEXOMRCB

US Trade in Goods (sa)	Datastream
Imports, total balance of payments basis	USIMPTBLB
Net adjustments	
Imports, total census basis	USIMPORTB
Foods, feeds, beverages	USIMFDFBB
Industrial supplies	USIMISMTB
Capital goods	USIMCPGDB
Automotive vehicles, etc.	USIMAUTMB
Consumer goods	USIMCNGDB
Other goods	USIMOMCHB

Petroleum and Non-petroleum End-Use Category (sa)	Datastream
Balance, total	USVISBOPB
Net adjustments	
Petroleum	USVSPETRB
Non-petroleum	
Exports, total	USEXPBOPB
Net adjustments	
Petroleum	USEXPETRB
Non-petroleum	
Imports, total	USIMPBOPB
Net adjustments	
Petroleum	USIMPETRB
Non-petroleum	

Exports and Imports of Goods by Principle End-Use Category (1996 Constant USD Basis, sa)	Datastream
Balance, total census basis	USVSBALND
Foods, feeds, beverages	
Industrial supplies	
Capital goods	
Automotive vehicles, etc.	
Consumer goods	
Other goods	
Exports, total census basis	USEXPRTSD
Foods, feeds, beverages	USEXFFBVD
Industrial supplies	USEXISUPD
Capital goods	USEXCAPGD
Automotive vehicles, etc.	USEXAUTOD
Consumer goods	USEXCONGD
Other goods	USEXOMRCD

Exports and Imports of Goods by Principle End-Use Category (1996 Constant USD Basis, sa)	Datastream
Imports, total census basis	USIMPORTD
Foods, feeds, beverages	USIMFDFBD
Industrial supplies	USIMISMTD
Capital goods	USIMCPGDD
Automotive vehicles, etc.	USIMAUTMD
Consumer goods	USIMCNGDD
Other goods	USIMOMCHD

Petroleum and Non-petroleum End-Use Commodity Category (1996 Constant USD Basis, sa)	Datastream
Balance, total census basis	USVSBALND
Net adjustments	
Petroleum	
Non-petroleum	
Exports, total census basis	USEXPRTSD
Net adjustments	
Petroleum	
Non-petroleum	
Imports, total census basis	USIMPORTD
Net adjustments	
Petroleum	
Non-petroleum	

US Trade in Goods (nsa)	Datastream
Balance, total balance of payments basis	USVSBALNA
Balance, total census basis	USVSBALNA
Exports, total balance of payments basis	USEXPTBLA
Net adjustments	
Exports, total census basis	USEXPRTSA
Foods, feeds, beverages	
Industrial supplies	
Capital goods	
Automotive vehicles, etc.	
Consumer goods	
Other goods	
Imports, total balance of payments basis	USIMPTBLA
Net adjustments	
Imports, total census basis	USIMPORTA
Foods, feeds, beverages	
Industrial supplies	
Capital goods	
Automotive vehicles, etc.	
Consumer goods	
Other goods	

Balance of Goods by Selected Countries (nsa, Census Basis)	Datastream
North America	
Canada	USBTPCCAA
Mexico	USBTPCMXA
Western Europe	USVBWEURA
Euro Area	
European Union	USVBEEC.A
Austria	USBTPCAUA
Belgium	USBTPCBEA
Finland	USBTPCFIA
France	USBTPCFRA
Germany	USBTPCGMA
Italy	USBTPCITA
Netherlands	USBTPCNLA
Spain	USBTPCSPA
Sweden	USBTPCSWA
United Kingdom	USBTPCUKA
European Free Trade Association	
Norway	USBTPCNOA
Switzerland	USBTPCSZA
Eastern Europe	
Hungary	USBTPCHUA
Poland	USBTPCPLA
Russia	USBTPCRSA
Pacific Rim Countries	
Australia	USBTPCASA
China	USBTPCCHA
Japan	USBTPCJAA
Newly Industrialized Countries (NICs)	
Hong Kong	USBTPCHKA
Korea	USBTPCKSA
Taiwan	USBTPCTWA
South/Central America	
Brazil	USBTPCBRA
OPEC	
Saudi Arabia	USBTPCSAA
Venezuela	USBTPCVEA
Other Countries	
South Africa	USBTPCSFA

Exports of Goods by Selected Countries (nsa, Census Basis)	Datastream
North America	
Canada	USEXCCA.A
Mexico	USEXCMX.A
Western Europe	USEXWEURA
Euro Area	
European Union	USEXEEC.A
Austria	USEXCAU.A
Belgium	USEXCBE.A
Finland	USEXCFI.A
France	USEXCFR.A
Germany	USEXCGM.A
Italy	USEXCIT.A
Netherlands	USEXCNL.A
Spain	USEXCSP.A
Sweden	USEXCSW.A
United Kingdom	USEXCUK.A
European Free Trade Association	
Norway	USEXCNO.A
Switzerland	USEXCSZ.A
Eastern Europe	
Hungary	USEXCHU.A
Poland	USEXCPL.A
Russia	USEXCRS.A
Pacific Rim Countries	
Australia	USEXCAS.A
China	USEXCCH.A
Japan	USEXCJA.A
Newly Industrialized Countries (NICs)	
Hong Kong	USEXCHK.A
Korea	USEXCKS.A
Taiwan	USEXCTW.A
South/Central America	
Brazil	USEXCBR.A
OPEC	
Saudi Arabia	USEXCSA.A
Venezuela	USEXCVE.A
Other Countries	
South Africa	USEXCSF.A

Imports of Goods by Selected Countries (nsa, Census Basis)	Datastream
North America	
Canada	USIMPCCAA
Mexico	USIMPCMXA
Western Europe	USIMWEURA
Euro Area	
European Union	USIMEEC.A
Austria	USIMPCAUA
Belgium	USIMPCBEA
Finland	USIMPCFIA
France	USIMPCFRA
Germany	USIMPCGMA
Italy	USIMPCITA
Netherlands	USIMPCNLA
Spain	USIMPCSPA
Sweden	USIMPCSWA
United Kingdom	USIMPCUKA
European Free Trade Association	
Norway	USIMPCNOA
Switzerland	USIMPCSZA
Eastern Europe	
Hungary	USIMPCHUA
Poland	USIMPCPLA
Russia	USIMPCRSA
Pacific Rim Countries	
Australia	USIMPCASA
China	USIMPCCHA
Japan	USIMPCJAA
Newly Industrialized Countries (NICs)	
Hong Kong	USIMPCHKA
Korea	USIMPCKSA
Taiwan	USIMPCTWA
South/Central America	
Brazil	USIMPCBRA
OPEC	
Saudi Arabia	USIMPCSAA
Venezuela	USIMPCVEA
Other Countries	
South Africa	USIMPCSFA

Exports and Imports of Goods by Principal SITC Commodity Grouping (nsa)	Datastream
Exports, total census basis	USEXPRTSA
Manufactured goods	
Agricultural commodities	
Mineral fuels	
Imports, total census basis	USIMPORTA
Manufactured goods	
Agricultural commodities	
Mineral fuels	

Exports, Imports and Balance of Advanced Technology Products (nsa)	Datastream
Balance	USVSADVTA
Exports	USEXADVTA
Imports	USIMADVTA

Imports of Energy-Related Petroleum Products, including Crude Petroleum (nsa)	Datastream
Total energy-related petroleum products	
Quantity (1000s of barrels)	
Value (USD1000s)	
Total crude petroleum	
Quantity (1000s of barrels)	
1000s of barrels per day average	
Value (USD1000s)	
Price unit (USD)	

Literature

DiLullo, Anthony J. and Henderson, Hugh, 'Reconciliation of the U.S.–Canadian Current Account, 1996 and 1997', US Department of Commerce, *Survey of Current Business* (November 1998), pp. 41–54.

Klitgaard, Thomas and Schiele, Karen, 'The Growing U.S. Trade Imbalance with China', Federal Reserve Bank of New York, *Current Issues in Economics and Finance*, Vol. 3, No. 7 (May 1997).

Pakko, Michael R., 'The U.S. Trade Deficit and the "New Economy"', *Federal Reserve Bank of St. Louis Review*, Vol. 81, No. 5 (September/October 1999), pp. 11–19.

Papaioannou, Stefan and Yi, Kei-Mu, 'The Effects of a Booming Economy on the U.S. Trade Deficit', Federal Reserve Bank of New York, *Current Issues in Economics and Finance*, Vol. 7, No. 2 (February 2001).

17.2 Balance of Payments

Data Source

Data are published by the Bureau of Economic Analysis at the Department of Commerce. The press release is available on the Internet at www.bea.gov/bea/di1.htm. The data are also published in Tables F and G in the Survey of Current Business.

Importance for the Financial Markets   C

Description

Balance of payment figures, which are published quarterly, represent the broadest measurement of international transactions. In addition to movements of goods and services, which are based on monthly figures, the balance of payments also includes capital transactions, foreign income transactions and other international transfers accompanying change of ownership. Transactions between the USA and abroad are always based on market prices. Included are the 50 states in the USA with the District of Columbia, Puerto Rico, Samoa, Guam, the Midway Islands and the Virgin Islands, along with US army areas abroad and diplomatic and consular representations abroad. In addition, foreign diplomatic and consular representations within the USA are excluded.

Data acquisition is based on the national resident concept. All persons living in the USA for more than one year and all USA citizens living abroad for less than one year are classed as national residents. Exceptions include government employees and students. Employees of the US government, such as diplomats and the military who are abroad for more than one year, are still classed as national residents. The same applies to US students, irrespective of the length of their studies. Legal entities, such as companies, are also classed as national residents where their commercial activity is subject to US law. Therefore foreign subsidiaries, in the sense of the balance of payments statistics, are foreign companies, whereas subsidiaries of foreign companies with a subsidiary or branch in the USA are classed as national resident companies. On the other hand, representatives of international organizations based in the USA, diplomatic representations of foreign states in the USA and foreign students studying in the USA are not classed as national residents.

The data are recorded where possible as they occur. The Bureau of Economic Analysis partly refers to figures made available by other bodies. The data on the balance of trade and services are based on the monthly statistics of the Bureau of the Census which are, however, modified in part (see Section 17.1). Capital flows are taken into account on the basis of statistics which the US Treasury Department charts with the Federal Reserve Bank of New York. The BEA also employs statistics from the US budget collected by the Federal Reserve Board, international organizations, foreign central banks or statistical offices, trade organizations and a series of other bodies.

The balance of payments statistics have been published in a new format since May 1999 to facilitate international comparison in accordance with international practice and the IMF recommendations. A capital account and financial account are also published in this new format. A number of transactions, for which there are no offsetting transaction trades and which were previously included in the current balance, are now booked in the capital account. As the individual transactions are statistically hard to classify, only the net balance is published for the capital account and no details are given. In addition to these three sub-balances, the total of unclassifiable transactions is also published. These occur both on the issuing and receiving side as international

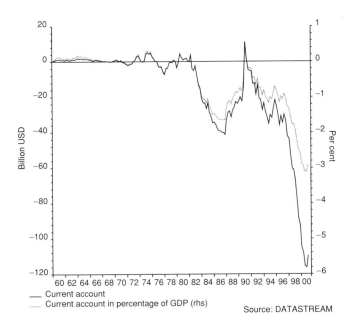

Figure 17.3 Current account balance in billions of USD and in percentage of GDP

transactions are always recorded twice. If both sides provide the same figures there is no statistical discrepancy. As this is not always possible due to the great number of transactions, or because time delays lead to transactions which belong together being entered at different times, there are statistical differences that need to be offset with the help of this balance. Another reason for such a difference is partial seasonal adjustment. The effects of such methods are recorded in explicit detail.

Periodicity/Revisions

The data are only published once every quarter, approximately $2\frac{1}{2}$ months after the end of the respective quarter. Revisions are conducted regularly for the previous publication, although there are revisions going back up to four years for benchmark revisions. Publication takes place at 10.00 ET (16.00 CET).

Seasonal Adjustment

Data are seasonally adjusted for individual categories where a statistically significant seasonal pattern is identified. The data series are revised every year. Visible exports and imports are currently seasonally adjusted. For services this is conducted on data on travel, passenger fares, other transportation, US government miscellaneous services, US government receipts from abroad as well as US

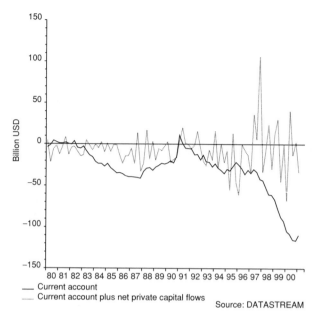

Figure 17.4   Current account balance and net private capital flows

government and private unilateral transfers. With the financial account balance, only payments for government credit and long-term assets (as well as reinvested income from direct US investment) are seasonally adjusted.

Notes

Relatively little notice is taken of the balance of payments statistics by the financial markets as they are already out of date at time of publication and values for the balance of trade and services are already known from the monthly values. The data are more suitable for analytical use. This applies mainly to the data on the financial account balance which can, for example, be used to identify the structure of ownership of the US Treasuries.

Data on trade with individual nations distort the actual transactions conducted in the individual nations. So, for example, goods transactions between the USA and the Netherlands also contain goods transactions from Germany or intended for Germany, which are shipped and freighted via Dutch ports. Capital transactions between, for example, the USA and the UK are also distorted as British banks execute many orders for companies and individuals not living in the UK who want to exploit the advantages of using London as a banking centre. For this reason, data on the investment habits of individual nations with US Treasuries are also distorted.

Balance of payment figures have existed since 1870, although in the early years they were still somewhat patchy. A summary in table form for the years 1870–1961 can be found in the Balance of Payments Statistical Supplement published by the Department of Commerce in 1963.

Key Datastream Mnemonics

Current Account (sa)	Datastream
Exports of goods and services and income receipts	USEXPTGSB
Exports of goods and services	USEXPGSBB
Goods, balance of payments basis	USEXMERCB
Services	USSVSRECB
Transfer under US military agency sales contracts	USSVRMILB
Travel	USTRVRECB
Passenger fares	USPSFRECB
Other transportation	USOTRRECB
Royalties and licence fees	USRAFRECB
Other private services	USOPRVSVB
US Government miscellaneous services	USMISRECB
Income receipts	USINCRECB
Income receipt on US-owned assets abroad	USIOVINVB
Direct investment receipts	USINCDIVB
Other private receipts	USINCOPRB
US government receipts	USINCGVRB
Compensation of employees	USINCWERB
Imports of goods and services and income payments	USIMPTGSB
Imports of goods and services	USIMPGSBB
Goods, balance of payments basis	USIMMERCB
Services	USSVSPAYB
Direct defence expenditures	USSVPDEFB
Travel	USTRVEXPB
Passenger fares	USPSFEXPB
Other transportation	USOTREXPB
Royalties and licence fees	USROYLICB
Other private services	USOPVSERB
US Government miscellaneous services	USMISEXPB
Income payments	USINCPAYB
Income payments on foreign-owned assets in the USA	USIFRINVB
Direct investment payments	USPAYDIVB
Other private payments	USPAYOPRB
US government payments	USPAYGVRB
Compensation of employees	USINCWEPB
Unilateral current transfer, net	USUNITTRB
US government grants	USGOVGRNB
US government pensions and other transfers	USGOVPENB
Private remittances and other transfer	USUNIPRVB

Capital Account (sa)	Datastream
Capital account transactions, net	USCATBALB

Financial Account (sa)	Datastream
US-owned assets abroad, net (increase/financial outflow (−))	USASSABRB
US official reserve assets, net	USRESVASB
Special drawing rights	USRSSDRBB
Reserve position in the IMF	USRSIMFBB
Foreign currencies	USRSFOXBB
US Government assets, other than official reserve assets, net	USGOVASSB
US credits and other long-term assets	USGVALTCB
Repayments on U.S. credits and other long-term assets	USGVALTRB
US foreign currency holdings and U.S. short term assets, net	USGVASTFB
US private assets, net	USPRVASSB
Direct investment	USDIRINVB
Foreign securities	USFORSECB
US claims on unaffiliated foreigner reported by U.S. non-banking concerns	USCLAIMFB
US claims reported by U.S. banks, not included elsewhere	USCLAIMRB
Foreign-owned assets in the United States, net (increase/financial inflow (+))	USFORNASB
Foreign official assets in the United States, net	USFROFASB
US Government securities	USGOVNSCB
US Treasury securities	USGOVSECB
Other	USGOVDBTB
Other US Government liabilities	USOTHGLBB
US liabilities reported by U.S. banks, not included elsewhere	USLBBANKB
Other foreign official assets	USOTHFOAB
Other foreign assets in the USA	USOTHFRAB
Direct investment	USDRINVSB
U.S. Treasury securities	USTREAFAB
U.S. securities other than U.S. Treasury securities	USSECOTHB
U.S. currency	USCURRFAB
U.S. liabilities to unaffiliated foreigners reported by U.S. non-banking concern	USLIBFORB
U.S. liabilities reported by U.S. banks, not included elsewhere	USLIBBNKB
Statistical discrepancy	USSTATDSB
Of which seasonal adjustment discrepancy	USSADISCB

Memoranda (sa)	Datastream
Balance on goods	USVSMERCB
Balance on services	USSVSBALB
Balance on goods and services	USGSBALBB
Balance on income	USIVIBALB
Unilateral current transfers, net	USUNITTRB
Balance on current account	USCURACBB

Literature

Andersen, P.S. and Hainaut, P., 'Foreign Direct Investment and Employment in the Industrial Countries', Bank for International Settlements, *BIS Working Papers* No. 61, November 1998.

Fieleke, Norman S.: 'What is the Balance of Payments?', *Federal Reserve Bank of Boston Special Report* No. 3.

Higgins, Matthew and Klitgaard, Thomas, 'Viewing the Current Account Deficit as a Capital Inflow', Federal Reserve Bank of New York, *Current Issues in Economics and Finance*, Vol. 4, No. 13 (December 1998).

International Monetary Fund, 'Determinants and Systemic Consequences of International Capital Flows', *Occasional Papers* No. 77, March 1991.

US Department of Commerce, Office of Business Economics, *Balance of Payments Statistical Supplement*, Washington, DC, 1963.

18
Inflation Indicators

18.1 Producer Price Index

Data Source

Data are published by the Bureau of Labor Statistics (BLS) at the Department of Labor. The press release is available on the Internet at stats.bls.gov.

Importance for the Financial Markets   A

Description

The Producer Price Index measures price trends which producers of goods and services receive. The index has been produced since 1902, although prices for the years 1890 to 1901 were also published retrospectively. In the course of time, more and more sub-indices have been added. The sub-indices for services have recently been redeveloped and incorporated. Until 1978 the indices were published as wholesale price indices and had a slightly different target. Since 1979 the focus has been on producer prices, so a large proportion of data is now collected in the production industry. In addition, prices are also collected from mining companies, supply companies and agricultural operations. The indices are based on fixed weightings which are aligned at regular intervals to actual production conditions. The latest update took place with the release of January 2002. The basis for this adjustment was the net sales values in the individual industries from 1997. Sales within an industrial sector are therefore not included. One exception to this is crude materials for further processing which are based on all sales (i.e., also in the crude materials sector).

Overall, several sub-indices are published and are based on various aggregate stages. The most important aggregates are the production level indices which are divided into crude materials for further processing; intermediate materials, supplies and components as well as finished products. Aggregates are also formed for types of goods and industrial sectors. With crude materials for further processing, goods that have not yet been processed are incorporated. Intermediate products, on the other hand, are goods that have been through at least one stage of production but cannot yet be delivered to the end user because they require further processing, or are to be used as a component in the production of other goods. For this reason fuel, paper and similar non-durable goods that do not require further processing but go into the production can be found under this category, too. In contrast, finished goods are goods not requiring further production which can be delivered to the end user. This category mostly includes goods which have gone through a production process. However, there is also a small proportion of unprocessed goods, such as eggs or other foods, which do not require processing. It is therefore possible to input individual goods with different weightings into different production levels. There are also investment goods, such as machinery, which are sold to companies and used for the production of other goods.

As only price changes relating to prices of US producers are included, tax due on sales is not included, whereas rebates and similar price-reducing agreements are. Imports are also excluded, as are services not relating to production. On the other hand, services such as goods transport, maintenance work, car rental, etc. (i.e., types which are required for production), are incorporated in the

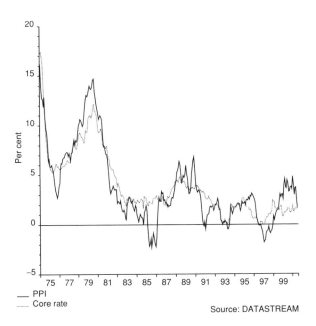

Figure 18.1 Change in total producer prices and core rate on preceding year

calculation of the indices. In the coming years the BLS wants to increase further the number of services to be taken into account for a comprehensive survey. One consequence of this is that sub-indices for services have to date had a brief history of normally less than five years only.

Reporting prices to the Bureau of Labor Statistics is voluntary. The likelihood that a company will be selected and requested to submit producer prices increases according to the size of the company. If it agrees, individual company goods are selected for which prices are to be reported. Around 30 000 companies currently report prices for around 100 000 goods and services to the Bureau of Labor Statistics. Upon data publication not all questionnaires sent out to companies will have been returned to the BLS. The missing prices are then produced on the basis of the preceding month's prices by taking the average price trend for similar goods as the basis.

Periodicity/Revisions

Data are always published at 08.30 ET (14.30 CET). They are announced shortly before the middle of the month following the survey month. Due to the survey method the data are largely based on prices which are due to be paid in the first half of the month. For the majority of the prices the data are reported on the Tuesday of the week of the thirteenth of the month. Revisions are minor. The monthly data are, however, revised regularly four months after publication. The reason for this method is that approximately 67 per cent of prices are known at the time of the first publication whereas, after four months, 90 per cent of the price figures have been reported. A study in the 1970s showed that the existing information was so extensive after four months that no further revision was required. In the light of this they decided to incorporate revisions with a time lag only. In addition annual revisions take place on a yearly basis.

Seasonal Adjustment

Data for most sub-indices are seasonally adjusted.

Notes

Along with the *Labor Market Report* and the Consumer Price Index, publication of the Producer Price Index has the greatest influence on the financial markets. The market focuses virtually exclusively on the monthly or yearly change in the prices of finished products. It is also worth noting the so-called core rate of finished goods, i.e., with the exception of food and energy goods. These two types of good are extremely volatile and can conceal the general price trend. In addition to these indicators the intermediate product indices also serve as an indicator of future price trends for finished products and there is a correlation, albeit not a very close one, between price trends for intermediate materials, supplies and components and crude materials for

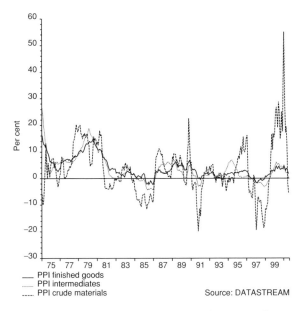

Figure 18.2 Change in producer prices for finished goods, intermediate goods and crude materials on preceding year

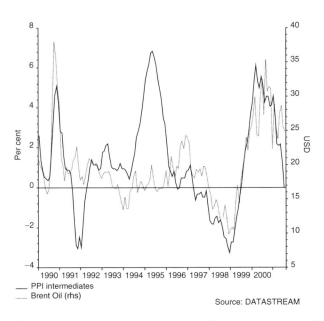

Figure 18.3 Change in producer prices for intermediate goods on preceding year and Brent Oil in USD

further processing. The reason for this is that crude materials only make up part of the costs incurred in production. It also depends on the competitive position of the individual companies as to whether they pass on crude materials price increases to their customers, or have to reduce their margins. The importance of the indices for crude materials, however, is also reduced by the fact that other indicators relating to crude material price trends (e.g., the ISM Purchasing Managers' Index) are published before the producer prices and therefore supply the first information on inflationary trends in the crude materials for further processing sector.

Producer price trends are frequently seen as a leading indicator of consumer price trends. However, the relation between the two indicators is distorted by a number of influencing factors. On the one hand, the indices are made up of different sub-indices, which in turn go into the calculation with different weighting. Consequently prices are obtained via the producer price indices which flow to the producers, whereas the Consumer Price Index reflects prices to be paid by consumers. Taxes and prices of imported goods are also contained in these data which are excluded from the producer prices. The consumer price indices also only take into account price trends of goods purchased by consumers, whereas the producer price indices include goods purchased by

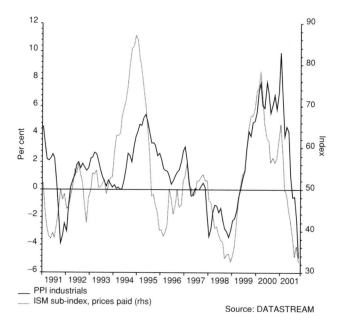

Source: DATASTREAM

Figure 18.4　Change in producer prices for industrial goods on preceding year and prices paid sub-index of the ISM Purchasing Managers' Index for Manufacturing Business

companies for production. One example of this is machinery or trucks. Thus all services of a consumptive nature are only included in the consumer price indices. For consumer prices there are also the profit margins and wholesale and retail costs which are not yet included in the producer prices. The different direction of the indices is expressed by the use of the indices by other bodies. The Producer Price Index, for example, is used as the basis for real development in economic growth, whereas consumer price indices are based on the calculation of real income and expenditure trends.

In addition to the differences as a result of data definition, different survey methods are also used for both indices. For producer prices, most of the data are obtained on the Tuesday in the week of the thirteenth day in the month. For consumer price indices, on the other hand, data are obtained within the first 18 working days. The method of questioning is also different. Producer prices are primarily obtained via a postal survey, whereas consumer prices are obtained via telephone poll or direct from BLS staff. A further difference is the way in which model modifications of goods are treated. For producer prices the new models are taken into account and the old models are omitted as soon as the producers stop selling the old models. In the automobile sector this regularly leads to disturbances in September/October as this is when new models come on to the market. For consumer prices, on the other hand, old models are

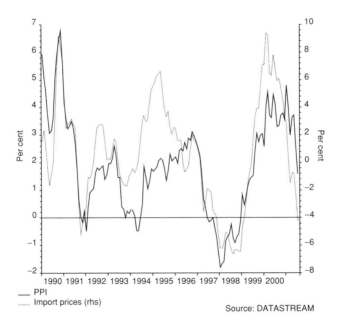

Figure 18.5 Change in producer prices and import prices on preceding year

included until they are no longer purchased. However, in the automobile sector, as soon as more new models begin to be bought than old ones, the old models no longer count. This means that new models are included in the producer prices in October, and only 4–6 months later with consumer prices.

The producer price indices are employed both by the President's office and Congress, as well as by the Federal Reserve as a basis for formulating economic policy. In addition, they serve as the initial basis for the calculation of real economic figures by the Bureau of Economic Analysis. And finally the inflation-indexed agreements are based on these indices.

Key Datastream Mnemonics

Producer Price Index, by Stage of Processing (sa)	Datastream
Finished goods	USFINGPRE
Finished consumer goods	USWPCONFE
Finished consumer foods	USPPIFCFE
Finished consumer goods, excluding foods	USPPICGFE
Capital equipment	USPSFCNDE
Manufacturing industries	USPSFEM.E
Non-manufacturing industries	USPSFEY.E
Intermediate materials, supplies, and components	USWPINTME
Materials and components for manufacturing	USPSPTM.E
Materials for food manufacturing	USPSPMMFE
Materials for non-durable manufacturing	USPSPMMNF
Materials for durable manufacturing	USPSPMMDE
Components for manufacturing	USPSPCM.E
Materials and components for construction	USPSPTC.E
Processed fuels and lubricants	USPSPFL.E
Containers	USPSPB . . E
Supplies	USPSPS . . E
Manufacturing industries	USPSPSM.E
Non-manufacturing industries	USPSPSY.E
Crude materials for further processing	USWPCRUDE
Foodstuff and feedstuff	USPSMFF.E
Non-food materials	USPPICXAE
Crude fuel	USPSMNL.E

Special Groupings	**Datastream**
Finished goods, excluding foods	USPPIFXFE
Intermediate materials less foods and feeds	USPPIIXFE
Intermediate foods and feeds	USPPIIFFE
Crude materials less agriculturals products	USPPICXAE
Finished energy goods	USPPIFEGE

Producer Price Index by stage of Processing (sa)	Datastream
Finished goods less energy	USPPIGXEE
Finished consumer goods less energy	USPPICXEE
Finished goods less foods and energy	USPPIGFFE
Finished consumer goods less foods and energy	USPPICFEE
Consumer non-durable goods less foods and energy	USPPINFEE
Intermediate enegy goods	USPPIIEGE
Intermediate materials less energy	USPPIIXEE
Intermediate materials less foods and energy	USPPIIFEE
Crude energy materials	USPPICEMF
Crude materials less energy	USPPICMXE
Crude non-food materials less energy	USPPICMXE

Producer Price Indices for Selected Commodity Groupings (nsa)	Datastream
Finished goods (1967=100)	
All commodities	USWPCOMMF
Major commodity groups	
Farm products and processed foods and feeds	USPPIFRMF
Industrial commodities	USWPINCMF
Industrial commodities less fuels and related products and power	USPPIICXF

Producer Price Indices for the Net Output of Major Industry Groups (nsa)	Datastream
Total mining industries	USPPIX .. F
Total manufacturing industries	USPPIM .. F
Services industries	

Literature

Cecchetti, Stephen G., 'The Unreliability of Inflation Indicators', Federal Reserve Bank of New York, *Current Issues in Economics and Finance*, Vol. 6, No. 4 (April 2000).

US Department of Labor, Bureau of Labor Statistics: 'Producer Prices', *BLS Handbook of Methods*, Ch. 14, April 1997, pp. 130–43.

18.2 Consumer Price Index

Data Source

Data are published by the Bureau of Labor Statistics (BLS) at the Department of Labor. The press release is available on the Internet at stats.bls.gov. The CPI Detailed Report, which contains detailed tables and in-depth analysis of price trends, is available around three weeks after publication of the BLS press release. Data are also published in the publication *The Monthly Labor Review* by the Bureau of Labor Statistics.

Importance for the Financial Markets   A

Description

The Consumer Price Index measures the level and change in monthly consumer prices. Consumer prices have been measured since 1913 so a number of time series are available since then. Goods of different weighting go in the basket of commodities. Until 2001, the weightings were aligned to the actual demand situation approximately every ten years on the basis of the results of a consumer survey of around 29 000 households. The price changes are also weighted according to their importance for the demand behaviour. For the years up to 2001, consumer demand was based on the basket of commodities from the years 1993–95. Starting in January 2002, the basket is based on consumer behaviour in 1999–2000. After this, it will be changed every two years. This means that in 2004 the basket from the years 2001–2 will be applied. As long as the basket of commodities is unchanged, the Consumer Price Index only measures the change in prices and not the resulting change in demand behaviour, as would a cost of living index.

Altogether, two different types of indices are published. The CPI-U (Consumer Price Index for all Urban Consumers) measures consumer expenditure of the whole population in or around urban conurbations. The consumer expenditure of the rural population (in communities with less than 2500 inhabitants), as well as military dependants and those imprisoned and institutionalized is therefore not included. Overall, the behaviour of around 87 per cent of the population is covered by this index. The CPI-W (Consumer Price Index for all Urban Wage Earner and Clerical Workers) only measures the costs for wage earners and clerical workers in and around urban areas. In order to take into account this category at least one member of the household has to be a wage earner or clerical worker and have been employed for at least 37 weeks within the last 12 months. This index only covers around 32 per cent of the population as it does not include members of company management, technical staff, the self-employed, the unemployed, pensioners or those not classed as part of the potential work force. For this reason the index has far less importance than the CPI-U, even though the differences measured in price trends between the indices are not very great.

The index measures the total consumer expenditure of consumers. Consequently, VAT and charges (including rebates and other deductions) are included. Data for the index have been produced since 1988 in 85 geographical regions with 88 districts in total (in New York there are three districts and in Los Angeles two). Every month staff at the Bureau of Labor Statistics record around 90 000 prices directly in around 23 000 shops. Goods for which prices are recorded are defined in terms of type, quantity and quality. If no price is reported for a particular good, a similar good of a different quality is reported instead. This change in the method is then documented.

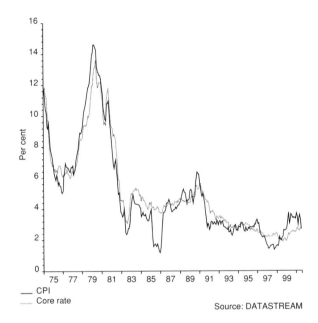

Figure 18.6   Change in total consumer prices and core rate on preceding year

In addition to the total indices, data on sub-indices and special aggregates are also published. In total prices are currently collected in around 200 categories, which are summarized in eight groups. These are:

- Food and beverages (eggs, juice, coffee, prepared foods, etc.)
- Housing (rent, fixtures and fittings, heating oil, etc.)
- Apparel (T-shirts, trousers, women's shoes, jewellery, etc.)
- Transportation (vehicles, fuel, flight tickets, etc.)
- Medical care (drugs, examinations, hospital costs, etc.)
- Recreation (televisions, sport equipment, pets, etc.)
- Education and communication (school fees, postal charges, telephone costs, computers, etc.)
- Other goods and services (tobacco, hairdressers, undertakers' costs, etc.)

In addition, sub-indices are also produced for 26 regions in the USA but they are not published every month.

With rent calculation, the fact that home-owners do not have to pay rent is taken into consideration. Here a rent equivalent is calculated, corresponding to the rent which would be payable if the home was rented. This rent equivalent is also part of the indicator.

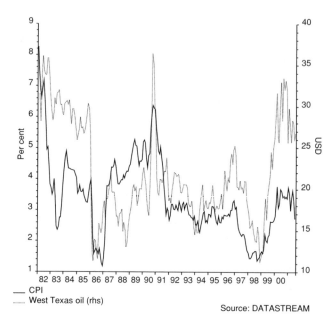

Figure 18.7   Change in consumer prices on preceding year and West Texas oil price in USD

Starting in August 2002 with the release of the data for July, the BLS publishes a supplemental index of consumer price change, the so-called Chained Consumer Price Index for All Urban Consumers (C-CPI-U). The C-CPI-U utilises expenditure data in adjacent time periods in order to reflect any substitution effect that consumers make across item categories in response to relative price changes. This index will be a closer approximation to a cost-of-living index than the other published indices. It will employ a December 1999=100 reference base. Data prior to December 1999 will not be available.

Periodicity/Revisions

The data are collected in the first 18 days of the month and published around the following mid-month, normally a few working days after publication of the producer prices. The non-seasonally adjusted data are not revised, whereas seasonally adjusted figures can be revised going back five years, as soon as the seasonal adjustment factors have been aligned. The composition of the underlying basket of commodities has also been aligned every ten years, according to changes in consumption patterns. The latest changes happened in the years 1940, 1953, 1964, 1978, 1987, and most recently 1998. As consumer behaviour changes continually, however, the indicator becomes increasingly unreliable the longer it has been since the last alignment. The BLS maintains that an alignment of the basket of commodities could be possible between the main

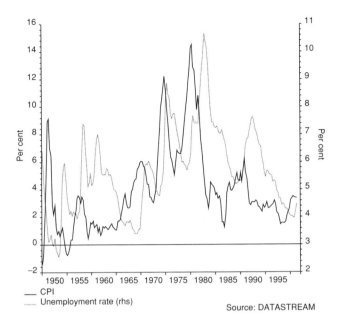

Figure 18.8 Change in consumer prices on preceding year and unemployment rate

revisions if consumption patterns change drastically. However, this has never occurred and, since the BLS decided to update the basket every two years starting in January 2002, this will no longer be a major problem. Due to the alignment of the basket of commodities a recalculation of the consumer price trends going back some years may be required. Publication is always effected at 08.30 ET (14.30 CET).

Seasonal Adjustment

In addition to the unadjusted figures, seasonally adjusted data are also published. The unadjusted data are not revised and represent therefore a suitable basis for agreements based on inflation trends. The unadjusted index also forms the basis for index-linked salary and pension agreements. The C-CPI-U is not seasonally adjusted.

A number of goods such as winter coats and snow shovels are not available all year round in all areas. The BLS therefore increases the number of listings to ensure that prices for such goods are available all year round.

Notes

The publication of consumer prices, in conjunction with the labour market figures and producer prices, has the greatest influence on the financial markets.

Consumer prices focus on the monthly and annual change in consumer prices as measured by the CPI-U and the so-called core rate, i.e. consumer prices excluding the volatile food and energy prices. In particular with unusual price changes from individual categories of expenditure, it is useful to monitor other summaries where special movements can be analyzed and eliminated, e.g., the Department of Energy releases prices for gasoline in advance. These numbers can be used to calculate the CPI energy cast gauge. As the expenditure data required for the calculation of the C-CPI-U are available only with a large time lag, the index will be published in a preliminary form using the latest data available. With the first publication from August 2002, final data are published for the twelve months of 2000. The months from 2001 are available as 'interim' values and the 2002 values are initial data. With the publication of the data for January, the values from the months two years before become "final" and the values of the previous years' months will become 'interim' data. These revisions will happen each February and are expected to be small.

As with changes in consumption patterns which are only taken into consideration for an alignment of the weightings, the method of calculation for the Consumer Price Index overrates price trends in the course of time. In 1998 a Commission came to the conclusion that the annual inflation rate was up to 1 percentage point too high. In the meantime initial measures have been

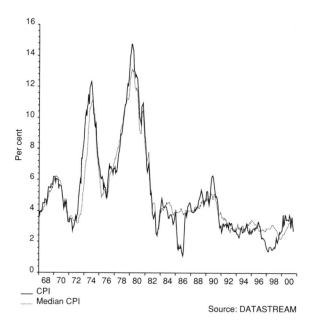

Figure 18.9 Change in total consumer prices and Median Consumer Price Index on preceding year

taken to conduct a more accurate measurement. Since January 1999 geometric averages were therefore used instead of arithmetic ones for around 61 per cent of the goods. This step meant the inflation rate is around 0.2 per cent under the price trends using the old method and therefore reflects actual trends more accurately. Further steps are scheduled.

In addition to the indices produced by the Bureau of Labor Statistics, indicators for ascertaining consumer price trends are also calculated by other organizations. The price index in the NAPM Purchasing Managers' Index, for example, is a good guide to consumer price trends. However, the so-called Median Consumer Price Index produced by the Federal Reserve Bank of Cleveland is also of interest. It excludes particularly volatile components from the price trends and thereby responds in a similar way to the core rate of consumer prices. The data on this indicator are available on the Internet at www.clev.frb.org/research/mcpipr.htm.

Key Datastream Mnemonics

Consumer Price Index for All Urban Consumers (CPI-U, sa)	Datastream
Expenditure categories	
All items	USCP....E
All items (1967 = 100, nsa)	USCP67..F
Foods and beverages	USCPFDBVE
Housing	USCPHOUSE
Apparel	USCPAPPLE
Transportation	USCPTRANE
Medical care	USCPMEDCE
Recreation	USCPR...E
Education and communication	USCPE&C.E
Other goods and services	USCPOGDSE
Commodity and service group	
Commodities	USCPCOMME
Food and beverages	USCPFDBVE
Commodities less food and beverages	USCPCXB.E
Services	USCPSERVE
Rent of shelter	USCPSRS.E
Tenants' and household insurance (nsa)	USCPHI..F
Gas (piped) and electricity	USCPSHE.E
Water and sewer and trash collection services (nsa)	USCPHWT.F
Household operations (nsa)	USCPHOP.F
Transportation services	USCPST..E
Medical care services	USCPSM..E
Other services	USCPSO..E

Consumer Price Index for All Urban Consumers (CPI-U, sa)	Datastream

Special Indices	**Datastream**
All items less food	USCPXF..E
All items less shelter	USCPXHS.E
All items less medical care	USCPXMEDE
Commodities less food	USCPCXF.E
Non-durables less food	USCPNXF.E
Non-durables less food and apparel	USCPNXP.E
Non-durables	USCPN...E
Services less rent of shelter	USCPSXS.E
Services less medical care services	USCPSXM.E
Energy	USCPENGYE
All items less energy	USCPXENGE
All items less food and energy	USCPXFDEE
Commodities less food and energy commodities	USCPCXE.E
Energy commodities	USCPEC..E
Services less energy services	USCPSXE.E
Purchasing power of the consumer dollar (nsa)	USCPPD..F
Purchasing power of the consumer dollar (old base, nsa))	USCPPD67F
Yearly inflation rate	USCPANNL

Consumer Price Index for All Urban Wage Earners and Clerical Workers(CPI-W, sa)	Datastream

Expenditure categories	
All items	USCPIW..E
All items (1967 = 100, nsa)	USCW67..F
Foods and beverages	USCWFB..E
Housing	USCWH...E
Apparel	USCWA...E
Transportation	USCWT...E
Medical care	USCWM...E
Recreation	USCWR...E
Education and communication	USCWE&C.E
Other goods and services	USCWO...E
Commodity and service group	
Commodities	USCWC...E
Food and beverages	USCWFB..E
Commodities less food and beverages	USCWCXB.E
Services	USCWS...E
Rent of shelter	USCWSRS.E
Tenants' and household insurance	USCWHI..F
Gas (piped) and electricity	USCWSHF.E

Consumer Price Index for All Urban Wage Earners and Clerical Workers(CPI-W, sa)	Datastream
Water and sewer and trash collection services	USCWWSTCE
Household operations (nsa only)	USCWHOP.F
Transportation services	USCWST..E
Medical care services	USCWSM..E
Other services	USCWSO..E

Special Indices

All items less food	USCWXF..E
All items less shelter	USCWXHS.E
All items less medical care	USCWXM..E
Commodities less food	USCWCXF.E
Non-durables less food	USCWNXF.E
Non-durables less food and apperal	USCWNXP.E
Non-durables	USCWN...E
Services less rent of shelter	USCWSXS.E
Services less medical care services	USCWSXM.E
Energy	USCWE...E
All items less energy	USCWXE..E
All items less food and energy	USCWXFE.E
Commodities less food and energy commodities	USCWCXE.E
Energy commodities	USCWEC..E
Services less energy services	USCWSXE.E
Purchasing power of the consumer dollar (nsa)	USCWPD..F
Purchasing power of the consumer dollar (old base, nsa)	USCWPD67F

Chained Consumer Price Index for All Urban Consumers (C-CPI-U, nsa)	Datastream
All items	USCCP...F
Foods and beverages	USCCPFB.F
Housing	USCCPH..F
Apparel	USCCPAPLF
Transportation	USCCPT..F
Medical care	USCCPM..F
Recreation	USCCPR..F
Education and communication	USCCPE&CF
Other goods and services	USCCPO..F
Services	USCCPS..F
Commodities	USCCPC..F
Durables	USCCPCD.F
Non-durables	USCCPCN.F
Addenda:	
All items less food and energy	USCCPXFEF
Energy	USCCPE..F

Literature

Blomberg, S. Brock and Harris, Ethan S., 'The Commodity-Consumer Price Connection: Fact or Fable', Federal Reserve Bank of New York, *Economic Policy Review*, Vol. 1, No. 3 (October 1995), pp. 21–38.

Boskin, M. *et al.*, *Toward a more Accurate Measure of the Cost of Living* (Advisory Commission to Study the Consumer Price Index), Washington, DC, 1996.

Bryan, Michael F., Cecchetti, Stephen G. and Wiggins, Rodney L., 'Efficient Inflation Estimation', *NBER Working Paper Series No. 6183*, Cambridge, MA, 1997.

Cecchetti, Stephen G., 'The Unreliability of Inflation Indicators', Federal Reserve Bank of New York, *Current Issues in Economics and Finance*, Vol. 6, No. 4 (April 2000).

Gillingham, Robert, *A Conceptual Framework for the revised Consumer Price Index*, Proceedings of the Business and Economic Statistics Section, American Statistical Association 1974, pp. 46–52.

Gordon, Robert J., 'The Boskin Commission Report and its Aftermath', Bank of Japan, *IMES Discussion Paper No. 99-E-27*.

Poole, Wiliam, 'Is Inflation too Low?', *Federal Reserve Bank of St. Louis Review*, Vol. 81, No. 4 (July/August 1999), pp. 3–10.

Steindel, Charles, 'Are There Good Alternatives to the CPI?', Federal Reserve Bank of New York, *Current Issues in Economics and Finance*, Vol. 3, No. 6 (April 1997).

Steindel, Charles, 'The Impact of Reduced Inflation Estimates on Real Output and Productivity Growth', Federal Reserve Bank of New York, *Current Issues in Economics and Finance*, Vol. 5, No. 9 (June 1999).

US Department of Labor, Bureau of Labor Statistics, 'The Consumer Price Index', *BLS Handbook of Methods*, Ch. 17, April 1997, pp. 167–202.

18.3   Employment Cost Index

Data Source

Data are published by the Bureau of Labor Statistics (BLS) at the Department of Labor. The press release is available on the Internet at stats.bls.gov.

Importance for the Financial Markets   B

Description

The Employment Cost Index is a fixed weighted index which represents a measure for the entire remuneration of employees in the private sector and state and local employees. Those employed in agriculture, government administration, the army and those employed in households are not included. In total, 90 per cent of employees are covered. Earnings and salaries, as well as social security contributions, are recorded to obtain the index. Earnings and salaries also contain bonus payments which are directly linked to work performance, whereas overtime supplements are classed as additional payments. Employers' contributions to social security and pensions, sick pay and holiday pay (as well as voluntary payments by the employer) are also included in this category. Stock options are not included (yet). In addition to the indices which are divided into the private sector and public sector employees, there are also data on the change in labour costs for employees who are trade union members and those who are not. Here the weightings are realigned quarterly so these time series are not fully comparable with the remaining indices.

Average hourly earnings are used as the basis for index calculation. For employees not paid an hourly rate the basic wage is divided by the number of working hours. Out of a total of 28 000 companies, 6500 companies were selected from private industries. From a total of 4100 state companies and bodies in the states and localities, around 800 were selected and surveyed. However, the composition of the companies surveyed changes regularly every five years.

The advantage of the Employment Cost Index is that reshuffles within the structure of the employed are not initially included and are only changed with a realignment of the weightings. This prevents a proportionally higher growth in the number of employed in the higher wage brackets being interpreted as a rise in wage costs, based on the individual employees.

The Employment Cost Index has been produced since 1976. At first only earnings and salaries in private companies outside agriculture were included and the states of Alaska and Hawaii were excluded. In 1978 these two states were incorporated and other statistical time series were provided, such as the

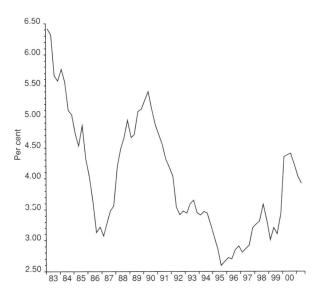

Source: DATASTREAM

Figure 18.10 Change in Employment Cost Index on preceding year

level of organization of employees. Social security contributions have been included since 1980 and after 1981 state and local authority employees were also finally included.

The index is still calculated in the form of a Laspeyere Index with fixed weighting, although studies aimed at implementing alternative calculation methods to obtain more accurate results are currently in progress. However, it could be some time before the Bureau of Labor Statistics is ready. This will possibly be when other expansions, such as the incorporation of holiday payment and some social security contributions, are improved.

Periodicity/Revisions

The index is published at the end of the first month following the end of a quarter. The data relate to labour costs occurring in the respective salary period in which the twelfth day in March, June, September and December falls. The change in labour costs between these respective periods is then compared. Revisions are only conducted with changes in the seasonal adjustment factors. The weightings in the index are based on the data from a survey in 1990. These weightings have been employed since March 1995. Since this time the indices have also been normed to June 1989 = 100. Publication is always effected at 08.30 ET (14.30 CET).

Seasonal Adjustment

Data have been seasonally adjusted only since December 1990. At the beginning of a calendar year the seasonal adjustment factors are recalculated. Seasonally adjusted data are revised going back five years.

Particularly with state and local authority employees it has been established that salary increases often take place in the third quarter. Non-adjusted data are thereby extremely distorted during this quarter. For those employed in private industry, salary rises are distributed over the whole year so a different seasonal pattern is thereby produced.

Notes

Since Alan Greenspan, Chief of the Federal Reserve, pointed out the importance assigned to the Employment Cost Index by the Federal Reserve in July 1996, the financial markets have shown renewed interest in this index. It reflects the pressure on labour costs better than, for example, the hourly earnings indices, as far more earnings and salary components are included. One of the limiting factors in terms of index importance is that it is only published quarterly. Particular attention is paid to the rates of change for the overall indices on the preceding quarter and preceding year. Furthermore, special movements of individual components are also monitored on the financial markets.

Key Datastream Mnemonics

Employment Cost Index (sa)	Datastream
Industry and occupational group	
Total compensation	
Civilian workers	USLCCV..E
State and local government	USLCGZ..E
Private industry	USLCPV..E
Industry	
Goods producing	USLCIQ..E
Construction	USLCIC..E
Manufacturing	USLCIM..E
Durables	USLCIMD.E
Non-durables	USLCIMN.E
Service producing	USLCIH..E
Non-manufacturing	USLCIY..E
Occupational group	
White collar	USLCPOW.E
Blue collar	USLCPOB.E
Service	USLCPOS.E
Wages and salaries	
Civilian workers	USLWCV..E
State and local government	USLWGZ..E
Private industry	USLWPV..E
Industry	
Goods producing (nsa only)	USLWIQ..F
Construction	USLWCON.E
Manufacturing (nsa only)	USLWIM..F
Durables (nsa only)	USLWIMD.F
Non-durables	USLWNDURE
Service producing	USLWSVP.E
Non-manufacturing	USLWNONME
Occupational group	
White collar	USLWWCW.E
Blue collar (nsa only)	USLWPOB.F
Service (nsa only)	USLWPOS.F
Benefit costs	
Civilian workers	USLBCV..E
State and local government	USLBGZ..E
Private industry	USLBPV..E
Industry	
Manufacturing	USLBGMFGE
Service producing	USLBLVP.E
Non-manufacturing	USLBNMN.E

Employment Cost Index (sa)	Datastream
Occupational group	
White collar	USLOWCW.E
Blue collar	USLOBCW.E
Service	USLOSVC.E

Literature

O'Connor, Karen and Wong, William, 'Measuring the Precision of the Employment Cost Index', *Monthly Labor Review*, March 1989.

Ruser, John W., 'The Employment Cost Index: What Is It?,' *Monthly Labor Review*, September 2001, pp 3–21.

Schwenk, Albert E., 'Employment Cost Index Rebased to June 1989', *Monthly Labor Review*, April 1990.

Schwenk, Albert E., 'Introducing 1990 Weights to the Employment Cost Index', *Compensation and Working Conditions*, June 1995.

US Department of Labor, Bureau of Labor Statistics, 'National Compensation Measures', *BLS Handbook of Methods*, Ch. 8, April 1997, pp. 57–69.

Wood, Donald, 'Estimation Procedures for the Employment Cost Index', *Monthly Labor Review*, April 1990.

18.4   Import/Export Price Index

Data Source

Data are published by the Bureau of Labor Statistics (BLS) at the Department of Labor. The press release is available on the Internet at stats.bls.gov.

Importance for the Financial Markets   D

Description

Indices have been produced for import/export prices since 1971. The aim was to create a tool that shows how international trade affects the production of goods and services, apart from price fluctuations. Therefore, indices were created to produce price trends for internationally traded goods and services. Both import and export prices are calculated using a fixed-weighted index. Until recently only prices for goods were included in the calculation. But since then, they have also started to publish indices for internationally traded services. In addition to the classification of types of goods, import price indices based on the country of origin have also been calculated for the leading nations since 1990. The data went on to be produced quarterly and figures have been available monthly since January 1993.

Prices of over 20 000 goods from more than 6000 primary and secondary sources are reported for calculation of the indices. In addition, up to 2000 prices for services have also been surveyed every quarter. Starting in 2002, the index calculation is currently weighted based on trading patterns from 2000. Therefore most indices are normed to 100 for the base year, 2000. The indices for goods prices are published in three different definitions: the 'harmonized' system, the system employed by the Bureau of Economic Analysis and the Standard International Trade Classification (SITC) system. The harmonized system, which has been in use since 1993, is a standard international method which aims to prioritize product groups. This classification is also used for the data survey. The SITC classification has been applied since 1974. The Bureau of Economic Analysis system, by contrast, is oriented more strongly to end-users and less production-oriented.

The price indices for services are published according to only two definitions. The balance of payments definition classifies transactions in terms of national residents and foreign residents, whereas the balance of trade statistics distinguishes between US importers and US exporters without further consideration of the nationality of individuals. The background to the different classifications is that indices are used by other authorities for other statistics with their own individual definitions. Imports of goods not in US dollars account for around 15–20 per cent of imports, excluding the crude oil sector. To calculate the prices of these imports in US dollars, the Bureau of Labor Statistics uses the average rate of exchange in the preceding month.

Import price indices are based on prices paid by US importers. The basis for this is the standard international definitions in goods transportation. Imports

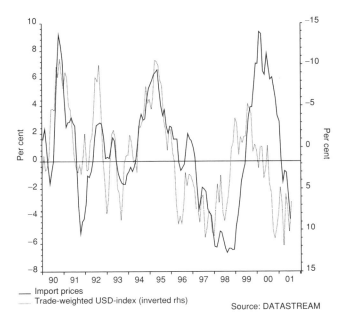

Figure 18.11 Change in import prices on preceding year and trade-weighted USD-index

are classed as 'free on board' (f.o.b.) or 'cost, insurance and freight' (c.i.f.), depending which definition is standard practice in the sector. For exports the definitions 'free alongside ship' (f.a.s.) or 'free on board' (f.o.b.) are employed. When calculating the prices, the BLS for crude oil imports resorts to the figures from the Department of Energy, and grain exports, excluding rice exports, are based on data from the Department of Agriculture. Indices for prices of services are only published quarterly and indices for oil tanker freight prices, which are based on Department of Energy data, are published with a time lag of three months.

Periodicity/Revisions

The monthly data are published at the end of the following month and relate to transactions conducted in the first week of the month. On publication, revisions of the three preceding publications are announced. Publication is always at 10.00 ET (16.00 CET).

Seasonal Adjustment

The indices are not seasonally adjusted.

Notes

The focus is on the change in the indices compared to the preceding period or preceding year. The figures on import prices are far more important than the export price figures as they are a guide to possible imported inflationary pressure. A rise in the prices of imported goods can occur for two reasons: first, because foreign companies increase prices, and second, because the national currency has chronically weakened. The prime importance of the export price statistics is due to the fact that they make a statement about the change in the competitiveness of the US economy. If prices of export goods rise more rapidly than imports in the medium term, the competitiveness of the national economy suffers as a result and this could spark off a cycle of lower economic growth in subsequent quarters.

Key Datastream Mnemonics

Import Price Indices (End Use, nsa)	Datastream
All commodities	USIPTOTLF
All imports excluding petroleum	USIPEXPTF
Foods, feeds and beverages	USIPFOODF
Industrial supplies and materials	USIPISUPF
Industrial supplies and materials excluding petroleum	
Industrial supplies and materials, durable	

Import Price Indices (End Use, nsa)	Datastream
Industrial supplies and materials, non-durable excluding	
Crude petroleum	USIPPETRF
Capital goods	USIPCAPGF
Automotive vehicles, parts and engines	USIPMOTVF
Consumer goods excluding automotives	USIPCONGF

Export Price Indices (End Use, nsa)	Datastream
All commodities	USEPTOTLF
Agricultural commodities	USEPAGRCF
Non-agricultural commodities	USEPNAGRF
Foods, feeds and beverages	USEPFOODF
Industrial supplies and materials	USEPISUPF
Industrial supplies and materials, durable	
Industrial supplies and materials, non-durable	
Non-agricultural Industrial supplies and materials	
Capital goods	USEPCAPGF
Automotive vehicles, parts and engines	USEPMOTVF
Consumer goods excluding automotives	USEPCONGF

Import Price Indices (SITC, nsa)	Datastream
All commodities	
Food and live animals	
Beverages and tobacco	
Crude materials, inedible, except fuels	
Mineral fuels, lubricants and related materials	
Chemicals and related products	
Manufactured goods classified chiefly by material	
Machinery and transport equipment	
Miscellaneous manufactured articles	

Export Price Indices (SITC, nsa)	Datastream
All commodities	
Food and live animals	
Beverages and tobacco	
Crude materials, inedible, except fuels	
Mineral fuels, lubricants and related materials	
Animal and vegetable oils, fats and waxes	
Chemicals and related products	
Manufactured goods classified chiefly by material	
Machinery and transport equipment	
Miscellaneous manufactured articles	

Import Price Indices (Harmonized System, nsa)   Datastream

Live animals, animal products
Vegetable products
Prepared foodstuff, beverages, and tobacco
Mineral products
Products of the chemical or allied industries
Plastics and articles thereof, rubber and articles thereof
Raw hides, skins, leather, fur, skins, travel goods, etc.
Wood, wood charcoal, cork, straw, basket and wicker
Woodpulp, recovered paper and paper products
Textile and textile articles
Footwear, headgear, umbrellas, whips, artificial
    flowers, etc
Stone, plaster, cement, asbestos, ceramic glass, etc
Pearls, stones, precious metals, imitation jewellery
    and coins
Base metals and articles of base metals
Machinery, electrical equipment, televisions, image and sound
    recorders, parts, etc.
Vehicles, aircraft, vessels and associated transport equipment
Optical, photo, measuring, medical and musical instruments, and
    timepieces
Miscellaneous manufactured articles

Export Price Indices (Harmonized System, nsa)   Datastream

Live animal, animal products
Vegetable products
Animal or vegetable fats and oils
Prepared foodstuff, beverages, and tobacco
Mineral products
Products of the chemical or allied industries
Plastics and articles thereof, rubber and articles thereof
Raw hides, skins, leather, fur, skins, travel goods, etc.
Wood, wood charcoal, cork, straw, basket and wicker
Woodpulp, recovered paper and paper products
Textile and textile articles
Stone, plaster, cement, asbestos, ceramic glass, etc.
Pearls, stones, precious metals, imitation jewellery and coins
Base metals and articles of base metals
Machinery, electrical equipment, televisions, image and sound
    recorders, parts, etc.
Vehicles, aircraft, vessels and associated transport equipment
Optical, photo, measuring, medical and musical instruments, and
    timepieces
Miscellaneous manufactured articles

US Import Price Indices by Locality of Origin (nsa)	Datastream

Developed countries
  Manufactured goods
  Non-manufactured goods
Developing countries
  Manufactured goods
  Non-manufactured goods
Canada
  Manufactured goods
  Non-manufactured goods
European countries
  Manufactured goods
  Non-manufactured goods
Latin America
  Manufactured goods
  Non-manufactured goods
Japan
Asian NICs

Literature

McCarthy, Jonathan, 'Pass-Through of Exchange Rates and Import Prices to Domestic Inflation in Some Industrialised Economies', Bank for International Settlements, *BIS Working Paper* No. 79, November 1999.

US Department of Labor, Bureau of Labor Statistics, 'International Price Indexes', *BLS Handbook of Methods*, Ch. 15, April 1997, pp. 154–9.

18.5   Agricultural Price Index

Data Source

Data are published by the Department of Agriculture. The press release is available on the Internet at usda.mannlib.cornell.edu/reports/nassr/price/pap-bb/.

Importance for the Financial Markets   E

Description

The Agricultural Price Index is calculated on fixed weightings. Current weightings correspond to the importance of agricultural products in the years 1990–92. For this period the indices are normed at 100. In addition, indices are obtained where prices are normed for the average in the years 1910–14 at 100. Overall, indices are obtained for two sub-sectors. One is an index based on prices that agricultural operations receive from their customers (prices received). All deductions and price reductions are already included in these prices. Sub-indices are also produced for crops, livestock and products and agricultural production items. The data are calculated for the whole of the

USA and the individual states. In addition, indices are based on prices payable by agricultural operations for purchases of goods and services and other operating costs (prices paid). These are therefore classed in terms of production goods, interest on credit taken up and land leased, tax and wages applied.

To calculate the indices based on prices received by agricultural operations, data were collected from over 2600 mills and silos for the grain statistics. Data for the prices of livestock and animal products are obtained from auctions, breeders and slaughterhouses. Prices for goods traded between various agricultural corporations are not included; however, they account for a small proportion only of total sales. Prices for fruit and vegetable products are obtained directly from producers and via surveys at sales outlets.

For the prices paid statistics, data are obtained from companies and operations selling goods to agricultural operations. Around 8500 operations are surveyed; the quota of responses is between 75 and 80 per cent. The weightings within the price indices are revised every year in April on the basis of the results of a more extensive survey.

Periodicity/Revisions

Data are published on the last working day of the month. In the current report, prices quoted apply to the middle of the month whereas, in the revised report a

Figure 18.12 Change in agricultural prices on preceding year: prices paid and prices received

month later, data apply to average agricultural prices of the entire month. With this method major revisions may be incorporated between the provisional and final report. Statistics on prices of goods and services may also be revised every year in April when weightings of the indices are redefined. Data are published at 15.00 ET (21.00 CET).

Seasonal Adjustment

Data are not seasonally adjusted.

Notes

The main focus of the financial markets is on the price change on the preceding year. As the indices are not seasonally adjusted, huge monthly fluctuations can result. However, the link between prices for agricultural products and the respective price components in the Producer and Consumer Price Index is not very close. Consequently, the importance of this index is also further limited.

Key Datastream Mnemonics

US Agricultural Prices (nsa)	Datastream
Prices received	USFMPR..F
All farm products	USFMPRFPF
All crops	USFMPRCPF
Livestock and products	USFMPRLUF
Prices paid	USFMPP..F
All items	USFMPPALF
Production items	USFMPPPDF

18.6   Productivity and Costs

Data Source

Data are published by the Bureau of Labor Statistics (BLS) at the Department of Labor. The press release is available on the Internet at stats.bls.gov.

Importance for the Financial Markets   D

Description

The publication provides a rough guide to labour productivity and the costs of producing goods. Since 1959, indices on output per hour (productivity), compensation per hour, labour costs per unit of output (unit labour costs), real compensation per hour and hours of all persons have been published. These indices are calculated for the entire business sector and the non-farm business sector. Non-profit making government sectors and institutions are excluded. In all, these indices are based on 76 per cent of the overall economy. In addition, there are indices for the manufacturing sector overall and classed by industry for durable goods and non-durable goods, as well as for companies outside the financial sector available.

Data on working hours are obtained from the Current Employment Statistics, which supply monthly information on the labour market situation. As these data do not relate to the agricultural sector the data required for this were taken from the Current Population Survey by the Bureau of Labor Statistics. In the non-farm sector, the National Income and Product Account released by the BEA and the Current Population Statistics are used to measure the labour input for government enterprises, proprietors and unpaid family workers. However, further calculation is necessary as the Current Employment Statistics are based on paid working hours and therefore contain paid holiday, etc. In the calculation of the indices on the hours worked, no distinction is made between different activities, it is purely a total of the number of hours worked. Both employed staff and self-employed, as well as unpaid family firm members, are included so the salaries of the self-employed are also taken into account. The reason for this is that in the agriculture and retail sectors the work output of the

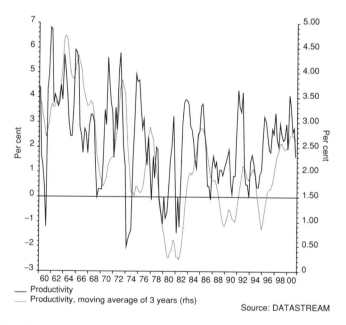

Source: DATASTREAM

Productivity
Productivity, moving average of 3 years (rhs)

Figure 18.13   Change in productivity excluding agriculture on preceding year

self-employed accounts for a large proportion of the total working time. If this were not included, the work performed and remuneration would be extremely distorted.

Data on the output are derived from an annual-weighted index by excluding from the GDP data the following sectors: general government, non-profit institutions, paid employees of private households, and the rental value of owner-occupied dwellings. For the non-farm business sector output, the farm sector is also excluded.

For calculating the indices, data from the input side (hours worked) are compared with data from the output side (production). The indices can be obtained using simple formulae. Productivity is total production divided by the number of hours worked. Unit labour costs correspond to total labour costs divided by production or remuneration per hour of work divided by productivity. The following therefore applies for growth rates:

Growth rate of unit labour costs = Growth rate of unit labour costs minus
                growth rate of production
              = Growth rate of hourly compensation
                minus growth rate of productivity
Growth rate of real compensation = Growth rate of compensation minus
                inflation rate

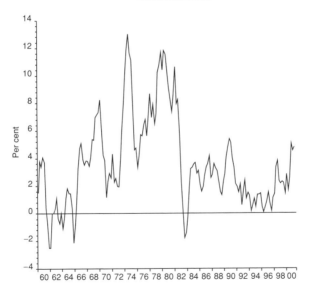

Source: DATASTREAM

Figure 18.14 Change in non-farm unit labour costs on preceding year

Periodicity/Revisions

The data always relate to individual quarters. The first data are published around 5 weeks after the end of the quarter and are therefore published approximately one week after the GDP advance report. The revised data are produced around one month later, after publication of the preliminary GDP figures. The final productivity and cost figures are only published with the first data for the coming quarter. Therefore two months of publications of this economic data are followed by one month without any publication. The revisions conducted between the individual publications are influenced by the GDP revisions and can be relatively major. Revisions of productivity and costs are possible going back for a number of years as they are based on the GDP revisions, which can relate to preceding years. Publication always takes place at 10.00 ET (16.00 CET).

Seasonal Adjustment

Data are seasonally adjusted.

Notes

The financial markets focus on the change in productivity and unit labour costs in the non-farm business sectors. Although the concept of productivity is relatively simple, it causes great problems with empirical surveys. Moreover, the underlying figures, such as the GDP results, are already known, so publication rarely contains surprises, although the data in terms of preceding quarters is very volatile and the source data will be modified.

Key Datastream Mnemonics

Productivity and Costs (sa)	Datastream
Business sector	
Output per hour of all persons	USOPHPBSE
Annualized change from preceding quarter	USOPHBS%G
Output	USOUTPBSG
Hours of all persons	USHRSPBSE
Compensation per hour	USCOMPBSE
Real compensation per hour	USRCMPBSE
Unit labour costs	USULCPBSE
Unit non-labour costs	USUNPPBSE
Implicit price deflator	USIPDPBSE
Non-farm business sector	
Output per hour of all persons	USOPHNBSE
Annualized change from preceding quarter	USOPHNB%G
Output	USOUTNBSG

Productivity and Costs (sa)	Datastream
Hours of all persons	USHRSNBSE
Compensation per hour	USCOMNBSE
Real compensation per hour	USRCMNBSE
Unit labour costs	USULCNBSE
Unit non-labour costs	USUNPNBSE
Implicit price deflator	USIPDNBSE
Manufacturing sector	
Output per hour of all persons	USOPHMANE
Annualized change from preceding quarter	USOPHIM%G
Output	USOUTMANG
Hours of all persons	USHRSMANE
Compensation per hour	USCOMMANE
Real compensation per hour	USRCMMANE
Unit labour costs	USULCMANE

Productivity and Costs (sa)	Datastream
Durable manufacturing sector	
Output per hour of all persons	USOPHDURE
Annualized change from preceding quarter	USOPHID%G
Output	USOUTDURG
Hours of all persons	USHRSDURE
Compensation per hour	USCOMDURE
Real compensation per hour	USRCMDURE
Unit labour costs	USULCDURE
Non-durable manufacturing sector	
Output per hour of all persons	USOPHNDRE
Annualized change from preceding quarter	USOPHIN%G
Output	USOUTNDRG
Hours of all persons	USHRSNDRE
Compensation per hour	USCOMNDRE
Real compensation per hour	USRCMNDRE
Unit labour costs	USULCNDRE
Non-financial corporations	
Output per hour of all persons	USOPHNFNE
Annualized change from preceding quarter	USOPHNF%G
Output	USOUTNFNG
Employees' hours	USHRSNFNE
Hourly compensation	USCOMNFNE
Real hourly compensation	USRCMNFNE
Unit labour costs	USULCNFNE
Unit non-labour costs	USUNPNFNE
Total unit costs	USTUCNFNE
Unit profits	USUPFNFNE
Implicit price deflator	USIPDNFSE

Literature

Steindel, Charles, 'The Impact of Reduced Inflation Estimates on Real Output and Productivity Growth', Federal Reserve Bank of New York, *Current Issues in Economics and Finance*, Vol. 5, No. 9 (June 1999).

Steindel, Charles and Stiroh, Kevin J., 'Productivity: What Is It, and Why Do We Care about It?', *Federal Reserve Bank of New York Staff Reports* No. 121 (March 2001).

Stiroh, Kevin J., 'What Drives Productivity Growth', Federal Reserve Bank of New York, *Economic Policy Review*, Vol. 7, No. 1 (March 2001), pp. 37–59.

US Department of Labor, Bureau of Labor Statistics, 'Industry Productivity Measures', *BLS Handbook of Methods*, Ch. 11 (April 1997), pp. 103–9.

US Department of Labor, Bureau of Labor Statistics, 'Productivity Measures: Business Sector and Major Subsectors', *BLS Handbook of Methods*, Ch. 10 (April 1997), pp. 89–98.

Webb, Roy II., 'National Productivity Statistics', *Federal Reserve Bank of Richmond Economic Quarterly*, Vol. 84, No. 1 (Winter 1998), pp. 45–64.

19
Financial Activity

19.1 Monetary Aggregates

Data Source

Data are published by the Federal Reserve Board. The press release is available on the Internet at www.federalreserve.gov/releases. Data are also published in Table 1.21 Money Stock and Debt Measures in the *Federal Reserve Bulletin*.

Importance for the Financial Markets   D

Description

The Federal Reserve Board publishes weekly data on the monetary aggregates in various definitions. The M1 monetary aggregate, the most narrow aggregate, includes cash which is held outside the banking sector, demand deposits, reserves in the form of travellers' cheques which are not issued by banks as well as other checkable deposits in banks. The M2 monetary aggregate includes savings deposits, time deposits up to a total of USD100 000 and deposits of private investors in money market funds, in addition to the M1 monetary aggregate. And finally, the M3 monetary aggregate includes time deposits from a total of USD100 000, Eurodollar deposits of investors from the USA, deposits of institutional investors in money market funds and deposits in the form of Repurchase Agreements, as well as the M2 monetary aggregate. In addition to these monetary aggregate definitions, federal and non-federal debt measures are released. The lending figures are only published monthly. The monetary aggregate data have been produced monthly since January 1959, although in a somewhat different form, and the weekly data date back to January 1975. At that time monetarism, which advocates the management of monetary aggregates, gained great significance within the central bank so the available data, on which monetary policy was based, had to be increased.

For analytical purposes, an additional aggregate called MZM (Money, Zero Maturity) is published, too. This aggregate includes zero maturity, or immediately available, components of M3. MZM equals M2 minus small denomination time deposits, plus institutional money market mutual funds, which are included in M3 but excluded in M2. MZM is a substitute for M1 in that since 1994 the level and growth of M1 have been depressed by retail sweep programs that reclassify transactions deposits (demand deposits and other checkable deposits) as savings deposits overnight, thereby reducing banks' required reserves.

Periodicity/Revisions

Data are published weekly on a Thursday with a time lag of 10 days. As these data are still based on a relatively small database, they are revised one week later. The alignment of seasonal factors and benchmarks also leads to revisions which are conducted in February and which can have effects going back several months. The revisions in February can accompany the methodological adjustments which also lead to revisions of data already published. Publication always takes place at 16.30 ET (22.30 CET).

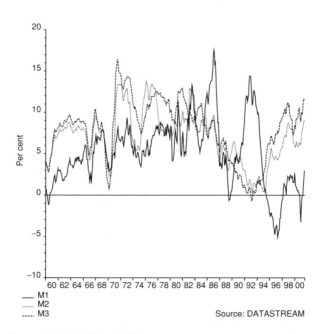

Figure 19.1　Change in M1, M2 and M3 monetary aggregates on preceding year

Seasonal Adjustment

Data are seasonally adjusted by seasonally adjusting individual components and then grouping these according to the individual monetary aggregate definitions.

Notes

The monetary aggregates are the best example of how the importance of individual indicators changes over time. Before 1975 they were nearly insignificant. As the monetary policy of the central bank began to concentrate on monetarism, the financial markets took more notice of these figures. In recent years the central bank has increasingly downplayed the significance so the importance of monetary aggregate figures is almost comparable to the period before 1975. The reason for this is that due to financial innovations and other structural changes the relation between monetary aggregate growth as well as economic growth and the inflation rate has declined. Only at times of exceptional trends in the monetary aggregates do monetarist theory supporters frequently point out possible wrong developments without this leading to too much irritation in the financial markets.

The trend of the M2 monetary aggregate is still followed most closely in the financial market. The Chairman of the Federal Reserve Board also has to

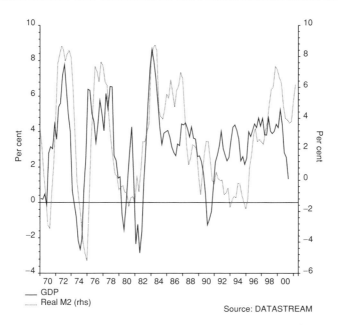

Figure 19.2   Change in GDP and real M2 monetary aggregates (with a lag of 12 months) on preceding year

announce target zones for the M2 and M3 monetary aggregates in his regular speech before Congress. In the meantime the Federal Reserve Board views these figures as orientation factors only rather than as strict target guidelines, and almost nobody in Congress would criticize the central bank for this policy. If the central bank fails to meet the target zones, it is the target zones and not the policy that will be realigned.

Key Datastream Mnemonics

Money Stock and Components (sa)	Datastream
Monetary Base	USM0...B
M1	USM1...B
Currency	USCURRNCB
Travellers cheques	USNBANKTB
Demand deposits	USDEMDEPB
Other checkable deposits	USOTHCHKB
M2	USM2...B
Total non-M1 M2	USM2NT.MB
Savings deposits	USDYDS.MB
Small-denomination time deposits	USDYDL.MB
Retail money funds	USMFRL.MB
M3	USM3...B
Total non-M2 M3	USM3NT.MB
Institutional money funds	USMFIL.MB
Large-denomination time deposits	USDYDB.MB
Repurchase Agreements	USDYRP.MB
Eurodollars	USBFED.MB
Money, zero maturity (MZM)	USM0M...B

Debt Components (sa)	Datastream
Federal	USFEDDEBB
Non-federal	USNFEDDBB

Weekly Money Stock Measures (sa)	Datastream
Monetary Base (Federal Reserve Bank of St. Louis)	USMYBSS
M1	
Week average	USMONEY
M2	
Week average	USM2WSA
M3	
Week average	USM3WSA

Literature

Anderson, Richard G. and Rasche, Robert H., 'Eighty Years of Observations on the Adjusted Monetary Base: 1918–1997', *Federal Reserve Bank of St. Louis Review*, Vol. 81, No. 1 (January/February 1999), pp. 23–9.

Cecchetti, Stephen G., 'Legal Structure, Financial Structure, and the Monetary Policy Transmission Mechanism', Federal Reserve Bank of New York, *Economic Policy Review*, Vol. 5, No. 2 (July 1999), pp. 9–28.

Clare, Andrew and Courtenay, Roger, 'Assessing the impact of macroeconomic announcements on securities prices and different monetary policy regimes', Bank of England, *Working Paper Series* No. 125, February 2001.

Dewald, William G., 'Historical U.S. Money Growth, Inflation, and Inflation Credibility' *Federal Reserve Bank of St. Louis Review*, Vol. 80, No. 6 (November/December 1998), pp. 13–23.

Haldane, Andrew G. and Read, Vicky, 'Monetary policy surprises and the yield curve', Bank of England, *Working Paper Series* No. 106, January 2000.

Nelson, Ed, *Direct Effects of Base Money on Aggregate Demand – Theory and Evidence*, Bank of England.

20
Address List

The Conference Board
845 Third Avenue
New York, NY 10022-6679
www.conference-board.org

Department of Agriculture
14th & Independence Avenue, SW
Washington, DC 20250
www.usda.gov

Department of Commerce
Bureau of the Census
P.O. Box 277943
Atlanta, GA 30384-7943
www.census.gov
www.doc.gov

Department of Commerce
Bureau of Economic Analysis
Washington, DC 20230
www.bea.gov
www.doc.gov

Department of Labor
Bureau of Labor Statistics
BLS Office of Public Affairs
Postal Square Building
2 Massachusetts Avenue, NE
Washington, DC 20212
stats.bls.gov

Department of Labor
Employment and Training Administration
ETA Office of Public Affairs
200 Constitution Avenue, NW
Washington, DC 20210
www.dol.gov

Federal Reserve Bank of Philadelphia
Ten Independence Mall
Philadelphia, PA 19106-1574
www.phil.frb.org

Federal Reserve Board
Eccles Building
20th Street
Washington, DC 20551
www.federalreserve.gov

Institute for Supply Management
PO Box 22160
Tempe, AZ 85285-2160
www.ism.ws

National Association of Home Builders
1201 15th Street, NW
Washington, DC 20005
www.nahb.com

National Association of Realtors
430 N. Michigan Avenue
Chicago, IL 60611
www.realtor.org

Purchasing Management Association of Chicago
2250 E. Devon Avenue
Suite 236
Des Plaines, IL 60018
www.napm-chicago.org

Office of Personnel Management
1900 E Street, NW
Washington, DC 20415-0001
www.opm.gov

University of Michigan
Institute for Social Research
Survey Research Center
PO Box 1248
Ann Arbor, MI 48106
www.isr.umich.edu

Part III
Euro-Zone

21
General Introduction

The Euro-zone is comparable to the USA in terms of its economic significance, number of inhabitants and area. There are, however, major differences between the sectors of economic statistics as statistics from the Euro-zone usually show a deficit. This is due, to some extent, to the creation of the European Monetary Union, an economic and statistical *terra incognita*. Completely new statistics had to be developed. In the EU official statistics are approved with the aid of legal directives. Therefore the necessary databases, the differences between individual nations, (which need to be eliminated where necessary), and the harmonization required in individual areas need to be considered in advance. Although EU-wide statistics have been available to a certain extent since the 1960s, harmonization was only accelerated a few years before the beginning of EMU. For this reason most time series only have a harmonized database of a few years. The statistical offices have calculated data series going back further, but in some cases they have to resort to national statistics, which do not include the individual figures required for calculation of individual aggregate figures and therefore have to be estimated.

Example

The monetary aggregates have been calculated according to uniform criteria since September 1997 for the entire Euro-zone. Monetary aggregates have been available throughout the Euro-zone since January 1980, however. These figures are obtained by aggregating national monetary aggregates and estimating individual figures.

Another equally important problem is that the exchange rates of EMU members still fluctuated in relation to one another before the beginning of the EMU. If national statistics are to be aggregated they have to be shown in the same units. Where monetary units are to be aggregated, the same currency has to be used. Since 1 January 1999 this has been the Euro. Prior to this, Eurostat used the ECU. The ECU was exchanged at a rate of 1:1 into Euro at the beginning of monetary union. Consequently, the method selected did not represent a problem at the time. The value of the ECU was, however, hit by the exchange rate fluctuations of currencies constituting the ECU. Consequently, the exchange rate had changed considerably, for example, in spring 1995 when the Italian Lira came under strong pressure. The weighting of Italian statistics was lower at this time, whereas the weighting of the other member state statistics tended to rise. The value of the ECU was not just affected by changes in the exchange rates of currencies which were then merged with the Euro. The currencies held in ECU by the nations who did not join the European Monetary Union (initially), i.e., Denmark, Greece, the UK and Sweden, also influenced the ECU. The influence the exchange rate fluctuations could have had on the value of the ECU can be seen in Figure 21.1, where the ECU-DEM and GBP–DEM rates are compared.

Apart from these problems, the method employed for most Euro-zone statistics is described below. The national statistical offices calculate the respective national statistics up to a certain time using a more or less uniform method, which now depends on the statistic. The statistical offices may make only the raw data available, or seasonally adjusted data and data including adjustments for the number of working days. These data are then passed on to Eurostat. There the figures are aggregated and seasonally adjusted where necessary for subsequent publication. The official Euro-zone statistics are normally published as overall aggregates as well as in terms of individual nations. Only monetary aggregates are not published as national aggregates but as an overall statistic for the Euro-zone.

Another problem arose in January 2001 when Greece joined the Euro-zone. The economic importance of Greece is limited. However, it had an impact one has to bear in mind. Euro-zone data up to the end of 2000 cover 11 Member States. With Greece's entry into the Euro-zone from the beginning of 2001, they cover 12 Member States. Eurostat treats the Euro-zone as an entity regardless of its composition. The growth rates for 2001 are calculated by comparing figures for the Euro-zone with 12 Member States in 2001 with the figures for the 11 Member States and Greece in 2000. For analytical purposes, Eurostat has made available historic series covering the current 12 Member States since 1990.

Eurostat faces the problem that the national data it publishes may not differ from the data from the statistical offices. For the non-adjusted data this problem is negligible, as the respective definitions of the individual statistics are largely uniform. By contrast the seasonally adjusted data are problematic. The national statistical offices normally use the X-12 ARIMA method or its predecessor, the X-11 ARIMA. Eurostat normally uses the TRAMO/SEATS method instead and the EU Commission uses the Dainties method for seasonal adjustment of survey results. Although the differences in the results are not great, there are always discrepancies which have to be taken into account.

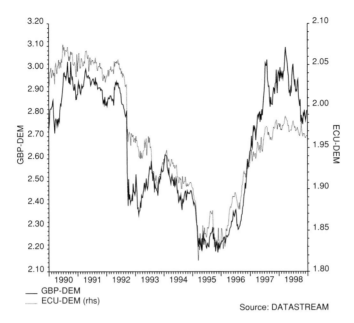

Figure 21.1   GBP and ECU performance against the German Mark

For the financial markets individual national statistics are frequently of greater importance than the aggregated Euro-zone data. The main reason for this is that national data are sometimes published well before the Euro-zone data. As soon as the data are published in the five largest nations, the Euro-zone data can be forecast accurately. For this reason the importance of the statistics published by Eurostat depends to some extent on how close its publication date is compared to the first national data. As a rule of thumb, it can be assumed that for the Euro-zone statistics Germany will be given a weighting of around 33 per cent, France a weighting of around 25 per cent, Italy 20 per cent, Spain 10 per cent and the Netherlands 5 per cent.

For the aforementioned it is clear that there are major differences between the Euro-zone and the USA. In the Euro-zone, regional data are normally published for individual member nations and only following this are the official statistics for the entire Euro-zone published. Consequently, it is possible to forecast with great precision in advance what the total value for the Euro-zone will be. This is not the case in the USA, where no detailed data are publicized before the actual publication and regional data are only announced after (or, at the earliest, alongside) the main publication. However, the statistical system of the USA is one of a small number of countries that is highly decentralized. More than 70 federal agencies or units within agencies collect statistical information.

For 10 agencies, collecting data and producing statistics is their sole mission and function. The statistical system in the EU follows a completely different approach. It applies the principle of subsidiarity and relies on co-operation between Eurostat and the national authorities. Statistical activities are carried out mainly by national authorities and there is only a very limited role for Eurostat to conduct statistical activities without the involvement of the national statistical institutions.

There is another problem with statistics from the Euro-zone, in that major methodological differences continue to exist. This sometimes applies even to statistics, which are already uniform throughout the Euro-zone. But the struggle towards harmonization at European level has been concentrated on the output side, leaving countries generally free to produce the results requested by statistical regulations by following different approaches. Worse still is the fact that Eurostat, and the national statistical offices or private research institutes which survey data for Eurostat, employ different seasonal adjustment methods. Although these do not produce any fundamental contradictions, the resulting values produced differ so greatly that diverging values can result. At the European level there are currently campaigns to introduce uniformity. The uniform method employed since the first quarter of 2000 by the German Federal Statistical Office and the Bundesbank to make seasonal adjustments to national accounting figures, is an example of a step in the right direction. The difficulty faced by the individual bodies in adapting their former methods to new circumstances or new findings can be seen in the fact that in Germany the industrial production figures are still seasonally adjusted with different methods, as in this area no agreement has yet been reached on what method to adopt.

Another important difference discovered during research for this book is the fact that individual data providers in the Euro-zone have different information polices. Whereas in the USA background information is frequently available on the Internet or in data publications or willingly made available on request, the data situation in the Euro-zone is considerably more difficult. On the one hand, methodical explanations are sometimes only published in part or are incomplete, or upon request you are told, for example, 'We do not give out detailed information on the indicator calculation, because anyone could come and calculate the indicator and we would lose our exclusivity.' In this respect the Euro-zone differs from the USA. This does not apply to all providers, although it shows how much progress still has to be made in the Euro-zone in terms of information policy.

The most important data provider in the Euro-zone is Eurostat, the statistical office of the European Commission. Eurostat works closely with the national statistical offices, the ECB and other Commission directorates supplying data. Information of differing quality is, however, available on the respective Internet sites and in the regular publications. In addition there are a series of private providers, such as research institutes, banks and media, supplying the information required for analysis of the economic situation in the Euro-zone.

The Euro-zone indicators were also assigned values for their respective importance for the financial markets, whereby A represents the most important and E the least important. Valuations between the USA and the Euro-zone are therefore intended to be comparable. Consequently, there is no Euro-zone indicator rated A, i.e., there is no publication in the Euro-zone which stands out clearly above the others. The most important indicators in the Euro-zone and the individual Member States are therefore:

- **B rating:**
  - National accounts
  - Industrial production
  - Ifo Business Survey
  - Labour market figures
  - Producer prices
  - Consumer prices
  - Monetary aggregates
- **C rating:**
  - *Handelsblatt* Leading Indicator
  - EU Industrial Survey
  - Reuters Purchasing Managers' Index
  - INSEE Industrial Trends
  - ISAE Industrial Trends
  - Retail sales
  - EU Consumer Survey
  - Balance of payments
  - Labour costs

The selection of the indicators described was based on their respective importance. National statistics are not listed separately if they appear subsequently in a Euro-zone-wide statistic. This is the case with the figures for the national accounts, for example, as the national data here forms the basis of the calculation of the GDP for the Euro-zone. Instead these national statistics are discussed with the Euro-zone data. In addition, no description was provided for data which are only published in one country and whose importance has clearly declined with the creation of European Monetary Union. Instead, a few key national indicators have been listed separately, such as the Ifo Survey on Business, whose publication still affects the financial markets.

For the Datastream mnemonics tables, the following method was selected. Detailed entries were only made for the EU overall, the Euro-zone and the five leading nations of Germany, France, Italy, Spain and the Netherlands. Only the key mnemonics are given for the other nations.

Literature

European Central Bank, *Statistical Information collected and compiled by the ESCB*, May 2000.

European Central Bank, *A Guide to Eurosystem Staff Macroeconomic Projection Exercises*, June 2001.

European Central Bank, 'The Euro area after the entry of Greece', *Monthly Report*, January 2001, p. 35–42.

Eurostat, *Short-term Statistics – Improving timeliness and cooperation*, 2001.

Fagan, Gabriel, Henry, Jerome and Mestre, Ricardo, 'An area-wide model (AWM) for the Euro area', *European Central Bank Working Paper* No. 42, Frankfurt-am-Main, January 2001.

22
Overall Activity

22.1 National Accounts

Data Source

The data for the Euro-zone are published by Eurostat, which publishes national data from the statistical offices of the individual nations. The Eurostat press release is available on the Internet at www.europa.eu.int/comm/euroindicators and some of the national data are available on the Internet sites of the respective statistical offices. In addition, data are published in Table 5.1 of the ECB *Monthly Report* as well as in the publication *Eurostatistics – Data on short-term economic analysis* issued by Eurostat.

Importance for the Financial Markets   B

Description

The GDP is the broadest aggregate of economic performance. Data on EU Member States are among the statistics which are not only produced by the national authorities, but also in aggregate form by Eurostat. Data published by Eurostat are based on the national statistics and are weighted according to the share of the GDP from 1998. However, with the national statistics real values are calculated using fixed price indices (in most countries 1995 is currently used as the base year), whereas Eurostat calculates the real values using a chain-type index. Consequently, there can be discrepancies if the national values are weighted and then compared with the official Eurostat statistics. Eurostat refers to data published by the respective national statistics offices. For Germany only, for the data up to the fourth quarter of 1999, the Deutsche Bundesbank statistics were used, as the German statistics office employed a seasonal adjustment method which differed substantially from those of the other statistics offices. Starting with the values for the first quarter of 2000 the Bundesbank and the Federal Statistical Office are now using the same seasonal adjustment method, so there is no longer a difference in the data. The data series are now shown in Euro, whereas for the period prior to 1999 data is given in ECU. This results in these values being distorted by exchange rate trends, and it explains why figures before and after the beginning of EMU are not fully comparable.

Table 22.1   Individual nation as a proportion of the Euro-zone GDP (2000)

Austria	3.35%
Belgium	3.96%
Finland	2.08%
France	21.93%
Germany	33.59%
Greece	1.73%
Ireland	1.31%
Italy	15.10%
Luxembourg	0.31%
Netherlands	6.25%
Portugal	1.61%
Spain	8.80%

The beginning of EMU was taken as a suitable occasion by statistical offices to reform and fundamentally revise the structure of national accounting in the individual Member States. Since then, the basis has been the European System of Accounts (ESA) 1995. As this system is binding on all Member States of the EU, via its use national statistics are largely unified and thereby more comparable. The 1995 ESA directive sets minimum requirements for national statistics which may not be undercut. Consequently, the national authorities are free to continue publishing their statistics with greater topicality and a more in-depth categorization of results. In addition, the 1995 ESA is based on the System of National Accounts of the UN. This facilitates greater comparability with data from other nations, although the 1995 ESA takes into consideration some of the anomalies in the respective European nations.

With the introduction of the 1995 ESA some new terminology was introduced replacing the classifications previously employed. For example, GNP is no longer used, but rather gross national income (GNI). A summary of the key terms can be found in Table 22.2. In addition to changes in terminology there is also a change in the definitions between various economic figures. The most important change is investment. Fixed asset investment now includes immaterial investment goods such as bought or self- produced software, which was not previously the case. Military equipment and buildings for civil use, such as trucks or military hospitals, also now count as fixed asset investment. As the level of depreciation increases with this extension of the definition, public consumer expenditure also rises and increases the values of the GDP or GNI compared with the old system. Table 22.3 shows the effects of the changes for 1995 for Germany.

Table 22.2 Previous and current national accounting terminology

Previous terminology	Current terminology as per 1995 ESA
Credit institutions and insurance enterprises +Financial auxiliaries +Civil servants' supplementary pension insurance	Financial corporations
Non-financial corporate enterprises + Non-financial non-corporate enterprises	Non-financial corporations
Compensation of employees	Compensation of employees
Gross wages and salaries	Wages and salaries
National income + Indirect taxes − Subsidies = Net national product at market prices	Balance of primary income (= Net national income)
GNP + Subsidies received from the rest of the world − Taxes on production and imports paid to the rest of the world	Gross national income
Exports of goods and services − Authorized export of commodity gold	Exports
Imports of goods and services	Imports
Final consumption	Final consumption expenditure
Purchases of resident households (excluding net acquisitions of valuables)	Final consumption expenditure of private households
Collective consumption of private non-profit institutions serving households	Final consumption expenditure of non-profit institutions serving households
Final consumption of households	Final consumption expenditure of private households and non-profit institutions serving households
Final consumption of general government	Final consumption expenditure of general government
Final consumption of households + Social benefits in kind	Actual individual consumption
Final consumption of general government − Social benefits in kind	Actual collective consumption

Table 22.2   Contd

Previous terminology	Current terminology as per 1995 ESA
Saving	Saving
Gross capital formation	Gross capital formation

Gross fixed capital formation
  + Net acquisitions of military
      equipment and building for civil use
  + Net acquisitions of mineral
      exploration, computer software and
      copyrights
	Gross fixed capital formation

Change in stocks
  + Growing plants
  – Harvest and timber felling
	Changes in inventories

Indirect taxes
  – Subsidies
	Taxes on production and imports
	    – Subsidies
	    = Net taxes on production

Direct taxes	Current taxes on income, wealth, etc.

Table 22.3   Effects of 1995 ESA conceptual change on GDP and GNI

	In billion DEM
Extension of investment definition	+32
Depreciation on roads, bridges, military hospitals, etc.	+26
Garages for own use, repairs by homeowners	+7
Other changes causing production to increase	+2
Use of copyrights	−12
Government levies	−9
Subsidies	−6
Increase of threshold value for investment goods	−1
Total effects on GDP	**+39**
Reinvested profits, booking date of interest	+8
Copyright use, licences with rest of world	+5
Subsidies and production expenses from/to rest of world	−21
Total effects on GNI	**+31**

According to this, Germany's GDP for 1995 increased as a result of the concept by a total of DEM 39 billion, whereas GNI in contrast increased by around DEM 31 billion. These account for +1.1 per cent (GDP) and +0.9 per cent (GNI) on the data published before. There was a similar impact on other EU nations.

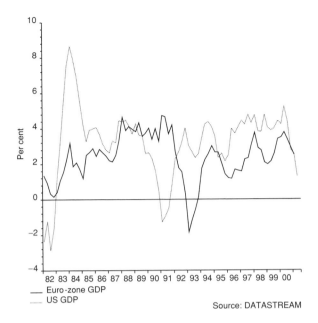

Source: DATASTREAM

Figure 22.1 Change in GDP for the Euro-zone and USA on preceding year

In addition to changes which affect the levels of the overall figures, the allocation of individual figures has also been restructured. Thus there is no closed company sector any more. Instead corporations will in the future be covered under the sectors of financial and non-financial corporations, whereas other companies without a legal identity, such as the self-employed and sole proprietors, will in future be assigned to the private household sector.

One problem with the calculation of economic flows in the Euro-zone is in surveying trading patterns between the Member States. These transactions are included in the calculation of the GDP figures. However, there are asymmetries between the individual nations (i.e., exports from one member state to another do not always correspond to the imports of the partner nations). For this reason, the effects of intra-Community trade on GDP are laden with uncertainty and should therefore be treated with caution.

The general problem for all statistical bodies producing national account data is that their main focus lies on the yearly data. But quarterly data have to be produced and these data have to be consistent with the yearly data. The quarterly accounts can be regarded as a simplified system of the yearly national accounts. They constitute a coherent set of transactions, accounts and balancing items, defined in both non-financial and financial domains, recorded on a quarterly basis. But the statistical methods used for compiling quarterly accounts may differ quite considerably from those used for annual accounts. However, as these two sets of data have to be consistent, in the case of flow variables, the sum of the quarterly accounts is equal to the annual figures for each year. To get this result, the same basic statistics should be used for the compilation of quarterly accounts as for annual accounts. The main problem is that these statistics are not always available on a quarterly basis or that they are less accurate when measured quarterly. This implies a different choice of basic statistics as, for quarterly accounts, the data must also be able to satisfy the demands of fast availability and reliability. To get such a result, the statistical offices have to rely on data that are published monthly, such as industrial production, retail sales statistics or, if no monthly data are available, the quarterly data are estimated by using extrapolations of annual estimates.

Periodicity/Revisions

Since the beginning of the EMU, national accounts data have been published somewhat earlier than before and now almost coincide with the data from

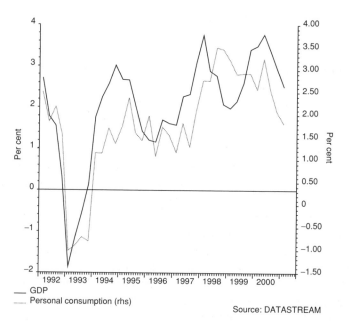

Figure 22.2   Change in Euro-zone GDP and personal consumption expenditure on preceding year

Germany, France and the Netherlands. Data publication takes place in the first week of the third month of the following quarter. One month later the initial revision of the Eurostat data is published, and a further revision follows one month later. The revision of the Eurostat data is primarily based on revised data from the individual states. By the first publication of the Euro-zone statistics, only three to four nations will have submitted data, so revisions are also necessary for a broader database. In addition, Austria, Ireland, Luxembourg and Portugal do not currently publish quarterly data, so some of the data have to be estimated by Eurostat. As the weighting of these nations is relatively small, Eurostat can resort to data for calculation of the quarterly statistics, accounting for over 90 per cent of the Euro-zone GDP. Publication of the EU statistics takes place at 12.00 CET (06.00 ET), whereas data from Germany are published at 08.00 CET (02.00 ET) data from France at 08.45 CET (02.45 ET) and data from Italy at 09.00 CET (03.00 ET).

Seasonal Adjustment

Data are seasonally adjusted. Until the end of 1999 Germany's data was supplied by the Bundesbank, as the German Federal Statistical Office used a completely different seasonal adjustment method compared to the other statistical offices. Starting with the values for the first quarter of 2000 the Bundesbank and the Federal Statistical Office now use the same seasonal adjustment method, so there is no longer any difference in the data. Data from the Netherlands, Spain and France are also adjusted in terms of calendar days by the national statistical offices, just like Germany's. The Eurostat data are seasonally adjusted by calculating aggregates for seasonally adjusted national statistics.

Notes

Histories of the national accounts reveal two problems. First, data were based on the ECU for the period before the beginning of EMU. As the exchange rates of participating Member States could still fluctuate within certain bandwidths and the value of the ECU was also affected by the exchange rate trends of currencies not participating in the EMU, comparisons of Euro-zone data with figures prior to the EMU are to be treated with caution. Second, Germany's figures surged forward as a result of reunification so care should also be taken with interpretation of longer-term studies.

The fact that Eurostat and the national authorities have agreed to adopt the 1995 ESA concept is a positive sign. This will ensure that data between EU Member States are comparable and facilitate international comparability.

Key Datastream Mnemonics

National Accounts (sa)	Datastream
Euro area	
GDP	EAESGD95D
GDP (since 1980)	EAGDP...D
GDP (%q/q)	EMESGDP.%
Domestic demand	EMEBDD..D
Private final consumption expenditures	EAESPN95D
Private final consumption expenditures (%q/q)	EMESPNCN%
Private final consumption (since 1980)	EACONEXPD
Government final consumption expenditure	EAESGV95D
Government final consumption expenditure (%q/q)	EMESGOVC%
Government final consumption expenditure (since 1980)	EAGOVCOND
Gross fixed capital formation	EAESGF95D
Gross fixed capital formation (%q/q)	EMESGFCF%
Gross fixed capital formation (since 1980)	EAGFCF..D
Changes in inventories	EAESCH95D
Changes in inventories (%GDP)	EMESCHIN%
External balance of goods and services	EAESET95D
External balance of goods and services (%GDP)	EMESTBAL%
External trade balance (since 1980)	EMEXTBALD
Exports	EAESEX95D
Imports	EAESIM95D
Gross value added:	
Total	EMEBVA..D
Agriculture, hunting, forestry and fishing activities	EMEBVAAGD
Manufacturing, energy and mining	EMEBVAMND
Construction	EMEBVACOD
Trade, repairs, hotels and restaurants, transport and communication	EMEBVATRD
Financial, real estate, renting and business activities	EMEBVAFID
Public administration, education, health and other services	EMEBVAPBD
Intermediate consumption of FISIM	EMEBFISID
Taxes less subsidies on products	EMEBTAXED
Deflators:	
GDP	EMESGDDFE
Domestic demand	EMEBDD..D
Private consumption	EAESPN95D
Government consumption	EAESGV95D
Gross fixed capital formation	EAESGF95D
Exports	EAESEX95D
Imports	EAESIM95D
Austria	
GDP	OEESGDP.D

National Accounts (sa)	Datastream
Belgium	
GDP	BGESGD95D
Finland	
GDP	FNESGD95D
France	
GDP	FRESGD95D
Domestic demand	FROCFFDD
Private final consumption expenditure	FRESPN95D
Government final consumption expenditure	FRESGV95D
Gross fixed capital formation	FRESGF95D
Change in inventories	FRESCH95D
External balance of goods and services	FRESET95D
Exports	FRESEX95D
Imports	FRESIM95D
Germany	
GDP	BDESGD95D
Domestic demand	BDOCFFDD
Private final consumption expenditure	BDESPN95D
Government final consumption expenditure	BDESGV95D
Gross fixed capital formation	BDESGF95D
Change in inventories	BDESCH95D
External balance of goods and services	BDESET95D
Exports	BDESEX95D
Imports	BDESIM95D
Greece	
GDP	GRESGD95
Ireland	
GDP	IRESGD95
Italy	
GDP	ITESGD95D
Domestic demand	ITOCFFDD
Private final consumption expenditure	ITESPN95D
Government final consumption expenditure	ITESGV95D
Gross fixed capital formation	ITESGF95D
Change in inventories	ITESCH95D
External balance of goods and services	ITESET95D
Exports	ITESEX95D
Imports	ITESIM95D
Luxembourg	
GDP	LXESGD95

National Accounts (sa)	Datastream
Netherlands	
GDP	NLESGD95D
Domestic demand	NLOCFFDD
Private final consumption expenditure	NLESPN95D
Government final consumption expenditure	NLESGV95D
Gross fixed capital formation	NLESGF95D
Change in inventories	NLESCH95D
External balance of goods and services	NLESET95D
Exports	NLESEX95D
Imports	NLESIM95D
Portugal	
GDP	PTESGDP.D
Spain	
GDP	ESESGD95D
Domestic demand	ESOCFFDD
Private final consumption expenditure	ESESPN95D
Government final consumption expenditure	ESESGV95D
Gross fixed capital formation	ESESGF95D
Change in inventories	ESESCH95D
External balance of goods and services	ESESET95D
Exports	ESESEX95D
Imports	ESESIM95D
EU15	
GDP	ECESGD95D
GDP (%q/q)	ECESGDP.%
Domestic demand	
Private final consumption expenditures	ECESPN95D
Private final consumption expenditures (%q/q)	ECESPNCN%
Government final consumption expenditure	ECESGV95D
Government final consumption expenditure (%q/q)	ECESGOVC%
Gross fixed capital formation	ECESGF95D
Gross fixed capital formation (%q/q)	ECESGFCF%
Changes in inventories	ECESCH95D
Changes in inventories (%GDP)	ECESCHIN%
External balance of goods and services	ECESET95D
External balance of goods and services (%GDP)	ECESTBAL%
Exports	ECESEX95D
Imports	ECESIM95D
Denmark	
GDP	DKESGD95D
Sweden	
GDP	SDESGD95C
United Kingdom	
GDP	UKESGD95D

Literature

Deutsche Bundesbank, 'Income, saving and capital formation in the nineties; results of the new ESA '95', *Monthly Report*, December 1999, pp. 49–62.

Essig, Hartmut, *et al.*, 'Revision der Volkswirtschaftlichen Gesamtrechnungen 1991 bis 1998', *Wirtschaft und Statistik* [Revision of national accounts 1991–1998, *Economics and Statistics*], 6/1999, pp. 449–78.

European Central Bank, 'The relative importance of domestic and foreign demand for output growth in the Euro area', *Monthly Report*, April 2000, pp. 27–9.

European Central Bank, 'Different ways of calculating the growth rate of GDP', *Monthly Report*, October 2000, p. 25.

Eurostat, *Handbook on Quarterly National Accounts*, Luxembourg, 1999.

Statistisches Bundesamt, 'Revision der Volkswirtschaftlichen Gesamtrechnungen 1999 – Anlass, Konzeptänderungen und neue Begriffe', *Wirtschaft und Statistik* [German Federal Statistical Office: Revision of national accounts 1999 – Reason, conceptual change and new terminology, *Economics and Statistics*], 4/1999, pp. 257–81.

22.2 Industrial Production

Data Source

Euro-zone data are published by Eurostat and national data are published by the statistical offices of the individual nations and the Deutsche Bundesbank. The press release by Eurostat is available on the Internet at www.europa.eu.int/comm/euroindicators. National data are available in part on the Internet sites of the respective statistical offices and the Deutsche Bundesbank. The data are also published in Table 5.2 of the ECB *Monthly Report* and in the publication *Eurostatistics – Data on short-term economic analysis* issued by Eurostat.

Importance for the Financial Markets   B

Description

Industrial production figures are a key economic indicator of monthly activity in the industrial sector, as the change in economic activity in the economy overall can normally be traced back to a change in industrial production. The index shows the value added at factor costs and at constant costs. Starting with the data for May 2001, the data are published for the following sectors:

- Total industry including construction
- Total industry excluding construction
- Manufacturing sector
- Construction
- Intermediate goods
- Capital goods
- Total consumer goods

Table 22.4 Individual nation as a proportion of
the total Index of Industrial Production,
excluding construction (2000)

Austria	3.3%
Belgium	4.0%
Finland	2.0%
France	18.9%
Germany	37.0%
Greece	0.7%
Ireland	1.5%
Italy	18.4%
Luxembourg	0.2%
Netherlands	4.8%
Portugal	1.6%
Spain	7.8%

- Durable consumer goods
- Non-durable consumer goods
- Energy

Thus not only data for the overall aggregate, but also some of the values of the key aggregate figures are published. The following sub-totals are added to calculate the factor costs:

- Turnover (excluding VAT)
- Immobilized production
- Other operating income
- Change in inventory
- Purchases of goods and services (negative sign)
- Tax on goods and production (negative sign)

However, in practice it is not always possible to define these totals accurately. This is why consumption of typical raw materials, energy or labour (input data) and volumes produced, deflated production values or sales values (output data) are often used instead.

Industrial production has the greatest influence on GDP fluctuations, even though the production sector does not account for the largest part of the economies. Starting with the data for May 2001, the composition of the published sectors (or Main Industrial Groupings – MIG) and the classification of the different activities by each Member State have been harmonized, The data covering the sectors have therefore been fundamentally revised. The weights of each MIG for the Euro-zone are as follows: intermediate goods 36.1 per cent, capital goods 25.2 per cent, durable consumer goods 4.4 per cent, non-durable

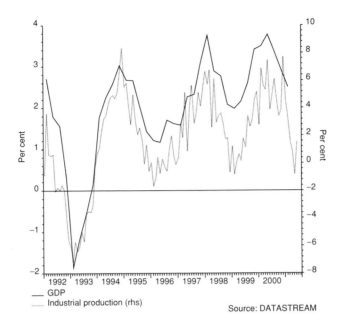

Figure 22.3   Change in Euro-zone GDP and industrial production on preceding year

consumer goods 22.2 per cent and energy 12.1 per cent. Eurostat converts the national figures into a weighted average, where the weighting from 1995 is currently used. Eurostat calculates the values for the Euro-zone, as soon as 60 per cent of the national data is received. The remaining data are first estimated and subsequently revised.

Data on construction is announced with a time lag of 1–2 months. These figures are based on statistics from nine of the twelve nations, as Ireland, Greece and Portugal do not produce construction figures. In addition, three nations calculate data only quarterly, so these values have to be estimated in the monthly publications.

Periodicity/Revisions

Eurostat produces its statistics with a time lag of 2–3 months. For this reason, only slight notice is taken of the Euro-zone data. The national statistics, on the other hand, are announced much earlier. Germany's data are normally published by the Deutsche Bundesbank in the first few days of the second month after the survey month, and the Netherlands and Italy then follow around one week later. A week after this France and Spain release their data. The national data are revised a number of times in the subsequent months. For the German data, for example, reasons for revisions include missing data. These are estimated on the basis of the preceding month's values. Consequently, the provisional values tend to show strong growth following months with high growth rates, whereas after weak months relatively weak growth is shown. These effects are then later compensated for in subsequent revisions. Revisions to national data mean that Eurostat data also have to be revised, so final data for the Euro-zone are only available after a time lag of several months. Publication of the EU data takes place at 12.00 CET (06.00 ET). Data from France are published at 08.45 CET (02.45 ET) and data from Italy at 09.00 CET (03.00 ET). There is no set time for publication of data from Germany.

Not all nations produce data every month. In the summer months, for example, the Netherlands and France have problems producing representative data due to temporary company closures for holidays and a lower than usual response rate. In France, therefore, for July and August only average values are published for the two months, while in the Netherlands the July data are announced one month later, with the August data.

Seasonal Adjustment

Data on industrial production are both seasonally and working-day adjusted. Eurostat publishes national seasonally adjusted data if available. (This is the case for Belgium, Denmark, Germany, France, Ireland, Italy, the Netherlands, Sweden, the UK and Finland.) For the other Member States Eurostat performs the adjustment. The seasonally adjusted Euro-zone and EU-15 data series are calculated using the so-called direct method. Therefore the working-day adjusted data are aggregated. Then the adjustment factors are calculated. Thus the Euro-zone and EU-15 seasonally adjusted growth rates might differ from the weighted growth rates based on the published national data. All Member States except Denmark calculate working-day adjusted series. For Denmark, Eurostat performs the working-days adjustment.

Notes

Fluctuations in GDP data occur largely due to fluctuations in industrial production. The importance of Eurostat data, however, is limited due to its late publication and the national statistics due to different definitions.

Key Datastream Mnemonics

Industrial Production (sa)	Datastream
Euro area	
Total including construction	EAESINPRG
Total excluding construction	EAESINXCG
Total excluding construction (% y/y, nsa)	EMESINXY%
Total excluding construction (% m/m, sa)	EMESINXM%
Total excluding construction (%, 3-month trend)	EMESINXC%
Manufacturing	EMESMNPRG
Manufacturing (% y/y, nsa)	EMESINPY%
Manufacturing (% m/m, sa)	EMESINPM%
Intermediate goods	EMEBIPM%H
Capital goods	EMEBIPI%H
Consumer goods	EMEBIPC%H
Durable consumer goods	
Non-durable consumer goods	
Energy	
Construction	EMESCONSG
Construction (% y/y, nsa)	EMESCONY%
Construction (% m/m, sa)	EMESCONM%
Austria	
Total including construction	OEOCFIPD
Total excluding construction	OEESINXCG
Belgium	
Total including construction	BGESINPRG
Total excluding construction	BGESINXCG
Finland	
Total including construction	FNESINPRG
Total excluding construction	FNESINXCG
France	
Total including construction	FRESINPRG
Total excluding construction	FRESINXCG
Manufacturing	FRESMNPRG
Construction	FRESCONSG
Germany	
Total including construction	BDESINPRG
Total excluding construction	BDESINXCG
Manufacturing	BDESMNPRG
Construction	BDESCONSG
Greece	
Total including construction	GROCFIPD
Total excluding construction	GRESINXCG

Industrial Production (sa)	Datastream
Ireland	
Total including construction	IRESINPRG
Total excluding construction	IRESINXCG
Italy	
Total including construction	ITESINPRG
Total excluding construction	ITESINXCG
Manufacturing	ITESMNPRG
Construction	ITESCONSG
Luxembourg	
Total including construction	LXESINPRG
Total excluding construction	LXESINXCG
Netherlands	
Total including construction	NLESINPRG
Total excluding construction	NLESINXCG
Manufacturing	NLESMNPRG
Construction	NLESCONSG
Portugal	
Total including construction	PTOCFIPD
Total excluding construction	PTESINXCG
Spain	
Total including construction	ESESINPRG
Total excluding construction	ESESINXCG
Manufacturing	ESESMNPRG
Construction	ESESCONSG
EU15	
Total including construction	ECESINPRG
Total excluding construction	ECESINXCG
Manufacturing	ECESMNPRG
Construction	ECESCONSG
Denmark	
Total including construction	DKESINPRG
Total excluding construction	DKESINXCG
Sweden	
Total including construction	SDOCFIPD
Total excluding construction	SDESINXCG
United Kingdom	
Total including construction	UKESINPRG
Total excluding construction	UKESINXCG

Literature

European Central Bank, 'Industrial production in the Euro area', *Monthly Report*, September 1999, pp. 28–30.

European Central Bank, 'Potential output growth and output gaps: concepts, uses and estimates', *Monthly Report*, October 2000, pp. 37–48.

22.3   Leading Economic Indicators

In Euro-zone, no 'official' leading indicator comparable to The Conference Board U.S. Index of Leading Indicators is available. There are, however, a number of indicators published by commercial banks and/or newspapers.

22.3.1   *Handelsblatt* Euro Economic Indicator

Data Source

The *Handelsblatt* Euro economic indicator is an indicator calculated by the *Handelsblatt* on the basis of economic data already published. It is published both on the Internet at www.handelsblatt.com and in the printed edition of the *Handelsblatt*.

Importance for the Financial Markets   D

Description

Since October 1999 the *Handelsblatt* Euro Economic Indicator (Eurokonjunktur-Indikator) for the Euro-zone has been published following the *Handelsblatt* Leading Indicator (see section 22.3.5). The reference value is therefore the seasonally adjusted moving average for the Euro-zone GDP. This method can lead to discrepancies between values in annual accounts for the Euro-zone GDP and the data published for this indicator. As the data employed are made available earlier and due to the great attention paid to seasonally adjusted data, this method is justifiable. The indicator is composed of six sub-indicators. These include:

- EU Industrial Confidence Indicator (with a weighting of 40 per cent)
- EU Consumer Confidence Indicator (10 per cent)
- EU industrial production excluding construction (20 per cent)
- M2 monetary aggregate (10 per cent)
- Inflation rate in Euro-zone, measured via Harmonized Consumer Price Index (10 per cent)
- Term-structure of interest rates, calculated as the difference in monthly average return on 10-year government securities in the Euro-zone minus the three-month Euribor rate (10 per cent)

The two confidence indicators are each input into the calculation as indicator values. Industrial production, the money supply and the inflation rate are taken into account in the form of a rate of change compared to the preceding month. With the Euro Economic Indicator the latest available values are input, whereby the structure of interest rates is based on the data published in the ECB *Monthly*

Report. This produces the following time lags between the economic indicator and the respective sub-indicators:

- EU Industrial Confidence Indicator   1 month
- EU Consumer Confidence Indicator   1 month
- EU industrial production excluding construction   4 months
- M2 monetary aggregate   3 months
- Inflation rate   2 months
- Term-structure of interest rates   2 months

Periodicity/Revisions

The indicator is published mid-month in the *Handelsblatt*. Revisions can extend over several months, as long as the sub-indicators are also revised.

Seasonal Adjustment

Some of the individual indicators are input into the calculation in their seasonally adjusted form. However, the overall index is not seasonally adjusted again.

Notes

The *Handelsblatt* Euro Economic Indicator, like many other indicators for the Euro-zone, only has a relatively short history to date. It is therefore not yet

Source: DATASTREAM

Figure 22.4 Change in *Handelsblatt* Euro Economic Indicator and Euro-zone GDP (moving annual rate) on preceding year

possible to estimate how the forecasting quality will develop in the coming months and years. Above all, with the growing database it is likely that a revision of the indicator structure will be necessary.

Unlike the *Handelsblatt* Leading Indicator for the GDP reference value, seasonally adjusted data are used for the calculation of the moving annual rate. This method was selected for the Leading Indicator to avoid the problem of seasonal adjustment. If the annual rate is produced using seasonally adjusted data for the Euro Economic Indicator, this now represents a form of 'double' seasonal adjustment.

The confidence indicators produced by the EU Commission have a very high weighting of 50 per cent. This can be explained primarily by the good forecasting results of these sub-indicators in the past. In contrast to the two other indicators produced by the *Handelsblatt*, no data are used on new orders. As such data are not yet available, industrial production is taken as the basis. The M2 monetary aggregate is taken into account and not the M3 definition used by the ECB as the target value. The reason for this is that the connection between M2 and economic growth is closer than the other monetary aggregates. As the lead of M2 to growth is relatively long and unstable, this sub-indicator is only used with a low weighting of 10 per cent in the calculation. The inflation rate is taken into account because purchasing power falls with rising price levels, thereby negatively affecting real economic growth. For this reason this sub-indicator is also entered as a negative figure in the calculation. Finally, the term-structure of interest rates is included because a reduction in the interest rate difference between the short and long end of the interest curve is normally a sign of more restrictive monetary policy, which then acts as a restraint on economic growth.

Key Datastream Mnemonics

Handelsblatt Euro Economic Indicator	Datastream
Euro Economic Indicator	EMHANDELR

Literature

Van Suntum, Ulrich, 'Die Konjunktur in der Eurozone hat zum Aufschwung angesetzt' [The economy in the Euro-zone prepares for recovery], *Handelsblatt*, 18 October 1999, p. 9.

Van Suntum, Ulrich, 'From the Handelsblatt Frühindikator for Germany to the Handelsblatt-Eurokonjunkturindikator for the Euro-zone', Stierle, Michael (ed.), *Wirtschaftsdaten, Konjunkturprognosen und ihre Auswirkungen auf die Finanzmärkte* [*Economic Indicators, Economic Forecast and the Impact on Financial Markets*], INFER Studies Vol. 2, Verlag für Wissenschaft und Forschung, 2000, pp. 55–65.

22.3.2   DZ Bank Euro Indicator

Data Source

The DZ Bank Euro Indicator is produced by the Economics Department of the DZ Bank and published in the *Frankfurter Allgemeine Zeitung*. The latest release of the indicator is available on the Internet at www.dzbank.de.

Importance for the Financial Markets   D

Description

Since the end of 1998 the DZ Bank (formerly DG Bank) has produced the Euro Indicator, which serves as a leading indicator for the economy in the Euro-zone. The calculation concept is similar to the US Index of Leading Indicators issued by the Conference Board where sub-indicators, which are already published, are standardized and totalled to form an overall indicator. All the available data at the time of calculation are included, which means that there is no fixed base month from which sub-indicators are used. The time lag can amount to up to three months, whereas for the daily available interest and share index, for example, no time lag is necessary.

   The aim of the indicator is to portray the trend in the entire economic area of the Euro-zone. This is why Europe-wide data series are used as far as possible. For the sub-indicators where this is not possible due to data not being available, indicators from the individual nations are aggregated using GDP weightings from 1997. The time series employed should cover the broadest possible spectrum of the economy and have the longest possible lead up to the actual trend.

   Five areas are included overall.

1. **Prospects in manufacturing sector**
   This sector is described by three indicator components:
   (a) Monthly new orders from Germany, France, the Netherlands, Italy, Spain, Belgium and Ireland;
   (b) Production expectations based on the EU Industrial Survey;
   (c) Reuters Purchasing Managers' Index for the Euro-zone.
2. **Prospects in construction**
   For this sector the monthly data on building permits in Germany, France and the Netherlands are used.
3. **Prospects for private consumption**
   This sector is calculated with the EU Consumer Confidence Survey.
4. **Labour market**
   The situation on the labour market is analyzed by looking at jobs available in Germany, France, Spain, Austria, Belgium, Finland and Luxembourg. However, only the data from Germany and France are taken into consideration

for the first publication of the indicator. Data from the other nations are only included in the revisions as they are announced later.

5. **Financial market indicators**

The sector covering the financial markets is described using three sub-indicators:

(a) M3 real monetary aggregate, i.e., the monetary aggregate deflated with the Harmonized Consumer Price Index for the Euro-zone;

(b) term-structure of interest rates, calculated from the difference in the monthly moving averages between the 10-year benchmark bond yield and the 3-month Euribor rate;

(c) MSCI stock index for the Euro-zone.

The sub-indicators go into an overall index in a weighted form. The basis of the weighting is the volatility of sub-indicators, measured in terms of their standard deviation. The standardization factors are calculated using a total normed to one of the reciprocal values of the standard deviations. The standardized change in a component is then the change in this sub-indices on the preceding month, multiplied by the respective standardization factor. The individual factors are shown in Table 22.5.

The standard deviation of the money supply is still distorted as there is only a short historical time series to date, and its variance is far less than the variance of the M2 money supply employed initially by the EMU 4 states (France, Germany, Italy, Spain). This figure now receives a far higher weighting than in the original version of the Euro Indicator. With the structure of interest rates there is the problem that the time series is even shorter, as no data are available for the time prior to the EMU. For this reason, DEM interest is taken as the basis in this case. The same applies to Reuters Purchasing Managers' Index,

Table 22.5 Weighting factors for sub-indices of DZ Bank Euro Indicator

Sub-indices	Standard deviation	Reciprocal	Weighting factor
New orders	1.815	0.551	0.053
Production expectations	2.116	0.473	0.047
Reuters Purchasing Managers' Index	1.097	0.912	0.104
Building permits	5.734	0.174	0.016
Consumer confidence	1.297	0.771	0.082
Jobs available	2.231	0.448	0.044
Monetary aggregate	0.398	2.511	0.239
Term-structure of interest rates	0.247	4.055	0.396
Stock index	4.708	0.212	0.020
Total		10.107	1.000

in which values from the German and Italian Purchasing Managers' Indices are included, which have a longer history than the EMU Index.

The calculation of the actual indicators is executed in eight steps.

1. In the first step the data used is collected, the data series is updated and any necessary transformations, such as seasonal adjustment, are carried out.
2. For the series, where necessary, data from the individual nations are aggregated using GDP weightings.
3. For the individual components the monthly change is obtained. For level figures a symmetrical percentage change is obtained based on the following formula:

$$x_t = \frac{X_t - X_{t-1}}{X_t + X_{t-1}} * 200$$

and for percentage figures, such as the structure of interest rates, a simple difference using the following formula is obtained:

$$x_t = X_t - X_{t-1}$$

4. The monthly changes are standardized in accordance with the method described above.
5. Only individual series with time lags are shifted to produce a value for the current month.
6. The total of standardized and shifted monthly changes is the monthly change in the Euro Indicator.
7. The level of the indicator is calculated for the base month from the formula below:

$$I[t] = \frac{200 + i[1]}{200 - i[1]}$$

and for the following months in accordance with the following formula:

$$I[t] = I[t-1] * \frac{200 + i[t]}{200 - i[t]}$$

8. The indicator is rebased to 100 for the average value for 1995.

Periodicity/Revisions

The indicator is published around the end of the month. As data are input in the calculation published by other bodies and also subsequently revised, revisions are conducted for the indicator as long as the sub-indicators are revised. In addition, the structure of the indicator is regularly revised. If the structure of the conditions no longer accurately reflects the Euro-zone economy, a structural change may be conducted which in turn leads to revision of the respective data.

Seasonal Adjustment

The sub-indicators are published in a seasonally adjusted form. The DZ Bank Euro Indicator is, however, not seasonally adjusted overall.

Notes

The DZ Bank Euro Indicator does not have a very long history. However, it covers the Euro-zone economy with a lead of around a quarter very efficiently, so it can be seen as a useful leading indicator of economic development. This should also change for the better, as soon as the database is broader and the structure of the indicator is aligned to changes in the data situation. The structure was last reviewed at the beginning of the year 2000 and the weightings were last updated in January 2001.

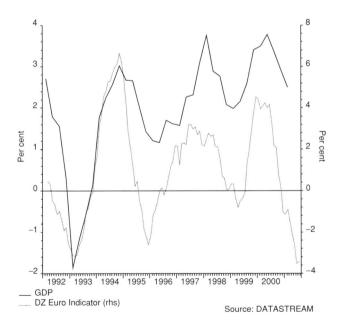

Figure 22.5 Change in Euro-zone GDP and DZ Bank Euro Indicator on preceding year

Key Datastream Mnemonics

DZ Bank Euro Indicator	Datastream
Euro Indicator	EMDKEMINA
m/m change	EMDKINDMR
y/y change	EMDKINDYY

Literature

Bahr, Holger, *Konjunkturelle Gesamtindikatoren* [Overall economic indicators], Verlag Peter Lang, 2000, pp. 104–8.

DG Bank, 'Der DG Bank Euro-Indikator: Ein neuer Frühindikator für die europäische Konjunktur', *Konjunktur und Kapitalmarkt* [DG Bank Euro Indicator – A new leading indicator for the European economy, *Economy and Capital Market*], September 1998, pp. 15–21.

DG Bank, 'DG Bank Euro-Indikator: Bisherige Entwicklung und anstehende Veränderungen', *Konjunktur und Kapitalmarkt* [DG Bank Euro indicator – Trend to date and future changes, *Economy and Capital Market*], January 1999, pp. 4–6.

Heise, Michael, Holstein, Michael and Jäckel, Hans, 'Ein Frühindikator für die europäische Konjunktur' [A leading indicator for the European economy], *Frankfurter Allgemeine Zeitung*, 5 October 1998, p. 21.

22.3.3   SZ-Euroland-Indicator

Data Source

The SZ-Euroland-Indicator is designed by the Economics Department of the DGZ•DekaBank and is published in the Süddeutsche Zeitung. The Indicator is available on the Internet at www.dgz-dekabank.com.

Importance for the Financial Markets   D

Description

In May 2000 the Economics Department of the DGZ•DekaBank presented the SZ-Euroland-Indicator. The objective of the composite indicator is that the peaks and troughs of cyclical swings should be signalled reliably and at an early stage. For this purpose, the turning points to be signalled by the index must be determined first. The GDP figures published quarterly would seem to be the most suitable variable for measuring economic performance at the level of the economy as a whole. However, in order to be able to work with data that are available on a monthly basis, the seasonally adjusted index of net output in the manufacturing sector (excluding the construction industry) within the Euro-zone is used. The objective is to transform the index of net output in such a way that an accurate evaluation of economic activity is possible or, in other words, that a so-called reference series can be obtained that reflects the performance of the economy as a whole. On both theoretical and empirical grounds, the deviation of net output from its trend was used. The reason for this is that when someone speaks of cyclical swings the reference is, in fact, to fluctuations in the economy's rate of capacity utilisation, measured here as the deviation from the trend line obtained with a Hodrick-Prescott filter (HP filter). The percentage deviations of net output from the trend line obtained in this way constitute the reference series for the SZ-Euroland-Indicator.

The sub-series of this composite indicator are selected if they mirror the fluctuations in economic activity satisfactorily. This means that their cyclical turning points lead those in the reference series and that this lead should be as stable as possible. Since July 2001, the SZ-Euroland-Indicator is based on five individual series:

- Ifo sub-indicator on business expectations for the manufacturing sector
- Reuters Purchasing Managers' Index for Manufacturing Sector in Euro-zone
- New orders in manufacturing industry in Germany, Italy and the Netherlands, included as a weighted 3-month rate of change
- Interest-rate differential, calculated with the 10-year government bonds yield and the 3-month Euro inter bank offered rate (Euribor)
- MSCI Stock Index for Euro-zone, calculated as the change in the end-of-month value on preceding year

The aggregation procedure follows sound arguments on the one hand for taking into consideration the time relationships that exist among the series involved, and on the other for determining an explicit weighting that takes into account the different degrees of volatility of the five individual series. Those series with the longest leads are shifted backwards, so they do not enter with their current values. The effect of this shift is that the cyclical swings that occur with the passage of time lie together as far as possible, with the result that, ideally, the turning points of all series will fall in the same month. It is this characteristic in the construction of the SZ-Euroland-Indicator that distinguishes it most clearly from other indexes of aggregate economic activity.

The method for the determination of the weights named 'principal components analysis' relies on the idea that the fluctuations of each series reflects two elements; namely fluctuations common to the group of variables on the one hand, and variable-specific developments on the other. The first part, the so-called 'principal component', can be deemed to represent developments in the business cycle. The so-called factor loads of this 'principal component' constitute a measure of the correlation between economic activity and individual series. By normalizing the factor loads to one, the weights of the five indicators to be included can be obtained directly.

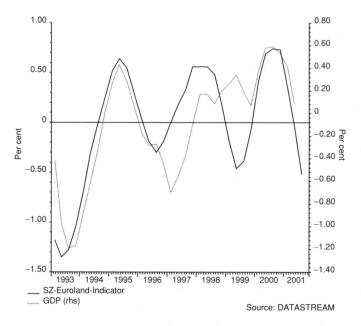

Figure 22.6   Standard deviation from trend of the SZ-Euroland-Indicator and GDP

Table 22.6   Weighting factors and lag structure of sub-indices of the SZ-Euroland-Indicator

Sub-indices	Difference between published and used data (in month)	Weighting factors (in per cent)
Ifo business expectations	2	24.5
Reuters Purchasing Managers' Index	1	24.2
New orders	6	20.9
Interest rate differential	7	19.6
MSCI stock index EMU	1	10.9

All five selected series lead the reference series by at least three months. For the current indicator value the latest available data are used, i.e., the new orders enter the composite indicator with a difference of five months to the stock index and the interest-rate differential with a difference of six months.

Periodicity/Revisions

The SZ-Euroland-Indicator is always published on a Saturday around the middle of a month. The indicator is revised as long as the sub-series are revised. This only is the case for the new orders statistics from Germany, Italy and the

Netherlands, which are subject to revisions by the national authorities. However, since the new orders enter the index with a time lag, the need for revision, which principally applies to the value for the previous month when the latest monthly value is published, ceases to be a relevant issue. The only remaining revisions to be considered are the annual revisions of new orders together with their seasonal adjustments, which subsequently may have a marginal influence on the historical data of the SZ-Euroland-Indicator.

Seasonal Adjustment

Three of the five components are seasonally adjusted, while the SZ-Euroland-Indicator by itself is not.

Notes

Since the SZ-Euroland-Indicator has a short history only, its impact on the financial markets is limited. Nevertheless, the SZ-Euroland-Indicator provides a clear description of economic activity in the nineties by measuring the fluctuations in capacity utilization through deviation from the trend. For the quarterly presentation the arithmetic mean is computed from the corresponding three monthly values of the SZ-Euroland-Indicator. This series is then subjected in a further step to smoothing with the moving asymmetric three-month average, before finally being standardized with the mean and the standard deviation of the trend deviation of real GDP. This results in an adaptation of the two series to each other which, however cautious someone may be with regard to quantitative interpretation, does nevertheless allow certain conclusions to be drawn concerning the strength of cyclical swings. The lead of the indicator with respect to the reference series does not apply equally to both peaks and troughs. Whereas in boom phases the index tends to turn downwards simultaneously with GDP with the result that the informational lead remains as the only analytical gain, troughs are signalled significantly earlier by the SZ-Euroland-Indicator.

Key Datastream Mnemonics

SZ-Euroland-Indicator	Datastream
SZ-Euroland-Indicator, monthly	EMSZINDMR
SZ-Euroland-Indicator, quarterly	EMSZINDQR

Literature

Bahr, Holger, *Konjunkturelle Gesamtindikatoren* [Overall economic indicators], Verlag Peter Lang, 2000, pp. 115–21.

Bahr, Holger, 'Der SZ-Euroland-Indikator in neuer Form' [The SZ-Euroland-Indicator with a new structure], in *Konjunktur – Zinsen – Währungen* [Business cycle – interest rates – Currencies], DGZ•DekaBank, August 2001, pp. 2–9.
Bahr, Holger and Huether, Michael, 'Indikator in neuer Form' [Indicator with a new structure], *Sueddeutsche Zeitung*, July 14–15 2001, p. 21.

22.3.4   *FAZ* Economic Indicator

Data Source

The *FAZ* Economic Indicator (*FAZ*-Konjunkturindikator) is produced by the Kiel Institute of World Economics and published monthly in the *Frankfurter Allgemeine Zeitung* (*FAZ*). The data are currently not available on the Internet.

Importance for the Financial Markets   D

Description

The Kiel Institute of World Economics has produced an overall economic index for West Germany since the end of 1989. Its construction is based on the US Index of Leading Indicators and predicts economic turning points. The reference figure is the difference in the trend of industrial net production in West Germany (excluding the construction sector). With the modification of the indicator in 1993 it was initially planned to extend the forecasting capacity to include the whole of Germany. However, due to problems with the database this project has been temporarily abandoned.

A total of six sub-indicators with different weightings are currently input into the indicator calculation:

- Number of jobs advertised in the *FAZ* (with a weighting of 5 per cent)
- New orders in the manufacturing sector in West Germany (18 per cent)
- *FAZ* stock index (5 per cent)
- Ifo Business Climate Index for the manufacturing sector in West Germany (32 per cent)
- Effective exchange rate of Euro (13 per cent)
- Interest-rate differential, expressed as difference of yield on bonds outstanding and interest rate for three months' money (27 per cent)

The sub-indicators were selected on the basis that the series should show a clear lead with a comparatively stable lead period. In addition, the series must be available after two months at the latest, so the values are always incorporated with a constant time lapse of two months. In addition, the sub-indicators may only undergo relatively minor revisions. Weighting was obtained via regression analysis for the years 1978–93. As the *FAZ* stock index and interest rates are available on trading days, these series are included in the calculation as monthly averages. Jobs vacancies are advertised weekly in the *FAZ*, although the number of vacancies does vary substantially. This value is therefore balanced out with a three-month moving average.

For the indicator calculation, changes compared to the preceding months are initially calculated for the individual series. For the interest-rate differential and the Ifo Business Climate Index this took the form of a difference. The effective exchange rate is input with inversed figures. Then the monthly changes are divided by the mean value of all absolute changes to make the fluctuations in the individual series comparable. Finally, the standardized rates of change are totalled and divided by the number of series included, thereby producing the monthly change in the overall index. The *FAZ* Economic Indicator has been calculated retrospectively going back to 1975. Since then the monthly changes have been totalled. The value of the *FAZ* Indicator was initially set at 1985 = 100; however, since the revision in 1993 the average for the year 1991 = 100 has been employed.

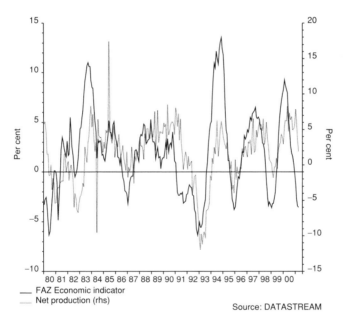

Source: DATASTREAM

Figure 22.7 Change in *FAZ* Economic Indicator and net production in the manufacturing sector of Germany on preceding year

Periodicity/Revisions

The indicator is always calculated in the first or second week of the month, as soon as all values for the reference month are available, and then published immediately. As with the selection of sub-indicators where revisions are comparatively minor, revisions to the overall indicator are limited, although revisions may be conducted over several months. These are also conducted with the alignment of the seasonal adjustment factors.

Seasonal Adjustment

Of the sub-indicators, only new orders and the Ifo Business Climate Index are seasonally adjusted. All other sub-indicators are incorporated without adjustment.

Notes

The *FAZ* Economic Indicator has the advantage that it has a long history to fall back on, although this advantage is offset, to some extent, by the fact that it only relates to West Germany. The indicator is very well suited to signalling economic turning points in advance, although due to the revision of the calculation method the lead has been shortened somewhat and now only accounts for around six months. In the past it showed that the economic turning point always occurred when the indicator turned by more than 2 per cent over a minimum period of five months. In addition, the indicator is only of limited use when changes of pace in economic growth are to be forecasted.

Key Datastream Mnemonics

FAZ Economic Indicator	Datastream
Economic Indicator	

Literature

Bahr, Holger, *Konjunkturelle Gesamtindikatoren* [Overall economic indicators], Verlag Peter Lang, 2000, pp. 86–90.

Langfeldt, Enno, 'Der *FAZ*-Konjunkturindikator – ein Hilfsmittel zur Prognose' [The *FAZ* economic indicator – a tool for forecasting], *Frankfurter Allgemeine Zeitung*, 11 December 1989, p. 19.

Langfeldt, Enno, '*FAZ*-Konjunkturindikator deutet auf vorsichtige Belebung' [*FAZ* economic indicator signals slight upturn], *Frankfurter Allgemeine Zeitung*, 9 September 1993, p. 17.

22.3.5   *Handelsblatt* Leading Indicator

Data Source

The *Handelsblatt* Leading Indicator (*Handelsblatt* Frühindikator) is a German indicator produced by the *Handelsblatt* on the basis of various published economic data. It is available on the Internet at www.handelsblatt.com and in the printed edition of the *Handelsblatt*.

Importance for the Financial Markets   C

Description

The financial paper, *Handelsblatt*, has published a leading indicator since January 1992 designed to forecast economic turning points in Germany on the basis of data already published. Since January 1995 it has also published the *Handelsblatt*- Konjunkturbarometer Ost [*Handelsblatt* Economic Barometer for the East], which specifically analyzes the situation in the former East German states and which, since November 1999, has been published together with the Leading Indicator. Data for the *Handelsblatt* Leading Indicator were calculated back to the year 1980 and for the Economic Barometer back to 1992. The indicator is designed to run ahead of actual economic development by around three months. It supplies information on the trend and level of GDP growth approximately six months prior to publication of the national German figures.

Since January 1993 the *Handelsblatt* indicator has been calculated on the basis of the following indicators, which show the following lead time attributes confirmed in empirical studies and theoretically proven in terms of the GDP:

- New orders in manufacturing industry (with a weighting of 20 per cent)
- New orders in construction sector (10 per cent)
- Real retail sales (30 per cent)
- Ifo Business Climate Index for the manufacturing industry (30 per cent)
- Term-structure of interest rates calculated as the difference between the monthly averages of yield on bonds outstanding and the three-month Euribor (10 per cent)

The indicator calculation therefore includes the latest available values in each case. This results in the following delays between the *Handelsblatt* Leading Indicator and the respective sub-indicators:

- New orders in manufacturing industry   3 months
- New orders in construction sector   4 months
- Retail sales   3 months
- Ifo Business Climate Index   2 months
- Term-structure of interest rates   2 months

This means, for example, that the Ifo Business Climate Index for February is used in the April indicator. The data for the structure of interest rates are also incorporated with a time lapse of two months, although they are available

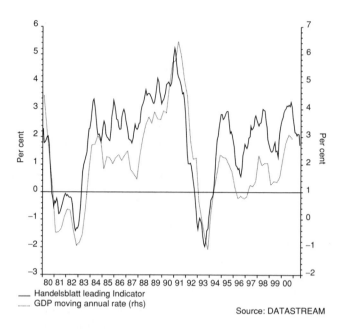

Figure 22.8 Change in *Handelsblatt* Leading Indicator and West Germany GDP (moving annual rate) on preceding year

on trading days. The reason for this is that data published by the Bundesbank and ECB in their monthly reports are incorporated into the calculation, and the 'latest values' of these are only available after a time lapse of several weeks.

Stock prices were also included in the original calculation. These are no longer included as they have a less stable influence on the GDP than the other figures. Values for new orders and retail sales go into the calculation in the seasonally adjusted Bundesbank form and as harmonized growth rates for the index values. The weighting is the result of a study of empirical links between these figures and the GDP trend for the period 1980–92. As the individual data series fluctuate to different degrees, they are standardized for the calculation of the *Handelsblatt* indicator using standard deviation and mean value, so that each sub-indicator is allocated the same influencing factor prior to weighting. A value of one is added to each standardized monthly value. Finally the sum of standardized and weighted sub-indicator values is multiplied by a value of 0.02. This factor corresponds to the average growth rate of the moving average annual GDP selected as the reference value so that the indicator almost fluctuates around this trend.

The moving average annual GDP rate, which is selected as the reference value for the *Handelsblatt* Leading Indicator, reflects the growth of the unadjusted actual GDP in the last four quarters respectively compared to the corresponding period from the previous year. This gets round the problem of seasonal adjustment as the value always covers twelve months, even if it only corresponds to a calendar year at year-end. The calculation of the average rates is based on the following formula:

$$\text{AAR}_t = \frac{\displaystyle\sum_{i=t-3}^{t} \text{GDP}_i - \sum_{i=t-7}^{t-4} \text{GDP}_i}{\displaystyle\sum_{i=t-7}^{t-4} \text{GDP}_i}$$

where
AAR_t = annual average rate at quarter t
GDP_i = value of GDP in quarter i

Four quarters are considered to eliminate the problem of seasonal fluctuations with the GDP and smooth the trend, so that individual quarters with special effects have only minor influence.

Whereas in the original *Handelsblatt* Leading Indicator calculation new order and retail sales figures are input in the form of indices, they are now incorporated as harmonized growth rates, even if they are still shown in the *Handelsblatt* publication as index figures. The harmonization is conducted on the seasonally adjusted figures from the Deutsche Bundesbank to obtain the monthly updated growth trend for the individual series. Consequently not just the latest values are included in the calculation of the *Handelsblatt* Leading Indicator. Extreme values of these three sub-indicators are thereby not given the opportunity to forecast changes in economic trends. With long recovery and downturn periods in particular, a strong reversal in these indicators could turn around this leading indicator.

In contrast to the *Handelsblatt* Leading Indicator, which relates to Pan Germany, the Economic Barometer for the East examines the situation only in the former East German states. Values for the barometer are available from the second quarter of 1992. Up to the end of 1998 the reference value for the Economic Barometer was the East German GDP. From this time special data were only made available in a limited form for the former East German states so the Economic Barometer no longer relates to a specific reference value but is just an indicator for the situation in these states. In 1998 the Economic Barometer underwent comprehensive revision as the forecasting quality kept declining with the rapid rate of change in the new states and the lack of adequate coverage of economic activity due to the sub-indicators previously used. Since the revision there are now five sub-indicators which are input into the calculation for the East German Economic Barometer. These are:

- New orders in the East German manufacturing sector (with a weighting of 15 per cent)
- New orders in the East German construction sector (40 per cent)
- Ifo Business Climate Index for the manufacturing sector (25 per cent)
- Ifo Business Climate Index for the East German retail trade (10 per cent)
- Ifo Business Climate Index for trade and industry in East Germany (10 per cent)

The Ifo Business Climate Index for trade and industry is a recent incorporation. This ensures that coverage of economic activities has risen, even though the service sector is no longer included.

The weighting of the individual time series diverging from the overall *Handelsblatt* Leading Indicator is produced from the peculiarities of the East German business cycle. The revised weightings are also very different from the original weightings. The reason for this is that economic structure changed so dramatically in the first few years after reunification that the original weightings no longer reflected the actual situation in East Germany. In addition, investment continues to be far less interest-elastic than in the former West German states due to the subsidies, so this figure has been abandoned.

The latest available values are also input into the calculation of the Economic Barometer. The following delays are thereby produced between the barometer and the respective sub-indicators:

- New orders in manufacturing industry   3 months
- New orders in construction sector   3 months
- Ifo Business Climate Index for manufacturing industry   2 months
- Ifo Business Climate Index for retail   2 months
- Ifo Business Climate Index for trade and industry   2 months

The standardization factors for the sub-indicators were also updated in the 1998 revision. In particular, the extreme growth rates in the first years of unification are no longer included as these were increasingly distorting current data. The economic indicator value for the East is obtained using two alignment factors for the sub-indicators. These factors are selected so that the data series is as close as possible both to the long-term level of the GDP as well as the progression pattern.

Periodicity/Revisions

The indicators are always published in the *Handelsblatt* at the beginning of the month. Revisions may extend over several months as long as the sub-indicators are also revised.

Seasonal Adjustment

With the *Handelsblatt* Leading Indicator new orders and retail sales are seasonally adjusted in accordance with the method used by the Bundesbank. The Ifo Business Climate Index is incorporated in the form adjusted by the Ifo Institute. These seasonally adjusted data are then included in the indicator calculation. The indicator itself is not seasonally adjusted again. The reference figure, the real GDP, is also used in its non-seasonally adjusted form. With the Economic Barometer for the East only the Ifo Business Climate Indices are seasonally adjusted. Data on new orders, on the other hand, are not adjusted prior to inclusion in the calculation.

Notes

The *Handelsblatt* Leading Indicator is one of the oldest economic indicators calculated by newspapers or news agencies to provide early turning signals on the economic cycle. With its long history and forecasting quality, it is highly regarded. Even so, precise forecasting of growth rates is neither possible nor desirable with the indicator. It is designed rather to provide reliable information on trends and the level of GDP growth, and above all to predict economic turning points. Moreover, in recent years it has suffered somewhat in terms of its forecasting quality, as it only showed the economic highs of 1995 and 1998 and the low of 1996 with a slight time delay. This will probably be taken as an opportunity for a critical appraisal of the composition of the sub-indicators and, where necessary, the model structure and modification of the indicator.

Since November 1999 the Handelsblatt Leading Indicator and the Economic Barometer have been published at the same time and no longer on different dates. This was triggered by the fact that the reference figure of the economic barometer (East German GDP) was no longer available after the beginning of 1999. This meant that the value for October 1999 became assigned to the month of November due to the change in the publication date. The preceding monthly values of the economic barometer and the assignment of the respective sub-indicators thereby lead by a month.

The Economic Barometer suffers from the fact that the history of the individual indicators relating to the specific situation in East Germany is very brief. For this reason the links between the Economic Barometer and the actual progression of the economy are not exactly modelled. This is also the reason why the term 'barometer' and not 'indicator' is used. The intention was to portray the qualitative differences between these two statistics. The Economic Barometer is important because it is the only statistic of its kind to refer exclusively to the former East German states. This importance will decline in time as differences between East and West Germany disappear.

Key Datastream Mnemonics

Handelsblatt Leading Indicator	Datastream
West Germany	BDHANDELR
East Germany	

Literature

Bahr, Holger, *Konjunkturelle Gesamtindikatoren* [Overall economic indicators], Verlag Peter Lang, 2000, pp. 91–100.

Van Suntum, Ulrich, 'Handelsblatt-Frühindikator bleibt abwärts gerichtet' [Handelsblatt leading indicator downturn continues], *Handelsblatt*, 18 January 1993, p. 8.

Van Suntum, Ulrich, 'Der Handelsblatt-Frühindikator signalisiert bevorstehende konjunkturelle Wendepunkte' [The Handelsblatt leading indicator signals future economic turning points], *Handelsblatt*, 24/25 January 1992, p. 5.

Van Suntum, Ulrich, 'Das Konjunkturbarometer Ost ergänzt den Handelsblatt-Frühindikator' [The economic barometer for the East supplements the Handelsblatt leading indicator], *Handelsblatt*, 27/28 January 1995, p. 6.

Van Suntum, Ulrich, 'Die sieben mageren Jahre im Osten gehen zu Ende' [The seven lean years in the East are over], *Handelsblatt*, 29/30 May 1998, p. 8.

Van Suntum, Ulrich, 'Konjunkturaufschwung gewinnt an Kraft' [Economic recovery is getting stronger], *Handelsblatt*, 4 November 1999, p. 7.

Van Suntum, Ulrich, 'From the Handelsblatt Frühindikator for Germany to the Handelsblatt-Eurokonjunkturindikator for the Euro-zone', Stierle, Michael (ed.), *Wirtschaftsdaten, Konjunkturprognosen und ihre Auswirkungen auf die Finanzmärkte* [Economic Indicators, Economic Forecast and the Impact on Financial Markets], INFER Studies Vol. 2, Verlag für Wissenschaft und Forschung, 2000, pp. 55–65.

23
Company Surveys

Within the EMU there are now several surveys for monitoring the economic situation. Most of the surveys are conducted at national level, although some of the results are summarized in an overall index by the EU Commission. The EU Commission not only publishes surveys on the situation in the industrial sector but also on consumer confidence and the situation in the construction sector. These surveys are conducted and published simultaneously. Details on surveys outside the company sector are shown subsequently.

23.1   EU Industrial Survey

Data Source

Data are surveyed by research institutes in the individual member countries within the context of their own survey. They then pass on the relevant parts of the results to the EU Commission, which aggregates the data, conducts seasonal adjustment and publishes the overall indices. A summary of the data is available on the Internet at europa.eu.int/comm/economy_finance/index_en.htm. More detailed data is published in the publication *European Economy*, Supplement B.

Importance for the Financial Markets   C

Description

Since 1962, the EU Commission has produced a survey of industrial companies in the respective Member States which can be used to analyze the economic situation. Whilst companies from only six countries took part in the initial survey, the number of countries has now increased to 15 with the new members. The survey is not, however, conducted by the Commission directly. Instead it uses the survey results of national institutes. Questions are therefore standardized across the EU to ensure comparability of data. Data is now surveyed from around 50 000 companies and sent to the EU Commission. For the individual indicators net values are calculated, (i.e., negative values are deducted from positive ones). The results for the individual indices are then published separately for the respective nations, the Euro zone and the whole of the EU.

Although the questions are standardized, it is still possible for the survey bodies to employ different formulations. In addition, further questions can also be incorporated. However, these additional questions may only be surveyed in accordance with the questions provided by the Commission so that the comparability of the responses is not impaired. For the survey in the industrial sector a number of subjects were analyzed based on the following points:

- Production trends in recent past: up/unchanged/down
- Order books: above normal/normal/below normal
- Export order books: above normal/normal/below normal
- Stocks of finished products: above normal/normal/below normal
- Production expectations for the months ahead: up/unchanged/down
- Selling price expectations for the months ahead: up/unchanged/down

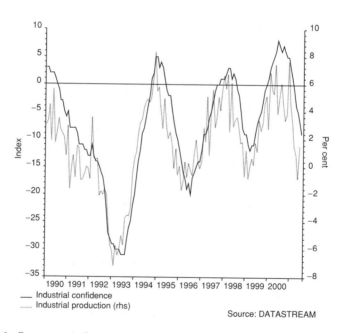

Source: DATASTREAM

Figure 23.1 Euro-zone industrial confidence and change in industrial production on preceding year

An index on industrial confidence is also produced, based on responses on production expectations, assessment of order books and responses on inventories. An average of seasonally adjusted net values is thereby obtained. However, the value of inventories is inversed as high inventories signal production cuts in the coming months, until they return to a 'normal' level.

In surveys in January, April, July and October additional information is collected on the following subjects:

- Capacity utilization: in per cent
- Duration of assured production: in months
- New orders in recent past: up/unchanged/down
- Export expectations for the months ahead: up/unchanged/down
- Production capacity: more than sufficient/sufficient/insufficient
- Limits to production: none/insufficient demand/shortage of labour/lack of equipment/other
- Competitive position in recent past:
  - on the domestic market: up/unchanged/down
  - on the foreign market inside the EU: up/unchanged/down
  - outside the EU: up/unchanged/down
- Employment expectations for the months ahead: up/unchanged/down

National data are used for the individual indices and are available around one week prior to publication of the EU indicators. Since January 2002, all national data are from the same month the Commission publishes the data.

Indicators on the position in the industrial sector are very useful for analyzing the economic situation, although they are inevitably limited to one subsector of the economy. Consequently the Commission also publishes an additional multi-sectoral EU Economic Sentiment Index which covers the entire economy. Prior to October 2001, this index was composed of:

- Index of Industrial Confidence with a weighting of one-third
- Index of Consumer Confidence with a weighting of one-third
- Index of Construction Confidence with a weighting of one-sixth
- Stock price index with a weighting of one-sixth

Starting in October 2001, the EU Commission published a modified Economic Sentiment Indicator. They have changed the weights of the single sub-indicators and replaced the stock price index with the EU Retail Trade Confidence Index. In addition, the composition of the EU Consumer Confidence Index has been changed.

The new EU Economic Sentiment Indicator composition is as follows:

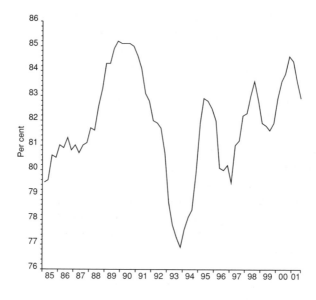

Source: DATASTREAM

Figure 23.2   Capacity utilization

- Index of Industrial Confidence with a weighting of 40 per cent
- Index of Consumer Confidence with a weighting of 20 per cent
- Index of Construction Confidence with a weighting of 20 per cent
- Index of Retail Trade Confidence with a weighting of 20 per cent

Periodicity/Revisions

Surveys are conducted by the economic institutes in the first half of each month and evaluated in the period from the tenth to the twenty-fifth day of each month. The results are then sent to the Commission shortly before the end of the survey month and the first results are published around one week after the end of the month. Revisions are normally only conducted in conjunction with seasonal adjustment factor alignment or a change in the base year. Publication is effected at 12.00 CET (06.00 ET).

Seasonal Adjustment

The data are aggregated and then seasonally adjusted by the EU Commission. However, the Commission uses the so-called Dainties method for seasonal adjustment. For this reason the values published by the national bodies are not fully comparable with the data published by the EU Commission.

Notes

Values in the surveys published by the Commission are very useful for assessing the economic situation and economic prospects in the Euro zone. In fact the raw data are already available prior to publication within the EU, as the national bodies obtaining the data publish the values in advance. The special value of the EU Commission data lies in the fact that they give an overall summary and are not limited to individual nations. The index, however, produces comparatively late signals of a change in the economic position. It can be seen that the index of industrial confidence normally only shows turning points immediately after industrial production turns. This disadvantage is not so serious given that industrial production has a time lapse and industrial confidence thereby has a lead on publication.

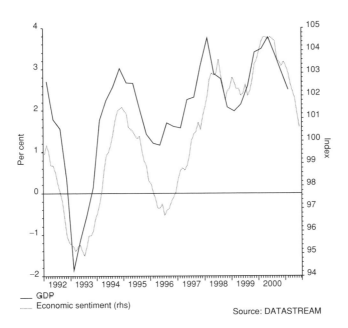

Figure 23.3 Change in Euro-zone GDP on preceding year and Euro-zone Economic Sentiment Index

Key Datastream Mnemonics

EU Industrial Survey (sa)	Datastream
Euro area	
Industrial confidence indicator	EAEUSICIQ
Production expectations	EAEUSIPAQ
Order books	EAEUSIOBQ
Stocks of finished products	EAEUSIFPQ
Production trends in recent past	EAEUSIPRQ
Export order books	EAEUSIEBQ
Selling price expectations	EAEUSISPQ
Capacity utilization	EAEUSICUQ
Production capacity	EAEUSICCQ
Limits to production	EAEUSILPQ
Duration of assured production	EAEUSIPDQ
New orders in recent past	EAEUSINOQ
Export expectations	EAEUSIEXQ
Employment expectations	EAEUSIEMQ
Competitive position in the recent past:	
On the domestic market	
On the foreign market inside the EU	
Outside the EU	
Austria	
Industrial confidence indicator	OEEUSICIQ
Production expectations	OEEUSIPAQ
Order books	OEEUSIOBQ
Stocks of finished products	OEEUSIFPQ
Belgium	
Industrial confidence indicator	BGEUSICIQ
Production expectations	BGEUSIPAQ
Order books	BGEUSIOBQ
Stocks of finished products	BGEUSIFPQ
Finland	
Industrial confidence indicator	FNEUSICIQ
Production expectations	FNEUSIPAQ
Order books	FNEUSIOBQ
Stocks of finished products	FNEUSIFPQ
France	
Industrial confidence indicator	FREUSICIQ
Production expectations	FREUSIPAQ
Order books	FREUSIOBQ
Stocks of finished products	FREUSIFPQ
Production trends in recent past	FREUSIPRQ
Export order books	FREUSIEBQ
Selling price expectations	FREUSISPQ
Capacity utilization	FREUSICUQ
Production capacity	FREUSICCQ
Limits to production	FREUSILPQ

EU Industrial Survey (sa)	Datastream
Duration of assured production	FREUSIPDQ
New orders in recent past	FREUSINOQ
Export expectations	FREUSIEXQ
Employment expectations	FREUSIEMQ
Competitive position in the recent past:	
On the domestic market	
On the foreign market inside the EU	
Outside the EU	
Germany	
Industrial confidence indicator	BDEUSICIQ
Production expectations	BDEUSIPAQ
Order books	BDEUSIOBQ
Stocks of finished products	BDEUSIFPQ
Production trends in recent past	BDEUSIPRQ
Export order books	BDEUSIEBQ
Selling price expectations	BDEUSISPQ
Capacity utilization	BDEUSICUQ
Production capacity	BDEUSICCQ
Limits to production	BDEUSILPQ
Duration of assured production	BDEUSIPDQ
New orders in recent past	BDEUSINOQ
Export expectations	BDEUSIEXQ
Employment expectations	BDEUSIEMQ
Competitive position in the recent past:	
On the domestic market	
On the foreign market inside the EU	
Outside the EU	
Greece	
Industrial confidence indicator	GREUSICIQ
Production expectations	GREUSIPAQ
Order books	GREUSIOBQ
Stocks of finished products	GREUSIFPQ
Ireland	
Industrial confidence indicator	IREUSICIQ
Production expectations	IREUSIPAQ
Order books	IREUSIOBQ
Stocks of finished products	IREUSIFPQ
Italy	
Industrial confidence indicator	ITEUSICIQ
Production expectations	ITEUSIPAQ
Order books	ITEUSIOBQ
Stocks of finished products	ITEUSIFPQ
Production trends in recent past	ITEUSIPRQ
Export order books	ITEUSIEBQ
Selling price expectations	ITEUSISPQ
Capacity utilization	ITEUSICUQ
Production capacity	ITEUSICCQ

EU Industrial Survey (sa)	Datastream
Limits to production	ITEUSILPQ
Duration of assured production	ITEUSIPDQ
New orders in recent past	ITEUSINOQ
Export expectations	ITEUSIEXQ
Employment expectations	ITEUSIEMQ
Competitive position in the recent past:	
On the domestic market	
On the foreign market inside the EU	
Outside the EU	
Luxembourg	
Industrial confidence indicator	LXEUSICIQ
Production expectations	LXEUSIPAQ
Order books	LXEUSIOBQ
Stocks of finished products	LXEUSIFPQ
Netherlands	
Industrial confidence indicator	NLEUSICIQ
Production expectations	NLEUSIPAQ
Order books	NLEUSIOBQ
Stocks of finished products	NLEUSIFPQ
Production trends in recent past	NLEUSIPRQ
Export order books	NLEUSIEBQ
Selling price expectations	NLEUSISPQ
Capacity utilization	NLEUSICUQ
Production capacity	NLEUSICCQ
Limits to production	NLEUSILPQ
Duration of assured production	NLEUSIPDQ
New orders in recent past	NLEUSINOQ
Export expectations	NLEUSIEXQ
Employment expectations	NLEUSIEMQ
Competitive position in the recent past:	
On the domestic market	
On the foreign market inside the EU	
Outside the EU	
Portugal	
Industrial confidence indicator	PTEUSICIQ
Production expectations	PTEUSIPAQ
Order books	PTEUSIOBQ
Stocks of finished products	PTEUSIFPQ
Spain	
Industrial confidence indicator	ESEUSICIQ
Production expectations	ESEUSIPAQ
Order books	ESEUSIOBQ
Stocks of finished products	ESEUSIFPQ
Production trends in recent past	ESEUSIPRQ
Export order books	ESEUSIEBQ
Selling price expectations	ESEUSISPQ
Capacity utilization	ESEUSICUQ

EU Industrial Survey (sa)	Datastream
Production capacity	ESEUSICCQ
Limits to production	
Duration of assured production	ESEUSIPDQ
New orders in recent past	ESEUSINOQ
Export expectations	ESEUSIEXQ
Employment expectations	ESEUSIEMQ
Competitive position in the recent past:	
On the domestic market	
On the foreign market inside the EU	
Outside the EU	
EU15	
Industrial confidence indicator	ECEUSICIQ
Production expectations	ECEUSIPAQ
Order books	ECEUSIOBQ
Stocks of finished products	ECEUSIFPQ
Production trends in recent past	ECEUSIPRQ
Export order books	ECEUSIEBQ
Selling price expectations	ECEUSISPQ
Capacity utilization	ECEUSICUQ
Production capacity	ECEUSICCQ
Limits to production	ECEUSILPQ
Duration of assured production	ECEUSIPDQ
New orders in recent past	ECEUSINOQ
Export expectations	ECEUSIEXQ
Employment expectations	ECEUSIEMQ
Competitive position in the recent past:	
On the domestic market	
On the foreign market inside the EU	
Outside the EU	
Denmark	
Industrial confidence indicator	DKEUSICIQ
Production expectations	DKEUSIPAQ
Order books	DKEUSIOBQ
Stocks of finished products	DKEUSIFPQ
Sweden	
Industrial confidence indicator	SDEUSICIQ
Production expectations	SDEUSIPAQ
Order books	SDEUSIOBQ
Stocks of finished products	SDEUSIFPQ
United Kingdom	
Industrial confidence indicator	UKEUSICIQ
Production expectations	UKEUSIPAQ
Order books	UKEUSIOBQ
Stocks of finished products	UKEUSIFPQ

Economic Sentiment Indicator (sa)	Datastream
Euro area	EAEUSESIG
Austria	OEEUSESIG
Belgium	BGEUSESIG
Finland	FNEUSESIG
France	FREUSESIG
Germany	BDEUSESIG
Greece	GREUSESIG
Ireland	IREUSESIG
Italy	ITEUSESIG
Luxembourg	
Netherlands	NLEUSESIG
Portugal	PTEUSESIG
Spain	ESEUSESIG
EU15	ECEUSESIG
Denmark	DKEUSESIG
Sweden	
United Kingdom	UKEUSESIG

Literature

European Commission: 'The joint harmonised EU programme of business and consumer surveys', *European Economy*, No. 6 (1997), Luxembourg.

23.2   Business Climate Indicator (Common Factor)

Data Source

Data is based on the EU Industrial Survey and is calculated by the EU Commission. A summary of the data is available on the Internet at europa.eu.int/comm/economy_finance/index_en.htm.

Importance for the Financial Markets   C

Description

The EU Commission has decided to construct a new indicator for the Euro zone, the Business Climate Indicator or Common Factor that is based on the information collected for the EU Industrial Survey. The Common Factor has been designed to analyze the information from the Industrial Survey and is thus clearly thought as a leading indicator for the industrial production. This Business Climate Indicator uses as input series the balance of opinions from the following sub-series from the EU Industrial Survey:

- Production trends in recent past

- Order books
- Export order books
- Stocks of finished goods
- Production expectations for the months ahead

The idea behind the Common Factor is that each series is the outcome of a 'common' component that summarizes the cyclical situation at a particular moment and a 'specific' component for each of the survey questions. This indicator tries to separate out the information that is common to each of the series, and is presented in the form of standard deviations.

The Common Factor was first released in November 2000. As with the data for Euro zone available going back to 1985, the indicator was recalculated since this date. The EU Commission decided to use the Industrial Survey only, and to limit the analysis to the industrial sector. The reason was that the other surveys available have not been calculated for the whole Euro zone for a considerable time. Nevertheless, the extension of the method to the construction sector and the retail trade sector is under consideration.

Periodicity/Revisions

The survey is released one working day after the release of the EU Industrial Survey, normally in the first week after the end of the reference month. Revisions are normally only conducted in conjunction with seasonal adjustment factor alignment or a change in the base year. Publication is effected at 12.00 CET (06.00 ET).

Seasonal Adjustment

The data of the Industrial Survey is seasonal adjusted, but the calculated data for the Business Climate Indicator is not seasonal adjusted further.

Notes

The Business Climate Indicator is one with a limited history. Thus, as yet, it has no great importance to the financial markets. The predicting power of the indicator, using the available history is fairly good, but it has to be shown whether this comes from the construction process during the back testing or whether this persists in the future.

Key Datastream Mnemonics

Business Climate Indicator (sa)	Datastream
Euro-zone	EAEUBCI.Q

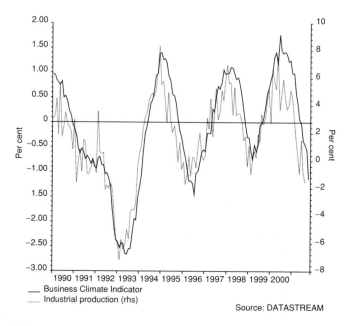

Figure 23.4 Euro-zone Business Climate Indicator and change in industrial production on preceding year

Literature

European Commission, 'The joint harmonised EU programme of business and consumer surveys', *European Economy*, No. 6, 1997, Luxembourg.

European Commission, *Business Climate Indicator for the Euro Area*, November 2000, Brussels.

23.3   Reuters Purchasing Managers' Index

Data Source

Data are commissioned by Reuters and produced by NTC Research in association with national purchasing associations and primarily published by Reuters.

Importance for the Financial Markets   C

Description

The news agency Reuters publishes similar indices to the ISM Purchasing Managers' Index on the USA for the UK, Germany, Italy and France and in aggregate form for the Euro zone. The questions are designed to find out how the business situation has changed compared to the preceding month. The results are published in the form of diffusion indices, which can fluctuate between 0 and 100. NTC began in September 1991 with a data survey on British industry. The results have been published since January 1992. In May 1997 Germany was added (with data from April 1996), in April 1999 France (April 1998), in November 1998 Italy (June 1997), in October 1999 Ireland (May 1998) and in November 1999 Austria (October 1998). In the meantime, data from other countries (e.g. Spain, the Netherlands, Greece and some non-EU countries) have been added. Since April 1997 figures on the service sector in the UK have also been published in addition to data on the industrial sector. The database for UK services goes back to July 1996. Data on the service sector for Germany have been published since April 1998 (with figures since June 1997) and for Italy since April 1999 (January 1998). In addition to these time series, NTC currently surveys data on the service sector in France, Spain and Ireland. These data are not, however, published separately. All the data are surveyed based on uniform methodology in order to be comparable.

By combining dates for the Euro-zone countries that it covers, NTC produces an overall composite Euro-zone PMI for both manufacturing and service sectors, plus an index for manufacturing and services combined. The countries together account for an estimated 92 per cent of total Euro-zone GDP. Companies taking part in the surveys are selected so that a breakdown by sector, region and company size reproduces the structure of the individual countries measured in terms of GDP. For the Euro zone indicators, over 5500 companies participate from the manufacturing and the service sectors combined.

The surveys are co-ordinated centrally by NTC Research which often works with a number of different national and international professional associations. These include, for example:

- Bundesverband Materialwirtschaft, Einkauf und Logistik (BME, the German association of materials processing, procurement and logistics) for the Purchasing Managers' Index for the production sector in Germany
- Compagnie des Dirigeants d'Appovisionnement et Acheteurs de France (CDAF, the French association of purchasing managers and buyers) for the Purchasing Managers' Index for the production industry in France
- Italian purchasing managers' association Associazione Italiana di Management degli Approvvigionamenti (ADACI) for the purchasing managers' indices for the production and service sector in Italy

For the manufacturing industry survey a series of questions is set on different variables, a number of them are weighted together to create the composite PMI (percentage share for the PMI in brackets).

1. **New Orders**

   Please compare the level of orders received this month with that of one month ago: higher/same/lower (30 per cent).

2. **Output**

   Please compare your production/output this month with the situation one month ago: higher/same/lower (25 per cent).

3. **Employment**

   Please compare the level of employment at your unit with the situation one month ago: higher/same/lower (20 per cent).

4. **Suppliers' Delivery Times**

   Please compare your suppliers' delivery times (volume weighted) with the situation one month ago: faster/same/slower (15 per cent).

5. **Stocks of Purchases**

   Please compare your stocks of purchases (in units) with the situation one month ago: higher/same/lower (10 per cent).

Values for suppliers' delivery times are inversed in the PMI calculation. In addition there are questions which are not included in the PMI calculation, although the responses are also published.

6. **New Export Orders**

   Please compare the level of export orders received this month with that of one month ago: higher/same/lower.

7. **Quantity of Purchases**

   Please compare the quantity of items purchased (in units) this month with the situation one month ago: higher/same/lower.

8. **Input Prices**

   Please compare the average price of your purchases (volume weighted) with the situation one month ago: higher/same/lower.

9. **Stocks of Finished Goods**

   Please compare your stocks of finished goods (in units) with the situation one month ago: higher/same/lower.

In the service industry survey the following questions are asked:

1. **Service Sector Business Activity**

   Please compare the level of business activity (i.e., gross income, chargeable hours worked, etc.) in your company with the situation one month ago: higher/same/lower.

2. **Incoming New Business/New orders**

   Please compare the level of orders placed during the month (whether already fulfilled or not) with the situation one month ago: higher/same/lower.

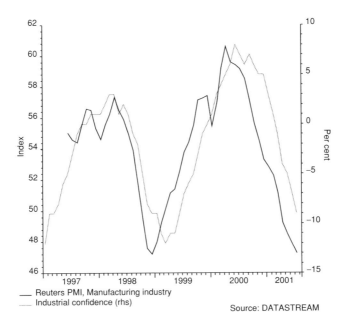

Figure 23.5 Euro-zone Purchasing Managers' Index on Manufacturing Industry and Industrial Confidence Index

3. **Outstanding Business**
   Is the level of outstanding business (i.e., work placed but not yet completed) higher, the same or lower than one month ago?
4. **Employment**
   Please compare the number of people employed at your company with the situation one month ago (treat two part-time as one full-time and ignore temporary labour): higher/same/lower.
5. **Average Prices Charged**
   Compare the average prices charged by your company (e.g., prices charged per item or unit or time) with the situation one month ago: higher/same/lower.
6. **Average Input Prices/Costs**
   Is the average price paid by your company for all inputs (purchases, wages and salaries, etc.) higher, the same or lower than one month ago?
7. **Service Sector Business Expectation**
   In twelve months time, do you expect the overall level of activity at your business unit to be higher, the same or lower than now?

Data from the manufacturing and service sectors can for a number of variables be combined to produce composite indices which provide greater coverage of the private sector economies in question. Composite indices are currently only produced for the Euro-zone as a whole. The following list shows those variables which are measured across both the manufacturing and the service sector, and outlines slight differences in their coverage.

1. **Output and business activity in the service sector**

   It is not always easy to measure production in the service sector. This is why there is no uniform definition of business activity for individual service companies. Instead companies should orientate themselves to what is most applicable for their business activity.

2. **New orders**

   With these questions the level of orders received in the manufacturing sector is compared with new orders in the service sector.

3. **Input prices**

   The largest cost factor in the manufacturing sector are material costs, whereas in the service sector wage costs constitute the main element.

4. **Number of employees**

   These sectors are identical both in the manufacturing and service sectors. Here, two part-time staff are counted as one full-time.

No other variables are recorded.

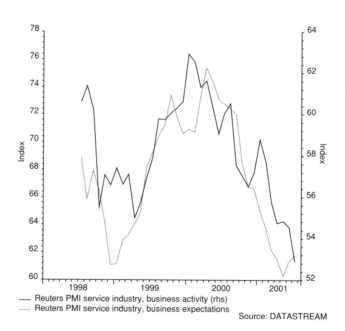

— Reuters PMI service industry, business activity (rhs)
······ Reuters PMI service industry, business expectations

Source: DATASTREAM

Figure 23.6   Euro-zone Purchasing Managers' Indices in Service Industry – business activity and business expectations

Periodicity/Revisions

Indices for the manufacturing sector are published on the first working day of the month, whereas indices for the service sector are published on the third working day of the month. The composite index for the Euro-zone is also published on the third working day. The index for France is published at 07.50 CET (01.50 ET) 07.45 GMT, the Italian indices at 07.45 CET (01.45 ET), the German indices at 07.55 CET (01.45 ET) and the Euro zone indices at 09.00 CET (03.00 ET). Revisions are normally only conducted in conjunction with alignments of the seasonal adjustment factors.

Seasonal Adjustment

The national data are seasonally adjusted; however, the values for the Euro-zone indicator are not seasonally adjusted again.

Notes

Data have only been available for a short period. The first data for the Euro-zone were surveyed in 1997, since which time a number of countries have been added. The Purchasing Managers' Indices have become more important since the ECB explicitly pointed out the informative content of these indices and noted that they should be taken into account in monetary policy decisions.

Key Datastream Mnemonics

Reuters Purchasing Managers' Index (sa)	Datastream
Manufacturing	
Output	
Employment	
New orders	
Suppliers' delivery times	
Stocks of purchases	

Reuters Purchasing Managers' Index (sa)	Datastream
Prices	
New export orders	
Stocks of finished goods	
Quantity of purchases	
Service	
Business activity	
New business	
Employment	
Input prices	
Prices charged	
Outstanding business	
Business expectations	

23.4   Ifo Business Survey

Data Source

The Ifo Business Survey (Konjunkturtest) is published by the Ifo Institute for Economic Research in Munich. A summary of the Ifo Business Climate Index in Industry and Trade is available on the Internet at www.ifo.de. In addition, staff at the Ifo Institute interpret survey results regularly in Ifo Institute publications.

Importance for the Financial Markets   B

Description

The Ifo Institute began conducting regular qualitative company surveys shortly after their foundation in 1949. Responses summarized in the Ifo Business Survey therefore represent one of the longest data series produced by a private organization on the economic position in Germany. Whereas only the situation in the manufacturing sector was surveyed at first, the retail sector was added in 1950. In 1951 came wholesale and in 1956 finally construction. Compared to December 1949, when just 88 companies were involved in the survey, now around 7000 companies take part. These sectors together thereby represent the industry and trade sector.

One of the aims of the Ifo Institute with this new type of survey was to gain information on procedures which are not covered by official statistics, or are only published with long time lapses, or are so disaggregated that they are virtually useless for economic policy decision-making processes. Primarily, these involve assessments of growth trends as well as opinions and expectations by entrepreneurs and top management. Quantitative information is the exception in this survey. Otherwise, questions are predominantly company-related. As participation in the survey is voluntary, there are two basic ways to motivate companies to participate. One is to ensure that internal company information will not be passed on to third parties. Second, aggregated data is available free of charge to participating companies in the form of a so-called economic mirror showing the individual market sectors and product groups immediately after evaluation of the data. This information is a particularly important source of operational market research for small and medium-sized companies. Sectoral and branch results are passed on to associations, organizations and departments and are available to everybody at a charge. The results from sparsely represented sectors are not published in tabular form.

The name 'business survey' clearly shows that the survey is targeted at economic development. Consequently, the aim is to use the survey to separate economic components from other components in the overall process, such as seasonal components and unique exogenous shocks. As a result only figures which are consistently important to management are requested. As the questionnaire is restricted to one A4 sheet, it is possible to have results ready around the middle of the month.

Companies within a product group are weighted differently depending on their size. Weighting is normally based on the number of staff employed in the respective areas, although in some cases market share or turnover weighting is used. The method therefore depends on market knowledge, number of companies, types of companies and association work. The reason for this weighting is that large companies contribute more to total output than smaller companies. However the weighting of growing individual companies does not rise proportionately, so smaller companies have a relatively high weighting compared to large ones. For the weighting of the larger aggregates, the gross production figures are used in the industry sector and sales are used in the trade and construction sector. Data for this are taken from the official statistics.

From the outset the survey was divided into a standard and specific question section. Standard questions were therefore set monthly, with special ones normally recurring every quarter. The standard questions are restricted exclusively to qualitative information. Consequently only trends or assessments are to be given and no figures. In the building sector, on the other hand, the level of equipment utilization and coverage of orders are set monthly, for which quantitative responses are required.

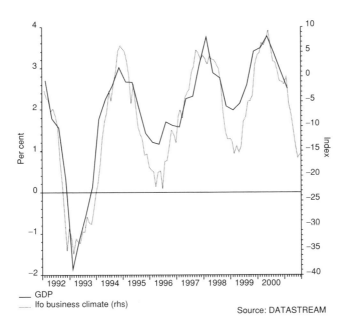

Figure 23.7 Change in the Euro-zone GDP on preceding year and Ifo Business Climate Index for Germany

Based on the survey questions, indicators can be derived to analyze economic trends. The most important indicator is the Ifo Business Climate Index, which is calculated as a geometric average from the balances of current business opinions and expectations for the coming six months. These balances are obtained as diffusion indices in the same way as the balances for the other set questions. Weighted responses to individual questions are therefore totalled to reflect positive development and the negative ones to produce negative development. The percentage of negative responses is then deducted from the percentage of positive responses. The Ifo Business Climate Index is then finally calculated using the following formula:

$$\text{Business Climate} = \sqrt{(CB + 200)(BE + 200)} - 200$$

where

CB = Sub-indicator for the current business situation (per cent)
BE = Sub-indicator for expected business situation in 6 months (per cent)

To avoid negative values in the square root term, the two sub-indicators are both increased by a value of 200 and then reduced again so that the index can fluctuate between −100 and +100. The evidence for the business climate is taken directly from the respective deviation from zero level. If there is a positive value, there are more responses with a positive estimate. This business climate is not just calculated for the overall sectors, but also for individual sub-sectors. From the business climate for the respective sectors of industry, trade and construction, the Ifo Business Climate Index is then calculated using the following formula:

$$\text{Ifo Business Climate} = \frac{\text{Business Climate}}{\text{Business Climate}_{1991}} * 100$$

where

Business Climate$_{1991}$ = Average value of business climate in 1991

The value of the business climate is also normed to the base year 1991. A value of 100 therefore corresponds to the average in this base year. In addition to the indices mentioned, the Ifo Institute has also calculated diffusion indices since 1979 by deducting negative opinions from positive ones.

The Ifo business survey is one of the surveys which the surveys published by the EU commission are based on. Prior to 2002, there has been no uniform survey month for the national surveys. Starting in 2002, the Ifo Institute has changed its survey period to harmonize with the other surveys. As a result, the following changes occurred:

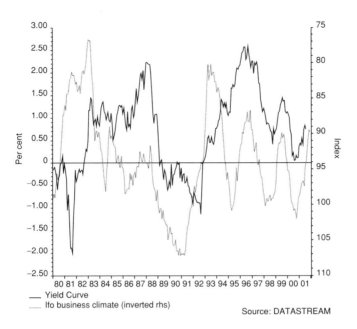

Figure 23.8 The yield curve and Ifo Business Climate Index with a lag of 5 months

1. There will be no longer a distinction between calendar month and reporting month.
2. The questionnaires will be sent to the reporting enterprises later than before to help them to report for the new time frame. The companies will have the reports around the fourth of the month.
3. The wording of some questions has changed.
4. The missing values for December are interpolated with the values for November and January.
5. All the quarterly specific questions that are incorporated into the EU surveys will be asked together in January, April, July and October.
6. The weights for the single companies as well as the weights for the sectors have been updated.
7. From mid-2002, the results were only published for Pan-Germany and for East Germany, and no longer for West Germany.

Since 2002, the following sectors are surveyed in the manufacturing business, using the following questions:

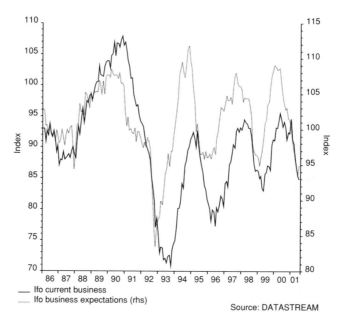

Figure 23.9   Ifo current business situation and business expectations

Actual situation

- **Business situation**
  In our opinion, the business situation for XY is good/satisfactory (typical for the season)/bad.
- **Stocks of unsold goods**
  Our stocks of unsold goods of XY in our opinion are currently too low/ adequate (typical for the season)/too high/no stocks held.
- **Orders (domestic and foreign)**
  Our domestic and foreign orders for XY in our opinion are currently disproportionately large (e.g. longer delivery times)/adequate (typical for the season) or not typical/too small.

Tendencies in the last month

- **Demand situation**
  The demand situation for XY improved/remained unchanged/worsened.
- **Value of orders**
  The value of our order stock (domestic and foreign) for XY is higher/about the same or atypical/lower.

- **Production**
  Our domestic production (excluding months of different lengths and seasonal fluctuations) for XY is higher/unchanged/lower/minimal production.
- **Domestic sales prices**
  Our domestic sales prices (net prices) for XY due to changes in conditions were higher/unchanged/lower.

Expectations for the next three months

- **Production**
  Our domestic production (excluding months of different lengths and seasonal fluctuations) of XY looks set to rise/stay around the same/fall/minimal domestic production.
- **Domestic sales prices**
  Our domestic sales prices (net prices) for XY over the next three months due to the changes in conditions look set to rise/stay around the same/fall.
- **Scope of export business**
  The scope of our export business with XY over the next three months in the light of exports concluded to date and current order negotiations looks set to rise/stay around the same/fall/we do not export to XY.
- **Employees (domestic operations only)**
  Employees (domestic operations only): The number of staff employed in the production of XY over the next 3 months will rise/stay the same/fall.

Expectations for the next six months

- **Trend in business situation**
  Our business situation for XY over the coming six months in economic terms looks set to improve/remain around the same/worsen.

Quarterly specific questions relate to three sectors:

- **Backlog of orders and capacity utilization**
  These questions are set in January, April, July and October and relate to the following factors:
  Coverage of orders in production months
  Capacity utilization as a percentage of standard full operating capacity
  Estimate of current technical capacity in terms of current orders and expected new orders over the next 12 months.
  Limits to production/reasons
  Competitive position

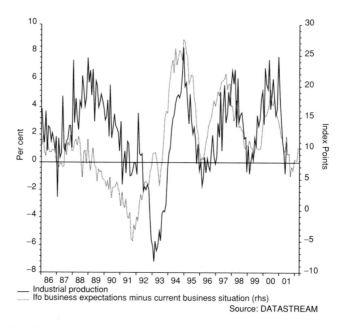

Figure 23.10 Change in Euro-zone industrial production on preceding year and difference of Ifo business expectations minus current business situation with a lag of 8 months

- **Inventories**

  These questions are set in February, May, August and November and relate to the following factors:

  Inventory levels in production weeks and opinion of key commodities and primary material inventories

  Inventory levels of finished products in production weeks.

- **Employment and labour market**

  These questions are set in March, June, September and December and relate to the following factors:

  Number of employees compared to expected sales over the next 12 months

  Overtime

  Short-time working

Different questions are mainly set for the trade sectors as opposed to the manufacturing sector, although the standard questions for wholesale and retail are the same.

The sectors' survey in retail and wholesale trade is the following:

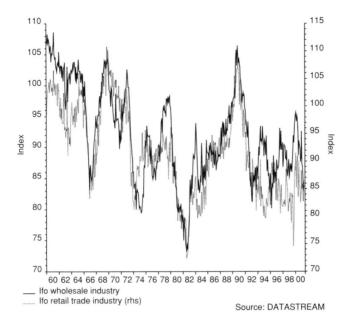

Figure 23.11   Ifo Business Climate Index in wholesale and retail trade industry

Actual situation

- **Current business situation**
  In our opinion, our business situation is currently good/satisfactory (or typical for the season)/bad.
- **Turnover compared to same month in the preceding year**
  Compared to the same month in the preceding year our turnover in the last month was higher/approximately the same/lower.
- **Inventories**
  In our opinion, our inventories are currently too small/adequate (or typical for the season)/too large
- **Sales price compared to preceding month**
  In the last month, our sales prices had been increased/were unchanged/had been decreased.

Expectations for the next three months

- **Sales prices**
  Our sales prices will probably rise/remain approximately the same/fall.
- **Orders**
  Compared to the same period in the preceding year, we will increase/not change/decrease our orders.

- **Employment situation**
  Excluding purely seasonal fluctuations the number employed by us will probably rise/remain approximately the same/fall.

Expectations for the next six months

- **Business situation**
  In the next 6 months excluding purely seasonal fluctuations our business situation will probably be more favourable/approximately the same/less favourable.

Each month, specific questions are asked in East Germany on sales activities and the number of employees.

In addition to surveys in industry and trade, the situation in the construction industry has also been surveyed since 1956. Questions are designed to obtain partial results for the following sectors:

Road construction
Other civil engineering
Public building constructions
Commercial building
Residential building

Residential building is also classified in terms of:

Residential building overall
Buildings with three or more flats

Companies operating in a number of sectors can respond to several sectors. Moreover, in contrast to the other questionnaires, questions are not categorized in terms of present and future, but by subject. These are:

- **Construction work**
  1. In the last month, construction work has increased/stayed the same/decreased.
  2. Construction work/execution of orders is currently obstructed (yes/no). If yes, due to: labor shortage/material shortage – inadequate technical equipment/unfavourable weather conditions/inadequate funding/shortage of orders/other reasons.
  3. Over the next three months compared to the preceding three months we will probably build more/about the same/less.

- **Building contracts**
  1. In the last month, the value of our building contracts has risen/stayed the same/fallen.

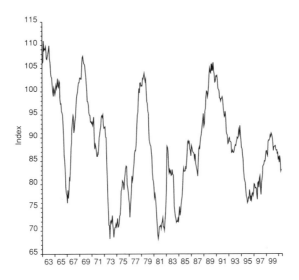

Figure 23.12   Ifo Business Climate Index for the construction industry

2. In our opinion, our orders are currently relatively high/adequate or typical for the season/too low.
3. Our orders at the end of the month under review under normal seasonal conditions would cover average production for . . . . . months.

- **Building prices**
  1. In the last month, our prices for new orders increased/stayed unchanged/decreased.
  2. Currently the prices charged on the market more than covered costs/covered costs/did not cover costs.
  3. In the next three months the building prices charged on the market will probably rise/remain about the same/fall.

- **Business situation**
  1. Our assessment of our current business situation is good/adequate or typical for the season/bad.
  2. In the next six months our business situation will probably be more favourable/remain about the same/be less favourable.

- **Equipment capacity**
  1. Our equipment capacity (full operating capacity = 100 per cent) amounted to around . . . . per cent on average in the reporting period (including classification: all equipment, equipment for civil engineering, equipment for building construction).

- **Employees**
    1. In the next 3–4 months the number of our employees will rise/remain about the same/fall (including classification: overall, trade employees, employed).
    2. Currently . . . . . per cent of our staff are ill.
    3. Number of people employed (including apprentices, temporary staff) Status: end of the month under review. We currently employ around . . . . . people in our business.

With the construction survey every month a large number of regularly recurring specific questions are also set on a broad range of subjects.

Periodicity/Revisions

Questionnaires are normally sent out to companies in the last week of the month. The exact date depends on the completion of results from the preceding month as these are sent out with the survey forms. Companies then have time to respond until around the seventh day of the following month, although many responses are often received somewhat later. By the tenth day of the month attempts are made to get outstanding replies back via fax reminders and ultimately by phone. Responses which are not received by the conclusion of the evaluation are no longer incorporated in the survey and there is therefore no revision of past months. As mentioned before, the Ifo Institute will change the survey time with the beginning of 2002. It is planned to send the questionnaires and publish the results approximately one week later then before.

Trials are currently under way to conduct the survey on the Internet. The results are published on a date announced in advance which varies between the seventeenth and twenty-second of the month (earlier in December), normally at 10.00 CET (04.00 ET).

Seasonal Adjustment

The data are seasonally adjusted.

Notes

The focus is on the level and monthly change of the overall index. The index of business expectations primarily gives an impression of future economic development. The qualitative questions have the advantage that extreme individual volumes or values do not go into the calculation to their full quantitative extent but with the weighting of the respective company. This therefore has a smoothing effect, in contrast to surveys with quantitative questions. However, this advantage unfortunately means that the survey cannot contain any information on the extent of economic change in terms of the volume or value, since the results only show what percentage of participating companies reported a certain situation or development. The index on net production is taken as the reference series for the Ifo Business Climate Index in Industry and Trade, whereas for the Business Climate Index in the Manufacturing Sector the GDP is employed. The Ifo Business Climate Index therefore has an average lead of two quarters, although the lead at the peak of the cycle was usually longer than at the trough. This is due to the fact that a worsening in a booming business climate is only registered in production with a certain time lapse due to the high order levels, whereas a resurgence in demand at the end of a weak economic period affects production rapidly. With 1991 as the base year, there is also the problem that this value is distorted by the euphoria of reunification and is clearly above the long-term average.

Another way of using the Ifo index as a forecasting tool is to derive the difference between the current business situation index to the business expectation index. As can be seen, this difference normally has a lead of 6–9 months to the year-on-year change of industrial production and has been a good leading indicator for overall activity.

The data provide an important analysis of economic development both in the recent past and in the near future. This is confirmed by the fact that the survey in the manufacturing sector is representative for around 40 per cent, whereas for trade and the building industry it currently represents around 15 per cent.

Key Datastream Mnemonics

Ifo Business Survey (sa)	Datastream
Industry and trade sector Pan Germany	
Business climate index	BDIFOIDXE
Diffusions index business climate	BDIFOIDX
Current business situation	BDIFOBUSE
Diffusions index current business situation	BDIFOBUS
Business expectations	BDIFOEXPE
Diffusions index business expectations	BDIFOEXP
Industry and trade sector East Germany	
Business climate index	EGIFOIDXE
Diffusions index business climate	EGIFOIDX
Current business situation	EGIFOBUSE
Diffusions index current business situation	EGIFOBUS
Business expectations	EGIFOEXPE
Diffusions index business expectations	EGIFOEXP
Manufacturing Pan Germany	
Overall business climate	BDIFOMTLE
Assessment of current business position	BDIFOMTAE
Business expectations over next 6 months	BDIFOMTKE
Production compared with previous month	BDIFOMTBE

Ifo Business Survey (sa)	Datastream
Assessment of stocks of finished goods	BDIFOMTCE
Demand compared with previous month	BDIFOMTDE
Orders in hand compared with previous month	BDIFOMTEE
Assessment of orders in hand	BDIFOMTFE
Assessment of export orders in hand	
Selling prices compared with previous month (nsa)	BDIFOMTGF
Production expectations over next 3 months	BDIFOMTHE
Selling price expectations over next 3 months (nsa)	BDIFOMTIF
Export expectations over next 3 months	BDIFOMTJE
Employment expectations	BDIFOBDSE
Capacity utilization	BDCAPUTLR

Manufacturing East Germany

Overall business climate	EGIFOINIE
Assessment of current business position	EGIFOINAE
Business expectations over next 6 months	EGIFOINHE
Production compared with previous month	EGIFOINBE
Assessment of stocks of finished goods	EGIFOINCE
Demand compared with previous month	EGIFOINDE
Orders in hand compared with previous month	EGIFOINEE
Production expectations over next 3 months	EGIFOINFE
Selling price expectations over next 3 months (nsa)	EGIFOINGF

Wholesale trade Pan Germany

Overall business climate	BDIFOWHLE
Diffusion index business climate	BDIFOWHIE
Assessment of current business position	BDIFOWHAE
Business expectations over next 6 months	BDIFOWHHE
Turnover compared with previous year (nsa)	BDIFOWHBF
Turnover compared with previous month	BDIFOWHCE
Assessment of stocks on hand	BDIFOWHDE
Selling prices compared with previous month (nsa)	BDIFOWHEF
Selling price expectations over next 3 months (nsa)	BDIFOWHFF
Orders expectations over next 3 months	BDIFOWHGE
Employment expectations	BDIFOEWTE

Retail trade Pan Germany

Overall business climate	BDIFORETE
Diffusion index business climate	BDIFORTIE
Assessment of current business position	BDIFORTAE
Business expectations over next 6 months	BDIFORTHE
Turnover compared with previous year (nsa)	BDIFORTBF
Turnover compared with previous month	BDIFORTCE
Assessment of stocks on hand	BDIFORTDE
Selling prices compared with previous month (nsa)	BDIFORTEF
Selling price expectations over next 3 months (nsa)	BDIFORTFF
Orders expectations over next 3 months	BDIFORTGE
Employment expectations	BDIFOERTE

Ifo Business Survey (sa)	Datastream
Construction Pan Germany	
Overall business climate	BDIFOBDQQ
Diffusion index business climate	BDIFOBDQE
Assessment of current business position	BDIFOBDOE
Business expectations over next 6 months	BDIFOBDPE
Activity compared with last 3 months	BDIFOBDAE
Impediment of building activity	BDIFOBDBE
Lack of manpower	BDIFOBDCE
Shortage of materials	BDIFOBDDE
Unfavourable weather	BDIFOBDEE
Insufficient financial resources	BDIFOBDFE
Lack of orders	
Other causes	BDIFOBDGE
Activity expectations over next 3 months	BDIFOBDHE
Orders in hand compared with previous month	BDIFOBDIE
Assessment of orders in hand	BDIFOBDJE
Extent of orders in hand (months)	BDIFOBDKE
Prices compared with previous month	BDIFOBDLE
Prime cost cover of prices achieved	BDIFOBDME
Price expectations over next 3 months	BDIFOBDNE
Utilization of plant and equipment	BDIFOBDRE
Expected number of all employees over next 3 months	BDIFOBDUE
Sickness figures	BDIFOBDVE

Literature

Nerb, Gernot, 'Konstruktion und Bedeutung des Ifo-Konjunkturtests' [Construction and Importance of the Ifo Business Survey], Stierle, Michael (ed.), *Wirtschaftsdaten, Konjunkturprognosen und ihre Auswirkungen auf die Finanzmärkte* [*Economic Indicators, Economic Forecast and the Impact on Financial Markets*], INFER Studies Vol. 2, Verlag für Wissenschaft und Forschung, 2000, pp. 31–53.

Oppenländer, Karl Heinrich and Poser, Günter (eds), *Handbuch der Ifo-Umfragen* [Handbook of Ifo surveys], Duncker & Humblot, Berlin and Munich 1989.

23.5   INSEE Industrial Trends

Data Source

The survey is conducted by the statistical office INSEE [Institut National de la Statistique et des Études Économiques, or National Institute of Statistics and Economic Studies] in France. The press release is available on the Internet at www.insee.fr.

Importance for the Financial Markets   C

Description

The INSEE surveys a large number of French companies each month on their assessment of the economic situation both in their own company and the economic situation in general. The following areas are surveyed:

- Estimate of current own production
- Expected own production
- Expected general business situation
- Expected general price trend
- Estimate of order levels overall
- Estimate of export order levels
- Estimate of inventories
- Expected about own price trend

The responses are summarized in diffusion indices by deducting the negative replies from the positive ones. Inventories are inversed. The fact that the responses are divided into sectors is useful as it provides a detailed analysis of the situation in French industry.

In addition to the monthly surveys additional questions are set around once a quarter for in-depth analysis. The subject areas covered are:

- Capacity utilization
- Number of companies with production bottlenecks
- Number of companies in financial difficulties
- Estimate of total demand
- Estimate of foreign demand
- Expected trend of total demand
- Expected trend of foreign demand
- Estimate of past wage trend
- Expected future wage trend

In the quarterly surveys diffusion indices are also obtained by deducting the negative replies from the positive ones.

Periodicity/Revisions

The survey is published in the last week of the month in which it is conducted. It therefore publishes early information on the economic situation.

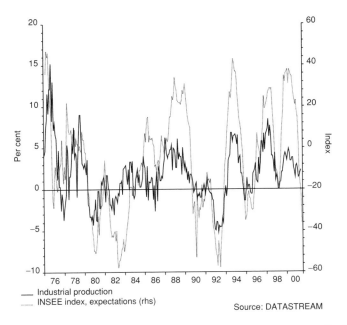

Figure 23.13 Change in French industrial production on preceding year and INSEE Index on Expected Overall Business Situation

The quarterly data are surveyed in January, April, July and October and are published in the first week of the following month. Publication is effected at 08.45 CET (02.45 ET). There are no revisions.

Seasonal Adjustment

Both the monthly surveys and the quarterly surveys are seasonally adjusted.

Notes

The focus is on the diffusion indices of the current business situation and the expected overall business situation. As the survey is only conducted in the industrial sector, it is a good indicator of production activity in this sector, although the replies to changes in conditions in their own business situation adapt far more rapidly than to the overall business situation. With the quarterly surveys capacity utilization is very important as it indicates the possible risk of a rise in inflation.

Key Datastream Mnemonics

INSEE Industrial Trends (sa)	Datastream
Total	
Recent trend in production	FRSURPINQ
Industry opinion of future production	FRSURTINQ
General prospects on probable trend in industrial production	FRSURGPDQ
General prospects on probable trend in industrial prices	FRSURGPRQ
Level of order book and demand	FRSURGINQ
Level of foreign order book and demand	FRSURFINQ
Level of finished stocks	FRSURSINQ
Probable trend in selling prices	FRSURCINQ
Manufacturing	
Recent trend in production	FRSURPMPQ
Industry opinion of future production	FRSURTMPQ
Level of order book and demand	FRSURGMPQ
Level of foreign order book and demand	FRSURFMPQ
Level of finished stocks	FRSURSMPQ
Probable trend in selling prices	FRSURCMPQ
Consumer goods	
Recent trend in production	FRSURPCSQ
Industry opinion of future production	FRSURTCSQ
Level of order book and demand	FRSURGCSQ
Level of foreign order book and demand	FRSURFCSQ
Level of finished stocks	FRSURSCSQ
Probable trend in selling prices	FRSURCCSQ
Capital goods	
Recent trend in production	FRSURPCGQ
Industry opinion of future production	FRSURTCGQ
Level of order book and demand	FRSURGCGQ
Level of foreign order book and demand	FRSURFCGQ
Level of finished stocks	FRSURSCGQ
Probable trend in selling prices	FRSURCCGQ

23.6   ISAE Industrial Trends

Data Source

The data are published by the Instituto di Studi e Analisi Economica (ISAE, or Institute of Economic Study and Analysis). It is available on the Internet at www.isae.it/english.html.

Importance for the Financial Markets   C

Description

The ISAE Industrial Trends for Italy are produced via a monthly survey of around 4000 industrial operations and mining companies throughout Italy. The responses are used by the EU Commission for the EU Industrial Survey. ISAE carries out surveys on a whole range of subjects relating to the current position and company expectations:

- Assessment of current domestic orders
- Assessment of current foreign orders
- Assessment of current total orders
- Stocks of finished goods
- Assessment of production levels
- Assessment of production levels compared to preceding month
- Expectations of order trends
- Expectations of production trends
- Expectations of sales price trends
- Expectations of trend in overall economic situation
- Change in unit labour costs within last 12 months
- Expected change in unit labour costs in next 12 months

The possible responses are 'rise', 'unchanged' and 'fall'. For stocks the possible responses are 'above normal', 'normal', 'below normal' or 'no stocks'. For the two questions on the change in unit labour costs, percentage changes are to be given which are then published as a weighted average. The questions on expectations relate to a period of 3–4 months. A diffusion index is produced from the response by deducting the percentage of negative responses from the positive ones. For the responses on stocks the percentage of the categories 'below normal' and 'no stocks' are totalled.

Additional questions on the following subjects are set quarterly:

- Competitive situation
- Production capacity
- Capacity utilization
- Number of hours effectively worked
- Incoming orders
- Export volume
- Employment situation

- Production restraints
- Production period for current orders

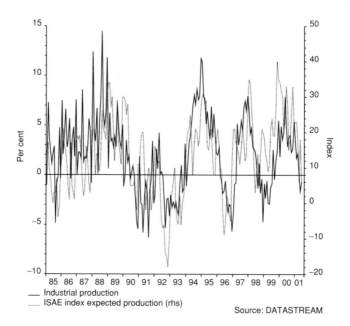

Figure 23.14   Change in industrial production in Italy on preceding year and ISAE expectations of production trends

Periodicity/Revisions

The survey is conducted at the end of the month and published at the end of the next month. There are no revisions.

Seasonal Adjustment

The data are seasonally adjusted using the X-11 ARIMA method.

Notes

ISAE does not publish an overall index. Consequently, no single subject is far more important than the others. For the analysis of industrial production the answers on production activity and on assesment of orders are important. There are always situations whereby individual questions temporarily gain in importance due to the overall economic circumstances.

Key Datastream Mnemonics

ISAE Industrial Trends (sa)	Datastream
Total	
Assessment domestic order books and demand level	ITDOMORD
Assessment export order books and demand level	ITFORORD
Assessment total order books and demand level	ITTOTORD
Assessment inventories of finished goods	ITLEVINV
Assessment production level	ITTOTPRDR
Assessment production changes on previous month	ITOTPRQR
Forecast order books	ITEXPORD
Forecast production	ITPRDEXP
Forecast selling prices	ITPRCEXP
Forecast economy	ITECONOP
Per capita labour cost	ITOTLABR
Capacity utilization	ITPURTID
Intermediate goods	
Assessment domestic order books and demand level	ITINTOBBR
Assessment export order books and demand level	ITINTEXOR
Assessment total order books and demand level	ITINTORDR
Assessment inventories of finished goods	ITINTSFGR
Assessment production level	ITINTPRDR
Assessment production changes on previous month	ITINTPRDR
Forecast order books	ITNTFOBR
Forecast production	ITNTFPRR
Forecast selling prices	ITNTFSPR
Forecast economy	ITNTFECR
Per capita labour cost	ITOTLABR
Capacity utilization	ITPURIVG
Investment goods	
Assessment domestic order books and demand level	ITINVOBBR
Assessment export order books and demand level	ITINVEXOR
Assessment total order books and demand level	ITINVORDR
Assessment inventories of finished goods	ITINVSFGR
Assessment production level	ITINVPRDR
Assessment production changes on previous month	ITINVPRDR
Forecast order books	ININVFOBR
Forecast production	ININVFPRR
Forecast selling prices	ININVFSPR
Forecast economy	ININVFECR
Per capita labour cost	ITINVLABR
Capacity utilization	ITPURIMG

ISAE Industrial Trends (sa)	Datastream
Consumer goods	
Assessment domestic order books and demand level	ITCONOBBR
Assessment export order books and demand level	ITCONEXOR
Assessment total order books and demand level	ITCONORDR
Assessment inventories of finished goods	ITCONSFGR
Assessment production level	ITCONPRDR
Assessment production changes on previous month	ITCONPRDR
Forecast order books	ITCONFOBR
Forecast production	ITCONFPRR
Forecast selling prices	ITCONFSPR
Forecast economy	ITCONFECR
Per capita labour cost	ITCONLABR
Capacity utilization	ITPURCGD

24
Labour Market Indicators

24.1 Employment and Unemployment

Data Source

The data for the Euro-zone are published by Eurostat and the national data by the statistical offices and the German Bundesamt für Arbeit (Federal Office of Labour) in Germany. The press release by Eurostat is available on the Internet at www.europa.eu.int/comm/euroindicators and some of the national data are available on the Internet sites of the respective statistical offices and German Bundesamt für Arbeit. The data series are also published in part in Table 5.4 of the ECB *Monthly Report* and in the publication *Eurostatistics – Data for short-term economic analysis* issued by Eurostat.

Importance for the Financial Markets   B

Description

Eurostat publishes standardized data on the labour market situation which are based on regular national data surveys, as well as an annual survey conducted in spring for the Euro-zone and the individual member countries. As the national data are published before the harmonized figures, it provides the earliest indications of the labour market situation. However, the national statistics are not uniform. Eurostat started in 2000 to adopt a new definition of unemployment that is fully compatible with the International Labour Organization (ILO) standards but which gives a more precise definition of unemployment. Most countries still have to adapt the labour force surveys slightly to comply with all the elements of this definition. The harmonization will go on in the next two years as more and more countries adapt their surveys to this new definition. When Member States takes corrective measures to match the definitions precisely, this may affect the published monthly series.

The basis for the calculation of the monthly unemployment rate is the Community Labour Force Survey, where the population of working age is divided into three groups: employed, unemployed and inactive. Employed persons are those who during the reference week did any job for pay or profit for at least one hour. In addition, people belong to this group if they were not working but had jobs from which they were temporarily absent. Family workers are also included. Unemployed persons comprise people aged 15 to 74 who were:

- Without work during the reference week
- Currently available for work before the end of the two weeks following the reference week
- Actively seeking work (i.e., had taken specific steps in the four week period ending with the reference week to seek paid employment or self-employment or who had found a job to start later but within a period of at most three months).

The following are considered as specific steps of actively seeking work:

- Having been in contact with a public employment office to find work
- Having been in contact with a private agency to find work
- Applying to employers directly
- Asking among friends, unions, etc., to find work
- Placing or answering job advertisements
- Studying job advertisements
- Taking a recruitment test or examination or being interviewed
- Looking for land, premises or equipment
- Applying for permits, licences or financial resources

Education and training are not considered as methods of seeking work but as ways of improving employability.

For the unemployment rate the figures for youth and adult unemployment, as well as for male and female unemployment, are shown separately. Youth is therefore defined as people under 25 years of age, whereas adults are 25 years and over. For these sub-groups the unemployment rate is calculated as a percentage of the people in work in the respective age groups. All data are also shown separately for men and women. In addition to the unemployment figures, Eurostat also publishes quarterly data on the employment situation. According to this, those in paid work and the self-employed in the reference period are classed as employed. The main time series are calculated for 11 countries until December 2000. Since that date, Greece has been included,

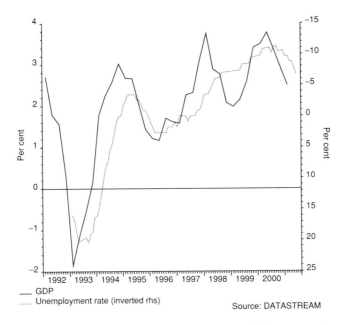

Figure 24.1   Change in Euro-zone unemployment rate and GDP on preceding year

but Eurostat has also published historical data for the 11 Member States plus Greece since 1991.

In addition, Eurostat also publishes data on people in paid employment. These include all those who were in paid employment or temporarily released from their occupation (sickness or maternity leave) over a reference period. In addition to the quarterly data, monthly data are also published for industry, production and construction. Particularly for the quarterly data, it should be noted that a very low level of harmonization has been achieved to date. Different concepts are therefore used in some cases (Germany and France) or individual sectors are not included (France). For Belgium, Ireland and Greece there are no data available at all and the data for the Netherlands and Austria are only published after a long time delay.

The differences between the national statistics and the Eurostat data are not just due to different definitions, but also the type of survey. Based on the annual survey conducted by Eurostat, the national statistics are used to extrapolate trends in the individual countries and the Euro-zone. However, as not all countries publish monthly data, this constitutes an additional source of uncertainty and can lead to revisions.

The information in the national statistics differs enormously in parts. Whereas in Germany information on the number of employed and unemployed, the unemployment rate, the number of short-time workers and the number of jobs vacant is published, and these data are only published in the national definition, the French INSEE, for example, makes the number of unemployed available both in the national definition and the ILO definition.

Periodicity/Revisions

The Eurostat data are published around the tenth day of the second month following the reference month, while the quarterly data are announced around $1\frac{1}{2}$ months after the end of the quarter. The data from Germany, France, Spain and the Netherlands have already been published by this time. In Spain, however, not all data are published on a monthly basis, the unemployment rate, for example, is only published quarterly. In addition, in the Netherlands only a moving average over three months is published. The data for the month of publication of February, for example, thereby relate to the average for the months January, February and March. Limited revisions are conducted both for the Eurostat data and the national data. Publication of the EU data is effected at 12.00 CET (06.00 ET). The data from Germany are published at 09.55 CET (03.55 ET), from France at 08.45 CET (02.45 ET) and Italy at 09.00 CET (03.00 ET).

Seasonal Adjustment

Both the Eurostat data and the national data are seasonally adjusted. Eurostat thereby uses TRAMO/SEATS, which is a different seasonal adjustment method from the other individual member countries. In addition, seasonal adjustment by Eurostat is conducted based on the so-called direct method, whereby unadjusted data are aggregated in the individual countries and only then seasonally adjusted.

Notes

The Eurostat data provide a good summary of the labour market situation in the individual member countries and the Euro-zone. The fact that the data are surveyed according to uniform criteria and are therefore comparable is also an advantage. In addition to the total unemployment rate, the markets are also interested in the national figures, although these are not completely standardized and therefore not fully comparable with the Eurostat data. In addition, they only relate to a limited part of the overall labour market. However, as they are partly published before the Euro-zone data and provide a good summary of the labour market situation in the larger member countries, they are still relatively important for the financial markets.

Figure 24.2 Unemployment rates in Euro-zone and the USA

Key Datastream Mnemonics

Employment and Unemployment (sa)	Datastream
Euro area	
Unemployment	EMEBUN . . O
Unemployment, percentage of labour force	EAEBUN . . Q
Total	EAESUNEMO
Adult	EMEBUNA.Q
Youth	EMEBUNY.Q
Employment	
Index whole economy (1995=100)	EMEBEM.XH
Industry (excluding construction)	EMEBEMI%P
Services	EMEBEMR%P
Unemployment rate (since 1993)	EMTOTUN%Q
Austria	
Unemployment, percentage of labour force	OEESUNEMO
Employment, index whole economy (1995=100)	OEESEMP
Belgium	
Unemployment, percentage of labour force	BGESUNEMO
Employment, index whole economy (1995=100)	BGESEMPIHI

Employment and Unemployment (sa)	Datastream
Finland	
Unemployment, percentage of labour force	FNESUNEMO
Employment, index whole economy (1995=100)	FNESEMPIH
France	
Unemployment, percentage of labour force	FRESUNEMO
Employment, index whole economy (1995=100)	FRESEMPIH
Germany	
Unemployment, percentage of labour force	BDESUNEMO
Employment, index whole economy (1995=100)	BDESEMPIH
Greece	
Unemployment, percentage of labour force	GRESUNEM
Employment, index whole economy (1995=100)	GRESEMPIH
Ireland	
Unemployment, percentage of labour force	IRESUNEMO
Employment, index whole economy (1995=100)	IRESEMPIH
Italy	
Unemployment, percentage of labour force	ITESUNEMO
Employment, index whole economy (1995=100)	ITESEMPIH
Luxembourg	
Unemployment, percentage of labour force	LXESUNEMO
Employment, index whole economy (1995=100)	LXESEMPIH
Netherlands	
Unemployment, percentage of labour force	NLESUNEMO
Employment, index whole economy (1995=100)	NLESEMPIH
Portugal	
Unemployment, percentage of labour force	PTESUNEMO
Employment, index whole economy (1995=100)	PTESEMPIH
Spain	
Unemployment, percentage of labour force	ESESUNEMO
Employment, index whole economy (1995=100)	ESESEMPIH
EU15	
Unemployment, percentage of labour force	ECESUNEMO
Employment, index whole economy (1995=100)	ECESEMPIH
Denmark	
Unemployment, percentage of labour force	DKESUNEMO
Employment, index whole economy (1995=100)	DKESEMPIH
Sweden	
Unemployment, percentage of labour force	SDESUNEMO
Employment, index whole economy (1995=100)	SDESEMPIH
United Kingdom	
Unemployment, percentage of labour force	UKESUNEMO
Employment, index whole economy (1995=100)	UKESEMPIH

Literature

Deutsche Bundesbank, 'The labour market in the Euro area', *Monthly Report*, October 1999, pp. 47–59.

European Central Bank, 'Developments in and structural features of the Euro area labour markets' *Monthly Report*, May 2000, pp. 57–74.

European Central Bank, 'Labour force developments in the Euro area', *Monthly Report*, June 2000, pp. 40–2.

European Central Bank, 'Revisions to employment figures', *Monthly Report*, September 2000, p. 44.

European Central Bank, 'Changes in the definition of unemployment in EU Member States', *Monthly Report*, March 2001, p. 37.

25
Consumer Indicators

25.1   Retail Sales

Data Source

The statistics on retail sales are produced by Eurostat. The press release is available on the Internet at www.europa.eu.int/comm/euroindicators. In addition, some of the data are published in Table 5.2 of the ECB *Monthly Report* and in the publication *Eurostatistics – Data for short-term economic analysis* issued by Eurostat.

Importance for the Financial Markets   C

Description

The retail sales index is an economic indicator of monthly retail sales covering around 40 per cent of total private consumer expenditure. Eurostat has

Table 25.1   Individual nation as a proportion of the total Retail Sales Index (2000)

Austria	3.2%
Belgium	4.2%
Finland	1.6%
France	22.9%
Germany	31.3%
Greece	1.4%
Ireland	1.0%
Italy	16.4%
Luxembourg	0.3%
Netherlands	5.7%
Portugal	1.8%
Spain	10.4%

produced this indicator since 1995. Before this, national data were employed. These data are not, however, fully comparable with the data after 1995 due to the lack of harmonization. The retail trade sector covers retail sales and repairs of non-durable goods. However, truck repairs, vehicle parts and fuel, trade with grain, ore, crude oil, techno-chemicals, iron and steel, industrial machinery and equipment, as well as sales of food and drink on the premises and takeaway services, are not included.

The statistics are divided into the following sectors:

- Food, beverages and tobacco
- Other goods
- Textiles, clothing and footwear
- Household equipment

The assignment of the individual categories is based on the main lines stocked by the companies surveyed so that product groups are not completely homogeneous. In addition, the data for the individual countries are published. The national weighting for the overall index is derived from annual structural data, other sales statistics or direct information from the member countries. The weighting is recalculated every five years. The present base year for the weighting and the index is 1995.

Turnover includes the total value of goods and services invoiced to third parties by the companies surveyed within a month. The following constitute turnover, for example:

- Product sales price
- Invoiced services provided
- Sale of by-products
- Packing and transport costs invoiced
- Assembly, installation and repair work invoiced
- Instalment payments invoiced
- Commission

These figures are shown including VAT. Price reductions, rebates, discounts and credit notes for returned goods or returned packaging are deducted, cash discounts, however, are not. Price reductions, rebates and bonus payments, which are only granted at the end of the year, are also excluded.

The data are published both in nominal and real terms. For the deflation, the national countries take the appropriate price indices as the basis and these are then calculated as weighted factors in the price indices for the respective economic sectors.

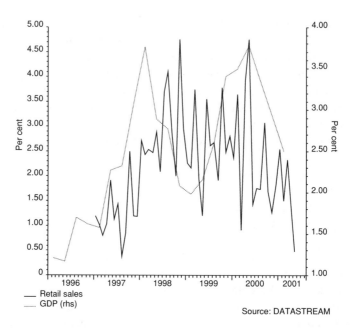

Figure 25.1 Change in Euro-zone retail sales and GDP on preceding year

Periodicity/Revisions

The aggregated data are sent to Eurostat at the latest two months after the end of the survey month. More detailed data are sent to Eurostat one month later. Member countries, whose added value in the retail sector within a given base year is less than 3 per cent of the EU-zone total, have to supply the data within 3 (aggregate data) or 4 (detailed data) months at the latest. Portugal does not currently produce these data. The data are published within three months of the reference month. As data for the smaller countries and detailed data are not yet available at this time, it is incorporated into later publications, so there are regular revisions. Publication is effected at 12.00 CET (06.00 ET).

Seasonal Adjustment

Member countries are obliged to submit working-day adjusted data to Eurostat. In addition, they may also submit seasonally adjusted data and indices in the form of cyclical trends based on the national seasonal adjustment method. Eurostat then publishes the data adjusted at national level, where available, otherwise it carries out the adjustment itself. For the aggregated data, national weighting is used for data with working-day adjustment. Then the time series is adjusted using the TRAMO/SEATS seasonal adjustment method. Consequently, seasonally adjusted growth rates published for the Euro-zone may differ from national seasonally adjusted weighted time series. Missing data are estimated using an ARIMA model.

Notes

The importance of retail sales is still somewhat limited due to its brief history. Eurostat publishes seasonally adjusted monthly growth rates as well as annual growth rates with working-day adjustments. The ECB, by contrast, publishes index values and seasonally adjusted annual growth rates in its monthly report. In addition, the ECB publishes data on new private car registrations, which are not included in the Eurostat retail statistics but are produced on the basis of statistics from the ACEA (European automobile producer association). These statistics create problems because the survey methods are not entirely harmonized. This will change in the coming months and years but, until then, certain distortions are inevitable.

Key Datastream Mnemonics

Retail Sales (sa)	Datastream
Euro area	
Total	EAESRSTTG
Food, beverages, tobacco	EAESRSFTG
Non-food	EAESRSNFG
Textiles, clothing, footwear	EAESRSTXG
Household equipment	EAESRSHEG
New passenger car registrations (nsa)	EANEWREGP
Austria	
Total	OEESRSTTG
Belgium	
Total	BGESRSTTG
Finland	
Total	FNESRSTTG
France	
Total	FRESRSTTG
Food, beverages, tobacco	FRESRSFTG
Non-food	FRESRSNFG
Textiles, clothing, footwear	FRESRSTXG
Household equipment	FRESRSHEG
New passenger car registrations (nsa)	FRNEWREGP

Retail Sales (sa)	Datastream
Germany	
Total	BDESRSTTG
Food, beverages, tobacco	BDESRSFTG
Non-food	BDESRSNFG
Textiles, clothing, footwear	BDESRSTXG
Household equipment	BDESRSHEG
New passenger car registrations (nsa)	BDNEWREGP
Greece	
Total	GRESRSTTG
Ireland	
Total	IRESRSTTG
Italy	
Total	IRESRSTTG
Food, beverages, tobacco	IRESRSFTG
Non-food	ITVD4031F
Textiles, clothing, footware	IRESRSTXG
Household equipment	IRESRSHEG
New passenger car registrations (nsa)	IRNEWREGP
Luxembourg	
Total	LXESRSTTG
Netherlands	
Total	NLESRSTTG
Food, beverages, tobacco	NLESRSFTG
Non-food	NLESRSNFG
Textiles, clothing, footware	NLESRSTXG
Household equipment	NLESRSHEG
New passenger car registrations (nsa)	NLNEWREGP
Portugal	
Total	PTESRSTTG
Spain	
Total	ESESRSTTG
Food, beverages, tobacco	ESESRSFTG
Non-food	ESESRSNFG
Textiles, clothing, footware	ESESRSTXG
Household equipment	ESESRSHEG
New passenger car registrations (nsa)	ESNEWREGP
EU15	
Total	ECESRSTTG
Food, beverages, tobacco	ECESRSFTG
Non-food	ECESRSNFG
Textiles, clothing, footware	ECESRSTXG
Household equipment	ECESRSHEG
New passenger car registrations (nsa)	ECNEWREGP

Retail Sales (sa)	Datastream
Denmark	
Total	DKESRSTTG
Sweden	
Total	SDESRSTTG
United Kingdom	
Total	UKESRSTTG

Literature

European Central Bank, 'Retail sales in the Euro area', *Monthly Report*, February 2000, pp. 27–8.

25.2   EU Retail Trade Survey

Data Source

Data are surveyed by research institutes in the individual member countries within the context of their own survey. They then pass on the relevant parts of the results to the EU Commission, which aggregates the data, conducts seasonal adjustment and publishes the overall indices. A summary of the data is available on the Internet at europa.eu.int/comm/economy_finance/index_en.htm. More detailed data are published in the publication *European Economy*, Supplement B.

Importance for the Financial Markets   D

Description

The EU Commission has conducted the survey in the retail sector since the beginning of 1984. Although the survey initially only covered Belgium, France, Germany and the UK, ten other countries have since been added. The only country not currently participating in the survey is Luxembourg. The results are then published by the EU Commission in conjunction with its other surveys. The surveys are not conducted by the Commission itself, however, but by research institutes in the individual countries. The data are surveyed according to uniform criteria so that they are comparable between the countries. The raw data are then sent to the EU Commission. For the individual indicators net values are then calculated (i.e., negative values are deducted from positive ones). The results of the individual indices are then shown separately for the relevant countries, the Euro-zone and the EU.

For the retail trade survey a number of subjects are analyzed using the following questions:

1. **Assessment of current business situation**
   We consider our present business (sales) position to be: good/satisfactory (normal for the season)/bad.
2. **Assessment of stocks of finished products**
   We consider our present stocks to be: too small/adequate (normal for the season)/too large.
3. **Scope of orders to be issued within the next three months to suppliers**
   We expect that our orders placed with suppliers during the next few (three) months excluding purely seasonal variations will be: up/unchanged/down.
4. **Business outlook over the next six months**
   Our business trend over the next six months, excluding purely seasonal variations will: improve/remain unchanged/deteriorate.

In addition, the employment situation is surveyed quarterly:

Source: DATASTREAM

Figure 25.2   Euro-zone Retail Trade Confidence Index

5. **Expectations of employment situation**
   In the next few (three) months, and compared with today, the number of persons we employ will: increase/remain unchanged/decline.

From the responses on the assessment of the current business situation, business outlook and the assessment of stocks, an Index of Retail Trade Confidence is also produced. An average of seasonally adjusted net values is calculated, whereby the value for stocks is inversed.

An indicator on the position in the retail trade sector is very useful for analizing the economic situation, although it is limited to one sub-sector of the economy. Consequently the Commission also publishes a multi-sectoral EU Economic Sentiment Index that covers the entire economy.

Starting in October 2001, the EU Commission published a modified Economic Sentiment Indicator. They have changed the weights of the single sub-indicators and replaced the stock price index with the EU Retail Trade Confidence Index. In addition, the composition of the EU Consumer Confidence Index has been changed.

The new EU Economic Sentiment Indicator composition is as follows:

- Index of Industrial Confidence with a weighting of 40 per cent
- Index of Consumer Confidence with a weighting of 20 per cent
- Index of Construction Confidence with a weighting of 20 per cent
- Index of Retail Trade Confidence with a weighting of 20 per cent

Periodicity/Revisions

Questionnaires are sent out by the national bodies shortly before the beginning of the month under review. The responses are evaluated in the second half of the month and sent to the EU Commission by the end of the survey month. The initial results are then published approximately one week after the end of the month. Revisions are normally only conducted in conjunction with seasonal adjustment factor alignments. Publication is effected at 12.00 CET (06.00 ET).

Seasonal Adjustment

The data are aggregated by the EU Commission and then seasonally adjusted. As the Commission does not use the X-12 ARIMA program but the so-called Dainties method, the figures published by the national bodies are not fully comparable with the data published by the EU Commission.

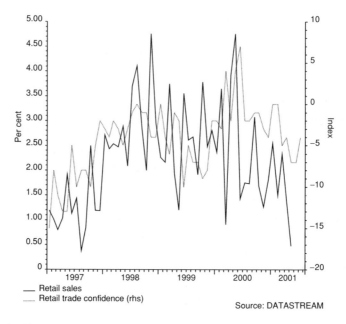

Figure 25.3 Change in retail sales on preceding year and Euro-zone Retail Trade Confidence Index

Notes

The retail trade survey is published in conjunction with the EU Industrial Survey, EU Construction Survey and the EU Consumer Survey. Overall, these surveys provide a good picture of the economic situation in the Euro-zone. However, the importance of the data on the retail trade sector is limited by its brief history.

Key Datastream Mnemonics

EU Retail Trade Survey (sa)	Datastream
Euro area	
Retail trade confidence survey	EAEUSRCIQ
Present business position	EAEUSRPBQ
Business trend over next six months	EAEUSREBQ
Present stock	EAEUSRSTQ
Expectations orders placed with suppliers	EAEUSROSQ
Number of persons employed	EAEUSREMQ

EU Retail Trade Survey (sa)	Datastream
Austria	
Retail trade confidence survey	OEEUSRCIQ
Present business position	OEEUSRPBQ
Business trend over next six months	OEEUSREBQ
Present stock	OEEUSRSTQ
Belgium	
Retail trade confidence survey	BGEUSRCIQ
Present business position	BGEUSRPBQ
Business trend over next six months	BGEUSREBQ
Present stock	BGEUSRSTQ
Finland	
Retail trade confidence survey	FNEUSRCIQ
Present business position	FNEUBRPBQ
Business trend over next six months	FNEUSREBQ
Present stock	FNEUSRSTQ
France	
Retail trade confidence survey	FREUSRCIQ
Present business position	FREUSRPBQ
Business trend over next six months	FREUSREBQ
Present stock	FREUSRSTQ
Expectations orders placed with suppliers	FREUSROSQ
Number of persons employed	FREUSREMQ
Germany	
Retail trade confidence survey	BDEUSRCIQ
Present business position	BDEUSRPBQ
Business trend over next six months	BDEUSREBQ
Present stock	BDEUSRSTQ
Expectations orders placed with suppliers	BDEUSROSQ
Number of persons employed	BDEUSREMQ
Greece	
Retail trade confidence survey	GREUSRCIQ
Present business position	GREUSRPBQ
Business trend over next six months	GREUSREBQ
Present stock	GREUSRSTQ
Ireland	
Retail trade confidence survey	
Present business position	
Business trend over next six months	
Present stock	
Italy	
Retail trade confidence survey	ITEUSRCIQ
Present business position	ITEUSRPBQ
Business trend over next six months	ITEUSREBQ
Present stock	ITEUSRSTQ
Expectations orders placed with suppliers	ITEUSROSQ
Number of persons employed	ITEUSREMQ

EU Retail Trade Survey (sa)	Datastream
Luxembourg	
Retail trade confidence survey	
Present business position	
Business trend over next six months	
Present stock	
Netherlands	
Retail trade confidence survey	NLEUSRCIQ
Present business position	NLEUSRPBQ
Business trend over next six months	NLEUSREBQ
Present stock	NLEUSRSTQ
Expectations orders placed with suppliers	NLEUSROSQ
Number of persons employed	NLEUSREMQ
Portugal	
Retail trade confidence survey	PTEUSRCIQ
Present business position	PTEUSRPBQ
Business trend over next six months	PTEUSREBQ
Present stock	PTEUSRSTQ
Spain	
Retail trade confidence survey	ESEUSRCIQ
Present business position	ESEUSRPBQ
Business trend over next six months	ESEUSREBQ
Present stock	ESEUSRSTQ
Expectations orders placed with suppliers	ESEUSROSQ
Number of persons employed	ESEUSREMQ
EU15	
Retail trade confidence survey	ECEUSRCIQ
Present business position	ECEUSRPBQ
Business trend over next six months	ECEUSREBQ
Present stock	ECEUSRSTQ
Expectations orders placed with suppliers	ECEUSROSQ
Number of persons employed	ECEUSREMQ
Denmark	
Retail trade confidence survey	DKEUSRCIQ
Present business position	DKEUSRPBQ
Business trend over next six months	DKEUSREBQ
Present stock	DKEUSRSTQ
Sweden	
Retail trade confidence survey	SDEUSRCIQ
Present business position	SDEUSRPBQ
Business trend over next six months	SDEUSREBQ
Present stock	SDEUSRSTQ
United Kingdom	
Retail trade confidence survey	UKEUSRCIQ
Present business position	UKEUSRPBQ
Business trend over next six months	UKEUSREBQ
Present stock	UKEUSRSTQ

Economic Sentiment Indicator (sa)	Datastream
Euro area	EAEUSESIG
Austria	OEEUSESIG
Belgium	BGEUSESIG
Finland	FNEUSESIG
France	FREUSESIG
Germany	BDEUSESIG
Greece	GREUSESIG
Ireland	IREUSESIG
Italy	ITEUSESIG
Luxembourg	
Netherlands	NLEUSESIG
Portugal	PTEUSESIG
Spain	ESEUSESIG
EU15	ECEUSESIG
Denmark	DKEUSESIG
Sweden	
United Kingdom	UKEUSESIG

Literature

European Commission, 'The joint harmonised EU programme of business and consumer surveys', *European Economy,* No. 6, 1997, Luxembourg.

25.3   EU Consumer Survey

Data Source

Data are surveyed by research institutes in the individual member countries within the context of their own survey. They then pass on the relevant parts of the results to the EU Commission, which aggregates the data, conducts seasonal adjustment and publishes the overall indices. A summary of the data is available on the Internet at europa.eu.int/comm/economy_finance/index_ en.htm. More detailed data are published in the publication *European Economy,* Supplement B.

Importance for the Financial Markets   C

Description

The EU Commission has conducted the Consumer Survey since May 1972 and it closely resembles that of the University of Michigan. Its aim is to acquire information on consumer expenditure and saving intentions and the factors affecting these figures. Initially, the survey was only conducted in Belgium, Germany, France, Italy and the Netherlands. All member countries except

Luxembourg now participate. In the early years the survey was only conducted three times a year. At the beginning of the 1980s Germany and the UK began to survey the data monthly and since July 1986 this survey period has been adopted by all nations. The survey is conducted on 2500 consumers in Germany, 2000 in Spain, France, Italy and the UK respectively, as well as 1500 in each of the remaining nations. The data are surveyed based on uniform criteria, so that they are comparable between the countries. The raw data are sent to the EU Commission which then calculates net values (i.e., negative values are deducted from positive ones). For this the responses showing substantial change, such as 'much better', are assigned a value of 1, whereas less positive responses, such as 'better', are assigned a weighting of 0.5. The results for the individual indices are then published for the individual countries, the Euro-zone and the EU.

For the survey a number of subjects are analyzed using the following questions:

1. **Assessment of financial position**
   How does the financial situation of your household now compare with what it was 12 months ago: got a lot better/got a little better/stayed the same/got a little worse/got a lot worse/don't know.

2. **Expectations of financial position**
   How do you think the financial position of your household will change over the next 12 months: get a lot better/get a little better/stay the same/get a little worse/get a lot worse/don't know.

3. **Assessment of overall economic situation**
   How do you think the general economic situation in this country has changed over the last 12 months: got a lot better/got a little better/stayed the same/got a little worse/got a lot worse/don't know.

4. **Assessment of economic prospects**
   How do you think the general economic situation in this country will develop over the next 12 months: get a lot better/get a little better/stay the same/get a little worse/get a lot worse/don't know.

5. **Assessment of price trends**
   Compared with what it was 12 months ago, do you think the cost of living is now: very much higher/quite a bit higher/a little higher/about the same/lower/don't know.

6. **Assessment of future price trends**
   By comparison with what is happening now, do you think that in the next 12 months: there will be a more rapid increase in prices/prices will increase at the same rate/prices will increase at a slower rate/prices will stay the same/prices will fall slightly/don't know.

7. **Expectations of employment situation**
   How do you think the level of unemployment in the country will change over the next 12 months. Will it: increase sharply/increase slightly/remain the same/fall slightly/fall sharply/don't know.

8. **Current buying intentions**
   Do you think that there is an advantage for people in making major purchases (furniture, washing machines, television sets, etc.) at the present time: yes, now is the right time/it is neither the right time nor the wrong time/no, it is the wrong time, the purchase should be postponed/don't know.

9. **Planned buying intentions**
   Over the next 12 months, how do you think the amount of money you spend on major purchases will compare with what you spent over the last 12 months? Will it be: much more/a little more/about the same/a little less/ much less/don't know.

10. **Current saving intentions**
    In view of the general economic situation, do you think this is: a very good time to save/quite a good time to save/rather an unfavourable time to save/ a very unfavourable time to save/don't know.

11. **Planned saving intentions**
    Over the next 12 months, how likely are you to be able to save any money: very likely/fairly likely/fairly unlikely/very unlikely/don't know.

12. **Assessment of current financial situation**
    Which of these statements best describes the present of your household: we are running into debt/we are having to draw on our savings/we are just managing to make ends meet on our income/we are saving a little/we are saving a lot/don't know.

On the basis of the responses given, a consumer confidence index is produced. Prior to October 2001, the following points had been included by calculating an average of seasonally adjusted net values:

- Assessment of financial position
- Expectations of financial position
- Assessment of overall economic situation
- Assessment of economic prospects
- Current buying intentions

Since October 2001, the new Consumer Confidence Indicator is calculated as the arithmetic average of the following points, thus using expectations only:

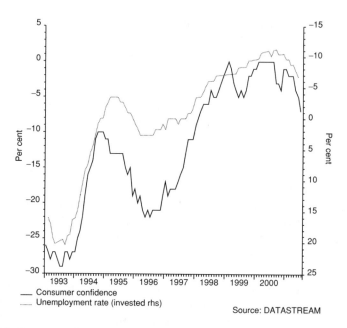

Figure 25.4   Euro-zone Consumer Confidence Index and change in unemployment rate on preceding year

- Expectations of financial position
- Assessment of economic prospects
- Expectations of employment situation
- Planned saving intentions

In the survey in January, April, July and October additional information is collected on the following subjects:

1. **Plans to buy a car**
   How likely are you to buy a car within the next two years: very likely/fairly likely/fairly unlikely/very unlikely/don't know.
2. **Plans to buy or build a house**
   Are you planning to purchase or build a home within the next two years (to live in yourself, for a member of your family, as a holiday home, to let, etc.): Yes, definitely/possibly/probably not/no/don't know.
3. **Plans to renovate**
   Over the next 12 months, how likely are you to spend any large sums of money on home improvements, such as central heating, sanitary equipment, etc.: very likely/fairly likely/fairly unlikely/very unlikely/don't know.

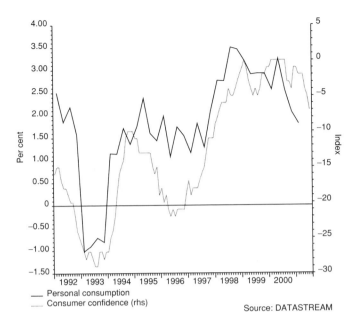

Figure 25.5 Change in personal consumption expenditures on preceding year and Euro-zone Consumer Confidence Index

The survey is conducted in such a way that the results are also shown in demographic and economic terms. The following categories are thereby included:

1. **Household income**
   (a) 1st quarter
   (b) 2nd quarter
   (c) 3rd quarter
   (d) 4th quarter
2. **Occupation of respondent**
   (a) Self-employed + professional
   (b) Self-employed farmer
   (c) Clerical + office employees
   (d) Skilled manual workers
   (e) Other manual workers
   (f) Total workers
   (g) Other occupations
   (h) Work full-time
   (i) Work part-time
   (j) Unemployed

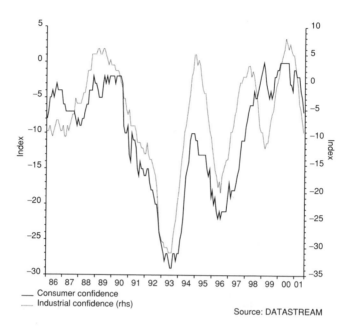

Figure 25.6 Euro-zone Consumer Confidence Index and Industrial Confidence Index

3. **Education of respondent**
   (a) Primary
   (b) Secondary
   (c) Further
4. **Age of respondent**
   (a) 16–29
   (b) 30–49
   (c) 50–64
   (d) 65+
5. **Sex of respondent**
   (a) male
   (b) female

Indicators on the position in the consumer sector are very useful for analyzing the economic situation, although they are inevitably limited to one sub-sector of the economy. Consequently the Commission also publishes another additional multi-sectoral EU Economic Sentiment Index which covers the entire economy. Prior to October 2001, this index was composed of:

- Index of Industrial Confidence with a weighting of one-third
- Index of Consumer Confidence with a weighting of one-third

- Index of Construction Confidence with a weighting of one-sixth
- Stock price index with a weighting of one-sixth

Starting in October 2001, the EU Commission published a modified Economic Sentiment Indicator. They have changed the weights of the single sub-indicators and replaced the stock price index with the EU Retail Trade Confidence Index.

The new EU Economic Sentiment Indicator composition is as follows:

- Index of Industrial Confidence with a weighting of 40 per cent
- Index of Consumer Confidence with a weighting of 20 per cent
- Index of Construction Confidence with a weighting of 20 per cent
- Index of Retail Trade Confidence with a weighting of 20 per cent

Periodicity/Revisions

Surveys are conducted by the economic institutes in the first half of each month and evaluated in the period from the tenth to the twenty-fifth of each month. The results are then sent to the Commission shortly before the end of the survey month and the first results are published around one week after the end of the month. Revisions are normally only conducted in conjunction with seasonal adjustment factor alignment or a change in the base year. Publication is effected at 12.00 CET (06.00 ET).

Seasonal Adjustment

The data are aggregated and then seasonally adjusted by the EU Commission. However, the Commission uses the so-called Dainties method for seasonal adjustment. For this reason the values published by the national bodies are not fully comparable with the data published by the EU Commission.

Notes

The figures in the surveys are very useful for assessing the economic position and economic prospects in the Euro-zone. The raw data are actually already known because the national bodies surveying this data publish the figures in advance. The EU Commission data are particularly valuable in that they provide an overall summary and do not only concentrate on individual countries. With consumer confidence there is also the advantage that predominantly uniform data have been available since 1972 for most of the member countries, so it also has a long enough history to analyze the situation. Due to the problems with the aggregation of real economic statistics in the consumer sector, the consumer confidence index is useful as it is surveyed according to uniform criteria. However, it should be noted that one of the main influencing factors affecting consumer confidence is the situation in the labour market.

Key Datastream Mnemonics

EU Consumer Survey (sa)	Datastream
Euro area	
Consumer confidence index	EAEUSCCIQ
Financial situation compared with 12 months ago	EAEUSCFNQ
Financial situation, expected change over 12 months	EAEUSCFYQ
General economic situation, change over the last 12 months	EAEUSCECQ
General economic situation, expected development over next 12 months	EAEUSCEYQ
Advantage in making major purchases at the present time	EAEUSCMPQ
Amount of money to be spent over the next 12 months	EAEUSCPCQ
Cost of living compared with 12 months ago	EAEUSCPRQ
Change of prices over the next 12 months	EAEUSCPYQ
Expected change in the level of unemployment	EAEUSCUNQ
Present savings situation	EAEUSCSAQ
Expected savings situation over the next 12 months	EAEUSCSYQ
Present financial situation	
Likelihood of buying a car within the next two years	
Planning to purchase a home within the next two years	
Expected spending of large sums of money on home improvement	
Austria	
Consumer confidence index	OEEUSCCIQ
Financial situation compared with 12 months ago	OEEUSCFNQ
Financial situation, expected change over 12 months	OEEUSCFYQ
General economic situation, change over the last 12 months	OEEUSCECQ
General economic situation, expected development over next 12 months	OEEUSCEYQ
Advantage in making major purchases at the present time	OEEUSCMPQ
Belgium	
Consumer confidence index	BGEUSCCIQ
Financial situation compared with 12 months ago	BGEUSCFNQ
Financial situation, expected change over 12 months	BGEUSCFYQ
General economic situation, change over the last 12 months	BGEUSCECQ
General economic situation, expected development over next 12 months	BGEUSCEYQ
Advantage in making major purchases at the present time	BGEUSCMPQ
Finland	
Consumer confidence index	FNEUSCCIQ
Financial situation compared with 12 months ago	FNEUSCFNQ
Financial situation, expected change over 12 months	FNEUSCFYQ
General economic situation, change over the last 12 months	FNEUSCECQ
General economic situation, expected development over next 12 months	FNEUSCEYQ
Advantage in making major purchases at the present time	FNEUSCMPQ

EU Consumer Survey (sa)	Datastream
France	
Consumer confidence index	FREUSCCIQ
Financial situation compared with 12 months ago	FREUSCFNQ
Financial situation, expected change over 12 months	FREUSCFYQ
General economic situation, change over the last 12 months	FREUSCECQ
General economic situation, expected development over next 12 months	FREUSCEYQ
Advantage in making major purchases at the present time	FREUSCMPQ
Amount of money to be spent over the next 12 months	FREUSCPCQ
Cost of living compared with 12 months ago	FREUSCPRQ
Change of prices over the next 12 months	FREUSCPYQ
Expected change in the level of unemployment	FREUSCUNQ
Present savings situation	FREUSCSAQ
Expected savings situation over the next 12 months	FREUSCSYQ
Present financial situation	
Likelihood of buying a car within the next two years	
Planing to purchase a home within the next two years	
Expected spending of large sums of money on home improvement	
Germany	
Consumer confidence index	BDEUSCCIQ
Financial situation compared with 12 months ago	BDEUSCFNQ
Financial situation, expected change over 12 months	BDEUSCFYQ
General economic situation, change over the last 12 months	BDEUSCECQ
General economic situation, expected development over next 12 months	BDEUSCEYQ
Advantage in making major purchases at the present time	BDEUSCMPQ
Amount of money to be spent over the next 12 months	BDEUSCPCQ
Cost of living compared with 12 months ago	BDEUSCPRQ
Change of prices over the next 12 months	BDEUSCPYQ
Expected change in the level of unemployment	BDEUSCUNQ
Present savings situation	BDEUSCSAQ
Expected savings situation over the next 12 months	BDEUSCSYQ
Present financial situation	
Likelihood of buying a car within the next two years	
Planing to purchase a home within the next two years	
Expected spending of large sums of money on home improvement	
Greece	
Consumer confidence index	GREUSCCIQ
Financial situation compared with 12 months ago	GREUSCFNQ
Financial situation, expected change over 12 months	GREUSCFYQ
General economic situation, change over the last 12 months	GREUSCECQ
General economic situation, expected development over next 12 months	GREUSCEYQ
Advantage in making major purchases at the present time	GREUSCMPQ

EU Consumer Survey (sa)	Datastream
Ireland	
Consumer confidence index	IREUSCCIQ
Financial situation compared with 12 months ago	IREUSCFNQ;
General economic situation, change over the last 12 months	IREUSCECQ
General economic situation, expected development over next 12 months	IREUSCEYQ
Advantage in making major purchases at the present time	IREUSCMPQ
Italy	
Consumer confidence index	ITEUSCCIQ
Financial situation compared with 12 months ago	ITEUSCFNQ
Financial situation, expected change over 12 months	ITEUSCFYQ
General economic situation, change over the last 12 months	ITEUSCECQ
General economic situation, expected development over next 12 months	ITEUSCEYQ
Advantage in making major purchases at the present time	ITEUSCMPQ
Amount of money to be spent over the next 12 months	ITEUSCPCQ
Cost of living compared with 12 months ago	ITEUSCPRQ
Change of prices over the next 12 months	ITEUSCPYQ
Expected change in the level of unemployment	ITEUSCUNQ
Present savings situation	ITEUSCSAQ
Expected savings situation over the next 12 months	ITEUSCSYQ
Present financial situation	
Likelihood of buying a car within the next two years	
Planing to purchase a home within the next two years	
Expected spending of large sums of money on home improvement	
Netherlands	
Consumer confidence index	NLEUSCCIQ
Financial situation compared with 12 months ago	NLEUSCFNQ
Financial situation, expected change over 12 months	NLEUSCFYQ
General economic situation, change over the last 12 months	NLEUSCECQ
General economic situation, expected development over next 12 months	NLEUSCEYQ
Advantage in making major purchases at the present time	NLEUSCMPQ
Amount of money to be spent over the next 12 months	NLEUSCPCQ
Cost of living compared with 12 months ago	NLEUSCPRQ
Change of prices over the next 12 months	NLEUSCPYQ
Expected change in the level of unemployment	NLEUSCUNQ
Present savings situation	NLEUSCSAQ
Expected savings situation over the next 12 months	NLEUSCSYQ
Present financial situation	
Likelihood of buying a car within the next two years	
Planing to purchase a home within the next two years	
Expected spending of large sums of money on home improvement	
Portugal	
Consumer confidence index	PTEUSCCIQ
Financial situation compared with 12 months ago	PTEUSCFNQ
Financial situation, expected change over 12 months	PTEUSCFYQ
General economic situation, change over the last 12 months	PTEUSCECQ
General economic situation, expected development over next 12 months	PTEUSCEYQ
Advantage in making major purchases at the present time	PTEUSCMPQ

EU Consumer Survey (sa)	Datastream
Spain	
Consumer confidence index	ESEUSCCIQ
Financial situation compared with 12 months ago	ESEUSCFNQ
Financial situation, expected change over 12 months	ESEUSCFYQ
General economic situation, change over the last 12 months	ESEUSCECQ
General economic situation, expected development over next 12 months	ESEUSCEYQ
Advantage in making major purchases at the present time	ESEUSCMPQ
Amount of money to be spent over the next 12 months	ESEUSCPCQ
Cost of living compared with 12 months ago	ESEUSCPRQ
Change of prices over the next 12 months	ESEUSCPYQ
Expected change in the level of unemployment	ESEUSCUNQ
Present savings situation	ESEUSCSAQ
Expected savings situation over the next 12 months	ESEUSCSYQ
Present financial situation	
Likelihood of buying a car within the next two years	
Planning to purchase a home within the next two years	
Expected spending of large sums of money on home improvement	
EU15	
Consumer confidence index	ECEUSCCIQ
Financial situation compared with 12 months ago	ECEUSCFNQ
Financial situation, expected change over 12 months	ECEUSCFYQ
General economic situation, change over the last 12 months	ECEUSCECQ
General economic situation, expected development over next 12 months	ECEUSCEYQ
Advantage in making major purchases at the present time	ECEUSCMPQ
Amount of money to be spent over the next 12 months	ECEUSCPCQ
Cost of living compared with 12 months ago	ECEUSCPRQ
Change of prices over the next 12 months	ECEUSCPYQ
Expected change in the level of unemployment	ECEUSCUNQ
Present savings situation	ECEUSCSAQ
Expected savings situation over the next 12 months	ECEUSCSYQ
Present financial situation	
Likelihood of buying a car within the next two years	
Planing to purchase a home within the next two years	
Expected spending of large sums of money on home improvement	
Denmark	
Consumer confidence index	DKEUSCCIQ
Financial situation compared with 12 months ago	DKEUSCFNQ
Financial situation, expected change over 12 months	DKEUSCFYQ
General economic situation, change over the last 12 months	DKEUSCECQ
General economic situation, expected development over next 12 months	DKEUSCEYQ
Advantage in making major purchases at the present time	DKEUSCMPQ
Sweden	
Consumer confidence index	SDEUSCCIQ
Financial situation compared with 12 months ago	SDEUSCFNQ
Financial situation, expected change over 12 months	SDEUSCFYQ
General economic situation, change over the last 12 months	SDEUSCECQ
General economic situation, expected development over next 12 months	SDEUSCEYQ
Advantage in making major purchases at the present time	SDEUSCMPQ

EU Consumer Survey (sa)	Datastream
United Kingdom	
Consumer confidence index	UKEUSCCIQ
Financial situation compared with 12 months ago	UKEUSCFNQ
Financial situation, expected change over 12 months	UKEUSCFYQ
General economic situation, change over the last 12 months	UKEUSCECQ
General economic situation, expected development over next 12 months	UKEUSCEYQ
Advantage in making major purchases at the present time	UKEUSCMPQ

Economic Sentiment Indicator (sa)	Datastream
Euro area	EAEUSESIG
Austria	OEEUSESIG
Belgium	BGEUSESIG
Finland	FNEUSESIG
France	FREUSESIG
Germany	BDEUSESIG
Greece	GREUSESIG
Ireland	IREUSESIG
Italy	ITEUSESIG
Luxembourg	
Netherlands	NLEUSESIG
Portugal	PTEUSESIG
Spain	ESEUSESIG
EU15	ECEUSESIG
Denmark	DKEUSESIG
Sweden	
United Kingdom	UKEUSESIG

Literature

European Commission, 'The joint harmonised EU programme of business and consumer surveys', *European Economy*, No. 6, 1997, Luxembourg.

26

Investment Indicators

26.1 EU Construction Survey

Data Source

Data are surveyed by research institutes in the individual member countries within the context of their own survey. They then pass on the relevant parts of the results to the EU Commission, which aggregates the data, conducts seasonal adjustment and publishes the overall indices. A summary of the data is available on the Internet at europa.eu.int/comm/economy_finance/index_en.htm. More detailed data are published in the publication *European Economy*, Supplement B.

Importance for the Financial Markets   D

Description

As early as 1966 the EU Commission decided to conduct a Construction Survey on similar lines to the Industrial Survey, as the data in this economic sector were inadequate. As all the Member States now take part in the survey, it is possible to summarize the survey results into an Index of Construction Confidence. For this the data are surveyed according to uniform criteria by the member countries so that they are also comparable between the countries. The raw data are then submitted to the EU Commission. Net values are then calculated for the individual indicators (i.e., negative values are deducted from positive ones). Then the results are shown separately for the individual indices for the individual countries, the Euro-zone and the EU.

A number of subjects are covered in the survey with the following questions:

1. **Development of activity compared with the preceding month**
   Compared with last month we have built: more/as much/less.

2. **Factors holding up activity**
   (a) Work has not been held up.
   (b) Work has been held up mainly by: insufficient demand/bad weather/ shortage of manpower/shortage of material and/or equipment/other factors.
3. **Evaluation of order books (or production schedules)**
   We consider that our present order book (production schedule) is: above normal/normal/below normal.
4. **Employment outlook**
   We reckon that over the next three or four months the numbers we employ will: go up/remain unchanged/go down.
5. **Price outlook**
   We reckon that over the next three to four months our prices will tend to: go up/remain unchanged/go down.

Using the responses to the assessment of orders and employment prospects, a construction confidence index is calculated by obtaining the average of the seasonally adjusted net values. For the index, national data are used which are available approximately one week prior to publication of the EU indicators.

Source: DATASTREAM

Figure 26.1   Euro-zone Construction Confidence Index

In addition, the following area is also surveyed in January, April, July and October:

6. **Operating time ensured by current backlog**
Within normal working hours, the work in hand and work already contracted for will account for approximately...months' operating time.

The data have to be surveyed in the individual countries to enable the responses to be assigned to the following sectors:

- **Building, total**
  (a) Residential
  (b) Non-residential
- **Public works (civil engineering)**
- **Construction as a whole**

Indicators on the position in the construction sector are very useful for analyzing the economic situation, although they are inevitably limited to one subsector of the economy. Consequently the Commission also publishes another additional multi-sectoral EU Economic Sentiment Index which covers the entire economy. Prior to October 2001, the index was composed of:

- Index of Industrial Confidence with a weighting of one-third
- Index of Consumer Confidence with a weighting of one-third
- Index of Construction Confidence with a weighting of one-sixth
- Stock price index with a weighting of one-sixth

Starting in October 2001, the EU Commission published a modified Economic Sentiment Indicator. They have changed the weights of the single sub-indicators and replaced the stock price index with the EU Retail Trade Confidence Index. In addition, the composition of the EU Consumer Confidence Index has been changed.

The new EU Economic Sentiment Indicator composition is as follows:

- Index of Industrial Confidence with a weighting of 40 per cent
- Index of Consumer Confidence with a weighting of 20 per cent
- Index of Construction Confidence with a weighting of 20 per cent
- Index of Retail Trade Confidence with a weighting of 20 per cent

Periodicity/Revisions

Surveys are conducted by the economic institutes in the first half of each month and evaluated in the period from the tenth to the twenty-fifth of each month. The results are then sent to the Commission shortly before the end of the survey month and the first results are published around one week after the end of the month. Revisions are normally only conducted in conjunction with seasonal adjustment factor alignment or a change in the base year. Publication is effected at 12.00 CET (06.00 ET).

Seasonal Adjustment

The data are aggregated and then seasonally adjusted by the EU Commission. However, the Commission uses the so-called Dainties method for seasonal adjustment. For this reason the values published by the national bodies are not fully comparable with the data published by the EU Commission.

Notes

The use of the Construction Confidence Index is primarily due to the fact that there was previously hardly any national information on construction activity. Time series with a long history are only available in Germany and France. No reference value can therefore be produced to which the index can refer. Consequently, the Construction Confidence Survey is the only source of EU-wide information on construction activity with a long history as the data on the Production in Construction Sector was only published from October 2001.

Key Datastream Mnemonics

EU Construction Survey (sa)	Datastream
Euro area	
Construction sentiment survey	EAEUSBCIQ
Evaluation of order books	EAEUSBOBQ
Employment outlook	EAEUSBEMQ
Development of activity compared with previous month	EAEUSBACQ
Price outlook	EAEUSBPRQ
Factors holding up activity:	
Work has not been held up	
Held up mainly by:	
Insufficient demand	EAEUSCIDQ
Bad weather	EAEUSCBWQ
Shortage of manpower	EAEUSCLBQ
Shortage of material	EAEUSCMTQ
Other factors	EAEUSCOTQ
Austria	
Construction sentiment survey	OEEUSBCIQ
Evaluation of order books	OEEUSBOBQ
Employment outlook	OEEUSBEMQ

EU Construction Survey (sa)	Datastream
Belgium	
Construction sentiment survey	BGEUSBCIQ
Evaluation of order books	BGEUSBOBQ
Employment outlook	BGEUSBEMQ
Finland	
Construction sentiment survey	FNEUSBCIQ
Evaluation of order books	FNEUSBOBQ
Employment outlook	FNEUSBEMQ
France	
Construction sentiment survey	FREUSBCIQ
Evaluation of order books	FREUSBOBQ
Employment outlook	FREUSBEMQ
Development of activity compared with previous month	FREUSBACQ
Price outlook	FREUSBPRQ
Factors holding up activity:	
Work has not been held up	
Held up mainly by:	
Insufficient demand	FREUSCIDQ
Bad weather	FREUSCBWQ
Shortage of manpower	FREUSCLBQ
Shortage of material	FREUSCMTQ
Other factors	FREUSCOTQ
Germany	
Construction sentiment survey	BDEUSBCIQ
Evaluation of order books	BDEUSBOBQ
Employment outlook	BDEUSBEMQ
Development of activity compared with previous month	BDEUSBACQ
Price outlook	BDEUSBPRQ
Factors holding up activity:	
Work has not been held up	
Held up mainly by:	
Insufficient demand	BDEUSCIDQ
Bad weather	BDEUSCBWQ
Shortage of manpower	BDEUSCLBQ
Shortage of material	BDEUSCMTQ
Other factors	BDEUSCOTQ
Greece	
Construction sentiment survey	GREUSBCIQ
Evaluation of order books	GREUSBOBQ
Employment outlook	GREUSBEMQ
Ireland	
Construction sentiment survey	IREUSBCIQ
Evaluation of order books	IREUSBOBQ
Employment outlook	IREUSBEMQ

EU Construction Survey (sa)	Datastream
Italy	
Construction sentiment survey	ITEUSBCIQ
Evaluation of order books	ITEUSBOBQ
Employment outlook	ITEUSBEMQ
Development of activity compared with previous month	ITEUSBACQ
Price outlook	ITEUSBPRQ
Factors holding up activity:	
Work has not been held up	
Held up mainly by:	
Insufficient demand	ITEUSCIDQ
Bad weather	ITEUSCBWQ
Shortage of manpower	ITEUSCLBQ
Shortage of material	ITEUSCMTQ
Other factors	ITEUSCOTQ
Luxembourg	
Construction sentiment survey	LXEUSBCIQ
Evaluation of order books	LXEUSBOBQ
Employment outlook	LXEUSBEMQ
Netherlands	
Construction sentiment survey	NLEUSBCIQ
Evaluation of order books	NLEUSBOBQ
Employment outlook	NLEUSBEMQ
Development of activity compared with previous month	NLEUSBACQ
Price outlook	NLEUSBPRQ
Factors holding up activity:	
Work has not been held up	
Held up mainly by:	
Insufficient demand	NLEUSCIDQ
Bad weather	NLEUSCBWQ
Shortage of manpower	NLEUSCLBQ
Shortage of material	NLEUSCMTQ
Other factors	NLEUSCOTQ
Portugal	
Construction sentiment survey	PTEUSBCIQ
Evaluation of order books	PTEUSBOBQ
Employment outlook	PTEUSBEMQ

EU Construction Survey (sa)	Datastream
Spain	
Construction sentiment survey	ESEUSBCIQ
Evaluation of order books	ESEUSBOBQ
Employment outlook	ESEUSBEMQ
Development of activity compared with previous month	ESEUSBACQ
Price outlook	ESEUSBPRQ
Factors holding up activity:	
Work has not been held up	
Held up mainly by:	
Insufficient demand	ESEUSCIDQ
Bad weather	ESEUSCBWQ
Shortage of manpower	ESEUSCLBQ
Shortage of material	ESEUSCMTQ
Other factors	ESEUSCOTQ
EU15	
Construction sentiment survey	ECEUSBCIQ
Evaluation of order books	ECEUSBOBQ
Employment outlook	ECEUSBEMQ
Development of activity compared with previous month	ECEUSBACQ
Price outlook	ECEUSBPRQ
Factors holding up activity:	
Work has not been held up	
Held up mainly by:	
Insufficient demand	ECEUSCIDQ
Bad weather	ECEUSCBWQ
Shortage of manpower	ECEUSCLBQ
Shortage of material	ECEUSCMTQ
Other factors	ECEUSCOTQ
Denmark	
Construction sentiment survey	DKEUSBCIQ
Evaluation of order books	DKEUSBOBQ
Employment outlook	DKEUSBEMQ
Sweden	
Construction sentiment survey	SDEUSBCIQ
Evaluation of order books	SDEUSBOBQ
Employment outlook	SDEUSBEMQ
United Kingdom	
Construction sentiment survey	UKEUSBCIQ
Evaluation of order books	UKEUSBOBQ
Employment outlook	UKEUSBEMQ

Economic Sentiment Indicator (sa)	Datastream
Euro area	EAEUSESIG
Austria	OEEUSESIG
Belgium	BGEUSESIG
Finland	FNEUSESIG
France	FREUSESIG
Germany	BDEUSESIG
Greece	GREUSESIG
Ireland	IREUSESIG
Italy	ITEUSESIG
Luxembourg	
Netherlands	NLEUSESIG
Portugal	PTEUSESIG
Spain	ESEUSESIG
EU15	ECEUSESIG
Denmark	DKEUSESIG
Sweden	
United Kingdom	UKEUSESIG

Literature

European Commission, 'The joint harmonised EU programme of business and consumer surveys', *European Economy*, No. 6, 1997, Luxembourg.
European Central Bank, 'The construction sector in the Euro area', *Monthly Report*, July 2000, p. 23.

26.2   Production in Construction Sector

Data Source

Data on the production in construction sector is produced by Eurostat on the basis of national statistics. The press release by Eurostat is available on the Internet at www.europa.eu.int/comm/euroindicators.

Importance for the Financial Markets   D

Description

Starting in October 2001, Eurostat published a new quarterly indicator for production in the construction sector. This indicator measures the volume trend in value added at factor costs. As this can only be approximated, Eurostat uses either input data, such as consumption of typical raw materials, labour or energy, or output data such as produced quantities, deflated production values or deflated sales values. To calculate the index of production at constant prices, Eurostat takes into account:

Table 26.1 Individual nations as a proportion of the total Index of Production in the Construction Sector (2000)

Austria	4.0%
Belgium	4.2%
Finland	1.0%
France	17.7%
Germany	38.2%
Greece	0.8%
Ireland	0.3%
Italy	14.7%
Luxembourg	0.3%
Netherlands	5.9%
Portugal	1.6%
Spain	11.3%

- Variations in type and quality of the commodity and the output materials
- Changes in stocks of finished goods and services and work in progress
- Changes in technical input-output relations (processing techniques)
- Services such as the assembling of production units, mounting, installations, repairs, planning, engineering or creation of software

In the year 2000, construction represented about 19 per cent of industrial production or roughly 5 per cent of the total economic output. The production index is divided into the production of building construction and civil engineering. In terms of the EU15 construction, building construction accounts for roughly 64 per cent of the total output and civil engineering accounts for the remaining 36 per cent.

The calculation of the production index is based on the data Member States transmit to Eurostat. Eurostat aggregates the working days adjusted data from the Member States. The reference period should be at least one quarter. Currently, only six Member States publish monthly data (Austria, Belgium, Deumour France, Germany and Luxemburg). Five other Member States publish quarterly data (Finland, Italy, the Netherlands, Spain and the United Kingdom), while data for the four remaining Member States are currently not available (Greece, Ireland, Portugal and Sweden) As the Member States not producing data are relatively small countries, the available data represents around 97 per cent of the total construction sector of the Euro-zone and 95 per cent of the EU15. It is intended to have the data available for all countries by mid-2003 at the latest.

Currently, the base year is 1995. The weights used for aggregation are based on the information from the Structural Business Statistics database or on information coming directly from the Member States. At present, the weights are also based on the data for the year 1995. The weights and base year are revised every five years.

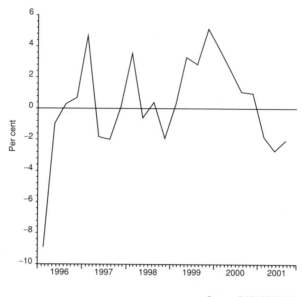

Source: DATASTREAM

Figure 26.2   Change in production in the construction sector on preceding year

In addition to the quarterly data, Eurostat will continue to publish monthly data for the Euro-zone and for the countries that supply monthly figures.

Periodicity/Revisions

The data will be published approximately 75 days after the end of a quarter. Between the quarterly releases, Eurostat will publish the monthly data approximately 60 days after the end of a month. Data are to be provided to Eurostat no later than two months after the end of the quarter. For those Member States whose total value added represents less than 3 per cent of the EU total, the deadline may be extended by 15 supplementary calendar days. Revisions can occur for several months. Publication is at 12.00 CET (06.00 ET)

Seasonal Adjustment

Member States are required to transmit working days adjusted data to Eurostat. They are also asked to transmit seasonally adjusted and trend data. Eurostat calculates the adjustment only when nationally adjusted data are not available. Eurostat aggregates the working days adjusted data to compile the Euro-zone and EU15 data. These aggregates are than seasonally adjusted with TRAMO/ SEATS.

Notes

The data on the production in the construction sector are not very important to financial markets due to its short history. The main element of its (limited) importance arises from the fact that there are hardly any other data available for the construction sector.

Key Datastream Mnemonics

Production in Construction Sector (sa)	Datastream
Euro area	
Total	EMESPICNG
Building Construction	
Civil Engineering	
Austria	
Total	OEESPICNG
Building Construction	
Civil Engineering	
Belgium	
Total	BGESPICNG
Building Construction	
Civil Engineering	
Finland	
Total	FNESPICNG
Building Construction	
Civil Engineering	
France	
Total	FRESPICNG
Building Construction	
Civil Engineering	
Germany	
Total	BDESPICNG
Building Construction	
Civil Engineering	
Greece	
Total	
Building Construction	
Civil Engineering	
Italy	
Total	ITESPICNG
Building Construction	
Civil Engineering	
Ireland	
Total	
Building Construction	
Civil Engineering	

Production in Construction Sector (sa)	Datastream
Luxembourg	
Total	LXESPICNG
Building Construction	
Civil Engineering	
Netherlands	
Total	NLESPICNG
Building Construction	
Civil Engineering	
Spain	
Total	ESESPICNG
Building Construction	
Civil Engineering	
Portugal	
Total	
Building Construction	
Civil Engineering	
EU15	
Total	ECESPICNG
Building Construction	
Civil Engineering	
Denmark	
Total	DKESPICNG
Building Construction	
Civil Engineering	
Sweden	
Total	
Building Construction	
Civil Engineering	
United Kingdom	
Total	UKESPICNG
Building Construction	
Civil Engineering	

27
International Transaction Indicators

27.1 Balance of Trade in Goods and Services

Data Source

Data on the balance of trade in goods and services are produced by Eurostat on the basis of national statistics. The press release by Eurostat is available on the Internet at www.europa.eu.int/comm/euroindicators. The data are also published in Table 9 of the ECB *Monthly Report* and in the publication *Eurostatistics – Data for short-term economic analysis* by Eurostat.

Importance for the Financial Markets   D

Description

Eurostat publishes data on nominal exports, imports and the balance of trade in goods and services. In addition, shipments within the Euro zone and the whole of the EU are published. Such shipments include trade between member countries and is therefore classed under the national balance of trade but at the same time it is also classed as intra-community trade in the aggregate balance of trade for the Euro zone and the EU. In addition to the aggregate totals for the Euro zone and the EU, data are also published on key product groups, trading partners and national aggregates. The data have been shown in Euro since January 1999 and prior to that they were given in ECU. The data have been produced in this form since January 1988. Belgium and Luxembourg have only published separate trading figures since January 1999. Prior to this the data were estimated.

The trade balances produced by Eurostat are supposed to cover trade between the Euro zone and/or the EU and the rest of the world. It is therefore necessary to exclude trading patterns from the data from the individual member countries as a result of trade with other member countries. In principle, national data could be aggregated and patterns would offset one another, as an export from one nation is an import to another one. However, this method produces major differences between the individual member countries. These occur, for example, on account of national rulings in data surveys, allocation of data to different periods, missing reports or allocation to different categories. For these reasons, Eurostat introduced the so-called Intrastat System, with which data could be collected direct from companies. As data obtained in this way can also be used by tax authorities, companies are obliged to complete the respective forms so that the trading patterns can be obtained extremely accurately using this system. However, with this system there are still differences in the national statistics and the exports (shipments) in the national statistics are more reliable than receipts (imports). Consequently, the data on intra-community trade are published on the basis of shipments.

The data are based on the international standard f.o.b./c.i.f. shipment terms, i.e., for exports (f.o.b., free on board) freight and insurance costs are only included up to the border. For imports, on the other hand, c.i.f. (cost, insurance, freight) applies. Insurance and freight costs are therefore included in full.

The balance of trade is part of the current account, so the figures are input into the balance of payments figures, although the balance of payments is

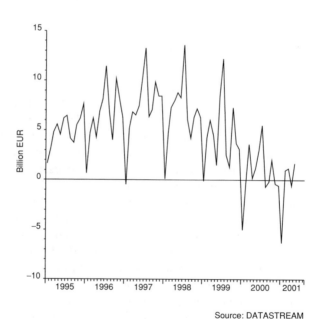

Source: DATASTREAM

Figure 27.1   Euro-zone balance of trade in goods and services

calculated on an f.o.b./f.o.b. basis (i.e., insurance and freight are not included in full for imports either). There are also further differences in the definition of data. Consequently, the balance of trade figures have to be aligned to the requirements of the balance of payment figures. This applies for all goods which are only exported temporarily for further processing without a change in ownership occurring, goods which are only being repaired abroad, goods for production in port areas and gold not for monetary use.

Another difference between the balance of trade and the balance of payment figures is due to the geographical definition. The balance of payment figures are based on the principle that exports are reported on the basis of the country of destination and imports on the basis of the country of origin. This principle also applies to trade with the rest of the world. Intra-community trade, by contrast, is based on shipment.

Example

German imports from the USA, for example, which are shipped first to Rotterdam by ship for final delivery in Germany, are reported in the Dutch balance of trade both as imports from the USA (Extra-Euro zone trade) and as exports to Germany (Intra-Euro zone trade). The same principle applies for German exports to Japan which are shipped via the Netherlands, for example.

Periodicity/Revisions

For some time now the data have been announced approximately two months after the end of the reference month. As not all national figures are available by this time, Eurostat estimates the figures for some countries. This means that substantial revisions over several months may be required. Publication is effected at 12.00 CET (06.00 ET).

Seasonal Adjustment

Starting with the data for May 2001, Eurostat now publishes seasonally adjusted data for the main aggregates.

Notes

The balance of trade figures account for approximately half of the current account figures, so that minor changes in the balance of trade can have a major effect on the current account. Due to the long time delay the importance of the data is limited. The national figures have also virtually lost their entire significance.

Key Datastream Mnemonics

EU Trade Balance (nsa)	Datastream
Euro area	
Extra-Euro area trade balance	EAESIEUBA
Extra-Euro area trade balance (sa)	
Primary products	
Food and drink	EMEBBTFTA
Crude materials	EMEBBTRMA
Energy	EMEBBTENA
Manufactured goods	
Chemicals	EMEBBTCHA
Machinery and vehicles	EMEBBTMQA
Other manufactured articles	EMEBBTOAA
Other	EMEBBTOTA
Extra-Euro area imports	EMESIEUMA
Extra-Euro area imports (sa)	
Primary products	
Food and drink	EMEBIMFTA
Crude materials	EMEBIMRMA
Energy	EMEBIMENA
Manufactured goods	
Chemicals	EMEBIMCHA
Machinery and vehicles	EMEBIMMQA
Other manufactured articles	EMEBIMOAA
Other	EMEBIMOTA
Import trade indices (1995 = 100)	
Value	EMEBIMVLF
Volume	EMEBIMVOH
Unit value	EMEBIMVUF
Extra-Euro area exports	EMESIEUXA
Extra-Euro area exports (sa)	
Primary products	
Food and drink	EMEBEXFTA
Crude materials	EMEBEXRMA
Energy	EMEBEXENA
Manufactured goods	
Chemicals	EMEBEXCHA
Machinery and vehicles	EMEBEXMQA
Other manufactured articles	EMEBEXOAA
Other	EMEBEXOTA
Export trade indices (1995 = 100)	
Value	EMEBEXVLF
Volume	EMEBEXVOH
Unit value	EMEBEXVUF
Intra-Euro area imports	EMESIEUAA
Intra-Euro area dispatches	EMESIEUDA
Intra-Euro area dispatches (sa)	

EU Trade Balance (nsa)	Datastream
Austria	
Imports	OEESIMPOA
Intra-Euro area imports	OEESIEUAA
Exports	OEESEXPOA
Intra-Euro area dispatches	OEESIEUDA
Belgium/Luxembourg	
Imports	BXESIMPOA
Intra-Euro area imports	BXESIEUAA
Exports	BXESEXPOA
Intra-Euro area dispatches	BXESIEUDA
Finland	
Imports	FNESIMPOA
Intra-Euro area imports	FNESIEUAA
Exports	FNESEXPOA
Intra-Euro area dispatches	FNESIEUDA
France	
Imports	FRESIMPOA
Intra-Euro area imports	FRESIEUAA
Exports	FRESEXPOA
Intra-Euro area dispatches	FRESIEUDA
Germany	
Imports	BDESIMPOA
Intra-Euro area imports	BDESIEUAA
Exports	BDESEXPOA
Intra-Euro area dispatches	BDESIEUDA
Greece	
Imports	GRESIMPOA
Intra-Euro area imports	GRESIEUAA
Exports	GRESEXPOA
Intra-Euro area dispatches	GRESIEUDA
Ireland	
Imports	IRESIMPOA
Intra-Euro area imports	IRESIEUAA
Exports	IRESEXPOA
Intra-Euro area dispatches	IRESIEUDA
Italy	
Imports	ITESIMPOA
Intra-Euro area imports	ITESIEUAA
Exports	ITESEXPOA
Intra-Euro area dispatches	ITESIEUDA
Netherlands	
Imports	NLESIMPOA
Intra-Euro area imports	NLESIEUAA
Exports	NLESEXPOA
Intra-Euro area dispatches	NLESIEUDA

EU Trade Balance (nsa)	Datastream
Portugal	
Imports	PTESIMPOA
Intra-Euro area imports	PTESIEUAA
Exports	PTESEXPOA
Intra-Euro area dispatches	PTESIEUDA
Spain	
Imports	ESESIMPOA
Intra-Euro area imports	ESESIEUAA
Exports	ESESEXPOA
Intra-Euro area dispatches	ESESIEUDA
EU15	
Extra-EU15 trade balance	ECESIEUBA
Primary products	
Food and drink	
Crude materials	
Energy	
Manufactured goods	
Chemicals	
Machinery and vehicles	
Other manufactured articles	
Other	
Imports	ECESIMPOA
Primary products	
Food and drink	ECESIMFTA
Crude materials	ESESIMRMA
Energy	ECESIMENA
Manufactured goods	
Chemicals	ECESIMCHA
Machinery and vehicles	ECESIMMQA
Other manufactured articles	ECESIMOAA
Other	
Import trade indices (1995=100)	
Value	
Volume	
Unit value	
Intra-Euro area imports	ECESIEUAA
Exports	ECESEXPOA
Primary products	
Food and drink	ECESEXFTA
Crude materials	ECESEXRMA
Energy	ECESEXENA
Manufactured goods	
Chemicals	ECESEXCHA
Machinery and vehicles	ECESEXMQA
Other manufactured articles	ECESEXOAA
Other	
Export trade indices (1995 = 100)	
Value	
Volume	
Unit value	
Intra-Euro area dispatches	ECESIEUDA

EU Trade Balance (nsa)	Datastream
Denmark	
Imports	DKESIMPOA
Intra-Euro area imports	DKESIEUAA
Exports	DKESEXPOA
Intra-Euro area dispatches	DKESIEUDA
Sweden	
Imports	SDESIMPOA
Intra-Euro area imports	SDESIEUAA
Exports	SDESEXPOA
Intra-Euro area dispatches	SDESIEUDA
United Kingdom	
Imports	UKESIMPOA
Intra-Euro area imports	UKESIEUAA
Exports	UKESEXPOA
Intra-Euro area dispatches	UKESIEUDA

Main Trading Partners – Euro area (nsa)	Datastream
Trade balance	
UK	UKESTEATA
USA	USESTEATA
Switzerland	SWESTEATA
Japan	JPESTEATA
Sweden	SDESTEATA
China	CHESTEATA
Russia	RSESTEATA
Poland	POESTEATA
Denmark	DKESTEATA
Hungary	HNESTEATA
Euro area exports to partner	
UK	UKESTEAXA
USA	USESTEAXA
Switzerland	SWESTEAXA
Japan	JPESTEAXA
Sweden	SDESTEAXA
China	CHESTEAXA
Russia	RSESTEAXA
Poland	POESTEAXA
Denmark	DKESTEAXA
Hungary	HNESTEAXA

Main Trading Partners – Euro area (nsa)	Datastream
Euro area imports to partner	
UK	UKESTEAIA
USA	USESTEAIA
Switzerland	SWESTEAIA
Japan	JPESTEAIA
Sweden	SDESTEAIA
China	CHESTEAIA
Russia	RSESTEAIA
Poland	POESTEAIA
Denmark	DKESTEAIA
Czech Republic	CZESTEAIA

Main Trading Partners – EU15 (nsa)	Datastream
Trade balance	
USA	USESTECTA
Japan	SWESTECTA
Switzerland	JPESTECTA
China	SDESTECTA
Norway	CHESTECTA
Russia	RSESTECTA
Poland	POESTECTA
Czech Republic	CZESTECTA
Hungary	HNESTECTA
Canada	
EU15 exports to partner	
USA	USESTECXA
Japan	JPESTECXA
Switzerland	SWESTECXA
China	CHESTECXA
Norway	CHESTECXA
Russia	RSESTECXA
Poland	POESTECXA
Czech Republic	CZESTECXA
Hungary	HNESTECXA
Canada	
EU15 imports to partner	
USA	USESTECIA
Japan	SWESTECIA
Switzerland	JPESTECIA
China	SDESTECIA
Norway	CHESTECIA
Russia	RSESTECIA
Poland	POESTECIA
Czech Republic	DKESTECIA
Hungary	HNESTECIA
Canada	

Member States' Trade (nsa)	Datastream
Trade balance	
Belgium	BGESTTBLA
Denmark	DKESTTBLA
Germany	BDESTTBLA
Greece	GRESTTBLA
Spain	ESESTTBLA
France	FRESTTBLA
Ireland	IRESTTBLA
Italy	ITESTTBLA
Luxembourg	LXESTTBLA
Netherlands	NLESTTBLA
Austria	OEESTTBLA
Portugal	PTESTTBLA
Finland	FNESTTBLA
Sweden	SDESTTBLA
UK	UKESTTBLA
Total exports	
Belgium	BGESTEXPA
Denmark	DKESTEXPA
Germany	BDESTEXPA
Greece	GRESTEXPA
Spain	ESESTEXPA
France	FRESTEXPA
Ireland	IRESTEXPA
Italy	ITESTEXPA
Luxembourg	LXESTEXPA
Netherlands	NLESTEXPA
Austria	OEESTEXPA
Portugal	PTESTEXPA
Finland	FNESTEXPA
Sweden	SDESTEXPA
UK	UKESTEXPA
Total imports	
Belgium	BGESTIMPA
Denmark	DKESTIMPA
Germany	BDESTIMPA
Greece	GRESTIMPA
Spain	ESESTIMPA
France	FRESTIMPA
Ireland	IRESTIMPA
Italy	ITESTIMPA
Luxembourg	LXESTIMPA
Netherlands	NLESTIMPA
Austria	OEESTIMPA
Portugal	PTESTIMPA
Finland	FNESTIMPA
Sweden	SDESTIMPA
UK	UKESTIMPA

Literature

European Central Bank, 'The openness of the Euro area with regard to external trade', *Monthly Report*, December 1999, pp. 53–4.

European Central Bank, 'The external trade of the Euro area: stylised facts and recent trends', *Monthly Report*, August 2000, pp. 51–61.

Statistisches Bundesamt, 'Erfassung der indirekten Importe (Rotterdam-Effekt) in der Aussenhandelsstatistik', *Wirtschaft und Statistik*, [Indirect import (Rotterdam effect) reporting in foreign trade statistics], Economics and Statistics 2/1999, pp. 85–91.

Statistisches Bundesamt, 'Durchführbarkeit der Intrahandelsstatistik auf Stichprobenbasis', *Wirtschaft und Statistik*, [Feasibility of intra-trade statistics on random sample basis], Economics and Statistics 8/1999, pp. 609–13.

27.2   Balance of Payments

Data Source

Balance of payment figures for the Euro-zone are published by the ECB, although the ECB and Eurostat produce the data jointly. The press release is available under 'Statistics' on the Internet at www.ecb.int. Data are also published in Table 8 of the ECB *Monthly Report* and in the publication *Eurostatistics – Data for short-term economic analysis*.

Importance for the Financial Markets   C

Description

As with the balance of trade, the problem when producing the balance of payments figures is that the statistics have to be produced on the basis of national figures which are not fully harmonized. The balance of payments figures for the Euro-zone include all transactions from the Euro-zone with the rest of the world. Initially, the method of aggregating the national statistics was used so that trade and financial movements within the Euro-zone would theoretically cancel each other out. Consequently, since the beginning of 2000 transactions with third countries have been explicitly incorporated as far as possible. Currently, the data incorporated in this way have been calculated back to the beginning of 1997. However, it should be noted that prior to 1999 the data were calculated in ECU and are therefore not fully comparable with the data in Euro.

The ECB and Eurostat are both involved in the production of the balance of payments figures. Whereas Eurostat is responsible for the current account and capital account data, the ECB calculates the data for the remaining sections and also co-ordinates publication of the Euro-zone data. The statistics are therefore published at three different intervals: monthly, quarterly and annually. The monthly figures in particular differ in structure from the other publications as the key figures are published, whereas the quarterly and annual data include more detailed information. In addition, the monthly national figures can also produce methodological differences and sub-sectors may be estimated, which is largely impossible in the quarterly and yearly publications.

The calculation of the balance of payments figures is based on the national resident concept (i.e., including transactions that natural and legal entities, whose economic base is in the Euro-zone, conduct with the rest of the world). However, of the EU institutions only ECB transactions are incorporated in the Euro-zone data. The transactions of all other EU institutions are not therefore included in the Euro-zone balance of payments. The figures are calculated at market prices (i.e., transactions are evaluated at the prices paid). For transactions where no market price can be calculated, the book value method or other standards of evaluation are applied.

Since 1999 the ECB has published additional information on the international investment position of the Euro-zone. This data can be used to analyze the structure of the external financial position of the Euro-zone. The change in the international investment position over one year and the balance of payments for this year should normally be very close. This relation is, however, impaired by the fact that changes in asset evaluation and the exchange rate fluctuations are treated differently. In addition, since April 2000 the ECB has published more specific information on the structure of the currency reserves held by the ECB and the national central banks.

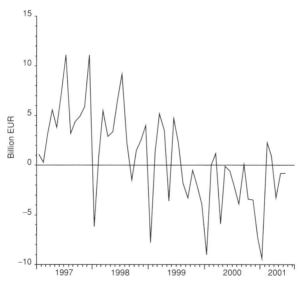

Source: DATASTREAM

Figure 27.2 Euro-zone current account balance

The categories calculated individually are grouped in individual sections in the balance of payments in accordance with international practice. The current account includes the balance of trade in goods and services, the income account as well as the current transfer account. The current account and the capital account are produced by Eurostat. The financial account, on the other hand, is produced by the ECB. This account includes transactions from direct investments, portfolio investments, financial derivatives and other capital movements as well as currency reserves.

The balance of trade in goods in the balance of payments constitutes the entire goods trade, irrespective of the level of processing, plus gold not for monetary policy use. It is based on the principle that transactions occur on change of ownership. Transactions are calculated on an f.o.b/f.o.b basis (i.e., at market prices at the border of the exporting country). Consequently, insurance premiums and transport costs are not included in full. Exports are based on the final country of destination and imports on the country of origin. In these two points the balance of payments and balance of trade therefore differ.

Whereas the balance of payments figures are calculated on an f.o.b./f.o.b. basis, for the balance of trade figures f.o.b./c.i.f. is taken as the basis (i.e., in the balance of trade, insurance and freight costs are included in full for imports). In addition, there are other differences in the definition of data. This applies to all goods which are only temporarily exported for further processing without change of ownership, goods which are only repaired abroad, goods which are erected in port areas and gold for non-monetary use and therefore included in the currency account.

Another difference between the balance of trade and the balance of payment figures is due to the geographical definition. The balance of payment figures are based on the principle that exports are reported on the basis of the country of destination and imports on the basis of the country of origin. This principle is also applied for trade with the rest of the world. Intra-community trade, by contrast, is based on shipment.

Example

German imports from the USA, for example, which are shipped first to Rotterdam by ship for final delivery in Germany, are reported in the Dutch balance of trade both as imports from the USA (Extra-Euro-zone trade) and as exports to Germany (Intra-Euro-zone trade). The same principle applies for German exports to Japan which are shipped via the Netherlands, for example.

So that the balance of trade figures comply with the requirements for the balance of payments statistics, the data are adjusted prior to calculation of balance of payments.

The services account consists of three main items. Transportation covers all services provided by residents of the Euro-zone for all other persons and vice versa. The same applies to the travel category, although this only affects travel for periods of less than one year. In this context, it should be noted that personal transport in connection with travel is not included under this item, but under transportation. The third category finally includes all other services, such as communications services, insurance and other financial services.

The income account covers two types of transactions between Euro-zone residents and non-Euro-zone residents. Compensation of employees includes wages and salaries as well as other labour costs which persons from the Euro-zone receive for their activities outside the Euro-zone and vice versa. Investment income incorporates income derived from a Euro-zone resident's ownership of a foreign financial asset and, vice versa, income derived from a non-Euro-zone resident's ownership of a domestic financial asset. This category includes all income flows from direct investments, portfolio investments and other financial investments. The only exception is interest payments on financial derivatives, which are included in the financial account. It should be noted that monthly statistics only include the total figures on income flows. More detailed information is published with the quarterly figures.

Current transfer payments are unilateral transactions in which one economic entity provides a real resource to another entity without receiving any real resource or financial item in exchange. These include, for example, transfers to international organizations, payments from international tax agreements, insurance premiums and insurance payments by property insurance companies.

The capital account covers transactions associated with the assignment of assets, the costs thereby incurred and transactions relating to loans, such as debt remission. In addition, all transactions concerning patent rights and leasing agreements are booked to this account.

The most important categories in the financial account are direct investments, portfolio investments and financial derivatives. Direct investments constitute all transactions relating specifically to long-term lending commitments to a company outside the Euro-zone. The commitment thereby must amount to at least 10 per cent of the total value of the company. Imports of direct investments relate on the other hand to commitments by foreigners to companies in the Euro-zone. Where a transaction is classified as direct investment, all other associated transactions are also classed as direct investment. Direct investment transactions include stock trading (as long as it exceeds 10 per cent of the total stock capital of the company), reinvestment of earnings from direct investments and other internal company capital movements between parents and subsidiaries.

Portfolio investments as a category covers all equity securities transactions and debt securities transactions in the form of bonds, notes and money market instruments which are not counted as direct investments or currency reserves. Financial market derivatives have their own category, however. Bonds and notes are, in principle, all securities, issued with an initial maturity of more than one year, whereas money market instruments only includes short-term instruments. Shortening the residual time to maturity to less than one year does not mean that a security is put into another category. The basis for the classification is the original term. The actual amounts traded are shown for the booking (i.e., the effective price plus any interest accrued less fees incurred).

Financial market derivatives are now given their own separate category due to their increased importance in recent years. Transactions are thereby applied on the date of booking in the accounts of the contracting party. One characteristic of derivatives is the so-called margin payments. In this case, the initial margin is assigned to the category of other capital transactions, as they are treated as a change in the currency position. The same applies to the variation margin for options. The variation margin for futures is classed as an integral part of the derivative business and therefore assigned to the category of financial derivatives. This method is only applicable when the respective payment flows can be identified.

'Other investment' is defined as a residual category that includes all other financial transactions or holdings not covered in the other categories of the

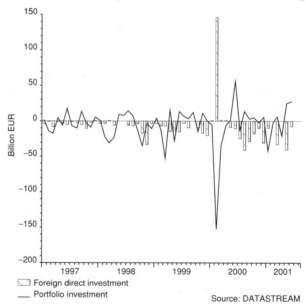

Figure 27.3 Euro-zone foreign direct investments and portfolio investments

financial account. The category also includes, for example, trade credits and repo-type operations (i.e., repurchase agreements with stocks, bonds or money market instruments or the assignment of equity capital by international organizations). So when the IMF wants to stock up its own reserves and the member countries of the Euro-zone transfer capital to this end, these transactions are booked as 'other investment'.

Finally transactions with ECB currency reserves and the national central banks in the Euro-zone are booked in the currency reserves category. Currency reserves include all assets directly administered by the central banks and in the form of highly liquid paper in a non-Euro currency. Only monthly net transactions are published in the financial balance. Additional information about the assets on which transactions are based are only provided in the quarterly figures. In addition, the figures are calculated on the basis of gross values without netting-off reserve-related liabilities. Currency reserves are valued at market prices. For transactions the respective transaction prices are applied, whereas stocks are based on the respective prices at the end of the quarter. The valuation rates are also regularly adjusted to new market conditions and the relevant up-to-date prices are then announced by the ECB.

As the balance of payments always balances overall, although this cannot be guaranteed entirely due to late bookings and no uniform harmonized booking method, there is an additional section within the balance of payments called errors and omissions. This offsets all anomalies incurred with the bookings.

Periodicity/Revisions

Balance of payments figures are published at the end of the second month after the reference month. Quarterly data are published as soon as all the monthly figures for a quarter are available, and the annual figures as soon as the figures for the calendar year are complete. Monthly figures are revised with publication of the quarterly figures, whereas quarterly figures are revised with publication of the annual figures. In addition, extensive revisions may occur when methodological changes are conducted. Publication takes place at 12.00 CET (06.00 ET).

Seasonal Adjustment

Beginning with the data for May 2001, seasonal adjusted data for the different categories of the current account are available.

Notes

Balance of payments figures are only of limited importance to the financial markets due to their relatively late publication. The figures are more suitable for analyzing underlying capital movements so their importance for background analysis is far greater than for day-to-day monitoring.

Key Datastream Mnemonics

Balance of Payments (nsa)	Datastream
Euro area	
Current account quarterly (since 1991, nsa)	EMCURBALA
Current account total (sa)	EMECBECAA
Credit	EMECBCCTA
Debit	EMECBCDTA
Goods	EMECBECGA
Credit	EMECBCCGA
Debit	EMECBCDGA
Services	EMECBECSA
Credit	EMECBCCSA
Debit	EMECBCDSA
Income	EMECBECIA
Credit	EMECBCCIA
Compensation of employees	EMEBWECQA
Investment income	EMEBIICQA
Total	EMEBIICQA
Direct investment	EMEBDICQA
Portfolio investment	EMEBPICQA
Other investment	EMEBOICQA
Debit	EMECBCDIA
Compensation of employees	EMEBWEDQA
Investment income	EMEBIIDQA
Total	EMEBIIDQA
Direct investment	EMEBDIDQA
Portfolio investment	EMEBPIDQA
Other investment	EMEBOIDQA
Current transfers	EMECBECCA
Credit	EMECBCCCA
Debit	EMECBCDCA
Capital account (nsa)	EMECBECBA
Credit	EMECBPCTA
Debit	EMECBPDTA
Financial account (nsa)	EMECBE.XA
Direct investment	EMECBEDIA
Abroad	EMECBDIAA
In the Euro area	EMECBDIEA
Portfolio investment	EMECBEPIA
Assets	EMECBPIAA
Equity	EMECBPEAA
Debt instruments	EMECBDATA
Liabilities	EMECBPTLA
Equity	EMECBPELA
Debt instruments	EMECBDLTA
Financial derivatives, net	EMECBEFDA
Other investment	EMECBEOIA
Assets	

Balance of Payments (nsa)	Datastream
Total	EMECBITAA
Eurosystem	EMECBIEAA
General government	EMECBIGAA
MFIs (excluding the Eurosystem)	EMECBMTAA
Other sectors	EMECBIOAA
Liabilities	
Total	EMECBITLA
Eurosystem	EMECBIELA
General government	EMECBIGLA
MFIs (excluding the Eurosystem)	EMECBMTLA
Other sectors	EMECBIOLA
Reserve assets	EMECBERAA
Errors and omissions (nsa)	EMECBEEEA

Reserve assets of the Eurosystem (nsa)	Datastream
Total	EMECBRESA
Monetary gold	EMECBMGLA
In fine troy ounces (millions)	EMECBMGLP
Special drawing rights	EMECBSDRA
Reserve position in the IMF	EMECBIMFA
Foreign exchange total	EMECBFEXA
Currency and deposits	EMECBCDMA
Securities	EMECBSECA
Financial derivatives	EMECBFXDA
Other claims	EMECBOTHA
Memo: Claims on Euro-area residents denominated in foreign currency	EMECBCEFA

Balance of Payments (nsa)	Datastream
Austria	
Current account	OEESCURBA
Belgium/Luxembourg	
Current account	BXESCURBA
Finland	
Current account	FNESCURBA
France	
Current account	FRESCURBA
Germany	
Current account	BDESCURBA
Greece	
Current account	GRESCURBA
Ireland	
Current account	IRESCURBA

Balance of Payments (nsa)	Datastream
Italy	
Current account	ITESCURBA
Netherlands	
Current account	NLESCURBA
Portugal	
Current account	PTESCURBA
Spain	
Current account	ESESCURBA
EU15	
Current account	ECESCURBA
Denmark	
Current account	DKESCURBA
Sweden	
Current account	SDESCURBA
United Kingdom	
Current account	UKESCURBA

Literature

Deutsche Bundesbank, 'Changes in the Methodology of the Balance of Payments', *Monthly Report*, March 1995, pp. 33–43.

European Central Bank, 'The balance of payments of the Euro area and international reserves of the Eurosystem: methodological issues', *Monthly Report*, May 1999, pp. 30–1.

European Central Bank, *European Union Balance of Payments/International Investment Position Statistical Methods*, Frankfurt, November 1999.

European Central Bank, 'The openness of the Euro area with regard to external trade', *Monthly Report*, December 1999, pp. 53–4.

European Central Bank, 'International investment position of the Euro area: methodological note', *Monthly Report*, December 1999, p. 56.

European Central Bank, *Statistical Information collected and compiled by the ESCB*, May 2000.

28
Inflation Indicators

28.1 Industrial Producer Prices

Data Source

Data are produced by Eurostat on the basis of national figures. The press release by Eurostat is available on the Internet at www.europa.eu.int/comm/euroindicators. In addition, the data are published in Table 4.2 of the ECB *Monthly Report*.

Importance for the Financial Markets   B

Description

Eurostat publishes monthly indices of producer prices for industrially manufactured goods. Agricultural products are not included. Producer prices for the construction sector are also shown separately. The Industrial Producer Price

Table 28.1 Individual nations as a proportion of the total Producer Price Index (2000)

Austria	2.3%
Belgium	3.3%
Finland	1.7%
France	20.9%
Germany	33.8%
Greece	1.0%
Ireland	0.7%
Italy	21.4%
Luxembourg	0.1%
Netherlands	3.7%
Portugal	1.8%
Spain	9.2%

Index, excluding the construction sector, measures ex-works sales prices for all products sold on the home market (for the period prior to 1999 in the local currency of the individual countries) in the member countries (excluding Austria, where no figures are available). Imports from intra-community trade are not included. The national statistics are weighted arithmetically in an overall index. The weighting is thereby produced from sales figures in the individual countries in 1995.

The data survey in the individual member countries is still not completely harmonized. They differ above all in the definition of the individual products for which prices are surveyed, and the individual sectors for which the sub-indices are calculated. However, harmonization is expected to continue in the coming months. The Index of Industrial Producer Prices is calculated as soon as approximately 60 per cent of data is received. Missing data are initially estimated using an ARIMA model and subsequently supplemented.

In addition to the overall index, sub-indices are produced for the manufacturing sector, intermediate goods, capital goods, consumer goods, durable consumer goods and non-durable consumer goods. It should be noted, however, that the Eurostat definition can sometimes differ from national definitions.

The Index of Producer Prices for the construction industry relates to sales prices of residential buildings. The overall index is a weighted arithmetic

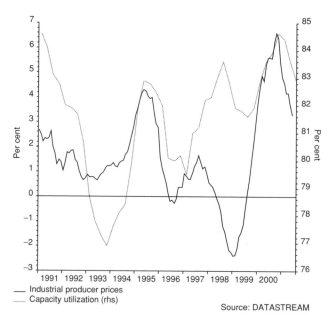

Figure 28.1 Change in Euro-zone industrial producer prices on preceding year and capacity utilization

average of the national indices (excluding Belgium and Portugal, where these statistics are not produced). The year 1995 is currently taken as the base year. It should also be noted that national statistics are not completely harmonized for these price indices either. Hence there are still differences in the definition of prices measured, the type of construction included and the frequency of the survey.

Periodicity/Revisions

The data are currently published around six to seven weeks after the end of the reference period. Due to missing data from some countries, revisions are always conducted in subsequent months. Publication takes place at 12.00 CET (06.00 ET).

Seasonal Adjustment

The data are not seasonally adjusted.

Notes

The Producer Price Index is a good indicator of shortages in individual goods and commodities. It can also be employed as a leading indicator for consumer price trends. Due to its late publication, the importance of the index is rather limited.

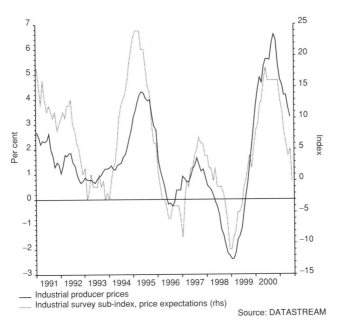

Figure 28.2 Change in Euro-zone industrial producer prices on preceding year and price expectations (EU Industrial Survey)

Key Datastream Mnemonics

Industrial Producer Prices (nsa)	Datastream
Euro area	
Total excluding construction	EAESPPIIF
Total excluding construction (% m/m)	EMESPPI.%
Total excluding construction (% y/y)	EMESPPIY%
Manufacturing	EAESPPIMF
Manufacturing (% y/y)	EMESPPMY%
Intermediate goods	EAESPPITF
Intermediate goods (% y/y)	EMESPPTY%
Capital goods	EAESPPICF
Capital goods (% y/y)	EMESPPCY%
Consumer goods	EMEBPPC%F
Durable consumer goods	EAESPPIDF
Durable consumer goods (% y/y)	EMESPPDY%
Non-durable consumer goods	EAESPPINF
Non-durable consumer goods (% y/y)	EMESPPNY%
Energy	
Construction	EMEBPPH%F
Austria	
Total excluding construction	
Belgium	
Total excluding construction	BGESPPIIF
Finland	
Total excluding construction	FNESPPIIF
France	
Total excluding construction	FRESPPIIF
Manufacturing	FRESPPIMF
Intermediate goods	FRESPPITF
Capital goods	FRESPPICF
Consumer goods	
Durable consumer goods	FRESPPIDF
Non-durable consumer goods	FRESPPINF
Germany	
Total excluding construction	BDESPPIIF
Manufacturing	BDESPPIMF
Intermediate goods	BDESPPITF
Capital goods	BDESPPICF
Consumer goods	
Durable consumer goods	BDESPPIDF
Non-durable consumer goods	BDESPPINF
Greece	
Total excluding construction	GRESPPIIF
Ireland	
Total excluding construction	IRESPPIIF

Industrial Producer Prices (nsa)	Datastream
Italy	
Total excluding construction	ITESPPIIF
Manufacturing	ITESPPIMF
Intermediate goods	ITESPPITF
Capital goods	ITESPPICF
Consumer goods	
Durable consumer goods	ITESPPIDF
Non-durable consumer goods	ITESPPINF
Luxembourg	
Total excluding construction	LXESPPIIF
Netherlands	
Total excluding construction	NLESPPIIF
Manufacturing	NLESPPIMF
Intermediate goods	NLESPPITF
Capital goods	NLESPPICF
Consumer goods	
Durable consumer goods	NLESPPIDF
Non-durable consumer goods	NLESPPINF
Portugal	
Total excluding construction	PTESPPIIF
Spain	
Total excluding construction	ESESPPIIF
Manufacturing	ESESPPIMF
Intermediate goods	ESESPPITF
Capital goods	ESESPPICF
Consumer goods	
Durable consumer goods	ESESPPIDF
Non-durable consumer goods	ESESPPINF
EU15	
Total excluding construction	ECESPPIIF
Manufacturing	ECESPPIMF
Intermediate goods	ECESPPITF
Capital goods	ECESPPICF
Consumer goods	
Durable consumer goods	ECESPPIDF
Non-durable consumer goods	ECESPPINF
Denmark	
Total excluding construction	DKESPPIIF
Sweden	
Total excluding construction	SDESPPIIF
United Kingdom	
Total excluding construction	UKESPPIIF

Literature

European Central Bank, 'The role of short-term economic indicators in the analysis of price developments in the Euro area', *Monthly Report*, April 1999, pp. 27–41.

28.2   Consumer Prices

Data Source

Figures are published by Eurostat on the basis of national data. The press release by Eurostat is available on the Internet at www.europa.eu.int/comm/euroindicators. In addition, data are published in Table 4.1 of the ECB *Monthly Report* and in the publication *Eurostatistics – Data for short-term economic analysis*.

Importance for the Financial Markets   B

Description

Harmonization of national figures is most advanced in the area of consumer prices monitoring. Eurostat therefore publishes a Harmonized Index of Consumer Prices (HICP) composed of weighted national inflation rates and used to calculate all kinds of consumer expenditure. In addition, around 100 subindices are available for individual consumer goods sectors, which are summarized into five main categories. In addition to unprocessed food (e.g., meat, fruit and vegetables), processed food is also included (e.g., bread, drinks and tobacco). Industrial goods excluding energy include, for example, footwear, trucks and computers. The energy sector is classed as one of the goods sectors (e.g., electricity, gas and other fuels), whereas housing, transport, communication, recreation and personal as well as miscellaneous constitute services. The reason for the extensive harmonization of statistics lies in the fact that this index was used as a reference value for checking convergence prior to the creation of the Monetary Union. In addition, HICP is used to determine price level stability. The ECB considers the price level stable when the inflation rate as measured with the HICP is below 2 per cent. The first harmonized figures were published in January 1997, although data have been calculated back to January 1995. Prior to this estimates were calculated by the ECB. However, these data are not fully comparable with the data after 1995. Because of the participation of Greece, HICP for the whole Monetary Union was chain linked in December 2000 so as to include Greece starting with the January 2001 index.

Beginning with the data for October 2001, Eurostat publishes a so-called 'flash estimate' for the Monetary Union HICP. To calculate this advance report, Eurostat uses early price information available. These are price data from Germany and Italy (and from other Member States, when available) as well as information on energy prices. The calculation procedure uses regression and time-series modelling. The outcome is limited to the year-on-year change of the total index for the Euro-zone. A detailed breakdown for the Member States is not available.

The flash estimates are published at the end of the reference months or at the beginning of the following month. Thus, the data are available two to three weeks before the complete results for the HICP are available. Simulations undertaken by Eurostat show the mean absolute error for a reference period (April 1999-September 2001) gave a result of 0.04 percentage points. The final result had been forecast 18 out of 30 times. In 11 other instances, the deviation was a mere 0.1 index points. The direction of the estimated trend was accurately forecast in all cases.

Expenses for private domestic consumer demand serve as weighting factors for the aggregation of the Euro-zone indicator. The HICP and nationalized indices are thereby constructed as chain-type indices, so the relevant weightings, both for the Euro-zone indices and the national indices are recalculated every year. The national weighting represents its proportion of total private, domestic consumer expenditure. As the accounting figures from which the weighting is produced are only available after a long delay, the country weighting is normally produced from data from two years before the reference year. In addition to the overall index, sub-indices are also calculated for individual product classes. These sub-indicators are also constructed as chain-type indices. However, the weighting in the individual countries differs. For example, expenditure on food in the southern member countries is weighted higher than in the northern countries, whereas the opposite applies to services.

Table 28.2 Comparison of national inflation figures and harmonized Index of Consumer Prices

Country	Weighting in year 2001	National inflation level May 2001 (y/y)	Harmonized Index of Consumer Prices May 2001 (y/y)
Austria	32.72	3.4	2.9
Belgium	33.26	3.1	3.1
Finland	15.91	3.4	3.3
France	204.73	2.3	2.5
Germany	309.28	3.5	3.6
Greece	24.46	3.9	3.9
Ireland	11.73	5.5	4.1
Italy	187.12	3.0	2.9
Luxembourg	2.62	3.3	3.8
Netherlands	52.55	4.9	5.4
Portugal	21.1	4.8	4.9
Spain	104.51	4.2	4.2

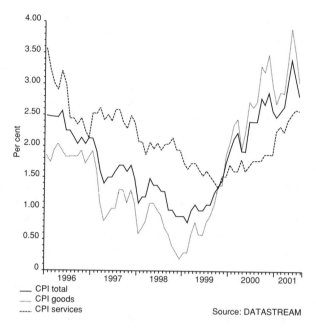

Per cent

Figure 28.3   Change in Euro-zone consumer prices and sub-indices on preceding year

Although a level of harmonization of approximately 95 per cent was initially assumed, the harmonization process has since advanced even further. Since January 2000 the survey sector has been expanded so that nearly 100 per cent of consumer expenditure in private households is now covered by the survey. The HICP and national sub-indicators cover all kinds of household expenditure. However, a number of incomparable areas had to be excluded up to now. The extended survey now includes goods and services, which were previously overlooked, and the geographical and demographic survey sectors have become completely harmonized. Specific additions were the sectors of healthcare, education and teaching, social security, specific insurance and financial services as well as tax-like charges associated with the home. With the revision of the methodology, the expenditure of the entire national resident population is included. According to the concept of consumer expenditure of private households in the economic area of a member country, expenditure by foreign visitors to member countries involving sales is now included. Expenditure on business trips abroad is still excluded as it is not counted as private consumption.

Periodicity/Revisions

Since February 2000 the statistics have been published earlier than before. The announcement is now made 17 to 19 days after the end of the reference month.

Revisions always take place with the publication of the next statistic. Extensive revisions are only conducted in exceptional cases, except where methodical revision occurs. Publication takes place at 12.00 CET (06.00 ET).

Seasonal Adjustment

Now the data are also published with seasonally adjusted figures.

Notes

The focus is on the change in the inflation rate for the Euro-zone compared to the preceding year. In early November 2001 Eurostat began publishing a flash estimate for the HICP. This early information will become increasingly import-ant for financial markets as it means that consumer price information in Euro zone is available before the corresponding information in the USA.

In addition to the trend in consumer prices, there is another factor on which the market is focusing. This is the difference between the highest and lowest inflation rate in the individual countries, which is a sign of possible different development in the individual regions of the currency area. The smaller the difference, the more scope the ECB has in implementing monetary policy. In this case, it can shape the monetary policy framework conditions so that they

Source: DATASTREAM

Figure 28.4   Change in consumer prices on preceding year and Euro-zone consumer price expectations (EU Consumer Survey)

apply to the entire currency area. However, inflationary trends in some countries and deflationary trends in others make the implementation of a single monetary policy by the ECB an ongoing struggle. As the Euro-zone HICP is the reference factor for the ECB in measuring the inflation rate, it is helpful to acquire early information on the anticipated price trend. In this context, the ECB is supported by the Eurostat industrial and consumer surveys and, above all, the survey on expected price trends. In this respect, it has been shown that above all sales price expectations in industry are a reliable indicator of future consumer price expectations.

In addition to the Euro-zone inflation figures the market also focuses on the national price figures, when they are published prior to the Eurostat data. The importance of national data thereby increases the earlier it is announced and the larger the country. However, the importance of these data has been limited somewhat since the publication of the Eurostat flash estimates for consumer prices, in which the national data are included.

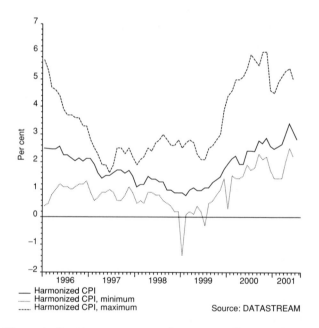

Figure 28.5   Change in Euro-zone consumer prices on preceding year: harmonized index, minimum and maximum

Key Datastream Mnemonics

Consumer Prices (nsa)	Datastream
Euro area	
All items (harmonized)	EAESHARMF
All items (harmonized, sa)	
All items (since 1960)	EMCP....F
Excl. energy	EAESCPXEF
Excl. energy, food, alcohol and tobacco	EAESCPXFF
Excl. tobacco	
Goods	EAESCPGDF
Goods (sa)	
Food (and non-alcoholic beverages)	EAESCPFBF
Processed food (including alcohol and tobacco)	EAESCPFAF
Unprocessed food	EAESCPUFF
Food, alcohol and tobacco	EAESCPFAF
Housing, water, electicity and other fuels	EAESCPUTF
Industrial goods	EAESCPINF
Non-energy industrial goods	EAESCPNEF
Energy	EAESCPENF
Services	EAESCPSVF
Services (sa)	
Housing (% y/y, harmonized)	EMEBSVHY%
Transport	EAESCPTPF
Communication	EAESCPCMF
Recreation and personal	EAESCPRCF
Miscellaneous	EMESCPMSF
Austria	
All items (harmonized)	OEESHARMF
Belgium	
All items (harmonized)	BGESHARMF
Finland	
All items (harmonized)	FNESHARMF
France	
All items (harmonised)	FRESHARMF
Germany	
All items (harmonized)	BDESHARMF
Greece	
All items (harmonized)	GRESHARMF
Ireland	
All items (harmonized)	IRESHARMF
Italy	
All items (harmonized)	ITESHARMF
Luxembourg	
All items (harmonized)	LXESHARMF
Netherlands	
All items (harmonized)	NLESHARMF
Portugal	
All items (harmonized)	PTESHARMF

Consumer Prices (nsa)	Datastream
Spain	
All items (harmonized)	ESESHARMF
EU15	
All items (harmonized)	ECESHARMF
All items (harmonized) (% m/m)	ECESHARM%
All items (harmonized) (% y/y)	ECESHARY%
Excl. energy	ECESCPXEF
Excl. energy food, alcohol and tobacco	ECESCPXFF
Goods (excluding services)	ECESCPGDF
Food (including non-alcoholic beverages)	ECESCPFBF
Processed food (including alcohol and tobacco)	ECESCPFAF
Unprocessed food	ECESCPUFF
Food, alcohol and tobacco	ECESCPFAF
Housing, water, electricity and other fuels	ECESCPUTF
Industrial goods	ECESCPINF
Non-energy industrial goods	ECESCPNEF
Energy	ECESCPENF
Services	ECESCPSVF
Housing	
Transport	ECESCPTPF
Communication	ECESCPCOF
Recreation and personal	ECESCPRF
Miscellaneous	ECESCPMSF
Denmark	
All items (harmonized)	DKESHARMF
Sweden	
All items (harmonized)	SDESHARMF
United Kingdom	
All items (harmonized)l	UKESHARMF

Literature

Deutsche Bundesbank, 'Problems with inflation measurement', *Monthly Report*, May 1998, pp. 51–64.

Deutsche Bundesbank, *On the discussion of using Consumer Price Index as indicator of inflation*, Deutsche Bundesbank, *Discussion Paper of the Economic Research Group of the Deutsche Bundesbank*, No. 3/1999.

Deutsche Bundesbank, 'Core inflation rates as a tool of price analysis', *Monthly Report*, April 2000, pp. 45–58.

Deutsche Bundesbank, 'The information content of survey data on expected price developments for monetary policy', *Monthly Report*, January 2001, pp. 35–49.

European Central Bank, 'Deriving inflation expectations from inflation index-linked bonds', *Monthly Report*, February 1999, pp. 16–17.

European Central Bank, 'The role of short-term economic indicators in the analysis of price developments in the Euro area', *Monthly Report*, April 1999, pp. 27–40.

European Central Bank, 'The effect of oil prices on the Harmonised Index of Consumer Prices (HICP)', *Monthly Report*, September 1999, pp. 23–4.

European Central Bank, 'Inflation differentials in a monetary union', *Monthly Report*, October 1999, pp. 35–45.

European Central Bank, 'Impact of import price developments on Euro area consumer prices', *Monthly Report*, June 2000, pp. 27–9.

European Central Bank, 'Trends in Euro area service price developments', *Monthly Report*, September 2000, p. 32.

European Central Bank, 'Why price stability', First ECB Central Banking Conference, November 2000.

European Central Bank, 'An analysis of price developments: the breakdown of the overall HICP into its Main components', *Monthly Report*, December 2000, p. 28.

European Central Bank, 'Inflation differentials within the Euro area', *Monthly Report*, December 2000, p. 32.

European Central Bank, 'Analysis of HICP developments based on seasonally adjusted data', *Monthly Report*, January 2001, p. 19.

European Central Bank, 'Changes in the coverage and methods for computation of the harmonised Index of Consumer Prices', *Monthly Report*, March 2001, p. 24.

European Central Bank, 'Measures of underlying inflation in the Euro area', *Monthly Report*, July 2001, pp. 49–59.

Junius, Karsten, *et. al.*, *Handbuch Europaische Zentralbank* [Hand book European Central Bank], Uhlenbruch Verlag, 2002.

Morana, C., 'Measuring core inflation in the Euro area', *European Central Bank Working Paper No. 36*, Frankfurt-am-Main, November 2000.

Smets, Frank, 'What horizon for price stability', *European Central Bank Working Paper* No. 24, Frankfurt-am-Main, July 2000.

Trecroci, C. and Veag, J. L., 'The information content of M3 for future inflation', *European Central Bank Working Paper* No. 33, Frankfurt-am-Main, October 2000.

Wynne, Mark A., 'Core Inflation: A Review of some Conceptual Issues', *European Central Bank Working Paper* No. 5, Frankfurt-am-Main, May 1999.

28.3   Labour Costs

Data Source

Data are published both by Eurostat and the national statistical offices, as well as the German Federal Office of Labour (Bundesamt für Arbeit). In addition, the ECB publishes its own data. Press releases are available on the respective Internet sites. The data series are also published in part in Table 5.4 of the ECB *Monthly Report*.

Importance for the Financial Markets   C

Description

In conjunction with the employment figures Eurostat also publishes information on labour productivity and labour costs, which can be used as indicators for existing or developing inflationary pressure. Labour costs, which are only produced quarterly and exclude the agricultural sector, public sector and health and education, are published by Eurostat on the basis of national figures, as soon as approximately 60 per cent of the required information is available. Labour costs include total gross compensation, bonus payments, employee social security contributions and all tax incurred. Employer contributions and the costs of vocational training, hiring staff and canteens are not however included. Data are principally surveyed from all types of company and level of staff. However, in Italy, for example, only companies with at least 500 staff are included. In Luxembourg only employees earning a maximum of five times the statutory minimum wage (currently approximately 5800 Euro) are surveyed, and in Germany, Ireland, Austria and Sweden certain individual sectors are not included. National data is weighted on the basis of the compensation for 1996 converted into Euro with the ECU rates of 1996. Quarterly data for Belgium and Ireland are only available with a huge time gap. In Portugal the data are treated confidentially and are therefore not published separately. Greek figures are not yet available, so the calculation of the Euro-zone aggregates before and after January 2001 is done without Greece. Data which arrive late are estimated using an ARIMA model, and missing data within a series are deduced via interpolation.

Total nominal hourly labour costs are obtained by dividing the total cost of all those employed in the respective member country by the number of hours worked. If data are not available for hours worked, the number of employed (Italy, Belgium and Ireland) or the number of paid working hours is taken as the measure. This data are published for the overall economy and the industrial sector separately. In addition, labour costs are divided up in terms of wages and other labour costs.

In addition to Eurostat, the ECB also publishes data which it calculates on the basis of national figures and which are weighted on the basis of the GDP figures for 1995. The database is not yet fully harmonized and statistics are only calculated quarterly on the basis of national data. Unit labour costs for the overall economy are obtained by dividing total compensation per employee by real GDP per employed person. Data from Belgium, Ireland, Luxembourg, Austria, Portugal and Greece are currently missing for the quarterly figures; Luxembourg and Greece are also not included for the annual data. For compensation per employee in the whole economy, all wages, salaries and employer contributions to social security are divided by the number of employers who receive compensation. Luxembourg also produces annual data on this data series. Labour productivity is defined as the GDP divided by the number of persons employed. For this Luxembourg and Greece do not supply any annual figures. Quarterly figures are missing from Belgium, Ireland, Luxembourg, Austria, Greece and Portugal. In addition to the statistics on unit labour costs, the ECB also calculates earnings per employee in the manufacturing sector.

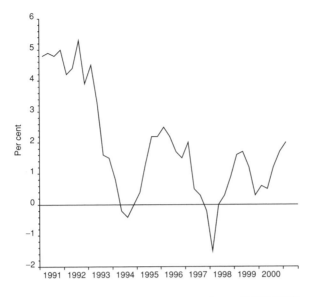

Figure 28.6   Change in Euro-zone unit labour costs on preceding year

This data series is defined as the sum of wages and salaries which are paid in the manufacturing sector divided by the number employed in this sector. Currently Euro-zone data are only available for ten nations, excluding Portugal and Greece, and are calculated on the basis of non-harmonized national figures. However, there are efforts under way to improve the scope of the database and harmonization.

Periodicity/Revisions

The Eurostat data are published around the tenth day of the second month following the reference month. The quarterly data are therefore announced around $1\frac{1}{2}$ months after the end of a quarter. The ECB data are announced with the publication of the monthly report. Limited revisions are conducted. Publication of the Eurostat data takes place at 12.00 CET (06.00 ET).

Seasonal Adjustment

The data are not currently seasonally adjusted, as the scope of the existing data does not permit this.

Notes

It should be noted that data published by Eurostat on wages and unit labour costs are not harmonized. Instead the most frequently used national series are employed. There are therefore differences in the definitions between the individual countries. These differences can relate to different types of employment, such as full-time employment, part-time employment or traineeships, the type of employment (manual workers, employees outside the trade) and the type of payment (normal remuneration, overtime pay, bonus payments, paid holiday). Consequently, very little notice is taken of the figures. This should change with the improvement in the data position and since the ECB has recently referred to the importance of the figures.

Key Datastream Mnemonics

Labour Costs (nsa)	Datastream
Euro area	
Total nominal hourly labour costs, whole economy	
Total nominal hourly labour costs, whole economy (% q/q)	EMESHLCW%
Wages	EMEBLCW%B
Other	EMEBLCO%B
Total nominal hourly labour costs, industry	EMESWAGRH
Total nominal hourly labour costs, services	EMEBLCS%B
Unit labour costs, whole economy	EMEBLCU%B
Compensation per employee, whole economy	EMEBWPE%B
Labour productivity, whole economy	EMEBLPY%B
Earnings per employee in manufacturing	EMEBWPM%B
Austria	
Total nominal hourly labour costs, whole economy	
Total nominal hourly labour costs, whole economy (% q/q)	OEESHLCW%
Wages	OEESWAGE%
Other	OEESOTHR%
Total nominal hourly labour costs, industry	OEESWAGRH
Belgium	
Total nominal hourly labour costs, whole economy	
Total nominal hourly labour costs, whole economy (% q/q)	BGESHLCW%
Wages	BGESWAGE%
Other	BGESOTHR%
Total nominal hourly labour costs, industry	BGESWAGRH
Finland	
Total nominal hourly labour costs, whole economy	
Total nominal hourly labour costs, whole economy (% q/q)	FNESHLCW%
Wages	FNESWAGE%
Other	FNESOTHR%
Total nominal hourly labour costs, industry	FNESWAGRH

Labour Costs (nsa)	Datastream
France	
Total nominal hourly labour costs, whole economy	
Total nominal hourly labour costs, whole economy (% q/q)	FRESHLCW%
Wages	FRESWAGE%
Other	FRESOTHR%
Total nominal hourly labour costs, industry	FRESWAGRH
Germany	
Total nominal hourly labour costs, whole economy	
Total nominal hourly labour costs, whole economy (% q/q)	BDESHLCW%
Wages	BDESWAGRH
Other	BDESWAGE%
Total nominal hourly labour costs, industry	BDESOTHR%
Greece	
Total nominal hourly labour costs, whole economy	
Total nominal hourly labour costs, whole economy (% q/q)	GRESHLCI%
Wages	
Other	
Total nominal hourly labour costs, industry	GRESWAGRH
Ireland	
Total nominal hourly labour costs, whole economy	
Total nominal hourly labour costs, whole economy (% q/q)	IRESHLCW%
Wages	IRESWAGE%
Other	IRESOTHR%
Total nominal hourly labour costs, industry	IRESWAGRH
Italy	
Total nominal hourly labour costs, whole economy	
Total nominal hourly labour costs, whole economy (% q/q)	ITESHLCW%
Wages	ITESWAGE%
Other	ITESOTHR%
Total nominal hourly labour costs, industry	ITESWAGRH
Luxembourg	
Total nominal hourly labour costs, whole economy	
Total nominal hourly labour costs, whole economy (% q/q)	LXESHLCW%
Wages	LXESWAGE%
Other	LXESOTHR%
Total nominal hourly labour costs, industry	LXESWAGRH
Netherlands	
Total nominal hourly labour costs, whole economy	
Total nominal hourly labour costs, whole economy (% q/q)	NLESHLCW%
Wages	NLESWAGE%
Other	NLESOTHR%
Total nominal hourly labour costs, industry	NLESWAGRH
Portugal	
Total nominal hourly labour costs, whole economy	
Total nominal hourly labour costs, whole economy (% q/q)	PTESHLCW%
Wages	
Other	
Total nominal hourly labour costs, industry	PTESWAGRH

Labour Costs (nsa)	Datastream
Spain	
Total nominal hourly labour costs, whole economy	
Total nominal hourly labour costs, whole economy (% q/q)	ESESHLCW%
Wages	ESESWAGE%
Other	ESESOTHR%
Total nominal hourly labour costs, industry	ESESWAGRH
EU15	
Total nominal hourly labour costs, whole economy	
Total nominal hourly labour costs, whole economy (% q/q)	ECESHLCW%
Wages	
Other	
Total nominal hourly labour costs, industry	ECESWAGRH
Denmark	
Total nominal hourly labour costs, whole economy	
Total nominal hourly labour costs, whole economy (% q/q)	DKESHLCW%
Wages	
Other	
Total nominal hourly labour costs, industry	DKESWAGRH
Sweden	
Total nominal hourly labour costs, whole economy	
Total nominal hourly labour costs, whole economy (% q/q)	SDESHLCW%
Wages	SDESWAGE%
Other	SDESOTHR%
Total nominal hourly labour costs, industry	SDESWAGRH
United Kingdom	
Total nominal hourly labour costs, whole economy	
Total nominal hourly labour costs, whole economy (% q/q)	UKESHLCW%
Wages	
Other	
Total nominal hourly labour costs, industry	UKESWAGRH

Literature

European Central Bank, 'Monitoring wage and labour cost developments in the Euro area', *Monthly Report*, October 1999, pp. 18–19.

European Central Bank, 'Price and cost indicators in the Euro area', *Monthly Report*, August 2000, pp. 33–50.

European Central Bank, 'Recent developments in Euro area labour cost indicators', *Monthly Report*, February 2001, p. 25.

29
Financial Activity

29.1 Monetary Aggregates

Data Source

Data are calculated by the ECB. The press release is available under 'Statistics' on the Internet at www.ecb.int. In addition, more detailed information is published in Tables 2.1 to 2.4 of the ECB *Monthly Report*.

Importance for the Financial Markets   B

Description

The ECB publishes monthly statistics on monetary aggregates. For this it uses three monetary definitions in accordance with standard international practice, for which separate time series are produced. The M1 monetary aggregate is the narrow type of monetary aggregate. It is composed of currency in circulation plus overnight deposits at monetary financial institutions (MFI). The intermediate M2 monetary aggregate includes all other short-term deposits, in addition to the M1 monetary aggregate. These include deposits with an agreed maturity of up to two years and deposits redeemable at notice over 3 months. Finally, the broad M3 monetary aggregate, which is more broadly defined, includes the M2 monetary aggregate and certain marketable instruments. These include repurchase agreements, money market fund shares/units and money market paper, as well as debt securities issued with a maturity of up to two years. Beginning with the data for June 2001, the ECB calculates the annual growth rates for most of the aggregates and parts on the basis of monthly stocks and flows. These data are adjusted for seasonal and end-of-month-calendar effects. Through this procedure the annual growth rates reflect the underlying pattern in a more accurate way than using the unadjusted data. The ECB plans to expend this way of calculation to all the items of the consolidated balance sheet of the MFI sector in the coming months.

For calculation of the monetary aggregate trends, only data relating to residents are included. Transactions and holdings of economic objects outside the Euro-zone are not included either. Data on monetary aggregate trends have been produced in a harmonized form since September 1997, so the annual rate for the growth of all balance sheet items can be calculated from September 1998. In addition, the ECB has calculated statistics for the monetary aggregate from January 1980. However, values prior to September 1997 are partly based on estimated national figures and not seasonally adjusted so these data are not fully comparable with the harmonized data.

Starting with the monetary developments for April 2001, the ECB announced that M3 had to be adjusted because its growth had to a significant extent been driven by demand from investors outside the Euro-zone. M3 is intended to measure the money holdings of Euro-zone residents. These holdings are relevant for an assesment of the implications of monetary policy for price stability within the Euro-zone. The idea behind this way of thinking is that in a large and relatively closed economic area such as the Euro-zone, domestic prices are most likely to be influenced by funds held at domestic banks by domestic depositors. Therefore, holdings by non-residents of the Euro-zone had to be excluded from M3. Prior to the start of EMU, the amount of these holdings were rather small and were subject to only moderate growth over time. But since the start of EMU,

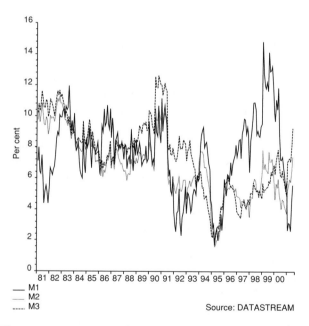

Figure 29.1   Change in M1, M2 and M3 monetary aggregates on preceding year

the expansion of the negotiable instruments held by non-residents of the Euro-zone included in M3 has become very dynamic.

In assessing the impact on M3 growth, a distinction needs to be made between the non-residents of the Euro-zone holdings of money market paper and short-term debt securities with an initial maturity of up to two years on the one hand, and money market fund shares/units on the other. For the former, reliable data are not yet available, although they are for the latter. The impact of holdings of money market fund shares/units of non-Euro-zone residents on the annual growth rate of M3 was very small until late summer 2000. Only after this date did the distortion gradually become more sizeable. In the beginning, the effect amounted to around half a percentage point. But only a few months later, the effect increased to 0.75 percentage points. Since October 2001, the ECB also excludes holdings of short-term debt instruments by non-residents of the Euro-zone. These holdings having accounted for an upward distortion of the annual growth rate of M3 of around 0.75 percentage points. At the time of writing the ECB publishes adjusted data, beginning with the statistics for January 1999. Prior to this date no adjustment is necessary owing to the limited value of holdings by non-resident investors included in M3.

For the monetary aggregate definitions the ECB introduced the term 'monetary financial institutions' (MFI), for which it has drawn up an aggregate balance which forms the basis of the calculation of the monetary aggregate. The MFI sector includes all institutions whose liabilities may be of a monetary nature (i.e., the national central banks and the ECB, credit institutions and other financial institutions). These include, above all, money market funds. The importance of the MFI sector for the monetary aggregate trend is also indicated by the fact that the ECB has named this sector the 'money-issuing' sector.

By contrast, the 'money holding' sector covers all non-MFIs resident in the monetary area, excluding central government. These primarily include private households, non-financial corporations, insurance companies and federal states, districts and social security offices in the national sector. Central governments are classed as the 'money-neutral' sector, apart from central government deposits in the MFIs of a monetary nature. These are taken into account in the calculation of the monetary aggregates.

In addition to the monetary aggregates, the ECB also publishes the balance sheet of counterparts of M3. These include, as liabilities, deposits with an agreed maturity over two years, redeemable deposits at notice of over 3 months, debt securities issued with a maturity of over 2 years and capital and reserves. These liabilities together form the longer-term financial liabilities against the other Euro-zone residents. In addition, there are the deposits of central government

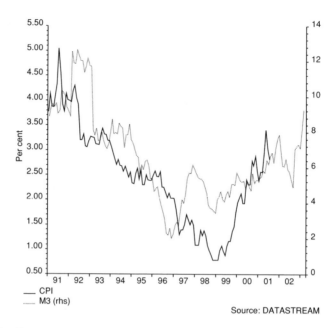

Figure 29.2   Change in Euro-zone consumer prices and M3 monetary aggregate (with a lag of 20 months) on preceding year

and external liabilities. They include credits to general government and credits to other Euro-zone residents. There are also external assets and other counterparts of M3 included as residuals. Here the difference between loans to the government and loans to other economic objects in the Euro-zone is also of interest.

Periodicity/Revisions

The data are published at the end of the month following the reference month. However, no set date or time is given so that the respective publication times can vary each month. Substantial monthly revisions may be required. The data are not published at a fixed time; instead, the time is announced shortly before publication.

Seasonal Adjustment

The data have been seasonally adjusted since September 1997. The ECB uses both the X-12 ARIMA method and the TRAMO/SEATS method, although only data obtained with the X-12 ARIMA program is officially published. Seasonal adjustment of the M3 monetary aggregate is indirectly obtained by aggregating the seasonally adjusted data for M1; M2 minus M1; and M3 minus M2. The seasonal adjustment factors are estimated using the indices for the adjusted stocks.

Notes

The focus is primarily on the percentage change in the M3 monetary aggregate compared with the preceding year, plus a moving average for this figure over three months as this is one of the pillars of the ECB monetary policy concept. Based on the monetarist assumption that inflation is always a monetary phenomenon in the long term, the ECB decided to fix a reference factor for the M3 monetary growth rate annually as a target. With the calculation of the reference value the ECB initially assumes that price level stability occurs when the inflation rate is below 2 per cent on the preceding year, according to their definition. In addition to this assumption, the growth rate in the real GDP and medium-term change in the velocity of circulation are estimated. With the help of these three figures the ECB then calculates the reference value for the coming year in December of each year. Deviation from this reference value does not automatically lead to a change in central bank interest rates. Instead, the value is only meant to be helpful in explaining interest rate decisions guaranteeing price level stability in the medium term. In case of a deviation further analysis is conducted, so decisions can be based on a comprehensive picture. This is why the ECB did not choose parameters, as it was feared that the public nature of these parameters would be falsely interpreted to mean that interest rates would be automatically changed as soon as monetary growth went outside the parameters.

Unlike other Euro-zone statistics the ECB does not publish any national data. What is a problem for the monetary policy concept is the fact that aggregate figures have only been directly surveyed since September 1997, although data were calculated prior to this. Thus, for the assessment of the Euro-zone transmission mechanism of the money and the change in the velocity of circulation, the only data available do not match the quality of the national data used before the beginning of the EMU.

The holdings of the individual components of the monetary aggregates and their counterparts are calculated from the MFI consolidated balance. The percentage change of monetary aggregates compared to the preceding year is not, however, calculated on the basis of these levels, but on the basis of monthly changes in holdings which are adjusted for regrouping, other revaluations, exchange rate fluctuations and all other movements not based on transactions.

Key Datastream Mnemonics

Euro zone: Financial Activity

Monetary Aggregates

Monetary Aggregates (nsa)	Datastream
M1	EAECBM1.A
Currency in circulation	EMECBM1CA
Overnight deposits	EMECBM1SA
M2	EAECBM2.A
Deposits with agreed maturity up to 2 years	EMECBM2DA
Deposits redeemable at notice up to 3 months	EMECBM2RA
M3	EAECBM3.A
Effect on M3 of holdings of money market fund shares/units by non-residents of Euro zone	
M3 (% y/y)	EMECBM3Y%
M3 (% y/y, 3-months average)	EMECBM3.%
Index (December 1998 = 100, nsa)	EMECBM3.F
Index (sa)	EMECBM3.F
Repurchase agreement	EMECBM3RA
Money market fund shares/units and money market paper	EMECBM3MA
Debt securities issued with maturity up to 2 years	EMECBM32A
Counterparts of M3	
MFIs liabilities	EMECBLIAA
Deposits of central government	EMECBLDGA
Longer-term financial liabilities against other Euro area residents	EMECBLOTA
Deposits with agreed maturity over 2 years	EMECBML2A
Deposits redeemable at notice over 3 months	EMECBML3A
Debt securities issued with maturity over 2 years	EMECBMLSA
Capital and reserves	EMECBMCRA
External liabilities	EMECBLEXA
MFIs assets	EMECBASSA
Credit to Euro area residents	EMECBAOTA
Credit to general government	EMECBMCGA
Of which loans	
Of which securities other than shares	
Credit to Euro area residents	EMECBMCOA
Of which loans	EMECBMCLA
Of which securities other than shares	
Of which shares and other equities	
External assets	EMECBAEXA
Other counterparts of M3	

Literature

Bindseil, Ulrich and Seitz, F., 'The supply and demand for eurosystem deposits – The first 18 months', *European Central Bank, Working Paper* No. 44, Frankfurt-am-Main, February 2001.

Bindseil, Ulrich, 'Central Bank Forecasts of liquidity factors: Quality, publication and the control of the overnight rate' *European Central Bank, Working Paper* No. 70, Frankfurt-am-Main, July 2001.

Brand, C. and Cassola, N., 'A money demand system for Euro area M3', *European Central Bank, Working Paper* No. 39, Frankfurt-am-Main, November 2000.

Clare, Andrew and Courtenay, Roger, 'Assessing the impact of macroeconomic announcements on securities prices and different monetary policy regimes', *Bank of England Working Paper Series* No. 125, February 2001.

Coenen, Günter and Vega, Juan-Luis, 'The Demand for M3 in the Euro zone', *European Central Bank, Working Paper* No. 6, Frankfurt-am-Main, September 1999.

Deutsche Bundesbank, 'Financial market prices as monetary policy indicators', *Monthly Report*, July 1998, pp. 49–66.

Deutsche Bundesbank, 'Taylor interest rate and Monetary Condition Index', *Monthly Report*, April 1999, pp. 47–63.

European Central Bank, 'Definitions of monetary aggregates for the Euro area', *Monthly Report*, January 1999, p. 21.

European Central Bank, 'The stability-oriented monetary policy strategy of the Eurosystem', *Monthly Report*, January 1999, pp. 43–56.

European Central Bank, 'Euro area monetary aggregates and their role in the Eurosystem's monetary policy strategy', *Monthly Report*, February 1999, pp. 29–46.

European Central Bank, 'The institutional framework of the European System of Central Banks', *Monthly Report*, July 1999, pp. 55–63.

European Central Bank, Statistical Information collected and compiled by the ESCB, 2000.

European Central Bank, 'The influence of base effects on annual monetary growth rates', *Monthly Report*, February 2000, pp. 8–9.

European Central Bank, 'The switch to variable rate tenders in the main refinancing operations', *Monthly Report*, July 2000, pp. 39–44.

European Central Bank, 'Monetary policy transmission in the Euro area', *Monthly Report*, July 2000, pp. 43–58.

European Central Bank, 'The two pillars of the ECB's monetary policy strategy', *Monthly Report*, November 2000, pp. 37–48.

European Central Bank, 'Annual review of the reference value for monetary growth', *Monthly Report*, December 2000, p. 10.

European Central Bank, 'The derivation and use of flow data in monetary statistics', *Monthly Report*, February 2001, p. 8

European Central Bank, 'Measurement issues related to the inclusion of negotiable instruments in Euro area M3', *Monthly Report*, May 2001, pp. 9–11.

European Central Bank, 'Adjustment of M3 for sales of negotiable instruments by non-residents of the Euro area', *Monthly Report*, November 2001, pp. 10–13.

Gaspar Vitor *et al.*, 'The ECB monetary policy strategy and the money market', *European Central Bank Working Paper* No. 69, Frankfurt-am-Main, July 2001.

Haldane, Andrew G. and Read, Vicky, 'Monetary policy surprises and the yield curve', *Bank of England Working Paper Series* No. 106, January 2000.

Junius, Kansten, *et. al.*, Handbuch Europaische Zentralbank [Handbook European Central Bank], Uhlenbruch Verlag, 2002.

Söderström, Ulf, 'Monetary Policy with uncertain parameters', *European Central Bank Working Paper* No. 13, Frankfurt-am-Main, February 2000.

Trecroci, C. and Veag, J. L., 'The information content of M3 for future inflation', *European Central Bank Working Paper* No. 33, Frankfurt-am-Main, October 2000.

30
Address List

EU Institutions

European Commission
200 Rue de la Loi
B-1049 Brussels
europa.eu.int

European Central Bank
Kaiserstrasse 29
D-60311 Frankfurt-am-Main
www.ecb.int

Eurostat
Joseph-Bech-Gebäude
L-2920 Luxembourg
europa.eu.int/comm/eurostat

Austria

Dr Fessel + GFK Institut für Marktforschung
Hainburger Strasse 33
A-1030 Vienna
www.gfk.at

Österreichische Nationalbank
Otto-Wagner-Platz 3
A-1090 Vienna
www.oenb.co.at

Statistik Austria
Hintere Zollamtsstrasse 2b
A-1033 Vienna
www.oestat.gv.at

WIFO Österreichisches Institut für Wirtschaftsforschung
Arsenal, Objekt 20
A-1103 Vienna
www.wifo.at

Belgium

ASPEMAR
Kunstlaan 2, Bus 16
B-1040 Brussels

Banque Nationale de Belgique
Bd de Berlaimont 5
B-1000 Brussels
www.bnb.be

National Institute for Statistics
Rue de Louvain 44
B-1000 Brussels
www.statbel.fgov.be

Denmark

Danmarks Nationalbank
Havnegade 5
DK-1093 Copenhagen K
www.nationalbanken.dk

Danmarks Statistiks
Sejrogade 11
Postbox 2550
DK-2100 Copenhagen Ö
www.dst.dk

GFK Danmark
Tolbodgade 10B
DK-1253 Copenhagen K
www.gfk.dk

Finland

Suomen Pankki
P.O. Box 160
SF-00101 Helsinki
www.bof.fi

Confederation of Finnish Industry and Employers (CFIE)
Eteläranta 10
SF-00130 Helsinki

Statistics Finland
Työpajakatu 13
SF-00580 Helsinki
www.stat.fi

France

Banque de France
F-75049 Paris Cedex 01
www.banque-france.fr

Compagnie des Dirigeants d'Appovisionnement et Acheteurs de France (CDAF)
2, Rue Paul Cezanne
F-93364 Neuilly-Plaisance Cedex

Institut National de la Statistique et des Études Économiques (INSEE)
18, Boulevard Adolphe Pinard
F-75675 Paris Cedex 14
www.insee.fr

Germany

Bundesverband Materialwirtschaft, Einkauf und Logistik (BME)
Bologarostrasse 82
D-65929 Frankfurt-am-Main
www.bme.de

Deutsche Bundesbank
Postfach 100602
Wilhelm-Epstein-Strasse 14–16
D-60006 Frankfurt-am-Main
www.bundesbank.de

DGZ-DeraBank
Economics Department
Mainzer Landstrasse 16
D-60325 Frankfurt-am-Main
www.dgz-derabank.de

DZ Bank
Economics Department
Am Platz der Republik
D-60325 Frankfurt-am-Main
www.dzbank.de

Frankfurter Allgemeine Zeitung
Hellerhofstrasse 2–4
D-60327 Frankfurt-am-Main
www.faz.net

GFK Gesellschaft für Konsumforschung
Postfach 2854
Nordwestring 101
D-90319 Nürnberg
www.gfk.de

Handelsblatt
Economics and Politics Editors
Postfach 102741
D-40018 Düsseldorf
www.handelsblatt.com

IFO Institut für Wirtschaftsforschung
Poschingerstrasse 5
D-81679 Munich
www.ifo.de

IfW Institut für Weltwirtschaft
Düsternbrooker Weg 120
D-24105 Kiel
www.uni-kiel.de/ifw

German Federal Statistical Office
Gustav-Stresemann-Ring 11
D-65189 Wiesbaden
www.statistik-bund.de

Greece

Bank of Greece
21 E. Venizelos Avenue
GR-10250 Athens
www.bankofgreece.gr

FEIR Foundation of Economic & Industrial Research
11, Tsami Karatasou
GR-11742 Athens

Nationaler Statistikdienst von Greece
14–16 Lykourgou Str.
GR-10166 Athens
www.statistics.gr

PAN MAIL
Poseidonos 1–2
GR-17564 Paleo Faliro, Athens

Ireland

Construction Industry Federation (CIF)
Federation House – Canal Road
IR-Rathmines, Dublin 6
www.cif.ie

Economic & Social Research Institute (ESRI)
4, Burlington Road
IR-Dublin 4
www.esri.ie

Irish Business & Employers' Confederation (IBEC)
Confederation House
84/86 Lower Baggot Street
IR-Dublin 2
www.ibec.ie

Central Bank of Ireland
P.O. Box No. 559
Dame Street
IR-Dublin 2
www.centralbank.ie

Central Statistical Office
Skehard Rd.
IR-Cork
www.cso.ie

Italy

Associazione Italiana di Management degli Approvvigionamenti (ADACI)
Viale Ranzoni 17
I-20149 Milan
www.adaci.it

Banca d'Italia
Via Nazionale, 91
I-00184 Rome
www.bancaditalia.it

Instituto Nazionale per lo Studio della Congiuntura (ISCO)
Piazza dell Indipendenza 4
I-00185 Rome

Instituto di Studi e Analisi Economica (ISAE)
Piazza Indipendenza 4
I-00185 Rome
www.isae.it

Instituto Centrale die Statistica (ISTAT)
Via Alessandro Volta 3
I-00185 Rome
www.istat.it

Luxembourg

Service Central de la Statistique et des Études Économiques (STATEC)
19–21 Boulevard Royal
L-2983 Luxembourg
statec.gouvernement.lu

Banque Centrale du Luxembourg
2 Boulevard Royal
L-2983 Luxembourg
www.bcl.lu

Netherlands

Centraal Bureau vor de Statistiek (CBS)
Prinses Beatrixlaan 428
NL-Voorburg
www.cbs.nl

Economisch Instituut voor de Bouwnijverheid (EIB)
De Cuserstraat 89
NL-1081 CN Amsterdam
www.eib.nl

INTOMART BV
Noordse Bosje 13–15
NL-1211 BD Hilversum
www.intomart.nl

De Nederlandsche Bank
Westeinde 1
NL-1017 ZN Amsterdam
www.dnb.nl

NIPO Grote
Bickersstraat 74
NL-1013 KS Amsterdam
www.nipo.nl

Portugal

Associacao de empresas de construcao e obras publicas do sul (AECOPS)
Rua Duque de Palmela, 20
P-1250 Lisbon
www.aecops.pt

Banco de Portugal
R. do Ouro, 27
P-1100–150 Lisbon
www.bportugal.pt

INE Instituto Nacional de Estatistica
Avenida Antonio Jose de Almeida, 2
P-1000–043 Lisbon
www.ine.pt

Spain

Banco de Espana
Alcala, 50
E-28014 Madrid
www.bde.es

Instituto Nacional de Estadistica
Paseo de la Castellana 160
E-28071 Madrid
www.ine.es

INTERGALLUP
Miguel Angel 21–4
E-28010 Madrid
www.gallup.es

Ministerio de Industria y Energia
Estudios y Promocion Industrial
Paseo de la Castellana 160
E-28071 Madrid
www.min.es

Sweden

NIER Konjunkturinstitutet (National Institute of Economic Research)
Kungsgatan 12–14
Box 3116
S-10362 Stockholm

Sveriges Riksbank
Malmskillnadsgatan 7
S-10337 Stockholm
www.riksbank.com

Statistics Sweden
Box 24300
S-10451 Stockholm
www.scb.se

United Kingdom

Bank of England
Threadneedle Street,
London EC2R 8AH, UK
www.bankofengland.co.uk

Confederation of British Industry (CBI)
Centre Point
103 New Oxford Street
London WC1A 1DU, UK
www.cbi.org.uk

Construction Forecasting & Research (CFR)
Vigilant House
120 Wilton Road
London SW1V 132, UK
www.construction-forecast.com

GFK Great Britain Limited
22 Stephenson Way
London NW1 2HZ, UK
www.gfk.com

NTC Research
Farm Road
Henley-on-Thames
Oxon RG9 1EJ, UK

Office for National Statistics
1 Drummond Gate
London SW1V 2QQ, UK
www.statistics.gov.uk

Thomson Financial Datastream
1 Mark Square
Leonard Street
London ECZA YEG, UK
www.thomsonfinancial.com

Appendix: Datastream Mnemonics for Other Important Indicators and Financial Data

This book is intended to help people who work in the field of financial markets to make the access to data on these markets more convenient. Thus, the appendix delivers a broad number of Datastream mnemonics on stock markets, bond markets, currency markets, commodities and other economic indicators that are not explained in the book. It is far from complete, but most of the major data series are included. In addition, there is space to add all the mnemonics a user personally needs.

Stock Indices	Datastream
World	
DJ Global Titans 50	DJTITAN
DJ Stoxx 50	DJSTO50
FTSE 100	FTSE100
Hang Seng	HNGKNGI
Nikkei	JAPDOWA
Topix	TOKYOSE
USA	
Dow Jones Industrial	DJINDUS
Dow Jones Transportation	DJTRSPT
Dow Jones Utilities	DJUTILS
Nasdaq 100	NASA100
Nasdaq Composite	NASCOMP
Russel 2000	FRUSSL2
S&P 500	S&PCOMP
Wilshire 5000	WILEQTY
Euro-zone	
CAC 40	CAC4016
CDax	CDAXGEN
Dax 30	DAXINDX
Dax 30 Xetra	XETRDAX
DJ Euro Stoxx 50	DJES50I
Auto	DJESAUT
Banks	DJESBNK
Basic Resources	DJESBRS
Chemicals	DJESCHM
Conctruction	DJESCNS
Cyclical Goods	DJESCYG
Energy	DJESEES

Stock Indices	Datastream
Financial Services	DJESFIS
Food	DJESFBV
Healthcare	DJESHCR
Industrial Goods	DJESIGS
Insurance	DJESINS
Media	DJESMED
Non-cyclical Goods	DJESNCG
Retail	DJESRTL
Technology	DJESTES
Telecom	DJESTLS
Utilities	DJESUTI
MDax	MDAXIDX
Nemax All Share	NMXALLP
Nemax 50	NEMAX50
SDax	SDAXIDX
VDax	VDAXIDX

Interest Rates	Datastream
USA	
Benchmark bond yield 30 years	USBRYLD
Discount rate	USDISCR
Eurodollar deposits	
1 month	FREDD1M
3 month	FREDD3M
6 month	FREDD6M
Federal funds rate	FRFEDFD
Federal funds target	USFDTRG
Mortgages, fixed rate 30 years	USMECF3
Prime rate	USPRIME
Swap rates	
1 year	ICUSD1Y
5 year	ICUSD5Y
10 year	ICUSD10
30 year	ICUSD30
Swap spreads against US Treasuries	
2 year	ICUSS2Y
5 year	ICUSS5Y
10 year	ICUSS10
30 year	ICUSS30
Treasury bills	
3 month	FRTBS3M
6 month	FRTBS6M
1 year	FRTBS1Y

Interest Rates	Datastream
Treasury bonds	
3 month	FRTCM3M
6 month	FRTCM6M
1 year	FRTCM1Y
2 year	FRTCM2Y
5 year	FRTCM5Y
10 year	FRTCM10
30 year	FRTCM30
Euro-zone	
Benchmark bond yield 10 years	BDBRYLD
Bundesbank federal bonds outstanding	DBFEDBD
ECB	
Marginal lending rate	EUROMLR
Overnight deposit rate	EURODEP
Main refinancing rate	EUROPS
Longer term refinancing rate	EURORPL
Main refinancing operations	
Fixed rate tender	EMYRFIX
Variable rate tender	
Minimum bid rate	EMYRVMI
Marginal rate	EMYRVAM
Weighted average rate	EMYRVAW
Bids (amount)	EMTRBID
Allotment (amount)	EMTRALO
Longer-term refinancing operations	
Fixed rate tender	EMYLFIX
Variable rate tender	
Marginal rate	EMYLVAM
Weighted average rate	EMYLVAW
Bids (amount)	EMTLBID
Allotment (amount)	EMTLALO
Eonia/Fibor overnight	FIBORON
Euribor/Fibor	
1 week	EIBOR1W
1 month	FIBOR1M
3 month	FIBOR3M
6 month	FIBOR6M
1 year	FIBOR1Y
Government bonds	
2 year	GBBD02Y
5 year	GBBD05Y
10 year	GBBD10Y
30 year	GBBD30Y

Interest Rates	Datastream
Euro-zone	
JEX bond index	JEXINDX
1 year	JEXA01Y
2 year	JEXA02Y
5 year	JEXA05Y
10 year	JEXA10Y
PEX bond index	PEXINDX
1 year	PEXA01Y
2 year	PEXA02Y
5 year	PEXA05Y
10 year	PEXA10Y
REX bond index	REXINDX
1 year	REXA01Y
2 year	REXA02Y
5 year	REXA05Y
10 year	REXA10Y
Swap rates	
1 year	ICDEM1Y
5 year	ICDEM5Y
10 year	ICDEM10
30 year	ICDEM30

Commodities	Datastream
Commodity indices	
Brent crude oil	LCRINDX
CRB Index	NYFECRB
Dow Jones	DJCMDTY
Dow Jones Future	DJFUTUR
Economist Commodities index	
All items	ECALLIE
Food	ECFOODE
Industrials	ECIALLE
MG Base Metal index, cash	LMGYSPT
MG Base Metal index, 3 month forward	LMG3MTH
Crude oil	
Brent, Spot	OILBRNP
Brent, current month	OILBREN
Brent, 1 month forward	OILBRNI
Brent, 2 month forward	OILBRNT
West Texas, Spot	CRUDOIL
West Texas, nearest month	OILWTXI
West Texas, 2 month forward	OILWTX2

Commodities	Datastream
Livestock	
Cattle, live	CATLIVE
Hog, live	LIVEHOG
Pork bellies	CPBCASH
	PORKBEL
Minor metals	
Aluminium	WALUING
Copper, cash	COPHGRD
Copper, 3 month forward	COPPR3M
Precious metals	
Gold	GOLDBLN
Gold, Krugerrand	LKRUGER
Palladium	PALLADM
Platinum	PLATFRE
Silver	SLVCASH
Softs	
Cocoa	COCOAIC
Cocoa, future	COCCAPR
Coffee, second future	COFFUTR
Coffee, Brazilian	COFBRAZ
Coffee, Colombian	CFCOLUM
Coffee, mild arabica	COFICML
Coffee, ICO composite	COFDICA
Corn, no. 2 yellow	CORNUS2
Wheat, soft white	WHEAT1S
Wheat, hard	WHEATMP

Currencies	Datastream
Nominal Trade-weighted Indices	
Bank of England	
Australian Dollar	BOEAUST
Canadian Dollar	BOECAN$
Euro	BOEEURO
German Mark	BOEDEUT
Japanese Yen	BOEJAPY
New Zealand Dollar	BOENEWZ
Sterling	BOESTER
Swiss Franc	BOESWSF
US Dollar	BOEUSA$

Currencies	Datastream
ECB	
Euro nominal trade-weighted effective exchange rate	
Narrow, nominal	EMECBEXNR
Narrow, real (CPI)	EMECBEXCR
Narrow, real (PPI)	EMECBEXPR
Narrow, real (ULC)	EMECBEXLR
Broad, nominal	EMECBEXBR
Broad, real (CPI)	EMECBEXRR
Federal Reserve	
Broad	USDCWBN
Major currencies	USDCWMN
Other trading partners	
Reserve Bank of Australia	
Australian trade-weighted index	RBAAUST
Reserve Bank of New Zealand	
NZ Dollar effective index	NZ$EFFI
Swiss National Bank	
Swiss Franc Index	CHFTRDW

Miscellaneous	Datastream
World	
Output gap, calculated by OECD	
Euro-zone	EMOCFOGP
Germany	BDOCFOGP
Japan	JPOCFOGP
UK	UKOCFOGP
USA	USOCFOGP
USA	
Economic Cycle Research Institute future inflations gauge	USECRIFIF
Federal Reserve Board Senior Loan Officer Survey	
Commercial and industrial loans	USFLBLT.R
Large and medium banks tightening credit	USFLBLT.R
Large and medium banks increasing rate/COF spread	USFLBLI.R
Large and medium banks reporting stronger demand	USFLBLS.R
Household loans	
Banks willing to make instalment loans	USFLCIW.R
Banks with stronger demand for mortgages	USFLCMS.R
Banks with stronger demand for consumer loans	USFLCCS.R
Banks tightening mortgage standards	USFLCMT.R
Marketable US Treasuries held in custody by the Federal Reserve	USCBGWN

Miscellaneous	Datastream
Stock market sentiment (American Association of Individual Investors)	
Percentage respondents bullish	USAAIIP
Percentage respondents bearish	USAAIIN
Percentage respondents neutral	USAAIIM
Weekly data	
Bank of Tokyo-Mitsubishi	
Retail chain store sales index	USSRMSA
Leading indicator of chain store sales	USSRLCA
LJR Redbook total store	USSRGJA
McGraw-Hill business week production index	USBWPRD
Money/ABC News consumer comfort index	
Overall index	USCCIMA
State of the economy	USCCISE
Personal finances	USCCIPF
Buying climate	USCCIBC